The Market and Temple Fairs of Rural China

During the early Communist period of the 1950s, temple fairs in China were secularized and/or suppressed. Temples were closed down by the secular regime and their activities classified as feudal superstition and this process only intensified during the Cultural Revolution when even the surviving secular fairs, devoted exclusively to trade with no religious content of any kind, were suppressed. However, once China embarked on its path of free-market reform and openness, secular commodity exchange fairs were again authorized, and sometimes encouraged in the name of political economy as a means of stimulating rural commodity circulation and commerce.

This book reveals how once these secular "temple-less temple fairs" were in place, they came to serve not only as venues for the proliferation of a great variety of popular cultural performance genres, but also as sites where a revival or recycling of popular religious symbols, already underway in many parts of China, found familiar and fertile ground in which to spread. Taking this shift in the Chinese state's attitudes and policy towards temple fairs as its starting point, *The Market and Temple Fairs of Rural China* shows how state-led economic reforms in the early 1980s created a revival in secular commodity exchange fairs, which were granted both the geographic and metaphoric space to function. In turn, this book presents a comprehensive analysis of the temple fair phenomenon, examining its economic, popular cultural, popular religious, and political dimensions, and demonstrates the multifaceted significance of the fairs which have played a crucial role in expanding the boundaries of contemporary acceptable popular discourse and expression.

Based upon extensive fieldwork, this unique book will be of great interest to students and scholars of Chinese religion, Chinese culture, Chinese history, and anthropology.

Gene Cooper is a Professor of Anthropology at the University of Southern California, USA.

ASIA'S TRANSFORMATIONS
Edited by Mark Selden, Cornell University, USA

The books in this series explore the political, social, economic and cultural consequences of Asia's transformations in the twentieth and twenty-first centuries. The series emphasizes the tumultuous interplay of local, national, regional and global forces as Asia bids to become the hub of the world economy. While focusing on the contemporary, it also looks back to analyse the antecedents of Asia's contested rise.

This series comprises several strands:

Asia's Transformations
Titles include:

1. **Debating Human Rights***
   Critical essays from the United States and Asia
   Edited by Peter Van Ness

2. **Hong Kong's History***
   State and society under colonial rule
   Edited by Tak-Wing Ngo

3. **Japan's Comfort Women***
   Sexual slavery and prostitution during World War II and the US occupation
   Yuki Tanaka

4. **Opium, Empire and the Global Political Economy***
   Carl A. Trocki

5. **Chinese Society***
   Change, conflict and resistance
   Edited by Elizabeth J. Perry and Mark Selden

6. **Mao's Children in the New China***
   Voices from the Red Guard generation
   Yarong Jiang and David Ashley

7. **Remaking the Chinese State***
   Strategies, society and security
   Edited by Chien-min Chao and Bruce J. Dickson

8. **Korean Society***
   Civil society, democracy and the state
   Edited by Charles K. Armstrong

9. **The Making of Modern Korea***
   Adrian Buzo

10. **The Resurgence of East Asia***
    500, 150 and 50 year perspectives
    Edited by Giovanni Arrighi, Takeshi Hamashita and Mark Selden

11. **Chinese Society, second edition***
    Change, conflict and resistance
    Edited by Elizabeth J. Perry and Mark Selden

12. **Ethnicity in Asia***
    Edited by Colin Mackerras

13. **The Battle for Asia***
    From decolonization to globalization
    Mark T. Berger

14. **State and Society in 21st Century China***
    Edited by Peter Hays Gries and Stanley Rosen

15. **Japan's Quiet Transformation***
    Social change and civil society in the 21st century
    Jeff Kingston

16. **Confronting the Bush Doctrine***
    Critical views from the Asia-Pacific
    *Edited by Mel Gurtov and
    Peter Van Ness*

17. **China in War and Revolution,
    1895–1949***
    Peter Zarrow

18. **The Future of US–Korean Relations***
    The imbalance of power
    Edited by John Feffer

19. **Working in China***
    Ethnographies of labor and workplace transformations
    Edited by Ching Kwan Lee

20. **Korean Society, second edition***
    Civil society, democracy and the state
    Edited by Charles K. Armstrong

21. **Singapore***
    The state and the culture of excess
    Souchou Yao

22. **Pan-Asianism in Modern Japanese History***
    Colonialism, regionalism and borders
    *Edited by Sven Saaler and
    J. Victor Koschmann*

23. **The Making of Modern Korea, second edition***
    Adrian Buzo

24. **Re-writing Culture in Taiwan***
    *Edited by Fang-long Shih,
    Stuart Thompson, and
    Paul-François Tremlett*

25. **Reclaiming Chinese Society***
    The new social activism
    *Edited by You-tien Hsing and
    Ching Kwan Lee*

26. **Girl Reading Girl in Japan***
    *Edited by Tomoko Aoyama and
    Barbara Hartley*

27. **Chinese Politics***
    State, society and the market
    *Edited by Peter Hays Gries and
    Stanley Rosen*

28. **Chinese Society, third edition***
    Change, conflict and resistance
    *Edited by Elizabeth J. Perry and
    Mark Selden*

29. **Mapping Modernity in Shanghai**
    Space, gender, and visual culture in the Sojourners' City, 1853–98
    Samuel Y. Liang

30. **Minorities and Multiculturalism in Japanese Education**
    An interactive perspective
    *Edited by Ryoko Tsuneyoshi,
    Kaori H Okano and Sarane Boocock*

31. **Japan's Wartime Medical Atrocities**
    Comparative inquiries in science, history, and ethics
    *Edited by Jing-Bao Nie,
    Nanyan Guo, Mark Selden and
    Arthur Kleinman*

32. **State and Society in Modern Rangoon**
    Donald M. Seekins

33. **Learning Chinese, Turning Chinese***
    Becoming sinophone in a globalised world
    Edward McDonald

34. **Aesthetic Constructions of Korean Nationalism**
    Spectacle, politics and history
    Hong Kal

35. **Popular Culture and the State in East and Southeast Asia**
    *Edited by Nissim Otmazgin and
    Eyal Ben Ari*

36. **Japan's Outcaste Abolition**
    The struggle for national inclusion and the making of the modern state
    Noah Y. McCormack

37. **The Market and Temple Fairs of Rural China**
    Red fire
    Gene Cooper

38. **The Role of American NGOs in China's Modernization**
    Invited influence
    Norton Wheeler

39. **State, Society and the Market in Contemporary Vietnam**
    Property, power and values
    *Hue-Tam Ho Tai and
    Mark Sidel*

Asia's Great Cities
Each volume aims to capture the heartbeat of the contemporary city from multiple perspectives emblematic of the authors own deep familiarity with the distinctive faces of the city, its history, society, culture, politics and economics, and its evolving position in national, regional and global frameworks. While most volumes emphasize urban developments since the Second World War, some pay close attention to the legacy of the *longue durée* in shaping the contemporary. Thematic and comparative volumes address such themes as urbanization, economic and financial linkages, architecture and space, wealth and power, gendered relationships, planning and anarchy, and ethnographies in national and regional perspective. Titles include:

1. **Bangkok***
   Place, practice and representation
   Marc Askew

2. **Representing Calcutta***
   Modernity, nationalism and the colonial uncanny
   Swati Chattopadhyay

3. **Singapore***
   Wealth, power and the culture of control
   Carl A. Trocki

4. **The City in South Asia**
   James Heitzman

5. **Global Shanghai, 1850–2010***
   A history in fragments
   Jeffrey N. Wasserstrom

6. **Hong Kong***
   Becoming a global city
   Stephen Chiu and Tai-Lok Lui

Asia.com is a series which focuses on the ways in which new information and communication technologies are influencing politics, society and culture in Asia. Titles include:

1. **Japanese Cybercultures***
   Edited by Mark McLelland and Nanette Gottlieb

2. **Asia.com***
   Asia encounters the Internet
   Edited by K. C. Ho, Randolph Kluver and Kenneth C. C. Yang

3. **The Internet in Indonesia's New Democracy***
   David T. Hill and Krishna Sen

4. **Chinese Cyberspaces***
   Technological changes and political effects
   Edited by Jens Damm and Simona Thomas

5. **Mobile Media in the Asia-Pacific**
   Gender and the art of being mobile
   Larissa Hjorth

Literature and Society
Literature and Society is a series that seeks to demonstrate the ways in which Asian Literature is influenced by the politics, society and culture in which it is produced. Titles include:

1. **The Body in Postwar Japanese Fiction**
   Douglas N. Slaymaker

2. **Chinese Women Writers and the Feminist Imagination, 1905–1948***
   Haiping Yan

Routledge Studies in Asia's Transformations
Routledge Studies in Asia's Transformations is a forum for innovative new research intended for a high-level specialist readership.
Titles include:

1. **The American Occupation of Japan and Okinawa***
   Literature and memory
   Michael Molasky

2. **Koreans in Japan***
   Critical voices from the margin
   Edited by Sonia Ryang

3. **Internationalizing the Pacific**
   The United States, Japan and the Institute of Pacific Relations in war and peace, 1919–1945
   Tomoko Akami

4. **Imperialism in South East Asia***
   'A fleeting, passing phase'
   Nicholas Tarling

5. **Chinese Media, Global Contexts***
   Edited by Chin-Chuan Lee

6. **Remaking Citizenship in Hong Kong***
   Community, nation and the global city
   Edited by Agnes S. Ku and Ngai Pun

7. **Japanese Industrial Governance**
   Protectionism and the licensing state
   Yul Sohn

8. **Developmental Dilemmas***
   Land reform and institutional change in China
   Edited by Peter Ho

9. **Genders, Transgenders and Sexualities in Japan***
   Edited by Mark McLelland and Romit Dasgupta

10. **Fertility, Family Planning and Population Policy in China***
    Edited by Dudley L. Poston, Che-Fu Lee, Chiung-Fang Chang, Sherry L. McKibben and Carol S. Walther

11. **Japanese Diasporas***
    Unsung pasts, conflicting presents and uncertain futures
    Edited by Nobuko Adachi

12. **How China Works***
    Perspectives on the twentieth-century industrial workplace
    Edited by Jacob Eyferth

13. **Remolding and Resistance among Writers of the Chinese Prison Camp**
    Disciplined and published
    Edited by Philip F. Williams and Yenna Wu

14. **Popular Culture, Globalization and Japan***
    Edited by Matthew Allen and Rumi Sakamoto

15. **medi@sia***
    Global media/tion in and out of context
    Edited by Todd Joseph Miles Holden and Timothy J. Scrase

16. **Vientiane***
    Transformations of a Lao landscape
    Marc Askew, William S. Logan and Colin Long

17. **State Formation and Radical Democracy in India**
    Manali Desai

18. **Democracy in Occupied Japan***
    The U.S. occupation and Japanese politics and society
    Edited by Mark E. Caprio and Yoneyuki Sugita

19. **Globalization, Culture and Society in Laos***
    Boike Rehbein

20. **Transcultural Japan***
    At the borderlands of race, gender, and identity
    Edited by David Blake Willis and Stephen Murphy-Shigematsu

21. **Post-Conflict Heritage, Post-Colonial Tourism**
    Culture, politics and development at Angkor
    Tim Winter

22. **Education and Reform in China***
    Emily Hannum and Albert Park

23. **Writing Okinawa: Narrative Acts of Identity and Resistance**
    Davinder L. Bhowmik

24. **Maid in China***
    Media, mobility, and a new semiotic of power
    Wanning Sun

25. **Northern Territories, Asia-Pacific Regional Conflicts and the Åland Experience**
    Untying the Kurillian knot
    Edited by Kimie Hara and Geoffrey Jukes

26. **Reconciling Indonesia**
    Grassroots agency for peace
    Birgit Bräuchler

27. **Singapore in the Malay World***
    Building and breaching regional bridges
    Lily Zubaidah Rahim

28. **Pirate Modernity***
    Delhi's media urbanism
    Ravi Sundaram

29. **The World Bank and the post-Washington Consensus in Vietnam and Indonesia**
    Inheritance of loss
    Susan Engel

30. **China on Video**
    Smaller screen realities
    Paola Voci

31. **Overseas Chinese, Ethnic Minorities and Nationalism**
    De-Centering China
    Elena Barabantseva

Critical Asian Scholarship

Critical Asian Scholarship is a series intended to showcase the most important individual contributions to scholarship in Asian Studies. Each of the volumes presents a leading Asian scholar addressing themes that are central to his or her most significant and lasting contribution to Asian studies. The series is committed to the rich variety of research and writing on Asia, and is not restricted to any particular discipline, theoretical approach or geographical expertise.

1. **Southeast Asia***
   A testament
   George McT. Kahin

2. **Women and the Family in Chinese History***
   Patricia Buckley Ebrey

3. **China Unbound***
   Evolving perspectives on the Chinese past
   Paul A. Cohen

4. **China's Past, China's Future***
   Energy, food, environment
   Vaclav Smil

5. **The Chinese State in Ming Society***
   Timothy Brook

6. **China, East Asia and the Global Economy***
   Regional and historical perspectives
   Takeshi Hamashita
   Edited by Mark Selden and Linda Grove

7. **The Global and Regional in China's Nation-Formation***
   Prasenjit Duara

* Available in paperback

The Market and Temple Fairs of Rural China
Red fire

Gene Cooper

LONDON AND NEW YORK

First published 2013 by Routledge

2 Park Square, Milton Park, Abingdon, Oxon OX14 4RN
711 Third Avenue, New York, NY 10017, USA

Routledge is an imprint of the Taylor & Francis Group, an informa business

First issued in paperback 2017

Copyright © 2013 Gene Cooper

The right of Gene Cooper to be identified as author of this work has been asserted by him in accordance with sections 77 and 78 of the Copyright, Designs and Patents Act 1988.

All rights reserved. No part of this book may be reprinted or reproduced or utilised in any form or by any electronic, mechanical, or other means, now known or hereafter invented, including photocopying and recording, or in any information storage or retrieval system, without permission in writing from the publishers.

Notice:
Product or corporate names may be trademarks or registered trademarks, and are used only for identification and explanation without intent to infringe.

British Library Cataloguing in Publication Data
A catalogue record for this book is available from the British Library

Library of Congress Cataloging in Publication Data
Cooper, Eugene, 1947-
The market and temple fairs of rural China : red fire / Gene Cooper.
    p. cm. – (Asia's transformations)
Includes bibliographical references and index.
1. Fairs–China–History. 2. Bazaars (Markets)–China–History. 3. Temples–China–History. 4. China–Social life and customs. 5. China–Rural conditions. I. Title.
GT4863.A2C66 2012
381′.1860951–dc23
                                                                2012004384

ISBN: 978-0-415-52079-9 (hbk)
ISBN: 978-1-138-10948-3 (pbk)

Typeset in Times New Roman
by Graphicraft Limited, Hong Kong

Contents

List of plates   xi
List of maps   xii
List of tables   xiii
Preface and acknowledgments   xiv

1   Introduction: conceptual framework   1

PART I
BACKGROUND AND SETTING   7

2   The field site—the Jinhua region: geographic, historical and political-economic background   9

3   Religion in Jinhua and perspectives for understanding it   34

4   Temple fairs in Chinese history and Chinese folklore studies   54

PART II
UNRAVELING THE STRANDS OF THE TOTAL SOCIAL PHENOMENON   63

5   Secular fairs: the commercial/economic dimension   65

6   The popular cultural dimension   95

7   More popular culture: Wuju (Jinhua opera)   113

8   The religious dimension: the temple fair of Hugong Dadi 胡公大帝   150

9	The political dimension: macro and micro	185
10	Fotang town: the resacralization of a commercial fair	194
11	Conclusions	210

Appendix 1: Selected Daoqing repertoire items   217
Appendix 2: Selected Wuju repertoire items   221
Bibliography   226
Index   239

Plates

2.1	Filming on the Guangzhou Street lot: Hengdian	23
2.2	Qingming Shanghe Tu lot under construction: Hengdian	24
2.3	Recreated palace walls: Hengdian	24
3.1	New Huang Daxian temple: Jinhua	43
5.1	Freaks of nature: Huqi	71
5.2	Toy vendor: Qianxiang	74
5.3	Winnowers for sale: Qianxiang	75
5.4	Dough artist: Qianxiang	76
5.5	Street peddler: Xiawang	83
5.6	Xiawang child contortionist in Zhudaishi	84
5.7	Child contortionist performing: Xiawang	85
5.8	Road to the fair: Zhudaishi	90
5.9	Draft animal market: Zhudaishi	91
5.10	Freaks of nature: Zhudaishi	92
5.11	Snake handler: Zhudaishi	92
5.12	Raising the circus tent: Zhudaishi	93
5.13	Trained monkey: Zhudaishi	93
6.1	Xiaoluo shu: Fotang	99
6.2	Taige children: Fangyan	111
6.3	The author with a Taige child: Fangyan	111
7.1	Putting on make-up: Xiawang	123
7.2	Opera performance: Luodian	124
7.3	Opera performance: Fotang	125
7.4	Opera performance: Luodian	125
7.5	Opera audience: Fotang	137
8.1	Hugong temple: Fangyan	163
8.2	Hugong Dadi: Fangyan	164
8.3	Pusa visiting: Fangyan	170
8.4	36 professions: Fangyan	179
8.5	18 foxes: Fangyan	180
9.1	Hugong temple: Huku	190
10.1	Dancing girls: Fotang	204
10.2	House of horror: Fotang	205
10.3	Goods on sale: Fotang	206
10.4	Street vendor: Fotang	206
10.5	Medicinal herbs for sale: Fotang	207
10.6	One-man band: Fotang	207

Maps

2.1	China with provinces	9
2.2	Zhejiang showing Jinhua	10
2.3	Jinhua with counties and townships	10
2.4	Zhejiang river systems	11
2.5	Hengdian	22
2.6	Urban Yiwu	30
8.1	Yongkang	151
10.1	Fotang with historic preservation area	199

Tables

2.1	Annual GDP for four county-cities in Jinhua Municipality (in ¥10,000)	16
2.2	Jinhua GDP, 1978–2007 (¥)	17
2.3	Jinhua trade volume, exports and imports (US$)	18
2.4	Hengdiang industrial APV (¥)	20
2.5	Yiwu trade volume (¥)	32
3.1	Temples in Jinhua, 1480	35
3.2	Daoist temples in Jinhua, 1480	40
7.1	The genres of Wuju	120

Preface and acknowledgments

The origins of this book go back to the late 1980s, when Professor Jiang Yinhuo of the department of economics at Zhejiang University and I spent several months trundling around Dongyang county on an itinerary set up for us by the county Foreign Affairs Office in a study of rural artisan and industrial enterprises (see Cooper and Jiang 1998). In the spring of 1989, as we proceeded through the southern townships of the county, from Hengdian on lunar 2/23, to Nanma on 2/25, to Huangtianfan on 3/3, to Louxi Zhai on 3/11, back to the county seat, Wuning on 3/28, by chance we encountered a secular commodity exchange fair in every town. Our itinerary also coincided with that of the many peddlers who appeared repeatedly at each successive venue, clearly taking advantage of the clustering of fairs in the region during the late spring to hit successive fairs one after another with their arrays of lumber, furniture, agricultural tools, medicinal preparations, clothing, shoes, etc. Distinct from the weekly standard market, these are annual or semi-annual events which in the days before the establishment of the People's Republic often coincided with the lunar calendar birthday of a deity, and a traditional festival held in its honor centered on a local temple.

As we made our way through the "mountains and seas of people" in each market town, the dynamism and press of the crowds that engulfed us, what the townsfolk of the Jinhua region identify as *honghuo* – "red fire", was electric. The display of goods on the streets and alleyways, the street performers, gongfu/qigong aficionados, circuses, trained animal acts, opera performances, one-man bands, snake oil salesmen, healers, fortune tellers, gambling and games of chance of all kinds, and nowadays mechanical carnival rides for the kids, and even itinerant night club acts performing in huge canvas tents, everything out there in the open, a showcase of rural society, popular culture and expression.

However, I had spent the previous five years trying to secure approval from Chinese authorities for a project on rural industry (see Cooper 2000), and having finally got the Ministry of Education to sign off on my collaboration with Prof. Jiang, changing the focus of our research in midstream was not an option. But my curiosity was engaged, and I was determined to return to Zhejiang at some point in the future to investigate this rural fair phenomenon.

With *The Artisans and Entreprenuers of Dongyang County* going to press, I succeeded in securing funding to carry out a multi-sited ethnographic research project in Jinhua municipality from July through December of 1998, and investigated market and temple fairs in the towns of Qianxiang and Huqi (Dongyang county), Fangyan and Huku (Yongkang county), Zhudaishi and Shangwang (Lanxi county), Fotang (Yiwu county), and Luodian (Jinhua county)[1]. That research would never have gone forward without the imprimatur of Professor Yu Binghui of the sociology department of what was then Zhejiang Agricultural University in Hangzhou, now one of several campuses in a consolidated Zhejiang University. The transition to consolidation was in process during the course of the research.

Upon arrival in Hangzhou however, it very quickly became clear that Professor Yu was too busy with a multitude of other projects to accompany me on repeated research forays from Hangzhou into the rural areas of Jinhua, and I was therefore left pretty much in the hands of the university Foreign Affairs Office to arrange for my reception by local authorities in the townships where I had determined there were fairs to visit. This was both a blessing and a curse.

On the one hand, it put me unequivocally in charge of my own affairs to manage as I saw fit, for which I was grateful. However, despite the loosening up of controls on social life experienced by Chinese citizens under the economic reforms of the past two decades, foreign researchers were still subject to regulations on their movements and actions similar to pre-reform regulations on the Chinese citizenry as a whole.

As a foreign researcher, someone was required to assume responsibility for my person at all times. Going out on my own to carry out unsupervised interviews in villages or towns of my own choosing was out of the question. My foreign visage meant unobtrusively poking around and asking questions in rural townships was quite impossible, and would immediately come to the attention of local authorities, and then... where would I hide? While there was almost complete freedom for backpackers to travel at will through the countryside, and put up at local inns and hotels, the movements of a "researcher" affiliated with a Chinese unit were considerably more circumscribed.[2]

In my case, for each locale I proposed to visit, it was necessary to get the Foreign Affairs Office (FAO) of the county in the loop to arrange for my local reception, and most importantly to take responsibility for the security of my person, or so they always said. In the initial stages of the work, much of the burden of arranging for my reception by local FAOs fell on the shoulders of Mr. Yu Yiwen of the Zhejiang Agricultural University FAO who did his best to cope with my seemingly endless stream of requests and demands for contacting his sister offices in the cities and towns where I hoped to conduct investigations. I subsequently discovered that the cultural offices (Wenhua bu) in these locales were often more effective and more well-informed than the local FAOs in making arrangements for the conduct of ethnographic fieldwork, and more sympathetic with its goals. For the latter two months of the project, I was able to take advantage of this new found knowledge in arranging for local reception in several different counties.

In crafting a suitable sequence of visits to the fair sites, I relied on a province wide schedule of market fairs in Zhejiang, printed for the benefit of merchants wishing to plan their own itineraries to maximize the sales of their wares at the fairs in the province. The schedule was quite indispensable in planning my own research itinerary.

I both began and concluded my forays out to the fairs of Jinhua with visits to Dongyang county, where my local contacts were most extensive, and where I was already familiar with the local geography, the result of my earlier researches on rural industry. The former chairman of cultural affairs (wenlian zhuxi), Mr. Lu Xibing, and his associate in the study of local folklore, Mr. Chen Chongren, were instrumental in arranging visits to the townships of Hengdian, Qianxiang and Huqi, and in providing flexible and knowledgeable "official" reception and guidance. In Hengdian, the ever ebullient local entrepreneur, Mr. Chen Tianhong provided encouragement, good humor, and assistance in arranging local reception in Hengdian and Qianxiang through his own local contacts.

During my earliest unofficial trip to Dongyang county in 1986, I had occasion to visit neighboring Yongkang county's Fangyan "scenic area", and to climb to one of its peaks where the temple of one Hugong Dadi was still being reconstructed after having been leveled during the Cultural Revolution. At the time I knew nothing of Hugong's significance in the region, and it was only later I discovered that he was a deified righteous official of the Northern Song Dynasty (960–1127 AD), one Hu Ze, whose worship was again widespread in central and southern Zhejiang, and that he had a place among the Five (imperially recognized) Marquises (Wu Hou) of Jinhua. Most importantly, the revived temple fair at Fangyan during the month surrounding Hugong's "birthday" on lunar 8/13 was one of the grandest in the region, and noteworthy for the popular religious dimension associated with it from the very inception of its revival, marking it as the definitive total social phenomenon. So there was to be no way I would miss the grand temple fair in Fangyan on lunar 8/13, and I organized my itinerary to be certain that I would have a chance to visit Yongkang at that time, and as it turned out I was able to spend three days at the temple site during the high tide of performances to entertain the deity (see Chapter 8).

Local Yongkang historians, Mr. Ying Baorong and Mr. Hu Guojun were both instrumental in my education regarding Hugong, and I have Professor Gong Jianfeng of Jinhua Normal University to thank not only for introducing Mssrs. Ying and Hu to me, but also for providing an endless stream of books, articles, information and contacts in the fields of local Zhejiang history, folklore and popular culture. And for introducing me to Professor Gong, I must thank Professor Peter Bol, who having by chance discovered my existence during his own researches in the region, has offered gracious encouragement of this project from its earliest stages.

During an extended stay in Yongkang to investigate the Hugong fair, in addition to Messrs Ying and Hu, I was also assisted in my local arrangements by Mr. Luo Haiying of the Yongkang FAO. Mr. Xu Bin of the Office of the Fangyan Scenic Area (Fengjingqu Bangongshi) served as my local guide (peitong), and Mr. Hu Jianfeng of the Scenic Area's Tourism Office (Luyouju) provided much useful information on the locale. My investigations in the Yongkang township of Huku where Hugong was born, were graciously assisted by Mr. Cheng Nanshan of the Huku township government.

In a second visit to Yongkang, Mr. Chen Weimin of the Yongkang cultural bureau was instrumental in arranging my local reception. For the introduction to Mr. Chen, I am thankful for the efforts of Ms. Su Weiqian of the Jinhua cultural bureau who also had a hand in making arrangements for my investigations in Luodian and Lanxi.

During my stay in Yongkang, I was invited to attend the opening ceremonies of the annual metal products exhibition (wujin bolanhui) at which I was fortunate to have been seated next to Mr. Kong Zhe, the party secretary of Lanxi city, and his office later proved indispensable in arranging for the Lanxi cultural bureau to formally receive me, and serve as my host unit during investigations there. Mr. Wang Xiaodi from the bureau was a delightful and helpful companion during my work in Xiawang and Zhudaishi townships. As a way of reciprocating his valued assistance, I was able to donate to his appreciative household the set of countertop gas burners to which one of my fair-bought raffle tickets entitled me.

In Fotang, my local arrangements were supervised by Ms. Chen Jianfeng of the Yiwu county FAO, and facilitated by her superior, Ms. Feng Meilan FAO director. Through their efforts, I was put in the care of cultural affairs personnel, Mr. Huang Meiyan and Mr. Fu Jian of the Yiwu Museum, the latter of whom served as guide in my Fotang investigations. Mr. Jin Shouxing, Mayor of Fotang and Mr. Zong Fengqin, Fotang party secretary encouraged my efforts, and placed Mr. Pan Yixi and Mr. Wang Chunping, of Fotang government offices at my service, whose efforts on behalf of the project were indeed substantial both in the field and in subsequent email correspondence. Mr. Jia Cangbin, co-editor of the local township gazetteer was a mine of information on local history and folklore.

In Luodian, the able assistance of Ms. Zhou Yaping of the Jinhua FAO helped to make my inquiries there both convenient and productive, despite the rain, over which she had no control. Luodian Mayor Wang Yueping and Vice Party Secretary Wang Caifu were extremely accommodating.

In a brief data collection trip to Jinhua in the summer of 2006, Mr. Zhang Zhulin provided untold riches regarding the performance genre, Jinhua Daoqing, of which he is a composer, documentarian and performer, and Mr. Huang Jianhua of the office of the local history journal *Wuxing* (Jinhua Star) provided indispensable materials on Wuju, the local Jinhua opera genre. Regarding Wuju, I was also assisted in post-fieldwork correspondence by Mr. Bao Huasheng of the Jinhua Arts Institute (金华艺术研究所) who brought to my attention, and graciously sent me several quite indispensable recently published volumes on the subject.

In addition to observations, fieldnotes, and photographs from my field outings I also brought back a substantial number of secondary source materials on the subject of temple fairs, and gazetteers on the local history of each community in the multi-sited study. There is a rich modern historical/ social science literature on rural market/temple fairs in China, since their academic study began in the 1920s when Professor Gu Jiegang led a team of students from Peking University to investigate the fair at the temple of Bixia Yuanjun at Miaofeng Shan (Gu 1928), thereby inaugurating the field of modern Chinese folklore studies. Chinese folklorists, historians and social scientists since that time have continued the study of the fairs in their varied dimensions (see Chapter 4) (see eg. Dong 1981; He and Jin 1983; Wang and Liu 1987; Gao 1992; Zhong 1999; Zhao 1996, 2002; Liu n.d.).

Before I dared write a word, I felt I must at least preliminarily acquaint myself with the literature on the study of temple fairs carried out by these forerunners, and to learn something of the history of the temple fair phenomenon, its constituent performance genres and religious practices, and of the various communities whose temple fairs I had observed. For providing the time and setting to carry out that work during the 2006–7 academic year, I must thank the Institute for Advanced Study in Princeton and Professor Joan Scott of the School of Social Sciences. Participants in Professor Scott's Third World Now Seminar and Professor Nicola di Cosmo's East Asian Studies Seminar were also important first audiences for many of the ideas and analyses that follow, and contributed a great deal to the effort through many a challenging and stimulating session of critical discussion.

The metaphor Red Fire (Hong huo) used to describe the excitement and commotion of the crowds at Chinese ritual events was a minor theme in my fieldnotes during my ethnographic investigation of temple fairs in Jinhua. It was not until I read Adam Chau's half tongue in cheek espousal of a "sociothermic theory" of Chinese sociality, with Red Fire as its basis, that I came to realize the salience of the metaphor in expressing what was distinctive about the market and temple fairs I had investigated. Thus, the book found its title, with some assistance from Mark Selden, my editor at Routledge.

Notes

1 The research in Jinhua was funded by a grant from the Committee on Scholarly Communication with China of the American Council of Learned Societies.
2 I had always thought that the restrictions I had to deal with were the result of my being a foreigner, until I read of the experiences of Professor Cao Jinqing of Shanghai Huadong University's sociology department, who in a study of the rural economy of Henan province (Cao 2005) encountered many obstacles and difficulties similar to mine gaining unfettered access to field sites and prospective interviewees, despite a network of personal contacts with local Communist Party officials. I confess to having taken great joy in Professor Cao's experience (Cooper 2005), and had the pleasure of visiting with him in Shanghai in 2006, and telling him so in person.

1 Introduction
Conceptual framework

In what follows, Chinese temple fairs are understood as total social phenomena in the sense in which Marcel Mauss (1928) used the term, combining the secular and the spiritual, the economic, popular cultural, artistic, religious, political, and social dimensions of rural life in a single event/institution.

The narrative arc of this book is an exploration of how, in the context of state economic reform efforts to revive and stimulate rural political economy in the early 1980s, secular commodity exchange fairs were accorded the geographic and metaphoric space to function. And once these truncated "temple-less temple fairs" (Cohen 2005: 92) were in place, they not only came to serve as venues for the proliferation of a great variety of popular cultural performance genres, but also as sites where a revival/recycling of popular religious practices and symbols, already underway in many parts of China, found familiar and fertile ground in which to spread, thereby reestablishing the "totality" of the traditional temple fair.

In these two senses then, the fairs have provided a setting in which practitioners of popular cultural performance genres and popular religion have begun to "improvise" new ways of behaving, what Bourdieu (1977: 8, 11) would have called a new "habitus," informed by the past, but at the same time stretching the envelope of contemporary popular cultural and popular religious expression.

In the end I will argue that as Chinese rural folk have moved to fill in the ideological interstices left by the delegitimization of Communist orthodoxy and the dismantling of collectivist institutions, the fairs have become sites where they engage in their version of "the struggle to control the concepts and symbols by which current experience is evaluated" (Scott 1985: 27).

The multifunctional totality of Chinese temple fairs is not something Chinese folklorists and historians would find controversial. As Li and Yan have expressed it, popular ideology, standards of value, modes of thought and behavior, moral values, aesthetics, religious sensibility, habit and custom are all on display at temple fairs, a veritable "window on society." To study the temple fair is nothing less than "to study the character and spirit of a place" (Li and Yan 1992: 186).

Thus I trust that by the end of this volume devoted to the study of the temple fairs of Jinhua, readers will come away having learned something of the character and spirit of the municipality, and of several of its constituent communities, as well as reflecting on broader patterns of a society in flux.

Yang has noted that the study of the multi-functionality of temple fairs requires multidisciplinary breadth:

> Those who would study the culture of temple fairs need expertise in fields related to anthropology, religious studies, sociology, history, philosophy, psychology, economics, art, [as well as music and theater] and the knowledge and theory of other social sciences; [one needs] a multidisciplinary theory and method to study the combined nature [of temple fairs].
>
> (Yang 1992: 15)

This book is a humble attempt to combine these various fields of expertise so as to convey the multiple dimensions of temple fair activity, and demonstrate how the multifunctional totality of the fairs has provided a setting in which the boundaries of the acceptable in contemporary popular cultural and religious expression in China have been expanded.

Along the way, in addition to Mauss and Bourdieu, I combine an engagement with the literature on popular religion in China (Brook 2009; Chau 2006a; Dean 2009; Gates 1995; Goossaert 2005; Overmyer 2009; Potter 2003; Yang 1967) with a discussion of the grotesque in temple fair entertainments (after Bakhtin 1965 and Zhao 2002), combined with a recognition of the importance of the fairs as temporary autonomous zones (after Dean 2003), characterized by an egalitarian and potentially counterhegemonic spirit (after Zhao 2002), venues congenial to sub-insurrectional forms of resistance (after Scott 1985).

My approach is ethnographic, but I attach particular importance to history. In China where every institution and performance genre has a long history, it is essential to combine the observations of ethnography with the historical background necessary to make those observations meaningful.

The relationship between anthropology and history was broached by E.E. Evans-Pritchard in his Marrett lecture of 1950, in an effort to encourage British Structure-Functionalist anthropology to abandon its ahistorical practice. At the time, he quoted Maitland approvingly to the effect that "Anthropology must choose between being history or being nothing" (quoted in Evans-Pritchard, 1962), and later also insisted that history must choose between being social anthropology or being nothing.

The recognition of that complementarity seems to have gained some additional traction in recent years. Most recently, Chinese historian Yao Ping (2011) immersed herself in the specialized literature on kinship, and effectively employed anthropological approaches in her interpretation of historical materials of the Tang dynasty (AD 618–907). And historian David Johnson found that his "aim of describing the most important rituals of a few North China villages as completely as possible" put him squarely within the realm of "what at least some anthropologists aspire to," although in combining the concerns of anthropologist and historian, Johnson feared he would satisfy neither (2009: 17).

Notwithstanding such anxieties, which I share, this book is also an argument for the importance of combining anthropology with history in the study of Chinese society, for providing sufficient historical detail of the communities, activities, rituals, performance genres, and deities discussed in the narrative to make the ethnographic observations in the present more meaningful.

The fairs

Temple fairs in China were suppressed or secularized during the early Communist period of the 1950s. Temples were closed down by the secular regime, their activities classified as feudal superstition. In some ways, this was merely a more efficient, and certainly more far-reaching, implementation of the anti-superstition campaigns of their Republican predecessors (Chapter 3). Thus only truncated secular commodity trade fairs were permitted in the early 1950s and were quite common, but even secular fairs were convened much less frequently after 1958 when the standard market towns in which they were held were closed down during the Great Leap Forward. In the early 1960s the fairs made a brief resurgence during the period of recovery from the disastrous effects of the Great Leap famine.

But during the cultural revolution (1966–76) even these secular fairs, devoted exclusively to trade with no religious content of any kind, were deemed to be the "sprouts of capitalist restoration" and suppressed, along with the "four olds"—old habits, customs, belief, and culture. Any temples or idols that had escaped destruction in the early period of secularization, or even the murals and carvings on rural dwellings, pavilions, and classical architectural specimens were destroyed, defaced or otherwise vandalized. Popular cultural expressive genres were muzzled except for those that celebrated the virtues of the workers, peasants and soldiers as interpreted in Cultural Revolution terms.

After Mao's death in 1976 and the repudiation of leftist Cultural Revolution policies at the Third Plenum of the Eleventh Central Committee in 1978, China embarked on its path of free-market reform, and secular commodity exchange fairs were again authorized in the interest of stimulating rural commodity production, circulation, and commerce, and boosting rural incomes and consumption. Hence, our repeated encounters with them during research in Dongyang in 1989. Authorizing, and in some cases, encouraging such fairs to revive, Communist authorities have been quite successful in stimulating rural commodity trade (see Chapter 5). Indeed, this vast traditional arena of commerce has reemerged and contributed to a significant growth in the spirit of consumerism.

At the same time, the dismantling of the collective sector and the ubiquitous Communist Party surveillance apparatus, along with the pull-back of the party from its attempts to control the myriad details of people's lives, left some space for people to begin to express themselves creatively, spiritually and ritually, and to legitimately pursue private gain, and the fulfillment of personal desire. And the revived fairs have become an important and legitimate venue for that expression and pursuit.

In present-day Jinhua the fairs usually last for three days, during which time the scale and reach of the market is far greater than the weekly "standard" market held in the same town three times during each ten-day "market week." The fairs attract merchants from distant provinces, and the diversity and level of specialization of goods offered for sale is substantially greater than that of the standard weekly market. In a sense, during the fair, once or twice a year, the standard market town is transformed into an "intermediate level" market (Skinner 1964–5: 38, 380). Households will often postpone major purchases to take advantage of the greater variety and selection of goods available at an upcoming fair. And once at the fair, it is common knowledge that prices drop toward the afternoon of the third day, as merchants look to unload their goods to avoid having to carry them elsewhere, and bargains can be had.

Some fairs are known for their specialized market in a particular local product, and perform important wholesaling functions, like the medicinal herb market of the Qianxiang fair (see Chapter 5). Fairs held in particular seasons tend to specialize in products associated with that time of year. Dowry goods—cloth, furniture, cosmetics—are plentiful at the fairs during fall and early winter, whereas spring fairs are dominated by agricultural tools, equipment, and draft animals. The fairs also serve as a time to visit relatives and friends across a broader region, and engage in more extensive social and commercial networking. It is said that when a fair is held in one's own locale, it is customary to lay in a supply of food and sweets well in advance to prepare to receive the sure to be many unannounced visitors and guests.

The fairs also reverberate with the performances of popular cultural genres of all kinds, operatic, narrative, divinational, martial, acrobatic, craft, artistic, and musical, not to mention games of chance, competing for the attention and patronage of the assembled multitudes. That reverberation, what Mauss would have called "effervescence," is precisely what the Chinese metaphor 'red fire' (*honghuo*) conveys, the sense of excitement and commotion, generated by large crowds enjoying the variegated entertainments. Indeed the fairs have become arenas where creative voices of the most disparate sort have had the opportunity of responding to, while further enlarging the scope for, individual initiative and expression offered by China's economic reforms.

Some of those voices might even be characterized as giving expression to alternative, potentially counter-hegemonic discourses, most notably those of popular religious practice, but others as well. C.K. Yang has characterized temple fairs historically as occasions when the regular rules of conventional sociality and morality were temporarily suspended, "removing participants from preoccupation with small-group, convention ridden, routinized daily life" (Yang 1967: 89). And no small number of the performances and exhibitions at the secular fairs of Jinhua pass muster as exemplars of the grotesque in a sense that Bakhtin (1965) would doubtless recognize, contortionists, one-man bands, houses of horror, displays of freaks of nature, trained animal acts, etc. (Chapters 5 and 6).

Opera performances to "entertain the deity" of the host temple were the high point of temple fair entertainment prior to the establishment of the People's Republic of China (PRC) (Lu 1922), and Jinhua still possesses its own distinctive group of local operatic genres known collectively as Wuju (Chapter 7). With men performing as women, and make-up and costume that transformed ordinary humans into gargantuan deities and heroes and heroines, Chinese opera provides an excellent example of Bakhtinian grotesquery on display at temple fairs. The opera also served to attract crowds to the secular market of the temple fair, and Wuju troupes remain in demand nowadays by local merchants' associations in the towns of the commercially revived secular fairs to do just that, absent their ritual and religious function of entertaining the deity.

The beliefs, discourse and practices of popular religion were at the core of pre-liberation temple fairs which were most prominently ritual occasions, celebrations of the "birthdays" of Buddhist deities, Daoist immortals, or deified historical personages of good Confucian character, and occasions for the performance of rituals at their temples, celebrating their deeds, seeking their general blessing for the year, or their intervention in relieving hardship, and vowing to reciprocate if the deity proved efficacious. Indeed, in the 1980s when the fairs were once again authorized for their commercial function, popular sentiment often required that they be scheduled according to their traditional lunar dates on the birthdays of the temple deities of the past, even when the temples no longer existed.

In some instances, revived fairs included a religious dimension from the very moment of their revival like the fair in Fangyan township, Yongkang county at which the deity Hugong Dadi is worshipped (Chapter 8). Elsewhere, as in the town of Fotang in Yiwu county, the revival of a secular fair for the sake of commerce helped to encourage the rebuilding of Shuanglin temple, and for the temple to resume providing the appropriate popular religious context to the secular fair, completing the total social phenomenon as it were (Chapter 10).

Thus, even while the commercial and recreational functions of such fairs have been celebrated and their religious elements downplayed in official contemporary media, the cooptation of this traditional institution of rural trade to serve the commercial interests of the modern secular state has added fuel to the revival of popular religion and a recycling of popular religious symbols and practices that fly in the face of state regulations against activities that promulgate "superstition."

For their part, state authorities have abandoned their adherence to the "teleology that assumed that the people would give up their opiate once the social relations of production had been revolutionized" (Brook 2009: 22), and adopted a policy I characterize as "circumscribed toleration" toward the popular religious revival (Chapter 9). Unlike Falun gong and the Christian churches, Chinese indigenous religions, popular cults and their temples do not seem to be perceived by the Communist state as constituting a significant threat to its power, and their temple fairs have even been noted for their potential in promoting tourism!

The fairs are thus an ideal window on the popular culture of contemporary Jinhua, both secular and religious, and by implication of contemporary China more broadly, from individual street performers (Chapter 6), to practitioners of local opera, both professional and amateur (Chapter 7), to the participation of ordinary villagers in entertainment of the temple deity, in both martial and culturally themed performances (Chapter 8).

The book unfolds in two parts:

Part I is devoted to providing background of the Jinhua region, its modern history, geographic endowments, and contemporary political economy (Chapter 2); its religious institutions and perspectives for understanding them (Chapter 3); and a brief coda on the history of Chinese temple fairs down through to the Republic, when in the 1910s and 1920s temple fairs were "discovered" by early practitioners of Chinese folklore studies as a quintessential specimen of popular culture (Chapter 4).

Part II unravels the various dimensions of the total social phenomenon, the economic/commercial (Chapter 5), popular cultural (Chapter 6 and 7), popular religious (Chapter 8 and 10), and political (Chapter 9), in the process revealing the sources of red fire that contribute to the success of the temple fair event.

In conclusion (Chapter 11), I argue that the many sources of red fire in turn make clear the multi-functional totality of temple fair activity and rural social life. As temporary autonomous zones, the fairs are sites where the improvisation of a new habitus proceeds in the hands of popular cultural performance artists, popular religious practitioners, their patrons and audiences, where the boundaries of acceptable contemporary discourse are stretched in the "struggle to control the concepts and symbols by which current experience is evaluated" (Scott 1985: 27).

Part I
Background and setting

2 The field site—the Jinhua region

Geographic, historical and political-economic background

Physical/geographical

Jinhua Municipality covers an area of 10,918 square kilometers in central Zhejiang, in the eastern part of the Jinhua–Quzhou Basin. Its territory is dotted by undulating hills which create a series of smaller basins surrounding the central city of Jinhua (Jinhua City webpage #2).

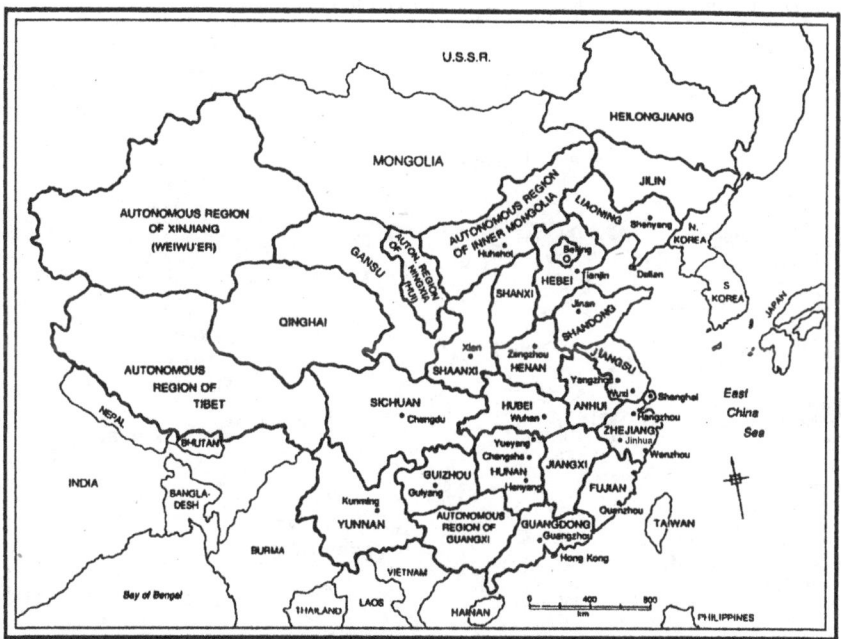

Map 2.1 China with provinces
Source: Cooper 1998

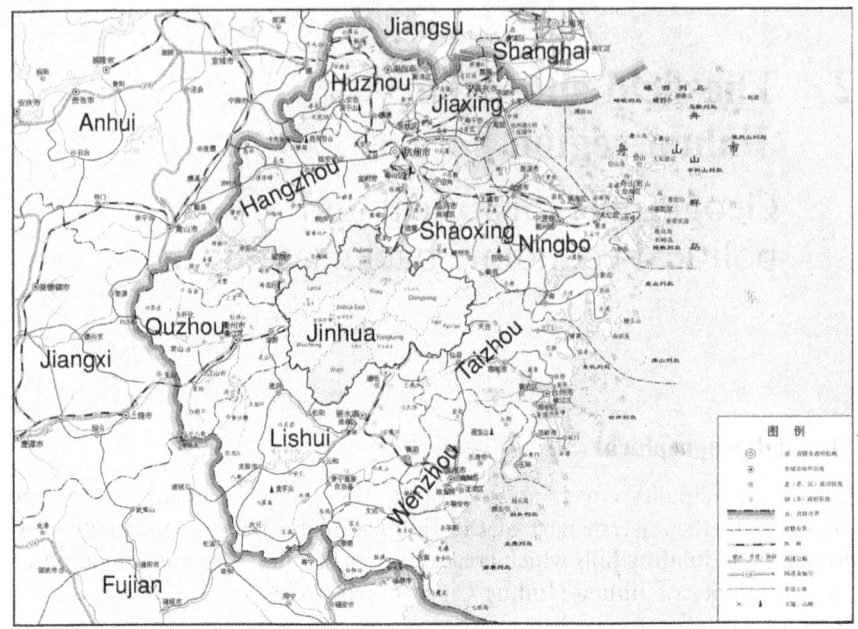

Map 2.2 Zhejiang showing Jinhua
Source: Jinhua City Local Names Committee Office, ed. 1998

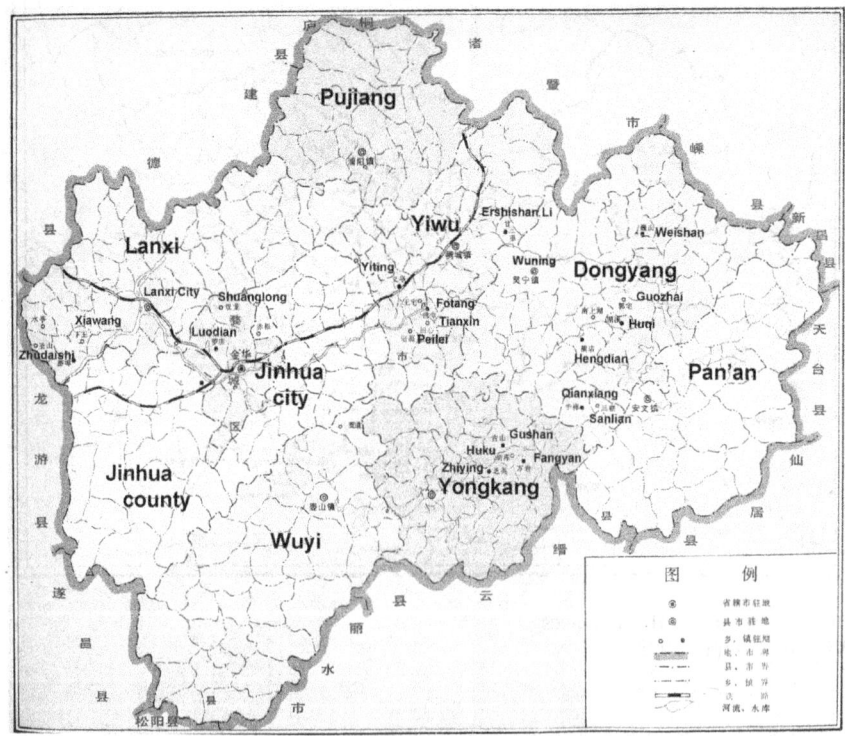

Map 2.3 Jinhua with counties and townships
Source: Jinhua Historical Annals Committee, ed. 1992

The field site—the Jinhua region 11

Climatically, Jinhua is located in the central Asian tropical monsoon zone, characterized by four distinct seasons. Annual temperatures are moderate. Spring comes early, and autumn is short; summers are long and hot, winters are mild. Rainfall is abundant, with clear rainy and dry seasons. The several basins are subject to variable weather patterns, and disastrous extremes occur frequently (Jinhua City webpage #1).

The Dongyang river flows from east to west through the municipality, passing through Dongyang, Yiwu, and Jinhua counties, meeting the Wuyi River in downtown Jinhua, to form the Jinhua River. The Jinhua river flows north to Lanxi where it joins the Qu river to become the Lan river. The Lan river flows north through Jiande city, where it joins the Xin An River at Meicheng town, which in turn becomes the Qiantang River on the way to Hangzhou.

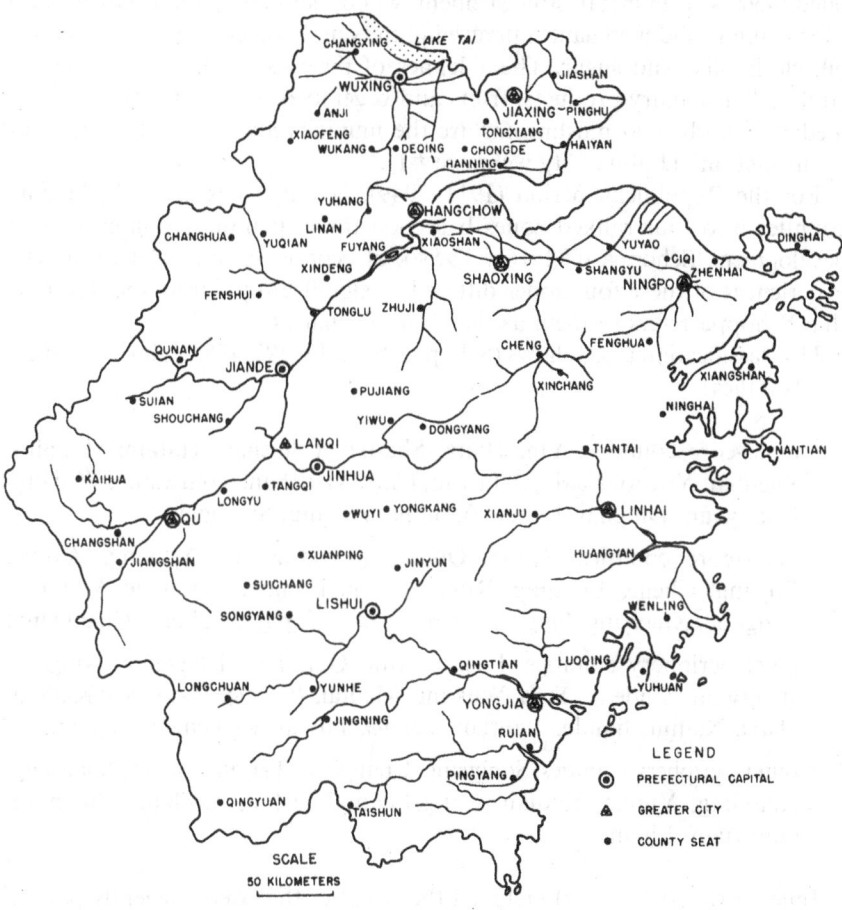

Zhejiang river systems

Map 2.4 Zhejiang river systems
Source: Schoppa 1982

Over the centuries, the territory of present-day Jinhua has variously been known as Dongyang, Jinhua or Wuzhou 婺州, assuming the name Jinhua in 1360 during the Yuan dynasty, which it has kept until today. At various times, both before and since the establishment of the PRC, Jinhua has been combined with the neighboring city of Quzhou in a single prefecture, but in the most recent bureaucratic reorganization of 1985, the two cities became independent administrative municipalities (Jinhua City webpage #1).

Jinhua has been known historically as the "prefecture of 100 skills." During the Tang (AD 618–907) and Song (AD 960–1278) dynasties, the region was known for its craft production of ceramics, silk and cotton goods, metal goods, casting, paper and printing, and during the Ming (1368–1644) and Qing (1644–1911) dynasties the scale of craft workshops expanded. Artisans plied their skills in metal, stone, cement, wood, bamboo, palm products, and wine making, and merchants purveyed pottery and porcelain, paper, vegetable oil, cloth, silk, and sugar. The sidelines of pig raising and meat products (Jinhua ham), dairy products, fruits and vegetables, decorative flowers, tea, medicinal herbs and mushrooms are the municipality's "six local products of distinction" (Jinhua City webpage #1).

For the Republican period (1911–1949), Schoppa has divided Zhejiang counties into four ranked zones based on three quantitative indicators of development (Schoppa 1982: 16).[1] The social, economic, political, and cultural experiences of these four zones differed so significantly during the Republic that Schoppa refers to them as the "four Zhejiangs."

His classification is as follows (Schoppa 1982: 18, 197–198; Jinhua's counties are in italics):

> inner-core counties: Yin, Hang, Shaoxing, Jiashan, Haining, Pinghu, Zhenhai, Yuyao, Jiaxing, Haiyan, Ciqi, Xiaoshan, Tongxiang, Wuxing, Huangyan, Dinghai, Linhai, Yongjia, Deqing, Shangyu;
>
> outer-core counties: *Lanxi*, Qu[zhou], Xiangshan, Yuhang, *Jinhua*, Fuyang, Cheng, Luoqing, Ruian, Zhuji, Longyu, Chongde, Wenling, Fenghua, Xinchang, Pingyang, Changshan, Tonglu, Yuhuan, Changxing;
>
> inner-periphery counties: Lishui, Anji, Qingtian, *Yongkang*, Ninghai, Jiangshan, Xindeng, *Yiwu*, Wukang, Tiantai, *Pujiang, Dongyang*, Kaihua, *Wuyi*, Xianju, Jiande, Nantian, *Tangqi*, Jinyun, Shouchang, Qunan;
>
> outer-periphery counties: Songyang, Changhua, Taishun, Suian, Xuanping, Xiaofeng, Yunhe, Yuqian, Longchuan, Fenshui, Suichang, Jingning, Qingyuan, Linan.

Inner core (20 counties) included the counties that were anciently part of the state of Wu, as well as Hangzhou and the coastal cities of Ningbo, Shaoxing, and Wenzhou of the ancient state of Yue, with Wenzhou at the lower end of the inner core ranking.

Outer core (20 counties) were centers that served as important commercial entrepots, handling large quantities of exported goods (tea, hams, wood products, vegetable tallows, and citrus fruits). Jinhua and Quzhou were included in this zone, as was Lanxi county.

Inner periphery (21 counties) were generally located on minor tributaries of major rivers or occasionally branches of these tributaries. The balance of Jinhua's constituent counties lay in this zone.

Outer periphery (14 counties) were marginal mountainous areas with little arable land (Schoppa 1982: 18–21).

In the early decades of the twentieth century, the inner-core counties experienced political change as the result of economic development which brought new constituencies with new interests into existence, whereas in the outer zones political change came about as a result of the penetration of the state into a milieu where "much tighter, less diverse elite oligarchical structures" prevailed (Schoppa 1982: 188). Magistrates in the inner core generally took a back seat to local gentry, whereas magistrates in the outer zones were somewhat more activist in initiating local projects and monitoring community affairs (Schoppa 1982: 102, 109).

Outer-core economic development lagged behind that of the inner core, and its cities and towns had far fewer same native place commercial associations (*huiguan* 会馆). The rising tide of nationalism that culminated in the 1911 revolution, and the development of the Guomindang nationalist party in the province during the Republic were basically inner-core phenomena (Schoppa 1982: 109, 168, 181).

The chief issue in the inner periphery, affecting all else, was order, coping with bandits and robbers, lineage vendettas, and organizing village defenses against violence and instability. The greater development of the outer core often attracted inner-periphery bandits who used their home counties as a base for attacks (Schoppa 1982: 199–120).

Until the mid-1920s elites from Jinhua, Quzhou, Yanzhou and Chuzhou prefectures controlled few provincial leadership posts and exercised little power in allocating provincial resources to their home areas. Their constituent counties were all located in the three outer zones (Schoppa 1982: 175). Perhaps because of their political weakness, in the late 1910s a combined native place association, the Jin–Qu–Yan–Chu association, was formed to look out for their collective interests in the provincial capital. This was a rather unusual arrangement in provincial politics at the time, but the association nevertheless became an important lobbying group and eventually a major force in Hangzhou politics (Schoppa 1982: 175).

Notwithstanding its relative political weakness, Jinhua prefecture also had its own independent *huiguan* in Hangzhou to look after the commercial interests of its residents (Schoppa 1982: 175), and in the early 1920s was "the only place outside of the inner core where a court functioned" (Schoppa 1982: 98). It was also well represented by same native place *huiguan* in the capital, Beijing.

Of some 500 such *huiguan* in Beijing during the Ming and Qing dynasties, Zhejiang had more than 40, and of these 40 odd, Jinhua had three: Jinhua *huiguan* in Tianlong Si (天龙寺金华会馆), built during the Ming Wanli period, 1573–1620; Jinhua *huiguan* in Banbi Street (半壁街金华会馆), present-day

Sujiapo Hutong 苏家坡胡同, built during the Qing Qianlong period, 1736–1796; and Lanxi Huguan 兰溪会馆 (Dai, ed. 1997: 70).

The *huiguan* functioned as headquarters for Jinhua merchants and other Jinhua natives with business in the capital, and as quarters where imperial examination candidates from Jinhua could reside during their examination ordeal. The Banbi Street *huiguan* was even equipped with a two-story shrine to Wenchang Dijun 文昌帝君, the deity said to control the fate of examination candidates (Dai, ed. 1998: 70).

Lanxi's 兰溪 status as an outer-core county, in advance of its neighbors in Jinhua both economically and politically, is marked by its independent *huiguan* in Beijing. With its thriving commercial port, Lanxi was said to outshine the prefectural government seat in Jinhua. The saying was:

Great Big Lanxi County, Tiny Little Jinhua Prefecture
Dada Lanxi Xian, Xiaoxiao Jinhua Fu 大大兰溪县, 小小金华府

Lanxi was such a busy commercial port that it was often referred to as "Little Shanghai" (Zhang and Hong 1985: 25; ZZL46).

According to an investigation conducted in 1929, Lanxi's trade volume of ¥12,890,000 was three times that of Jinhua's ¥4,370,000. And in 1933, Lanxi's shops and enterprises had a total capital of ¥2,700,000 compared to Jinhua's ¥460,000 (*Jinhua Shizhi* 1992: 644).

In 1937, when the anti-Japanese war began, large numbers of coastal folks fled inland to Jinhua, Lanxi, and Yongkang. Jinhua became an important transfer point linking the inland to the coast. Markets were lively and commerce flourished. In the fall of the following year the city wall was torn down, the streets broadened and improved, and many store fronts repaired. The city had a new face (*Jinhua Shizhi* 1992: 644).

But by 1942, the entire region was occupied by Japanese forces. Resident merchants from other places returned home, and local merchants dispersed to the hills. Urban–rural trade dwindled, and people met their needs largely through itinerant peddlers who purveyed here and there what wares they could secure. After the Japanese defeat, the merchants returned, but money and goods were lacking, sidelines were in difficult straits, and many of the remaining shops closed down. Commerce in the region was only about 10–20 percent of the prewar total (*Jinhua Shizhi* 1992: 644).

And before long, the civil war left another round of destruction, disruption of trade, and increased taxes. Still more shops closed, and commerce was hard hit. But on May 7, 1949, Jinhua was liberated, and the 8th Administrative District of Zhejiang Province was established, renamed the Jinhua Special District several months later (*Jinhua Shizhi* 1992: 645), and a modicum of stability was restored.

The greater Jinhua Municipality of today straddles the outer core and inner periphery of Schoppa's Republican-period classification, with Lanxi and Jinhua City in the outer core, and the rest of its constituent counties in the inner periphery. A legacy of the Republican period core–periphery structure of the province is the persisting inequality between northeastern and southwestern regions of Zhejiang. During the Maoist–socialist period, the state sector was much stronger in the northeast, and the southwest was "largely left to its own devices." Since the economic reforms have been instituted, the southwest has been characterized by the prominence of its private sector (Forster 1998: 99–100), which has given the region some new dynamism.

Jinhua's relatively poorer inner-peripheral counties (Dongyang, Yiwu, and Yongkang) have by all accounts taken greater advantage of the opportunities offered by economic reform since the 1980s than the agriculturally and commercially better endowed "outer-core" western county of Lanxi. The relatively backward peripheral counties were also helped by the recent development and expansion of land-based transport, both road and rail. But until very recently, there were still very few foreign-funded enterprises in the "more backward" inland areas of Zhejiang such as Jinhua, Quzhou, and Lishui (Forster 1998: 102).

Lanxi's decline relative to Yiwu, Dongyang, and Yongkang since the early period of economic reform is revealed in the following figures for GDP of each county-city. From the chart it can be seen that Lanxi began the period of economic reform in advance of its three relatively poor eastern neighbors, but it was exceeded by Yiwu in 1988, by Dongyang in 1991, by Yongkang in 1995.

In a bureaucratic reorganization that began in May 1985, Lanxi county (xian 县) was promoted administratively to Lanxi city (shi 市) (county level). In May 1988 Yiwu and Dongyang counties were similarly promoted to the status of city (county level). And in October 1992, Yongkang County became Yongkang City. At the end of 2004, Jinhua Municipality established the two districts of Wucheng (Jinhua's urban district), and Jindong (Jinhua East) what had previously been Jinhua county. The municipality also contained the counties of Wuyi, Pujiang, and Pan An, as well as the four newly designated cities of Lanxi, Yiwu, Dongyang, and Yongkang (Jinhua City webpage #1) where our field investigations of market and temple fairs were carried out. (See Map 2.3.)

Altogether, there are 109 towns and townships in Jinhua's eight constituent counties/cities, and close to 6000 administrative villages with a population in 2008 of 4.6 million of whom 923,800 were urban residents.

Economy and industry

Jinhua Municipality has more than 25,000,000 hectares of arable land, some 15,000,000 of which are planted in grain, with an annual output 85,330,000 tons. There are more than 400 local markets with a commodity trade volume of ¥114,502,000,000, among which 45 markets had annual trade volumes exceeding ¥100,000,000 (Jinhua City webpage #1).

The contemporary Jinhua economy is characterized by eight key industries arrayed as:

Table 2.1 Annual GDP for four county-cities in Jinhua Municipality (in ¥10,000)

Year	Lanxi	Yiwu	Dongyang	Yongkang
1978	16,361	12,809	15,115	9,643
1979	20,229	16,607	19,992	12,256
1980	23,639	18,763	22,801	14,395
1981	25,117	19,859	23,221	14,677
1982	28,620	23,058	29,315	17,330
1983	32,837	28,163	30,789	18,304
1984	41,904	38,449	35,773	21,212
1985	54,199	50,578	48,198	30,531
1986	68,820	60,609	57,429	36,591
1987	82,300	79,001	70,879	45,265
1988	100,798	**109,860**	90,268	60,523
1989	114,001	133,496	96,183	66,693
1990	120,383	160,025	108,934	74,527
1991	129,474	192,583	**130,983**	88,885
1992	149,878	274,972	162,773	110,299
1993	193,208	408,990	234,890	158,703
1994	290,584	625,752	352,196	240,964
1995	389,797	831,658	482,009	**405,261**
1996	485,098	977,021	582,287	506,747
1997	489,515	1,024,798	629,442	566,405
1998	500,333	1,087,085	682,878	615,104
1999	507,484	1,146,070	728,792	664,262
2000	530,504	1,309,848	820,473	752,837
2001	549,703	1,495,491	894,374	842,015
2002	590,872	1,737,700	1,005,799	936,735
2003	663,634	2,106,143	1,187,517	1,102,466
2004	785,521	2,603,585	1,421,322	1,359,233
2005	883,615	3,034,475	1,598,447	1,563,212
2006	1,030,542	3,528,644	1,835,725	1,788,308
2007	1,273,938	4,221,060	2,097,216	2,117,159

Source: Jinhua City webpage #7

> One base, two centers and five great industrial zones.
> The one base is the central Zhejiang automobile industry.
> The two centers are the Yiwu small commodities market and production center (described below), and the metal goods center in Yongkang.
> The five great industrial zones are the modern pharmaceutical and chemical industrial zone; the electronic media zone; the food processing zone; the construction materials zone; and the high value-added zone.
>
> (Jinhua City webpage #4)

Industries are distributed with different characteristics among the different counties or county-level cities. Jinhua City proper is characterized by its pharmaceuticals, construction materials and industrial measuring devices; Yiwu by its light-industrial commodities; Yongkang by its automobile and motorcycle accessories, and mechanical and electrical tools; Dongyang by its clothing, architecture/construction, and magnetic materials; Lanxi by its non-ferrous metal, cement, towels, and daily use chemicals; Pujiang by its textiles, lockmaking, and crystal ornaments (Jinhua City webpage #11). In 2003 industrial Annual Production Value (APV) was ¥40,836,332,476, rising to ¥47,656,000,000 in 2004, somewhat more than 50 percent of gross domestic product (GDP) ¥92,558,550,000 for the year (Jinhua City webpage #1).

There are 32 mines in use in the municipality which annually produce more than 30,000,000 tons of fluorite and some 200,000,000 tons of calcareous sandstone used in the production of cement (Jinhua City webpage #1).

By 2007 industrial APV had expanded to ¥72,532,126,000 and rose to ¥80,148,000,000 in 2008 (Jinhua City webpage #4).

Rural per capita income rose from ¥4156 in 2002, to ¥5018 in 2004, and urban per capita income rose from ¥11,262 to ¥12,445 during the same period (Jinhua City webpages #1 and 3).

From the beginning of the reform period to 2007, municipality GDP expanded by a factor of 148, from a little less than ¥1,000,000,000 to over ¥146,000,000,000.

Cultural affairs have also developed. At the end of 2004, the municipality had five specialized performance arts troupes, ten arts and culture centers (Wenhua guan), nine public libraries, eight opera houses, one city radio station, one city TV station; seven county-level radio stations (Jinhua City webpage #1), and was the site of one of China's major TV and movie production studios, Hengdian township (discussed below).

Foreign trade

Foreign trade has been an important factor in Jinhua's post-reform economic development. In the five years between 2003 and 2008, exports expanded by nearly a factor of four.

Table 2.2 Jinhua GDP, 1978–2007 (¥)

Year	GDP
1978	984,820,000
1979	1,239,050,000
1980	1,424,860,000
1985	3,096,170,000
1990	7,464,350,000
1995	31,963,640,000
2000	50,934,950,000
2005	106,353,970,000
2006	123,469,570,000
2007	146,574,680,000

Source: Jinhua government webpage #7

18 Background and setting

Table 2.3 Jinhua trade volume, exports and imports (US$)

Year	Total trade volume	Exports	Imports
2003	2,529,249,828	2,322,680,024	206,569,804
2004	3,675,000,000	3,348,000,000	327,000,000
2007	7,963,305,708	7,543,313,708	419,992,000
2008	9,548,000,000	8,969,000,000	579,000,000

Source: Compiled from Jinhua City webpages #1 and 5

In 2008, there were 187 enterprises exceeding US$10,000,000 in export volume (Jinhua City webpage #5).

Foreign investment

As pointed out above, foreign investment came somewhat late to the inland outer-core region of Zhejiang. Jinhua's first Chinese/"foreign" joint venture was a business-card printing company, established in 1985 by an overseas Jinhua native living in Hong Kong, with an initial capital investment of US$21,000. It was targeted at the domestic market exclusively, and went out of business two years later.

In 1988 five new and larger-scale joint-venture enterprises were begun with a total investment of US$5,010,000, of which the foreign investment share was US$1,465,000 (*Jinhua Shizhi* 1992: 738–739). These included Huatong Electrical Co. 华通电子有限公司, Jintong Electrical Co. 金通电子有限公司, Dongxiao Home and Room Co. 东晓组合房屋有限公司, Sanlian Woven Belt Co. 三联织带有限公司, and Yimei Leather 义美皮件有限公司.

In 1989, two more foreign-invested firms and two Taiwan-invested firms brought the total capital invested in joint ventures to US$7,162,000 (*Jinhua Shizhi* 1992: 738–739).

In 2003 Jinhua City's new Industrial Park came on line. The park occupies 11 sq km, with foreign investment in 2003 of US$101,930,000, roughly 40 percent of the municipality's total foreign investment of US$257,500,000.[2] In the same year, 19 new projects involving foreign capital with investments of US$10,000,000 were approved, and the pace of foreign investment began to pick up (Jinhua City webpage #3).

In 2004, 225 new foreign-invested enterprises were approved in machinery, electronics, chemicals, pharmaceuticals, and modern construction materials, and new contracts involving foreign investment totaled US$563,520,000 (although it is not clear what percentage of this total investment is actually foreign capital), and the municipality was proud to have attracted investments by five *Fortune* 500 firms in seven enterprises (Jinhua City webpage #1).

For the year 2008, 95 new enterprises with foreign participation were approved with a total investment of US$834,580,000, and another US$140,000,000 of foreign investments were made in hi-tech electronics, infrastructure, and computer software. Four enterprises in the municipality received approval from the Commercial bureau to establish investment companies trading in the stocks of foreign-invested enterprises (Jinhua City webpage #5).

During the eleventh five-year plan (2005–2010) some 200 projects per year in technical innovation were slated for implementation, with industrial investment of more than ¥20,000,000,000 per year. By the year 2010, industrial APV was expected to exceed ¥100,000,000,000, with annual increases of more than 14 percent, doubling the basis of 2005. And the scale of enterprises was also expected to increase, with enterprises of APV greater than ¥100,000,000 exceeding 100 in number, among which those with APV of ¥1,000,000,000 should exceed 50, and those with APV of ¥10,000,000,000 should exceed ten.

Home of Hengdian—China's Hollywood

One of Jinhua's more noteworthy places of interest is the once obscure market town of Hengdian which, after a decade of shrewd investment in rural industrialization, improbably exploded into the Chinese cinematic world as a major production site during the mid- to late 1990s. While this experience is unrelated to temple fairs, it does speak to the phenomena of modernization and globalization in which the constituent counties and townships of Jinhua have been active participants. I thus hazard a brief digression.

Hengdian is located in the central part of Dongyang county, 18 km from the county seat, with an area of 39 sq km, 12,340 mu of cultivated land, a population of 24,300, and 40 administrative villages under its jurisdiction (Hengdian GYGS 1988). The township lies in the shadow of Bamian Shan 八面山, a dormant volcano that looks the same from all eight compass directions, also called Da Yu Shan 大禹山, mountain of Great Yu, mythical controller of the waters and founder of the Xia dynasty whose temple is nearby (Fieldnotes 5/31/88).

Hengdian figured in the research Professor Jiang and I conducted in the late 1980s on rural industrial enterprise in Dongyang county. During three separate visits to Hengdian in 1986, 1988 and 1989, I spent a total of about a month in the township, and in 1988 had the honor of interviewing Mr. Xu Wenrong, general manager of the township's industrial office (Gongye Gongsi), and the architect of Hengdian's spectacularly successful venture in the development of township and village enterprises. In that interview Mr. Xu set out for me the historical trajectory of Hengdian's success up to that point.

Prior to 1980 Hengdian's citizenry depended exclusively on agriculture, producing mulberry and silk, and raising some pigs for the production of Jinhua hams. The town was also a center of traditional woodcarving and construction, an important sideline occupation. Annual per capita income was less than US$10.

Heng Dian's "development" began in 1975, before the actual implementation of economic reform, when the town, still formally a commune, opened a silk reeling factory. In Manager Xu's periodization, the years 1976–83 were the township's first stage. In 1978, with the new flexibility provided by the economic reforms, they diversified into the production of other finished silk commodities, which boosted township industrial APV to what at the time was an impressive ¥1,500,000 (DDZGZJ 1989: 298).

In 1981, a knit goods factory began production, and in 1982, an underwear factory was added, all of which succeeded in boosting township industrial APV in 1983 to ¥10,000,000 (Fieldnotes 6/2/88 interview with Xu Wenrong). Profits of these early enterprises provided the capital for the township industrial office to expand into new areas, likened metaphorically to a "mother hen laying eggs to hatch new chickens" (Hengdian GYGS 1988). And Mr. Xu was at pains to point out that the industrial office was totally self-reliant; they received no money from the central or provincial governments.

In 1984, as new enterprises were added industrial APV doubled, and redoubled, and redoubled again, over four years, achieving the second highest production value in the Jinhua region, behind only Dongyang's county town of Wuning.

Between 1986 and 1988, what had been the little Township Industrial Office grew into the Township Industrial Company (Gongye Gongsi), with nine offices administering 30 township-run enterprises, 34 village-run enterprises, and 346 joint household/private enterprises. Among these, there were 19 township-run and four-village run enterprises whose APV surpassed ¥1,000,000 (Hengdian GYGS 1988).

The township-run sector was composed of five product lines: silk products (spun and woven); cotton and polyester knit products; electrical products; chemical products, and miscellaneous products (including feather and down clothing, and wood carving).

By 1987 township residents were earning almost 90 percent of their income from industrial employment rather than agriculture, a pretty remarkable achievement for this once exclusively agricultural community (Hengdian GYGS 1988).

In 1993, the Industrial Company underwent another transformation incorporating into the rural conglomerate, the Hengdian Industrial Group of Companies (Hengdian Jituan). The Jituan has become absolutely ubiquitous in town. Everywhere one looks one sees the signboards (*paizi*) with the Group's name emblazoned on it, on the gateways of enterprises, shop fronts, hotels. And the headquarters of the Group's administration was moved to

Table 2.4 Hengdiang industrial APV (¥)

Year	APV
1984	19,000,000
1985	38,000,000
1986	62,000,000
1987	110,000,000

a new tastefully luxurious building located just in front of Da Yu's temple (Fieldnotes 8/1/98).

This was all very impressive in its own way, and in fact the creation of the Hengdian Industrial Group (Gongye Jituan) in 1993 was an innovation in rural enterprise management widely copied in other parts of China in subsequent years, vaulting Mr. Xu Wenrong into the status of national celebrity (Dagong Bao 1998a, 1998b). Yet, my familiarity with Hengdian, its leadership, citizenry and success in rural industrialization, had left me totally unprepared for the shock served up to me, together with a gin and tonic, by the young bartender in the provincial capital Hangzhou in 1998, who informed me of Hengdian's new aspirations:

"Hengdian," he said with a broad grin. "You mean China's Hollywood!"

In the intervening ten years since my last visit, Hengdian town had transformed itself from an eminently successful rural industrial center into a major TV and film production center, and the town was scarcely recognizable. The main street was built up well past the old "suburbs" and extended another kilometer out to the new "movie city" guesthouse and recreation center, complete with bowling alley, dance hall, sauna, and its own travel agency.

Initially in the hope of promoting tourism, the Hengdian Group of Companies had invested a portion of the profits from its rural enterprises in the construction of a modest theme park called "The Village of Culture" (Wenhua cun 文化村). Two fine specimens of classical rural architecture—the traditional ancestral halls Rui Ai Tang 瑞霭堂 of Hengdian's Xiali Shu village 夏厉墅村 and Rui Zhi Tang 瑞芝堂 of Hutoulu village 湖头陆村 were moved into the park, restored, and enclosed in "Enjoy the Moonlight" garden (Shangyue Yuan 赏月园). The garden is dotted with pavilions, covered passageways, lotus ponds, groves of willow and bamboo, all executed strictly according to Ming and Qing period styles. With an eye toward increasing tourism, a public swimming pool was added to the village in the following year. But at the time of the construction of the Village of Culture theme park, few Hengdian residents could have imagined what future these structures held in store.

The events that would decisively launch the town on its new cinematic career happened quite by chance, when in 1995, noted film director Xie Jin came through Dongyang to explore locations suitable for his film project *The Opium War*. The Hengdian Group was especially eager to secure this particular contract because the film's production was linked to, and gave Hengdian's citizenry the opportunity to participate in the national celebration of Hong Kong's "return to the motherland" in 1997. The leadership assured Xie that the Hengdian Industrial Group had the economic capability and the indigenous skilled labor force to handle the design and construction of whatever movie sets he might require, and guaranteed speed in execution.

Xie was evidently convinced. In January 1996, a contract was signed, and the Hengdian Group got to work immediately. They finished construction of what came to be known as "Guangzhou Street" in four months, much to Xie Jin's delight. He began shooting in early August, and given the film's

22 *Background and setting*

high political profile, more than 200 news crews from all over China came to cover the story. Hengdian basked in the attention (Interview with Mr. Zhang Xiliang, the General Manager of the Hengdian Group's TV and Film Studio, Fieldnotes 8/7/98).

After completion of the filming of *The Opium War*, word began to circulate among Chinese film insiders about this little dynamo of a town, and it wasn't long before Hengdian received another significant boost in its aspirations to greatness. In 1997, film director Chen Kaige arrived in search of a locale to film a historical epic, *The Assassin*, involving China's first unifier and emperor, Qinshi Huangdi. Chen had come to see if the Hengdian Group could be

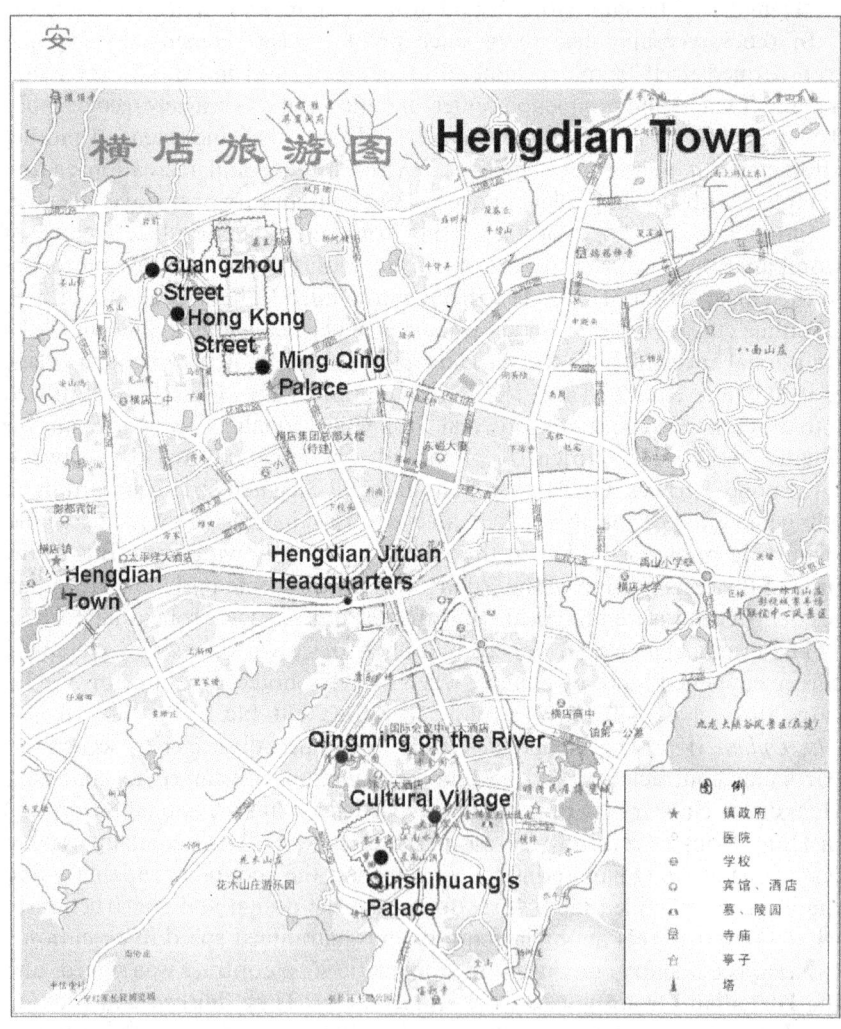

Map 2.5 Hengdian

The field site—the Jinhua region 23

persuaded to build him the historically accurate set he required. The 326-acre Palace of Qinshi Huang with its impressive 50-foot walls, 80-foot corner towers, and 1800 foot long courtyard was the result, and by the fall of 1997, all was in readiness for Chen Kaige and his cast of film stars, including director/actor Zhang Yimou and actress Gong Li to take over the set, and recreate a legend of the second century BC (Hengdian Jituan Bao 1997).

In 1998, three new lots were added.

"Hong Kong Street" is an 80,000-square-meter lot which recreates settings of late-nineteenth-century British colonial Hong Kong, the Hong Kong Shanghai Bank building, the governor's house, St. John's Cathedral, and Victoria Barracks, as well as scenes on Pedder Street, Connaught Road, Queen's Road, and Statue Square (Hengdian Jituan Bao 1997; Jinhua City webpage #12).

"Qing Ming (festival) on the River" is a life-size three-dimensional recreation of scenes from the famous Song Dynasty (AD 960–1280) scroll painting of the same name, undertaken in conjunction with a Beijing TV/Taiwan TV joint-venture serial. The location brings to life the original painting by Zhang Zeduan, vividly capturing the prosperous life of the Song dynasty capital city of Kaifeng. The set covers an area of 162,500 sq m divided into 12 sections, each centering on a particular structure recreated from the original painting, the Fan Tower, the City Gate, Rainbow Arch Bridge, the Opera Stage, the Fandan Temple, the city Yamen, the market, etc. (Hengdian Jituan Bao 1997; Jinhua City webpage #12).

Figure 2.1 Filming on the Guangzhou Street lot: Hengdian

Figure 2.2 Qingming Shanghe Tu lot under construction: Hengdian

Figure 2.3 Recreated palace walls: Hengdian

"The Forbidden City," a recreation of the original in Beijing, was just beginning construction in 1998, in the hope of attracting films requiring the backdrop but unable to secure permission to film at the real national shrine.

The Hengdian Group has also created a training school for extras, martial arts performers, and make-up artists, designed to prepare local residents for future employment. The training school occupies 16 acres, and contains a 2700 seat air-conditioned sports arena for performances and competitions, as well as a movie/opera theater with make-up rooms, dressing rooms and classrooms (Hengdian Jituan Bao 1997). Extras I talked to from nearby villages on the set of Guangzhou Street made 25 Yuan (US$3) per day for the privilege of being pushed around by the director's lackeys.

In 1999, Hengdian hosted 200 TV productions, and more than ten feature films on its various lots. The TV and Film Studio venture has become known nationally and internationally, vaulting the town of Hengdian to prominence in the world of international cinema, a fitting reward to the Group's vision, innovative thinking, and willingness to undertake risk.

Home of Yiwu small commodities market

Jinhua is also home to the nationally famous small commodities market in Yiwu, discussion of which merits a second somewhat longer digression for several reasons, first and foremost of which is the remarkably dramatic trajectory that the city of Yiwu has charted during the course of the economic reforms. Second, we will have occasion to visit Yiwu again when we discuss the performance genres Chang Daoqing and Xiaoluo Shu in Chapter 6 and the temple fair at Fotang town in Chapter 10, so a discussion of Yiwu's present circumstances is clearly in order as background. And finally, our extended digression will nevertheless circle around again to link up with our study of temple fairs in the end.

Yiwu

Of Jinhua's constituent counties, Yiwu stands out as perhaps the most successful in charting a dramatically new course that adapted China's economic reform policies to the distinctive characteristics of the locale. Located at the eastern edge of the Jinhua–Quzhou basin, its total area is roughly 1,100 sq km, of which 339,000 mu (226,113 sq km) is arable. In 2006 its total population was 1.5 million. Grain, sugar, and pigs are the principal agricultural products (Mao ed. 1996: 148).

Yiwu is known as the hometown of Zong Ze 宗泽 (1059–1128), the putative inventor of Jinhua ham, who was also a participant in the ultimately unsuccessful defenses of the Song dynasty capital, Kaifeng (Mao ed. 1996: 7). It is told of Zong Ze that, after visiting relatives while on leave in his native Yiwu, they sent him off with a large quantity of pork leg. Unable to consume it all, on the road he instructed his underlings to cover the pork in salt, and when they arrived at the capital, the meat had changed into a delectable ham. When he distributed it to his wounded soldiers, remarkably their wounds quickly healed. This hometown pork (Jiaxiang rou) made its way to Song emperor Gaozong who was profuse in his praise and, noting the fiery red color of the meat when it was sliced, conferred on it the name it has borne since—"fire leg" huotui 火腿 (Mao ed. 1996: 62).

The drum/rattle (Bolang Gu 拨浪鼓) and the sugar clique

If there is a quintessential symbol of Yiwu county's history and traditions of commerce, it is the noisemaker/drum-rattle Bolang Gu 拨浪鼓 wielded by purveyors of Yiwu "red sugar" in their perambulations through the region, the "bing-bong" sound of which announced their presence in the township streets and village lanes, across several provinces.

According to the Kangxi (1662–1723) and Yongzheng (1723–1736) reign period gazetteers for Yiwu, the cultivation of sugar was imported from Wenzhou during the early Qing Shunzhi reign period (1644–1662), by a Fotang township native, Jia Weicheng 贾惟承 of Yanli Village 燕里村 (Fu 1995 excerpt from Yiwu Bao; Mao ed. 1996: 59).

Yiwu's rural folk were poor, and land was insufficient to meet their basic subsistence needs. As early as the Qianlong reign period (1736–1796), during agricultural slack seasons in the winter and spring, Yiwu residents would take to the road with large cakes of the town's "red sugar" and confections made from it, going from village to village, into lanes and up to the doors, sounding their drum-rattles (Bolang Gu), trading sugar for feathers, animal bones, old clothes and shoes, waste metal, jade fragments, calligraphy specimens, whatever. During the Qianlong period, there were said to be some 10,000 people involved in the trade (Mao ed. 1996: 75; YWFSZ 1985: 163).

The "sugar" exchanged was of two types. One was a confection made with grain, nuts, and sesame mixed in, molded into large cakes, carried on a shoulder pole, up to the door, where pieces were sliced off with a knife, and generally sold for cash. The second type was pure "red sugar," sold in larger bricks, and more commonly exchanged for other commodities. From the chicken, duck, and goose feathers gathered, the best quality were extracted and marketed in Hangzhou and Shanghai, made into feather dusters or jacket padding, and in later years sold internationally. The rest was ground up for fertilizer (Mao ed. 1996: 75–76; YWFSZ 1985: 163).

Beginning in the 1850s, the goods carried by sugar traders expanded to include daily use items required by rural women, pins and needles, cosmetics, combs and other small commodities (Mao ed. 1996: 75), and such traditions of trade are said to have conferred on Yiwu residents a commercial personality.

Over the years the profession became organized into what was known as the "sugar clique" (Qiaotang Bang 敲糖帮), with a hierarchical internal structure and a set of regulations. There were four levels in the hierarchy of Dantou 担头 (carriers): the lowest rung were the Tangdan 糖担 who went up to household doors to trade sugar for goods, rattling their Bolang Gu on their rounds. They went where and did what they were told. Their assignment was in the hands of the Bodan 拔担 and his assistant the Nianbo 年伯, all of whom were under the command of the Laolutou 老路头 or route master (Mao ed. 1996: 75–76; YWFSZ 1985: 163).

Specialized shops (Zuofang 坐坊) and inns affiliated with the clique sprang up along three service routes, north, central, and south, to serve the needs of sugar traders out in the field, reprovisioning their supplies of sugar in exchange for cash or collected merchandise, making arrangements for packing and shipment of goods back to Yiwu, providing accommodation (Mao ed. 1996: 76; YWFSZ 1985: 163).

There were short and long routes, the short requiring one to several months to complete a circuit, the long requiring six to ten months. Each Tangdan was assigned his own fixed route and place to stay by the Nianbo, going out during the day, and reassembling at night to be given their assignments for the next day. Poaching on the routes of others, or stopping work without authorization were strictly punished. Life out on the road was tough, and profit was not inevitable. But still, at the sound of his rattle drum in the village lanes, gleeful children would all flock around crying out "Tangdan Tangdan" (Mao ed. 1996: 76; YWFSZ 1985: 163).

At the beginning of the twentieth century, the sugar cultivation area was centered in Fotang township's Yiting village (Mao ed. 1996: 59), and in the decade from 1915 to 1925 Yiwu "red sugar" won a series of prizes at the annual Westlake Exposition in the provincial capital, Hangzhou (Fu 1995). In the 1930s the area planted in sugar expanded, and gradually came to encompass the entire county, reaching a peak in 1935 when more than 60,000 mu (9,882 acres) were planted in sugar cane. On the eve of the anti-Japanese war in the late 1930s there were said to be as many as 30,000 people engaged in the "sugar for feathers" trade (Mao ed. 1996: 59, 75).

During the mid-1940s, the area planted in cane expanded to some 66,700 mu, producing about 10,000 metric tons of sugar per year. By contrast, in 1995 the annual planted area of cane cultivation had shrunk to only 30,000 mu, but due to selection and advanced cultivation techniques, now produce a ton of sugar per mu (Fu 1995).

In 1957, three state run sugar enterprises were set up in Yiting, Wangzhai, and Jiting villages, replacing the ox-powered mills with modern machine presses. The three factories merged in the next year, to become the Yiwu Sugar and Paper Factory with a daily processing capacity of 50 tons (Fu 1995).

In November 1965, the Yiwu Sugar Factory was begun in Fotang's Yangzhai village. In 1967, it merged with the Yiwu Sugar and Paper Factory and the combined enterprise had an annual capacity of 1,700 tons. The two-month period required to process cane was reduced to 20 days (Fu 1995).

During the Cultural Revolution, the traders of the sugar clique were attacked as capitalist roaders, and criticized, but there were still many who carried on the trade in secret, with rural cadres turning a blind eye. With the advent of reforms in the late 1970s, the "bing-bong" of the Bolang Gu rattle drums was once again heard in the rural lanes (Mao ed. 1996: 77), and after many years of quiescence the tradition of commercial activity came back to life. An informal market sprang up in the suburban village of Ershisan Li, where sellers offered a variety of presorted kits to provision the sugar traders, who not only vended sugar, but also other small articles of daily use (Mao ed. 1996: 133).

In the late 1970s, the "underground market" at Ershisan Li would begin an expansion and transformation beyond the wildest dreams of the feather trading Bolang Gu rattlers, first quietly emerging from underground into public, then from selling out of baskets to fixed street stalls, then to multistory fully enclosed markets, and finally to international wholesale marketing center. But it was nonetheless the itinerant sugar trade that provided the kernel from which the Yiwu Small Commodities Market would spring, giving the Bolang Gu drum/rattle special symbolic significance to Yiwu residents.

Nowadays the sugar-processing season begins around the solar term Dongzhi (winter solstice) when the sugar cane ripens. There are two stages to the processing, squeezing out the juice in a mill, and then cooking it down. During the sugar-processing season, stoves in all the villages become active throughout the day and night. Each stove holds five to eight woks in line, with the sugar liquid moved from large to small in stages as it thickens. The resulting "red sugar" is actually yellow with a greenish tinge, and so it is also called "Yiwu green" 义乌青. The processing season is the busiest time of the year in these villages, and everywhere the heightened activity around the stoves and the sweet smell of sugar in the air attracts onlookers from near and far (Mao ed. 1996: 59–61).

In 1995 APV of sugar in Yiwu was ¥10,000,000, more than twice the value of the county's production of tea leaves, mulberry, and fruit combined. Sugar is now considered one of Yiwu's "fist commodities," although it is no longer traded for chicken feathers by Bolanggu-wielding itinerants (Fu 1995).

Progressive relaxation of regulations on trade

> Don't seek property, but seek its circulation,
> the circulation of people, goods, capital, information, knowledge;
> property must be simple, as long as it circulates through Yiwu, all is development.
> 不求所有，但求所流，
> 人流，物流，资金流，信息流，知识流；
> 所有要素，只要流经义乌，都是发展.
>
> (Yang 2006)

In the 1960s and 1970s, because of the influence of the "left" ideology, private commerce was strictly regulated, and the concerned departments adopted policies to "suppress, expel, obstruct, prohibit" (wei, gan, du, jin 围, 赶, 堵, 禁) private commerce (Mao ed. 1996: 133).

When the Gang of Four were overthrown in 1976, the underground market which had developed in Ershisan Li to reprovision sugar traders with supplies came out in the open, and a broader selection of goods began entering the market. What had been the anti speculation office was transformed into the Industry and Trade Office (Gongshang Suo 工商所), and soon found itself the object of a request that it approve the expansion of the market onto the drying ground of the production brigade where it had already begun overflowing. In the new political climate, a "temporary" market on the drying ground was approved (Ma 1997: 312–313).

After the Third Plenum of the Eleventh Central Committee established reform and openness as state policy in 1978, the Ershisan Li market prospered, and was once again judged too small. But many leaders still suffered from the Gang of Four's influence, and it took repeated appeals to higher authorities before approval was finally granted for construction of a covered market on five mu of additional land. It immediately became very active, dealing in toys, buttons and metal goods (Ma 1997: 309–313).

In early 1982, there were suddenly 320 stalls at Ershisan Li market, and the business grew from simple retail to wholesale. Outsiders began appearing to engage in the small commodities trade, and the first generation of the Yiwu small commodities market began to take shape. The market expanded so fast that it was soon moved to Xianqian Street 县前街 (Chenlie guan 2006; Mao ed. 1996: 26), and before long a group of traders applied for permits to legally trade outside the state-run Baihuo (drygoods) Co.'s purview.

Facing the reality of "the more it was prohibited, the more it would proliferate," in 1982 the Yiwu County party committee and government made the fateful decision that rural commerce was Yiwu's greatest asset (Mao ed. 1996: 133), and boldly devised and implemented a policy of "four allows" (Sige Yunxu 四个允许) (Chen ed. 1994: 36; Mao ed. 1996: 134):

- allow peasants to participate in commerce;
- allow them to participate in long distance transport of goods for sale;
- allow the opening of urban and rural markets;
- allow many channels of competition.

Once the "four allows" "legalized" non-state sector commerce, more and more stalls began springing up on Xianqian Street, and before long they had overflowed to Chaoqing Men and the north end of Xin Malu. At that point, the county Industry and Trade Office invested ¥5,000 to create concrete street-side stalls (Mao ed. 1996: 134), and moved the market from Xianqian Street to Beimen Street 北门街 (Chen ed. 1994: 36).

On September 5, 1982, the county government approved an investment of ¥20,000 to formally inaugurate the Small Commodities Market of Choucheng 稠城 Town (the name of Yiwu's county town in dynastic times) at Huqing men 湖清门. It covered an area of 4,252 sq m, with 750 stalls. Businesses ranged from those dealing in articles of daily use, to hardware,

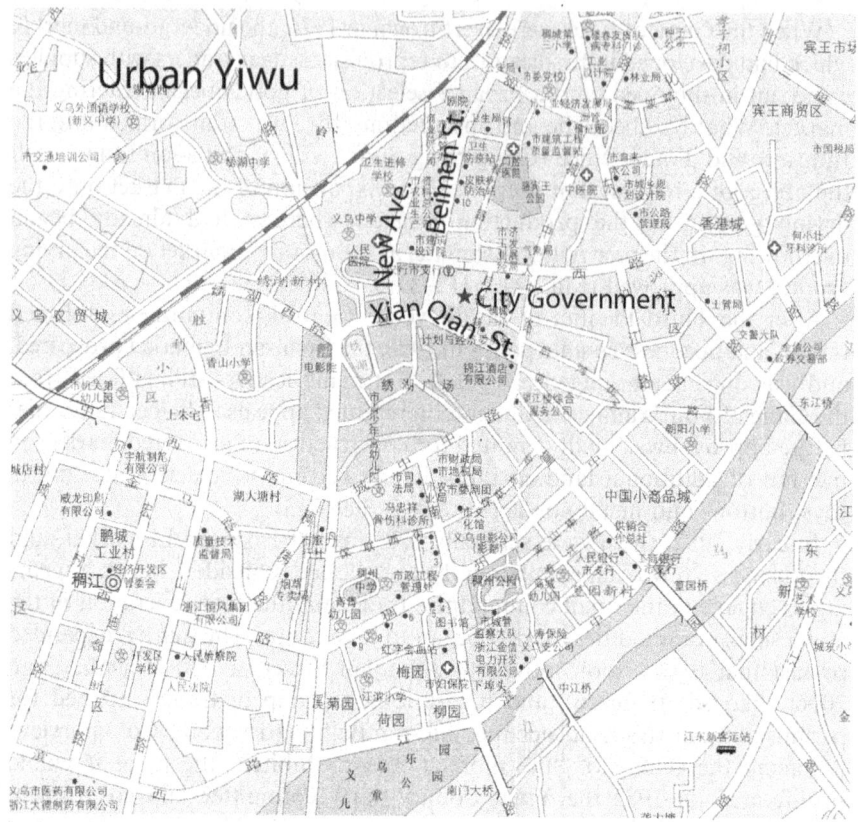

Map 2.6 Urban Yiwu

knitwear, plastic products, toys and clothing, and in 1982 the trade volume of the market was ¥3.92 million.

In 1983, the number of stall spaces expanded to 1,027, and the trade volume reached ¥14.44 million. The small commodities market had become a national distribution center.

In 1984, the county government put forward the slogan "make commerce prosper to build the city" (Xingshang Jianshi 兴商建市), and trade volume for the year reached ¥23.21 million (Chenlie guan 2006; Mao ed. 1996: 27, 134).

From that point forward the Yiwu small commodities market went through three more "generations" of expansion in 1984, 1986, and 1992–4 emerging at the completion of the fourth generation market with an area of more than 100,000 sq m, more than 23,000 stall spaces, a trade volume of ¥10.117 billion, a new name, "China Small Commodities City", and a China Small Commodity City Stock Corporation 股份有限公司, (Chenlie guan 2006). And of all the commodities traded, 30–40 percent originated in Yiwu (Chen ed. 1994: 49; Chen ed. 2005: 86).

To keep up with the increased traffic through the city, the Yiwu railroad station was modernized and upgraded in the late 1980s (Mao ed. 1996: 141), and commensurate with its growing stature as a city, the Yiwu airport was opened in April 1991. Expanded in October 1994, the airport now has flights to and from Guangzhou, Shenzhen, Wenzhou, Beijing, Xiamen, and Wuhan (Mao ed. 1996: 141). Forster has characterized the construction and modernization of Zhejiang province's airports as a manifestation of a kind of cargo cult mentality among local cadres (Forster 1998: 106). Build an airstrip so the planes will land and deliver cargo to the people, but in the case of Yiwu at least, it would appear that the cargo is very real indeed, and its airport will most definitely play an increasing role in Yiwu's internationalization.

Then in January 1994, with a capital investment of ¥2,300,000,000, construction began on Binwang 宾王 21st Century Trade Center in a formerly poor, yellow-earth, hilly area in the north of the city. The Center occupies 66 hectares, and 1,300,000 sq m of built space, equal in size to the entire city of Yiwu in 1985.

Opened in November 1995, Binwang Center consists of five specialized trade areas and one international trade center, with more than 9,000 stalls, and over 20,000 employees. The main product lines include apparel, knit goods, underwear, neckties, woolen yarn, towels, leather, textiles, lace, bedding, non-staple foods, dried fruits, candies and confections, roasted seeds and nuts, groceries and furniture (Binwang Market from Yiwu government webpage).

The Center takes its name from Yiwu native son, Luo Binwang 骆宾王 (619–ca. 687), one of the four great poets of the early Tang dynasty (618–907) (Chutang Si Jie Zhiyi 初唐四杰之一). (The other three were Lu Zhaolin 卢照邻, Wang Bo 王勃 and Yang Jiong 杨炯 (Chen ed. 2005: 3).)

By 1995, China Small Commodities City had nearly 100 specialized commodities markets, a trade volume of ¥15,200,000,000, employing more than 100,000 people (Mao ed. 1996: 134–135).

Yiwu International Trade City 国际商贸城

But the Yiwu party committee was still not satisfied, and in recognition of growing economic globalization, and motivated by China's new membership of the World Trade Organization, they adopted a policy of internationalization built on the "Three Foreigns" — foreign trade, foreign capital, foreign economy (三外 – 外贸, 外资, 外经) (Mao ed. 1996: 145), and in 2001 began planning the construction of Yiwu International Trade City 国际商贸城.

Between 2002 and 2008, through four stages International Trade City added 1,900,000 sq m of market space and 30,000 stalls to the Yiwu market, which registered a trade volume in 2008 of ¥49,230,000,000 (Yiwu city webpage).

Table 2.5 Yiwu trade volume

Year	Volume
2001	21,197,000,000
2002	22,998,000,000
2004	26,687,000,000
2007	46,000,000,000
2008	49,230,000,000

Source: compiled from Chenlie guan 2006; DVD 2004; and Woicha webpage

Up to the end of 2004, there were more than 6000 foreign businessmen from more than 200 countries and regions in Europe, America, Middle East, Southeast Asia, and Africa permanently based in Yiwu, and nearly 500 authorized foreign agents, one third of all such agencies in Zhejiang province. In 2005, the United Nations High Commission for Refugees set up its purchasing information center in the market (Chen ed. 2005: 8; Chenlie guan 2006; Yang 2006).

Yiwu's small commodities market has moved six times and expanded nine times, growing into the largest and most modern commodity distribution center and export hub in the nation. Since the early 1980s, it has kept a step ahead in the development of infrastructural facilities, functional innovation, and reform of its management system, and since 1991 its commodity trade volume has ranked first among all of the professional wholesale markets in China (Chenlie guan 2006).

In the process Yiwu's urban area has expanded from only 2.84 sq km in 1984 to 6.55 sq km in 1990, to 10 sq km in 1993, to 15 sq km in 1996, to 20+ sq km in 2000, with a population of 250,000. The urban area was slated to expand to 35–40 sq km by the year 2010, with a target population of 350–400,000 (Chen ed. 1994: 49; Mao ed. 1996: 137, 139, 141, 181–2).

In recent years, Yiwu has also become a center for the convening of specialized modern trade fairs and exhibitions (Bolanhui 博览会). In 2004, there were 24 trade fairs and ten national conferences convened in Yiwu, including the international small commodities fair, the hosiery and socks fair, the metal and electrical appliances fair, the toys fair, and the home products fair, and in 2007, over 80 fairs and expositions were held in its facilities (Chen ed. 2005: 8; Yang 2006; Yiwu government webpage overview).

The strategy of "Building a city by encouraging commerce" 兴商建市 has succeeded in turning what was a small agricultural county town in 1982 into one of the most prosperous county-level cities in the nation, home to "the largest supermarket in the universe" (Chenlie guan 2006; Mao ed. 1996: 132).

And all this was the outfall from the small illegal market that provisioned the Bolang Gu wielding itinerants who traded sugar for chicken feathers.

Central provisioning center for temple fair merchants and peddlers all over Jinhua and beyond

Yiwu's national and international profile is indeed impressive, and places the municipality of Jinhua clearly in the circuit of international capital, but for our purposes one of its more significant functions is serving as a provisioning and restocking station for local and regional merchants and peddlers who frequent the many market and temple fairs in the region. Whether one is a purveyor of clothing, shoes, cosmetics, woven and knit goods, or hardware, it is relatively easy to stock up, and restock by making a stop at Yiwu's China small commodities city.

Notes

1 The three indicators are population density; highest postal ranking of county seats or of non-administrative towns; and a financial institution index, determined by the number of pawnshops and native banks in proportion to population (Schoppa 1982: 16).
2 Thus the other cities and counties of the municipality accounted for about US$155,500,000 of total foreign investment.

3 Religion in Jinhua and perspectives for understanding it

In contemporary China the government requires that religious practice be conducted only in officially approved churches and temples, the sphere of legitimate religion, encompassed by the same five state-sanctioned religions so designated during the pre-Communist Republic (Buddhism, Daoism, Islam, Protestantism, and Catholicism). All else is illegitimate superstition.

But before dealing with the ambiguous case of popular religious practice which hovers in what Chau (2006a: 213) has called a "huge grey area" between legitimate religion and superstition, it may be useful to first discuss something of the history of Buddhism and Daoism in Jinhua, the two religious traditions deemed legitimate by the contemporary Chinese state, and the temples of which were historically sites of our temple fairs.

The orthodox religions

Buddhism

Buddhism entered Jinhua beginning in the Eastern Han (AD 58–75). The earliest extant Buddhist temple in Jinhua is Faxing Yuan 法兴院, constructed in the eastern part of Wuning town (today's Dongyang county seat) in AD 238 during the Three Kingdoms period. In AD 412, during the Eastern Jin dynasty, Fachuang Si 法幢寺 was constructed in Dongyang county's Hengdian town, and in the same period Xiangyan Si 香岩寺 was constructed in Pujiang. These were the earliest recorded Buddhist temples in the region (*Jinhua Shizhi* 1992: 1086).

Buddhist temples proliferated in the sixth century, during the Northern and Southern dynasties (AD 420–589). In AD 503 Jiufeng Si 九峰寺 was constructed in Tangqi; in AD 506 Tiangong Si 天宫寺 was constructed in Wuning (Dongyang's county town); in AD 520 Shoushan Si 寿山寺 was built in Yongkang's Fangyan (*Jinhua Shizhi* 1992: 1086; Wang and Liu 1997: 42).

Shuanglin Fodian 双林佛殿 also dates from this period, constructed in AD 534 in Fotang town of Yiwu county. It is associated with the career of Fuxi 傅翕, on whom the title Dashi 大师 was later conferred, transforming him into one of the Three Buddhas of Jinhua (*Jinhua Shizhi* 1992: 1086). Fu Xi's career and the history of Shuanglin Fodian will be dealt with in detail in Chapter 10 in the discussion of the temple fair of Fotang.

During the Song dynasty (AD 960–1279) many temples of local deities came to the attention of the court as a result of increasingly frequent requests by local gentry that the court provide inscriptions and titles for the local temples and deities in their bailiwicks. And for the most part, the court complied, greatly expanding the number of popular cults deemed legitimate. For common folk, official recognition was seen to enhance the spiritual power of the deity (Zhao 2002: 32).

By the Ming dynasty Jinhua had 639 Buddhist temples, plus another 190 local cult shrines, distributed among its various counties as shown in Table 3.1.

Significant temple construction continued through the late Ming and early Qing dynasties leaving Jinhua with a total of 720 Buddhist temples by the middle Qing (*Jinhua Shizhi* 1992: 1087).

In the late 1920s and early 1930s Chinese Buddhist "associations" were organized in Lanxi and Dongyang (Dongyang Shizhi 1993: 727; Lanxi Shizhi 1988: 688), and by the mid-1930s such associations also existed in Jinhua, Wuyi, and Yongkang (*Jinhua Shizhi* 1992: 1087), undoubtedly part of the movement to formalize Buddhism as a "modern" religion with an organizational structure recognized as legitimate by the Republican state.

But over the course of the Republican period, Buddhism declined, most likely under pressure from secularizing state campaigns to "destroy temples— establish schools" and other Confucian-inspired anti-superstition initiatives. Nevertheless, in 1946, after the defeat of Japan, the monks and nuns of Jinhua assembled at Xihua Si 西华寺 within the city limits and held a (typically Daoist) Jiao ritual 打醮 to save the souls of those who had died at the hands of the Japanese invaders (see section below on syncretism) (*Jinhua Shizhi* 1992: 1087).

The anti-religion and anti-superstition campaigns of the late Qing and subsequent Nationalist governments eliminated many temples, and in the

Table 3.1 Temples in Jinhua, 1480

Jinhua county	Buddhist temple	Cult shrine
Jinhua	150	33
Lanxi	17	34
Dongyang	72	22
Yiwu	35	22
Yongkang	57	23
Pujiang	92	31
Wuyi	55	14
Tangqi (founded in 1471, abolished after 1949)	61	11
Totals	639	190

Source: Professor Peter Bol, private communication

early years of the People's Republic, land reform and the confiscation of temple property contributed further to the declining fortunes of Buddhist temples and convents, many of whose buildings were converted to other functions or torn down altogether, and whose remaining monks and nuns took on other occupations. During the Cultural Revolution, many of the temples which had managed to survive were further vandalized or destroyed, and public expressions of faith in the deities were out of the question.

But in the early 1980s, after the policies of "reform and openness" had been enacted, some "good men and faithful women" of Dongyang on their own initiative collected funds to refurbish a small number of abandoned or destroyed temples and convents (Dongyang Shizhi 1993: 727; *Jinhua Shizhi* 1992: 1087).

And beginning in 1985, the local state began to take an interest in the refurbishing and rebuilding of temples, perhaps so as not to let the spontaneous activities of the masses get out of control, or at least to better monitor the process already underway. In October 1985, the Dongyang county government conducted its own investigation of temples and convents at important scenic spots in the county. (Dongyang Shizhi 1993: 727). In the same year, the Yiwu county government conducted a similar survey, and moved to protect nine sites where temples existed as religious and tourist spots (Wu, ed. *Yiwu Xianzhi* 1987: 599). Presumably spurred on by such developments, after 1985, the Jinhua municipality government moved to protect and refurbish 33 sites of Buddhist activity across the region according to its own plan.

Three Buddhas and Five Marquises of Jinhua 金华的三佛五侯

Of all of Jinhua's deities, over the centuries Three Buddhas and Five Marquises (Jinhua de Sanfo Wuhou 金华的三佛五侯) have come to hold pride of place. According to myth each was responsible for bringing good fortune to the rural folk, and/or relieving their hardship. Thus their temples were found everywhere in Jinhua prefecture, and most were commemorated annually at temple fairs in greet/welcome/entertain the deity performances.

The three Buddhas are: Fu Dashi 傅大士 (or Dashi Fo 大士佛), Dingguang Fo 定光佛, and Huiguang Fo 慧光佛—the last two husband and wife deities (Cao 1929: 20).

Fu Dashi, again, is associated with Shuanglin Chan Buddhist temple in Yiwu's Fotang town where a temple fair is held in his honor on lunar 10/10, to be dealt with in Chapter 10. But there is also a temple fair in his honor held on lunar 1/18 in Jinhua, on which day each year supplicants go to Black Cloud Temple 黑云寺 to greet/welcome Fu Dashi with drums, dance, and song, and to watch the opera performed for his entertainment.

There is no temple fair for the husband and wife deity pair, Dingguang Fo and Huiguang Fo. They are worshiped all year round, but as they are husband and wife, it is considered unlucky to worship one without the worshipping the other (Cao 1929a: 20).

Dingguang Fo is said to be the deity of Jidao Mountain 积道山 where he attained enlightenment. Yongzheng period (1723–1736) sources record that in life he was surnamed Xu 徐, of Jinhua county's Fengpu township 澧浦镇 Wantang 弯塘 village. He "left home" for life as a Buddhist monk at Xiangfu Temple 祥符寺 (the remains of which are at present occupied by Sipailou Primary School in Jinhua). He lived for 30 years in Jinhua, and enjoyed donning the fine silks of his monk's attire to go around the city telling fortunes to make a little extra money (Jinhua East Government webpage).

Dingguang was able to divine a person's fate with great accuracy. During the reign of Song dynasty emperor Zhenzhong in 1006 he is said to have rambled to Quzhou's Jixiang temple 吉祥寺 in an increasingly deranged state of mind. He chanced upon a sedan chair carrying a new bride crossing the street, whereupon he parted the curtain, and bit the new bride on the neck. The chair bearers were shocked and chased him away. He sang as he fled: "Three lengths of cord, two broken. One remains to harm those in the world." Nobody understood the meaning at the time, but a month later, the new bride hanged herself, and everyone thought again of the song and the one cord that remained.

With such things happening too often on his watch, the Quzhou magistrate was greatly concerned, and he invited this monk Dingguang to dinner, to see what he was about. Accompanying the magistrate was his 19-year-old daughter, a mute, who no sooner had she laid eyes upon monk Dingguang than she spoke for the first time, calling out: "This master is Dingguang Fo." Dingguang thought to himself, "She has revealed my secret. This is some heaven girl." She sat with legs crossed, having already assumed the pose of a Buddha. Dingguang returned to Jinhua, and after bathing he also assumed his Buddha identity. After seven days, the smell of strange incense filled the house. The magistrate's daughter was none other than Huiguang Fo (Jinhua East Government webpage).

In another account, it is said of the magistrate's daughter that she went to Jidao Mountain to pray to Buddha, but kneeling in front of Dingguang Fo's pusa she fainted. As her attendants rushed to help, she spoke the following words: "If the Pusa wants to marry, [let him] choose a day and send it along after my bath." She woke up from her faint immediately, went back to town and, just as she was finished bathing, she died (presumably joining Dingguang Fo as his wife). Later people placed an image of her on Huiming Yan 慧明岩 directly facing Jidao Mountain. When the magistrate went to pray to Dingguang Fo and saw his daughter and Dingguang Fo sitting facing one another in this way, he thought it indecent. So he took his daughter's paper fan to block the view of her face, and to this day, Paper Fan Mountain 纸扇山 stands between Jidao Shan and Huiming Yan, so that even though Dingguang Fo and Huiguang Fo are facing each other, they cannot see one another (Jinhua East Government webpage).

The five Marquises of Jinhua are:

- Xing Hou 刑侯 (official imperial title Gangying Hou 刚应侯) whose principal temple is in Jinhua, Dong Zi Yan 东紫岩. He is regarded as a patron deity of the military, and is also worshipped as a water deity 水神 (Cao 1929: 30).
- Zhaoli Hou 招利侯 (official imperial title Lingkuang Hou 灵贶侯) whose principal temple in Jinhua, Baisha 白沙 was first constructed during the Wu dynasty (ca. AD 222–277), and given imperial recognition during the Tang dynasty (AD 618–907) (Cao 1929: 31).
- Qian Hou 钱侯 (official imperial title Huoying Hou 火应侯) whose principal temple is in Jinhua is approached by rural folk for assistance during natural disasters and plagues (Cao 1929: 32).
- Chen Hou 陳侯 (official imperial title Tieying Hou 铁应侯) whose principal temple is in Jinhua, Gu Ban Shan 古盤山.
- Hu Hou 胡侯 (official imperial title Youshun Hou 佑顺侯) whose principal temple is on Fangyan 方岩 peak in Yongkang county. Hu Hou, or Hugong as he is known colloquially, is the object of widespread veneration, and Hugong temples were historically the most numerous among the Five Marquises, and remain so today (Cao 1929: 24, 30–32; Zhang and Hong 1985: 13–14). The designation Hou (侯—marquis) was one conferred by the Emperor, and represented his recognition of a local deity and its worship as incorporated into the category of Zhengsi (official orthodoxy).

Three of the five Marquises, Hu Hou, Xing Hou, and Qian Hou, were historical figures of the Song dynasty (AD 960–1278), Hu Hou a beneficent official of the northern Song (AD 960–1126), Xing Hou a successful military commander during the southern Song (1127–1278), and Qian Hou honored for his role in fighting a fire in Lin An 臨安 (a suburb of the southern Song capital, Hangzhou) in 1243.

Four of the five Marquises, Xing Hou, Zhaoli Hou, Qian Hou, and Chen Hou are celebrated in simultaneous temple fairs on the occasion of the Mid-Autumn festival, lunar 8/15 and 8/16, when each is taken from his respective temple on a procession of inspection, ending at the deity's principle temple where an exchange of incense between branch and principal temple is carried out. The last but by no means least of the five Marquises, Hu Hou, is celebrated in a temple fair whose activities last more than a month centered around his "birthday", lunar 8/13 (the subject of Chapter 8) (Cao 1929: 30–32).

Daoism

Throughout its history, Daoism has been closely linked to popular religious expression, and the distinction between the two is often blurred. The anti-authoritarian, anti-Confucian character of Daoist theology often led to its association with local cult deities outside the register of imperially approved cults. During the Republican period Daoism's recognition as China's one "indigenous religion" succeeded in conferring some additional legitimacy on Daoism at a time when China sought to bring its religions in line with modernist notions as to how religion ought to be institutionalized.

Most scholars now date the earliest institutionalization of the Daoist religion to the second century AD and the founding of the Zhengyi Tianshi Dao (正一天师道—Orthodox Unity Celestial Master) movement in Sichuan by Zhang Daoling and Zhang Lu (Dean 2009: 179). But the earliest Daoist temples recorded in the Jinhua region were not built till the sixth century AD in Yongkang county—Yanzhen Guan 延真观, Chongdao Guan 崇道观, and Zixiao Guan 紫霄观 (*Jinhua Shizhi* 1992: 1087). Chen Liang, founder of the southern Song dynasty Yongkang school of Confucianism, studied at Zixiao Guan as a child in 1152, during which time the temple was refurbished.[1]

First Tang emperor Gaozu (AD 618–627) promulgated a religious ranking in which Daoism came first, and over the next two centuries Daoism flourished, Buddhism somewhat less so. But at the time of Tang Wenzong (AD 827–841) there were nearly 40,000 temples, with more than 700,000 monks and nuns of both faiths nationwide (Gao 1999: 47).

There was some Daoist temple construction in Jinhua during the Tang dynasty (618–907), sufficient to leave Dongyang county alone with 13 Daoist temples by the mid-tenth century (*Dongyang Shizhi* 1993: 727).

During the Song (960–1278), in another flurry of temple construction, Haoran Guan 浩然观 was constructed in Lanxi; Qizhen Guan 栖真观, Jingxing Guan 景星观, and Zhenyi Guan 真一道观 were constructed in Dongyang; and Shanxiang Guan 善祥观 was constructed in Yongkang (*Jinhua Shizhi* 1992: 1087).

The late Song dynasty witnessed the founding of the Quanzhen (全真—Complete Perfection) school of monastic Daoism by Wang Zhe (1113–70) (Dean 2009: 179), and during the subsequent Yuan dynasty (1280–1368), the two schools, Quanzhen Dao 全真道 and Zhengyi Dao 正一道 continued their evolution.

The Quanzhen Daoists were concerned with creating elixirs and pills to achieve immortality/transcendence, and were characterized by fairly strict religious discipline. They did not permit marriage, and ate no meat or fish. The Zhengyi Daoists were ritual specialists called upon to conduct exorcisms to expel evil spirits, or to perform rituals seeking good fortune. Their discipline was more lax, and practitioners were permitted to marry (*Jinhua Shizhi* 1992: 1087). Zhengyi Dao practitioners were also called Huoju Dao 火居道 (Fire in the Home Dao). They lived at home rather than in a temple, worked the land, married, and had children, and their customary clothing and food were the same as ordinary folk (*Lanxi Shizhi* 1988: 688).

Most of Jinhua's Daoists were of the Zhengyi school and lived among the people, throughout the various locales of the municipality. They performed rituals on a fee for service basis—Jiao rituals of renewal 建醮, rituals for the tempering of souls (*lian hun* 炼魂), exorcisms (逐煞 *zhusha*), "destroy hell" rituals (*poyu* 破狱) or "full sand flaming mouth" rituals (*Misha Fang Yankou* 弥沙放焰口) to release tormented souls from purgatory, summoning supernatural soldiers for assistance (*xingxi* 行檄), funerals (*song bin* 送殡) and the post-funeral rituals of "performing sevens" (*zuoqi* 作七) on the seventh, 14th, 21st, up to the 49th day following a death (*Jinhua Shizhi* 1992: 1087; Sai 1992: 11; Wu, ed. *Yiwu Xianzhi* 1987: 599).

If one can judge from the experience of Yongkang and Lanxi counties, the Yuan was a significant period in the expansion of Daoism in Jinhua. In Yongkang four existing Daoist Guan (temples) (Yanzhi Guan 延直观, Chongdao Guan 崇道观, Zixiao Guan 紫霄观, Shanxiang Guan 善祥观) were refurbished, and two new Daoyuan (Daoist cloisters) constructed—Quanzhen Daoyuan 全真道院 and Xiuzhen Daoyuan 修真道院 (Huang 1986: 256; Wang ed. 1997: 173). Of Lanxi's 19 Daoist Guan mentioned in its gazetteer, 12 were constructed in the Yuan dynasty (*Lanxi Shizhi* 1988: 688).

The Ming dynasty Jinhua gazetteer for the year 1480 indicates that there were 77 Daoist temples in Jinhua during the middle Ming distributed in the various counties as shown in Table 3.2.

By the Qing dynasty, the number of Daoist Guan in Jinhua had expanded to more than 170, with resident Daoist monks and nuns numbering 202 (*Jinhua Shizhi* 1992: 1088).

For the most part, during the Republican Era through to the late 1940s the Zhengyi Daoist practitioners in Jinhua were seldom associated with a temple in their ritual practice. But their rituals were subject to pressure from the atheist state in the early years of the People's Republic, and many had no choice but to abandon their ritual practice and revert to working the land full time. Dongyang's four Daoist Guan survived into the 1950s (*Dongyang Shizhi* 1993: 727), but with land reform and the confiscation of temple property most Daoist Guan in Jinhua were put to other uses, and many simply deteriorated and collapsed (*Jinhua Shizhi* 1992: 1088).

Table 3.2 Daoist temples in Jinhua, 1480

County	Number of Daoist temples
Jinhua	26
Lanxi	16
Dongyang	4
Yiwu	4
Yongkang	6
Pujiang	12
Wuyi	7
Tangqi 汤溪 (county founded in 1471, abolished after 1949)	2
Total	77

Source: Professor Peter Bol, private communication

The Eight Immortals are probably the best-known figures of the Daoist pantheon in the Jinhua region, and a performance of "Dance the Eight Immortals" is the opening act of every Wuju opera performance (see Chapter 7), so there is a constant reminder of their existence and of the specific skills and personality traits of each. And they have become a part of popular culture and folklore more broadly as decorative elements in housing, as didactic instructors of morality, objects of metaphoric allusion, bringers of good fortune in general, and across a much broader region than Jinhua alone (see Cooper and Jiang 1998).

Huang Daxian 黄大仙

At present, the best-known Daoist deity with roots in Jinhua is Huang Daxian (Great Immortal Huang). Hong Kong residents will recognize him immediately as among the deities considered most efficacious in Hong Kong where his temple is the best attended in the entire former colony/SAR. The Kowloon district of Wong Tai Sin takes its name (in Cantonese dialect) from his temple, as does a subway station, but very few Hong Kong devotees of the Immortal are aware of his origins in the village of Huangpen 黄溢村 in Jinhua's Lanxi county.

And it is clear that the rediscovery of Huang Daxian in Jinhua and the inspiration to resuscitate the cult were a product of the cult's vitality in Hong Kong. While the financing of new temple construction in China has often enough come from overseas Chinese communities in Taiwan and Southeast Asia, making this example from Hong Kong unsurprising, the resuscitation of his cult in his native village provides a somewhat unusual scenario of popular religious revival, due to its cooptation by local authorities in its early stages to achieve clearly secular goals, and the folkorification/museification of the deity in that context.

As a mortal, Huang Daxian was said to have lived during the Eastern Jin dynasty (AD 265–420) as Huang Chuping 黄初平 together with his brother Huang Chuqi 黄初起. The younger brother, Huang Chuping, is said to have attained the ability to turn rocks into goats, either as the result of having received instruction in the Way from an old Daoist while caring for goats on Chisong 赤松 mountain (Yuanyuan Yuan temple leaflet), or through self cultivation over 40 years in a cave, finally achieving transcendence/immortality (*Jinhua Shizhi* 1992: 1087; Shi 1997: 126).

In either case, elder brother Huang Chuqi saw his brother's success in cultivation and followed his example, in the end also becoming an immortal. The two brothers returned to their village to dispense aid and encourage good deeds in others. They left to posterity a "Two Immortals Well" spring fed with sweet water, a "green in the soup" vegetable that can cure illness and promote strength, a grove of yellow sandalwood trees planted to protect against flooding, and a spirit earth container in which rice would not spoil (Yuanyuan Yuan temple leaflet).

In commemoration of their good deeds, at the place where the two brothers became transcendents/immortals, the rural folk constructed the Daoist temple called Chisong Guan 赤松观. During the Song dynasty the name was changed to Baoji Guan 宝积观, the largest Daoist temple in Jiangnan at the time (*Jinhua Shizhi* 1992: 1087).

An actual well with a stone inscription "Two Immortals Well" (Er Xian Jing 二仙井) was excavated in Huangpen village, giving some credence to the legends. The well has been enclosed by a simple but elegant Two Immortals Pavilion, beside which is the recreation of the old home of Huang Chuping, with exhibits and artifacts of his life. At the entrance to the village is a stone stele on Tend Goats Road with the huge inscription "Chishi Chengyang" (叱石成羊—command rocks to transform into goats) (Yuanyuan Yuan temple leaflet).

In the 1600-plus years since the Jin dynasty, Huang Daxian has been enshrined in various places as a "wealth producing deity" 生财之神, a "deity of luck" 吉祥之神, or an "all powerful deity" 万能之神, and his temples were ubiquitous in southeastern China in dynastic times (Shi 1997: 126).

Interestingly, Huang Daxian was also worshiped as the patron deity of some opera troupes. The myth has it that Huang Daxian, after having attained the Dao, invited the Eight Immortals to come to his home, and altogether over nine days they wrote nine operas to discourage bad behavior—laziness, greed, murder, stealing, etc. They constructed a stage outside the gate of Chisong temple to perform them, and many people came to attend. After the performances, the villages all around Chisong mountain were peaceful, calm, and prosperous, and later generations of opera performers claimed Chisong Huang Daxian as the founding ancestor of their profession (Hong 1997: 86).

But the attacks on superstition during the early years of Communist rule and the Cultural Revolution campaigns against religion in the 1960s took their toll. Thus, notwithstanding his popularity with Chinese in Hong Kong, in 1984 there was not a single Huang Daxian temple anywhere in mainland China (Yang 2006: 109). And even Huangpen villagers had no memory of Huang Daxian prior to the rediscovery of his historical links to the village brought to light by a local Lanxi intellectual in the late 1980s (Chan and Lang 2007: 45).

By 2001, however, at least a dozen Huang Daxian temples had been rebuilt in Guangdong and Zhejiang Provinces (Yang 2006: 109). In Chan and Lang's analysis Huang Daxian's rise from a "country bumpkin" local Jinhua deity to a cosmopolitan urban deity popular in Hong Kong and Singapore conferred on him a certain exotic international panache which has been a factor in his increased popularity in the mainland (2007: 53).

In 1992, when the villagers of Huangpen, inspired by the rediscovery of their links to the immortal, proposed building a small temple dedicated to Huang Daxian in the middle of the village, and raised ¥40,000 for the purpose, township and municipal authorities applauded the move because they were keen to have a temple that would attract overseas pilgrims, tourists, and potential investors (Chan and Lang 2007: 51).

The Lanxi area, which was among the wealthiest of Jinhua's constituent counties in imperial and Republican times, was not as quick off the mark as the poorer eastern Jinhua counties of Yiwu, Dongyang, and Yongkang to take advantage of opportunities for development offered by the economic reforms, and in recent decades had lost ground in comparison to its eastern neighbors. Thus officials were particularly anxious to find ways of reversing Lanxi's downward trend, and hoped that Huang Daxian might be of assistance (Chan and Lang 2007: 47).

However, once Lanxi officials took charge of the project, Huangpen villagers had little further say in the planning, construction, or management of the temple. The scale of the project expanded with an eye to attracting "thousands" of pilgrims from Hong Kong and elsewhere, and was necessarily relocated to a larger site on the outskirts of the village, said to be the place where Huang Daxian and his brother had farmed.

Construction of the Huang Daxian Temple and its surrounding Garden of the Origin of Fate (Yuanyuan Yuan—缘源园) was begun in 1994, and completed in June 1995, with the opening ceremony held on 17 September 1995 (Lunar 8/23—ten days after his "birthday").

The total cost of construction was around ¥1.5 million, the majority of which, around ¥1.3 million, was solicited by township officials from the wealthy management board of the Huang Daxian Temple in Hong Kong (Chan and Lang 2007: 51–52). Presumably in imitation of the Hong Kong temple, the

Figure 3.1 New Huang Daxian temple: Jinhua

formal worship of Huang Daxian in Huangpen village was established in the spring on lunar 3/18, the day on which Huang Chuping was said to have attained immortality, and in the autumn on lunar 8/13, his "birthday" (Shi 1997: 127).

But all has not gone smoothly for Huang Daxian in his new venue. The expected flow of "thousands" of pilgrims into the area did not materialize in sufficient numbers to support the temple and its staff, let alone impart to the region any broad positive economic stimulus. There was insufficient traffic even to sustain the merchant stalls erected on the road to the temple in expectation of great throngs, so that they were never even occupied. The temple soon began to show signs of disrepair due to poor maintenance, further reducing its appeal (Chan and Lang 2007: 61, 57).

And there was an admission charge for entrance to the temple grounds, which even Huangpen villagers were forced to pay. When the villagers protested this outrage, they were given the "privilege" of entering the grounds free of charge before 7.30 a.m. Not surprisingly, villagers instead installed a *pusa* of Huang Daxian at their own village temple, Gonglu temple, which had been vandalized and put to other uses during the Cultural Revolution, but which had been rebuilt and re-opened in 1990, and refurbished in 1992 and 1994. Villagers for the most part ignored the larger *pusa* of Huang Daxian in Yuanyuan Yuan (Chan and Lang 2007: 57, 61, 66).

Thus, the new temple never achieved engagement with the rhythms of rural life, with a temple fair anticipated by large numbers of rural folk as a red fire occasion, where throngs of regional crowds would gather to shop, watch opera, and approach the deity with expressions of desire or gratitude. The revival of the cult of Huang Daxian was largely a phenomenon organized from the top-down, rather than one instigated and carried out by the grass-roots practitioners (Chan and Lang 2007: 47).

It has only been more recently that the township officials have started to realize the importance of local participation, after which they began to actively involve the locals in their temple promotion efforts (Chan and Lang 2007: 61). Perhaps a brighter future for the temple lies further down the road.

Understanding modern Chinese religion

Goossaert (2005) invokes five "paradigms" that have been used to conceptualize modern Chinese religious history and state–religion relationships in particular. These make a good starting point in evaluating perspectives for understanding modern Chinese religious institutions and practices. There are first of all several dichotomous (contrasting binary) paradigms, the most important of which for Goossaert are orthodox/heterodox, religion/superstition, elite/popular, institutional/diffused, doctrinally pure/syncretic. And then, completing his inventory, there are also a secularization paradigm, a continuity paradigm, a renewal paradigm, and a repression–negotiation paradigm (Goossaert 2005: 16).

Orthodox and heterodox/religion and superstition/elite and popular

The imperial period distinction between orthodox (Zhengsi 正祀) and heterodox (Yinsi 淫祀) was the work of Ming dynasty founder Zhu Yuanzhang, who as first Ming emperor Hong Wu (1368–1399) issued regulations governing rituals and sacrifices that sought to distinguish between deities whom one must pray to—zheng si 正祀—those one was allowed to pray to—za si 杂祀—and those that were forbidden—yin si 淫祀 (Goossaert 2005; Zhao 2002: 16; 3). During the second year of Hongwu's reign (1370) many popular deities, previously classified as Yinsi, attained official recognition and were incorporated into the imperially recognized pantheon, most prominent among whom were the Chenghuang deities (City gods), and Dongyue (God of the Eastern Peak—Taishan) (Zhao 2002: 32).

In the third year of Hong Wu, the emperor sent down an edict ordering every district in accord with the scale of its Yamen to construct a Chenghuang temple (Gao 1999: 64). All the Chenghuang deities in the nation were ranked in a system consistent with local officialdom, giving each local deity a title: Huang 皇; Jun 君; Wang 王; Sheng 圣; Di 帝; Gong 公; Xian 仙; Ye 爷. Female deities were entitled: Yuanjun 元君; Tianhou 天后; Taibao 太保 (Gao 1999: 187).

By the middle Ming, Chenghuang temples began appearing in large numbers in the cities and towns of the commercially advanced regions of Jiangnan, and the Chenghuang temple fair became a large scale annual event in which local officials often participated (Gao 1999: 64). Thereafter, Chenghuang deities served as a kind of hinge between the official sacrificial system and the local hierarchy of popular deities (Dean 2009: 183).

In any event, during most of the Ming dynasty, the distinction between Zhengsi and Yinsi was not strictly observed, and there was little enforcement of regulations against and few outright attempts to suppress the latter (Zhao 2002: 59).

The Qing dynasty initiated a new vigilance with regard to folk religion and popular belief largely as a reaction to their proliferation since the mid-Ming (Zhao 2002: 265). As an alien dynasty the Qing may have been especially concerned with the potential of popular religious cults to turn anti-dynastic in their rhetoric and rituals, and measures were taken periodically to suppress temple fairs and other manifestations of popular religious expression.

The late imperial Qing state was committed to protecting Confucianism, Buddhism and Daoism, but the latter two clearly took a back seat to the state cult of Confucianism. Buddhism, and Daoism were subject to a rather strict, if often unimplemented, system of control, and the late imperial state continued the practice of classifying local popular religious cults as heterodox/Yinsi (Goossaert 2005: 3). Still, in late imperial times, the majority of local temples were built without the state's approval, enshrining deities and spirits that were not part of the imperially approved pantheon (Chau 2009: 212). And as the late Qing state found itself besieged by foreign powers, and its intellectuals began a critical examination of the values that had led it to that point, an anti-religious discourse emerged. "Traditional fundamentalist Confucian anti-clericalism aimed at Buddhists, Daoists, and the spirit mediums of local communal religion, here began to combine with modern nation-state cultural nationalism" (Dean 2009: 189).

In 1898, Kang Youwei attacked Daoism, Buddhism, and local communal religion, proposing instead a cult of state Confucianism that would be based in Confucian academies in converted temples (Dean 2009: 189). Following Kang's proposal, the state reforms initiated in 1898 called for a movement to "Destroy temples to build schools" (*huimiao banxue* 毁庙办学) or "Build schools with temple property" which began in earnest in 1901, and grew continuously through the 1930s, despite the end of the dynasty and the establishment of the Republic in 1911 (Goossaert 2005: 14).

Early Republican leaders attempted to create religious policies congruent with various Western models of the secular nation-state which equated religion with the church, and presupposed the institutional separation of church and state. Provided they conformed to the criteria established by the state for "legitimate" churches, (i.e., organized along western lines with their own clergy, laity, places for worship, educational institutions, etc.), five organized religions (Buddhism, Daoism, Catholicism, Protestantism, and Islam) might enjoy a privileged legal status in Republican China.

For Goossaert the policies of the Chinese Republican government "amounted to a radical reinvention of the religious field, redrawing boundaries between acceptable, legitimate religion, and otherwise unacceptable superstition". While seeming quite similar to the imperial dichotomy that opposed Zhengsi orthodoxy to Yinsi heterodoxy, this reconfiguration relegated the great majority of local deities worshiped in village or neighborhood temples to the category of unacceptable superstition, including many that had been recognized as orthodox by the Qing court (Goossaert 2005: 4).

As such the cults were not only deprived of legal protection, but became the object of superstition eradication campaigns by the Guomindang regime (Goossaert 2005: 3–5), which in 1928, adopted a law calling for "the closing of temples in which purely legendary persons and spirits were worshipped" (Schneider 1971: 150). According to Dean, by 1937 perhaps half of the temples in China had been destroyed in such campaigns (Dean 2009: 189).

As Chau points out, "popular religious practices had struggled with issues of legitimacy for centuries before the modernist regimes (Republican, the Communist mainland, or Nationalist Taiwan) began their efforts to suppress them" (Chau 2009: 212).

Institutional/diffused dichotomy

In several oft quoted passages, C.K. Yang characterizes Chinese popular religion as a "religion having its theology, cultus, and personnel so intimately diffused into one or more secular social institutions that they become a part of the concept, rituals and structure of the latter" (Yang 1967: 295).

Diffused religion differs from "institutional" religion, in that "instead of hierarchical institutional organizations there is a complex network of local temples dedicated to a rich pantheon of gods. Rather than a hierarchical priesthood one finds local leaders rotating into positions of responsibility for the organization of localized communal rituals" (Dean 2003: 339).

Yang argues that in China institutional religion was relatively weak, and diffused religion the dominant form of practice (Yang 1967: 294), even if in many situations the institutional and diffused religions of China were interdependent in their theological concepts, inventory of gods, rituals, and sacrifices (Yang 1967: 295).

The notion of "diffused religion" is by Yang's own admission Durkheimian in inspiration (Yang 1967: 295), and the concept reverberates sympathetically with the Durkheimian/Maussian notion of "total social phenomenon," a phenomenon in which the religious, political, economic, and social dimensions/functions are so enmeshed, intertwined, embedded in one another that it is difficult to analyze them separately. From the fact that this book is engaged in "unraveling a total social phenomenon," the reader can judge where my chips are stacked.

The notion has had its detractors. Overmyer is critical of the institutional–diffused distinction because it "simply applies to China a sectarian definition of religion derived from Christianity that is not relevant to the mainstream of Chinese religion which has always been community-based, inclusive and non-sectarian" (2009: 4–5).

The notion is hardly derived from Christianity. It simply expresses a contrast with it. As an anthropologist, I have no problem with that.

Perhaps more damning is Overmyer's contention that diffused implies lack of organization. While Overmyer concedes that C.K. Yang was aware that Chinese community religion is organized at many levels and in various ways, he still contends that the term "diffused" "can give a misleading impression because of its meaning 'widespread or scattered'" (Overmyer 2009: 4).

Goossaert and Dean each echo this complaint, pointing out that while "Chinese local religion may be 'diffused' as opposed to 'institutional', ... at the village level, it is extremely organized" (Dean 2003: 343), with congregations, corporate resources, internal elections for leadership positions and regional networks of alliances and cooperation, leading Goossaert to conclude that the label diffused is purely arbitrary (Goossaert 2005: 18).

Overmyer is also concerned that local traditions of ritual and belief so categorized might therefore not be considered important in their own right, or devalued as a foundation of traditional Chinese ideas, values and social relationships. He concludes his critique by stating: "These local traditions are persistent and deeply institutionalized in their own ways, and do not deserve misleading comparisons based on the experience of other cultures" (Overmyer 2009: 4–5). Apart from the adjective "misleading", it would appear that Overmyer seems prepared to dispense with the discipline of anthropology. I simply do not agree.

Chau is much more sympathetically inclined toward C.K. Yang's characterization of Chinese religion as diffused, suggesting that the symbiosis between secular institutions and religious life is "even more intimate" than Yang might have been inclined to suggest (Chau 2006: 143). For Chau, the resilience of popular religion in the face of suppression/persecution by orthodox Confucianism, elite Daoism or Buddhism, or by the Nationalist and Communist governments, lies in its intrinsic socially *embedded* nature and organizational simplicity (Chau 2006: 146). There are no elaborate and symbolically complicated rituals; there are no intricate theological maneuvers; there is typically no priesthood. Chinese popular religion is a *minimalist* religion in this sense (Chau 2006a: 7, 146; 2009: 217).

And Dean seems to be expressing something similar when he states that in requiem services and exorcistic rites "the performative element prevails over the expression of specific beliefs. There is no exposition of the meaning of scripture, or interpretation to the public of the features of the liturgy" (2009: 191).

And despite Dean's misgivings about the notion of diffused implying lack of organization, he nevertheless also describes the ritual events of Chinese communal religion as *embedded* in elaborate local systems of social organization and regional networks of temples (Dean 2003: 355).

For Chau the building of temples and the staging of temple festivals rely on, extend and elaborate on the same principles of informal networking and mechanisms of organization as a funeral or wedding (Chau 2006: 143). And Dean would seem to concur in this as well, since for him the ritual events of rural Fujian are an "intensification of everyday relations," or an "intensification of the ritual core of everyday life," "moments for the confrontation of the ever-new in the always the same" (Dean 2003: 184, 356).

But while "minimalist" in its organizational, theological and ritual sense, for Chau, popular religion is also characterized by a "functional expansiveness," providing the community with services in agriculture, commerce, education, entertainment, and reforestation (Chau 2009: 215). I see no contradiction in this. In addition to being a site of both individual and communal worship, a temple is also a political, economic, and symbolic resource and resource-generator (Chau 2006: 243).

A beautifully built temple and a well-attended temple festival attest not only to the efficacy of the deity, and the state of blessedness of the community, but also to the organizational ability of the temple association and the strength of the community (Chau 2006: 243; 2009: 216). Symbolically, "temples are cultural monuments around which social labor and meanings coalesce" (Chau 2009: 222), and "It is no exaggeration to characterize temples as . . . a major locus of peasant cultural productions" (Chau 2009: 218), as we will see in great detail in examining temple fairs in the chapters to follow.

Dean provides an example of this functional expansiveness when he characterizes the networks of local temple and lineage halls in Fujian as a kind of "second government," "in that they have over the past several hundred years provided a growing range of social and cultural services and infrastructural improvements" (Dean 2009: 184). Considering such evidence, Chau concludes that temples are important elements of the local "cultural nexus of power" (Chau 2009: 214).

Thus, while the characterization of Chinese popular religion as diffused has had its critics, it seems to me that when all is said and done there is no way around it. Call it minimalist (Chau), imbedded (Chau and Dean), intertwined (Chau), functionally expansive (Chau), or second government (Dean); all seem to be groping at the same meaning Yang sought to express with the adjective "diffused." So let us then reaffirm C.K. Yang's (and Durkheim's) useful contrastive notion of the "diffused" nature of Chinese popular religious practice, conceding that it is highly institutionalized and organized, but according to patterns of organization distinctly different than those of Christian Europe.

Syncretism vs. doctrinal purity

There seems little argument with the empirical observation that the practice of Chinese popular religion exhibits a high degree of syncretism. Chau goes so far as to describe the Daoist and Buddhist syncretism in popular religion as "indiscriminate" (Chau 2006: 216), "a hodgepodge of different practices that have their origins in different traditions" (Chau 2009: 219). Dean sees a little more structure in the hodge podge, and characterizes the syncretic field of Chinese religion as ". . . stretched between polar attractors of Confucian sheng (hierarchical, ordering, centering power) and ling (immediate, localized, unpredictable spiritual efficacy), marked by complex, hybrid forms (read "hodge podge") of religious ritual and collective experimentation" (Dean 2003: 353).

This lack of a sectarian doctrinal basis for Chinese popular religious practice is reflected in the observation by C.K. Yang that the first striking characteristic of religious life in China is "the general absence of any membership requirement for worshiping in a temple or convent" (Yang 1967: 327). The issue would seem to come down to whether the term syncretic implies a pejorative meaning in comparison to the "pure" sectarianism of Christianity, or whether it can be used in a purely descriptive analytical sense. I believe opting for the latter does not in any way distort our attempt to understand contemporary Chinese popular religion.

Secularization paradigm

The secularization paradigm sees the modern state as removing itself from the religious sphere, giving that sphere a certain autonomy within a broader legal framework, and assumes that religion will ultimately succumb to the secularizing forces of modern science and reason. Arguing against the utility of this paradigm, Goossaert quotes Duara's neat metaphor in which "the realm of popular religion turns out . . . to be a reef upon which the enlightenment project in China repeatedly crashes" (Goossaert 2005: 8).

Continuity paradigm

The continuity paradigm emphasizes the commonalities in the Chinese state–religion relationship through the late Imperial, Republican, and Communist periods (Goossaert 2005: 12). There is undoubted similarity in the ways Republican and Communist governments defined "religion" and "superstition," and both regimes were responsible for anti-religion and anti-superstition campaigns. There may be less continuity with the Imperial period, but the overall similarity of the binary division of the field into two segments, one legitimate, the other heterodox, marks a certain continuity.

Renewal paradigm

The renewal paradigm attributes to the late Qing a state of decay of the major religious traditions, and a process of renewal and restructuring ushered in by state policies and local elite activists during the Republic, in which their engagement with the secularizing nation state was institutionalized in new ways (Goossaert 2005: 18). And now, having undergone several bouts of repression under the Communist state, religion in China might once again be said to be in a state of renewal/revival.

Something new

Still, there is consensus that the present popular religious scene in rural China is something new and different from anything seen in the past, since "Chinese agrarian society today differs considerably from . . . the Maoist period, the Republican era and the late imperial era" (Chau 2006: 9).

Chau cites approvingly the argument of Helen Siu that the apparent revival of traditional practices consists of "cultural fragments recycled under new circumstances," and Emily Chao's suggestion that the notion "ritual bricolage" might well be applied to the circumstances of the contemporary popular religious revival in China (Chau 2006: 10). For Chau, the feudal tradition that was suppressed during the Maoist period and reinvented in a piecemeal, haphazard fashion in the reform era is

> a complex, dynamic, ever-changing cluster of institutions, practitioners and consumers, knowledge and practices fully amenable to innovations, inventions and reinventions . . . [and] although many of these practices assume a traditional form, they carry meanings different from those of the past, and therefore we should not mistake the return of these practices as a revival of unadulterated tradition.
>
> (Chau 2006: 6)

For Chau, contemporary rural social institutions are part of a new power field in which the local state interacts with local society in new ways and with new rules (Chau 2006: 10). Dean's observation that "the ritual events of Chinese popular religion are not remnants of a rapidly vanishing traditional past but are instead arenas for the active negotiation of the forces of modernity" (Dean 2003: 342) would seem to be in very much the same spirit.

Something different

Dean recognizes that "Capitalism operates as a powerful expanding immanent logic within the realm of everyday life in contemporary China". But he argues that local popular religious ritual need not necessarily give way to the immanence of capital, since rather than being an obstacle to the movement of capital, the ritual event is "a different kind of movement altogether" (Dean 2009: 202). For Dean "ritual events generate distinct worlds with alternative spatial and temporal parameters of experience", providing an occasion to think in terms of "a-modern" temporalities, neither traditional nor modern (Dean 2009: 200). And, "extraordinarily, these seemingly impossible worlds coexist with the worlds of increasing capitalism and modernization" (Dean 2009: 199), thus confounding the secularization paradigm (the reef on which the enlightenment project crashes).

Ritual events are the site of an ongoing negotiation with the forces of modernity either in the form of global capitalism or the authoritarian atheist state (Dean 2009: 202). Their worlds of alternative a-modern temporal parameters seem "ever in danger of being captured ... caught between the state apparatus and global capital," in which contexts, they are represented as "something like heritage, local color, folk custom or quaint tradition". Thus temples in many places "have been reduced to a mummified, museum like existence, selling tickets to tourists" (Dean 2009: 200).

Indeed, such appears to have been the fate of the revival of the cult of Daoist deity Huang Daxian in his native village in Lanxi, discussed above. Goossaert sees such museification as one of the strategies used by the state to emasculate popular culture (Goossaert 2005: 18), but Chau sees the representation of superstitious activities as "folk custom" (*fengsu xiguan*) or "popular belief" (*minjian xinyang*) as an attempt to protect such activities by rendering them quaint and harmless, "colorful regional cultural attractions for tourists" (Chau 2006: 217).

Repression and resistance paradigm

The repression and resistance paradigm sees the state as acting predatorily toward popular religious institutions either as a result of anti-religious ideology, or the desire to "seize social, economic, and political resources that form the basis for local power and cultural/political autonomy in the towns and countryside". The reaction of religious institutions to this predation, both historically and in the present, is understood as resistance in the broadest sense, encompassing sub-insurrectional, "everyday" forms of resistance, rhetorical subversion, humor, indirection and metaphor, apparent compliance hiding defiance, etc. (Goossaert 2005: 14). We will take up repression and resistance in Chapter 9.

Money as symbol, symbol as money

The near universal penetration of the Chinese ritual sphere by petty-capitalist values is plainly expressed in the extremely positive view taken of money (Gates 1995: 168). Money is a magical and sacred substance in Chinese folk life, offered to gods and spirits and ancestors, "used for purification and to symbolize productive and reproductive increase . . . as something very like capital" (Gates 1995: 168).

Lest we forget, Gates reminds us of the role of money as a magical and sacred substance in our own society with a well-placed quote from Marx: "From its servile role in which it appears as a mere medium of circulation, [money] suddenly changes into the lord and god of the world of commodities, while they represent its earthly form . . ." (Gates 1995: 174). It is well to remember that paper money in our own society is "symbolic" of commodity value in its daily use. The use of spirit money as a medium for communicating/ carrying on transactions with deities is merely an extension of the already symbolic character of money (more of the same).

In the ritual sphere burning paper spirit money is a medium for finessing obligations of reciprocity. One gives offerings, one expects returns. One makes a vow (*xuyuan*) to sponsor a "fulfilling vow" opera, or to make a donation to the temple with real world money, if the deity responds. Or one burns spirit money as an offering to ancestors so that they might be better able to bribe the officials of the netherworld—subversive in the netherworld as in life.

Both Dean and Chau note that the provision of spiritual services in much of popular religion in China involves "fee for service" transactions in which payment is made on the spot to ritual specialists usually hired from outside the village to conduct particular rites—communicating with ancestors, performing exorcisms, divination rituals, fortune telling or providing protective talismans (Chau 2006: 9; Dean 2003: 339). This service provider perspective, for Chau, "points to the undeniable fact that [Chinese] religion is business in addition to involving beliefs and sacred symbols" (Chau 2006: 9).

Gates also suggests that the great quantities of ritual goods and services produced and consumed annually by individual households and by temples as corporate bodies make folk religion a big business (Gates 1995: 232). For Gates,

> In dealing with gods, and also with the ghosts and ancestors with which they are so complexly linked, people accept the hierarchical parameters of a tributary cosmos. Yet they valorize petty capitalism [and money] . . . because . . . Money subverts the rigid rules of tributary inequality, offers greater distributive justice, and thus glows with a luster brighter than virtue.
> (Gates 1995: 175)

Money effects this subversion in two senses; first, through enabling bribery of officials in the tributary hierarchy in this world as well as the next; and, second, through the control and circulation of extra-tributary resources and wealth.

Folk rituals support the virtues of getting rich (Gates 1995: 34), and in one's pursuit of wealth "one is most likely to petition Daoist gods, or [local] shen" for assistance; "Buddhist Fo (like ancestors) are primarily responsible for family well-being and tranquility" (Gates 1995: 168).

"Sacrifices made in the state cult, supportive of the tributary mode of production, included only consumable commodities—never money" (Gates 1995: 174).

A sociothermic theory of sociality

In his study of the Black Dragon Temple in Shanxi, Chau proposes what he calls a "sociothermic" theory of Chinese sociality (Chau 2006: 156), based on the Chinese notion of "*honghuo*" 红火 (red fire, red hot) "a condition of social co-presence ... the gathering of a group of people in one social space" (Chau 2006: 147).

> Crowdedness is the necessary condition of honghuo making ... The convergence of people generates honghuo, and honghuo generates a greater convergence of people because people are disposed to be attracted to the noise and colors of honghuo. A small crowd is sure to generate a bigger crowd ... whose members come to 'see the commotion' (kan honghuo or kan renao).
>
> (Chau 2006: 148)

People are drawn to temple fairs to experience "the most desirable mode of sociality: red-hot sociality ... Intense co-presence ... social heat endows popular religious sites and the deities with heightened aura and appeal" (Chau 2006: 147–148).

And while not expressing the meaning of *honghuo* in quite so concise a concept as "sociothermy," Dean, also recognizes that "Many of the rituals of local communal religion are intense, chaotic and stimulating events, filled with the smoke of incense and the sound of firecrackers, the simultaneous performance of opera, rituals and processions, and the participation of crowds" (Dean 2003: 339).

The temple fair is perhaps the most potent example of the appropriateness of Chau's sociothermic theory of Chinese sociality, making this a good segue to a discussion of temple fairs in Chinese history.

Note

1 One evening as Chen Liang was studying by candlelight at Zixiao Guan, two green frogs suddenly jumped up on his table, and called out to him. Although he shooed them away, they refused to go. So Chen Liang took up his brush and painted a red dot on the head of each, happily exclaiming: "Gotcha both!" Ever since, the frogs near Zixiao Guan all have a clear red dot on their heads. Later when Chen Liang achieved Zhuang Yuan status in the imperial examinations at the age of 50, the story came down as "Zhuang Yuan dots the frogs" (Wang ed. 1997: 173).

4 Temple fairs in Chinese history and Chinese folklore studies

The history of Chinese temple fairs runs parallel to the development of Chinese religion outlined in the previous chapter, and what we know of that history is the work of Chinese folklorists and historians of the Republican period and their latter-day practitioners who since the beginning of the period of economic reform and openness have resumed and carried forward that work.

Chinese temple fairs began taking shape after the Han dynasty, during the Wei (AD 220–264), Jin (AD 265–419), and Northern and Southern dynasties (AD 420–588) when organized Daoism was gradually coming into being (Wang and Liu 1997: 3, 44), and Buddhism had established its presence in China (Gao 1999: 25).

As early as the Northern Wei (AD 386–534) the ritual processions in which the *pusa* was removed from the temple and paraded around the city and countryside "*hang xiang*" 行像 in a tour of inspection are said to have been employed by practitioners of both Buddhism and Daoism as a means of bringing the local populace out, and expanding the influence of the temples (Wang and Liu 1997: 4).

The Sui (AD 589–618) and Tang (AD 618–907) eras brought to a close the long phase of division of the Northern and Southern dynasties (220–588), and initiated a rather long period of relative political stability, flourishing economic and cultural life, and imperial encouragement, during which temple fairs honoring and worshiping Daoist and Buddhist deities flourished (Gao 1999: 46, 48). As the fairs spread through town and countryside, the literate classes took notice, and left behind rather detailed descriptions that document the coexistence of the temple fair with the temple market (*miaoshi* 庙市), making clear the presence of the commercial dimension in the temple fairs of the period, especially so in the Jiangnan region (Gao 1999: 48–49; Zhao 1996: 133).

The reciprocal interaction and mutual influence of sacrifice and belief, economy and trade, culture and arts in temple fairs can be said to have begun in earnest during the Tang (Zhao 2002: 118). By the later Tang period temple fairs had established a close connection to local popular festival days, and this served to solidify their place in the annual cycle of rural activity (Gao 1999: 48–51).

Song dynasty (AD 960–1278) fairs were noteworthy for the elaboration of popular cultural performance genres, in particular for the development of opera as a means of entertaining the deity, and for the consolidation of the temple fair market in the south (Gao 1999: 51). A Song dynasty text cited by Wang and Liu describes more than 20 art and performance genres at a single temple fair (Wang and Liu 1997: 70, 83), among which were the traditions of song and dance then crystallizing into southern opera (*Nanxi*). The addition of the opera greatly enlivened the entertainment at southern temple fairs, while raising the overall standard of the opera performances (Gao 1999: 57, 252; Zhao 1996: 136).

During the Song, the dates during the year when the temple fairs of particular deities were convened became established and fixed, and the commercial dimension of the southern temple fair continued to expand (Gao 1999: 59), while the fairs of the north lagged behind in the elaboration of their commercial features (Wang and Liu 1997: 8).

Song emperors encouraged popular religion, conferring titles and legitimacy on local popular deities, and bringing forward and elaborating the practice of their Tang dynasty predecessors, of writing inscriptions for the "*hengban*" (橫版 horizontal signboards) of local temples, either in four-character or three-character form, expressing ideas of luck, good fortune, and security (Gao 1999: 176).

Yuan dynasty (1279–1368) temple fairs maintained the basic form of the Song dynasty fairs. The gods and spirits worshipped did not change, but evidence from Yuan dynasty temple and funerary inscriptions suggest that Yuan style opera 杂剧 was added to the repertoire of entertainments, and thereafter became inseparable from the culture of temple fairs. The Quanzhen sect of Daoism achieved widespread influence in north China during the Yuan dynasty, and temple fairs celebrating the feats of Daoist transcendants/immortals were plentiful (Gao 1999: 59–60). It may very well have been such developments that gave rise to the saying: "The temple fairs of the South honor Buddha; those of the North honor [Daoist] immortals" (Gao 1999: 190).

During the Ming dynasty (1368–1644) the temple fair as total social phenomenon reached its maturity, and set the standard for the temple fairs of subsequent centuries and the modern day. The regime of Ming founder Zhu Yuanzhang not only extended legitimacy to a host of local cult figures, but also encouraged the convening of Buddhist and Daoist temple fairs (Gao 1999: 64; 374–375).

Beginning in the Ming and continuing into the Qing, more or less coincident with the early period of the sprouts of capitalism in the Jiangnan region, and something of a climax in the movement of the important economic centers of the empire to the south that began in the Tang and Song dynasties, significant differences in scale arose between the temple fairs of Jiangnan and those of north China (Gao 1999: 249; Zhao 1996: 138).

The central plain in the north was the socio-political center from ancient times, the place of the primordial national ancestors. Thus the temple fairs of gods like Pan Gu, Fu Xi, Nu Wa, Huang Di, and Da Yu are relatively numerous, whereas in the south historical and cultural traditions of this kind are much weaker, and the temple fairs of local notables and local deities are more prominent (Gao 1999: 253). While the economic centers had already begun shifting south during the Song and Yuan, the important centers of political control were still in the north, and the northern cultural centers were still the equal of those in the south (Zhao 1996: 136). But during the Song and Yuan, as southern economic prosperity overtook the north, the scale and luxury of the southern temple fairs gradually eclipsed those of the north, a development that climaxed during the Ming (Zhao 1996: 131).

By Ming times, the south had surpassed the north in the number of Jinshi degrees awarded, and in the cultural sphere was experiencing a renaissance in local popular opera, fiction and pictorial art (Zhao 1996: 138). This in turn was reflected in the grandeur of southern temple fairs where the offerings were conspicuously more generous, the ceremonies of worship more diverse, and the expenditures involved in sponsorship of the entertainment and provision of sacrificial goods greater by many magnitudes than in the north. The relative grandeur of southern fairs has persisted down to the present (Gao 1999: 256).

The religious dimension of the temple fair was common to the fairs of north China and Jiangnan. The commercial component of the Jiangnan fairs was already present beginning in the Tang (618–907), but it was not until the Ming and Qing that northern temple fairs took on greater economic functions, although once they did many temple fairs of the northern plains maintained a very strong commercial flavor down to the present (Gao 1999: 251; Zhao 1996: 131, 133).

The recreational dimension of the temple fair also expanded during the Ming. But this also led to a concern by the central state that the excessive enjoyment of the fairs would produce a multitude of troubles, the spread of superstitiously inspired rumors, and the neglect of agriculture and sericulture. Thus, in the Ming Jiajing period (1522–1567) there suddenly appeared prohibitions forbidding the convening of temple fairs (Wang and Liu 1997: 8–10).

The Qing dynasty (1644–1911) initiated a new vigilance with regard to folk religion and popular belief and official pronouncements condemning or prohibiting temple fairs and their associated activities were increasingly common (Zhao 2002: 265). Tang Bin, an official of the Kangxi reign period (1662–1723), complained of the extravagance of temple fairs which wasted a great deal of money and caused severe damage. The performance of opera caused a rumpus far and near, with men and women gathering to watch together! "The people all seem crazy, they waste time, delay their work, and destroy the crops in the field" (quoted in Zhao 2002: 261).

Tian Wenqing, an official in the subsequent reign of Yong Zheng (1723–1736), issued a "Strict prohibition on temple fairs for the rectification of custom" which warns of the disaster that will result if such fairs and the "evil religions originating in them" were not prohibited (Zhao 2002: 265).

Perhaps for reasons such as these Gao (1999: 66–67) asserts that Qing dynasty temple fairs in both their secular and religious dimensions were somewhat less dramatic than their Ming predecessors. But despite periodic attempts at suppression during the Qing temple fairs proved quite resilient (Liu 1996: 193, in Liu ed. 1996), and remained an important fixture in rural culture. The regional variation between north and south continued, and prosperity, stability and cultural fluorescence in the south were manifest in more frequent fairs and an elaboration of ritual and entertainment activities.

Despite the relaxation of standards of behavior that often characterized the fairs, and the potential for mob violence or other forms of anti-dynastic activity, it must also be recognized that the values promulgated at temple fairs were for the most part consistent with Confucian concepts of righteousness, loyalty, and filial piety (Gao 1999: 68).

The temple fairs of the Republican period (1911–1949) did not differ significantly from those of the late Qing (Gao 1999: 70), although in the Nationalist government's reconfiguration of traditional understandings of orthodoxy-heterodoxy many local cults came to be classified as "superstition" and their temple fairs suppressed. But indeed it was during the Republican period that the temple fair was "discovered" by practitioners of the emerging field of academic folklore studies as a quintessential example of popular folk religion and folk culture.

Chinese folklore studies

Chinese folklore studies was the child of the May 4th "enlightenment" movement (Lü 1996: 29). Its raison d'être "was the belief that it was only the masses, the great unwashed and untutored but vital and spontaneously creative body of the nation whose efforts were necessary if innovation in the cultural realm were to succeed" (Schneider 1971: 123). Its practitioners believed that the very same principles of individual liberty, equality and democracy that May Fourth Movement reformers advocated could be discovered in the traditional popular culture of the masses. Thus from the beginning, folklore studies was closely related to the movement for democracy (Lü 1996: 22, 26, 29).

Beginning in 1919, the year of the May Fourth Movement, "a variety of populist student organizations sprang up, each in its own way devoted to removing the intellectual from his traditional position 'aloof from the masses' and ignorant of physical labor" (Schneider 1971: 122). The proper Chinese tradition of the masses had been usurped and suppressed by the upper classes and their intellectual accomplices. "The new intelligentsia would set things aright through the dual process of simultaneously educating and being educated by the long suffering masses" (Schneider 1971: 13). The inevitable result of this intellectual logic was that intellectuals should "go among the people," get close to the masses, understand the masses, to achieve that goal of mutual education (Lü 1996: 22–23, 29).

As Franz Boas was the founder of academic empirical anthropology in the US, Gu Jiegang played a similar role with respect to academic empirical folklore studies in China. But under the influence of the May Fourth democratic intellectual tide, Gu also "led his associates in a serious campaign to substitute the culture ... of the people for that of the aristocrats" (Schneider 1971: 123).

Gu first became interested in the study of popular folklore after discovering the work that some of his colleagues at Peking University were doing collecting folksongs and ballads. In 1918, Professor Liu Pannong began publishing folksongs gathered from various parts of China, in the Peking University student daily (Schneider 1971: 124), and Liu Fu published "Selected songs and ballads" in Beijing Rikan (Liu 1996: 183). This activity was very much in synch with the contemporary New Culture Movement of which it became an important component, recording the creativity of the masses (Liu 1996: 181, in Liu ed. 1996).

"It never occurred to me," Gu Jiegang wrote, "that such verses were meritorious enough to put into print" (Schneider 1971: 124). Within a short time, however, Gu himself was an avid folksong collector, among the first to devote serious scholarly effort to the classification and analysis of the genre. He joined a small group of Peking University professors including Liu Pannong, Chen Juntian, and Zhou Zuoren, who decided to coordinate their private studies of Chinese folksong by establishing the Department of Folksong Collection in February 1918 (Schneider 1971: 124). A Peking University song and ballad study group was subsequently organized in 1920 under Liu Fu's leadership (Liu 1996: 183).

Zhang Jingsheng soon after assembled a questionnaire designed to investigate popular habits and customs, which led in May 1923 to the organization of the Peking University Society for the Investigation of Popular Habits and Customs. According to Liu (1996: 183), the Society suffered from inexperience and never organized any empirical investigations of their own, tending to rely more on the analysis of the collections of amateurs and dilatants, but Naquin (1992: 356) credits the Society with sponsoring Gu Jiegang's 1925 investigation of the temple fair at Miaofengshan (described below).

The first issue of the journal *Songs and Ballads* (*Ge yao zhoukan* 歌谣周刊) appeared in December 1922, and its preface "heavily emphasized the need to gather folk materials, no matter how crude their appearance, with an open mind, for the purpose of pure research ... it hinted that out of the folksongs, and the popular feelings which they represented, a new national poetry would be born." Gu Jiegang's writings dominated the journal from late 1924 until its demise in the following year, and included his "impressively thorough study of the legend of Lady Meng Jiang, and his pioneering collection of folksongs from the Suzhou area" (Schneider 1971: 137).

However, if Gu Jiegang and his fellow folklorists came to consider all that was good in literature and the arts to be "of the people," "they were far from considering all that was 'of the people' to be good" (Schneider 1971: 123). While Gu and the new educated elite sought to create a modern identity for the intelligentsia, based on the relationship of intellectuals to the common people, their embrace of the people was rather "stiff" at first (Schneider 1971: 7, 13). Their going among the people wasn't so much among the people, as standing on the side and observing, maintaining a certain distance from the people, although Lü (1996: 24) claims that some of this reticence was overcome in subsequent studies as the researchers became more familiar with the ethnographic method.

Because at this time folklore investigations and research was still a new phenomenon, many people did not understand why any reasonable intellectual would concern himself with such matters. "What do these things have to do with you? You've already eaten your fill and you've nothing [better] to do" (*chibaole, meishi zuo*) (Lü 1980: 619).

By the late 1920s, the Nationalist regime had come to regard folklore, in Eberhard's words, "as a dangerous field." Eberhard writes that "folklorists were accused of keeping alive superstitious beliefs and attitudes of an era which should not be cherished but, instead, should be allowed to die" (quoted in Schneider 1971: 149).

For the early Chinese folklorists and Gu Jiegang, the temple fair epitomized the folk culture of the people, and the nearby fair at Miaofengshan came to be a proving ground for their early efforts at going among the people in actual ethnographic investigation. This was quite unheard of in Chinese scholarly life, where truth was commonly sought in the analysis of texts (Liu 1996: 183).

The temple fair at Miaofengshan was the scene of two virtually simultaneous ethnographic investigations during the spring of 1925, one by a team of five scholars from the Guoxue 国学 Studies unit of the Beijing University Research Institute under the leadership of Gu Jiegang, and one carried out by sociologist Li Jinghan, at the instigation of American sociologist/reformer Sidney Gamble (Gao 1999: 388).

The inspiration for the Beijing University study occurred when Gu Jiegang had the previous year by chance found himself in the Western Hills of Beijing just at the high tide of the worship of Miaofengshan's host goddess, Bixia Yuanjun, on lunar 4/8. Already an aficionado and collector of folk songs, he was captivated by the singing and spirit of the supplicants in one of the many tea stalls lining the route up the mountain (Lü 1996: 10), and determined to return for a systematic investigation.

In the history of Chinese folklore studies, Gu Jiegang's team study, including contributions from Sun Fuyuan, Rong Xibai, Rong Yuantai, and Zhuang Yan, represented the first systematic application of the ethnographic method, and a division of labor among team members organized to carry out specific goals (Lü 1980: 617; Liu 1996: 183). The study was a "banner," opening the way to the scientific study of folklore through empirical investigation (Liu 1996: 184). At the same time it also established the temple fair "as a splendid example of popular folklore, worthy of the intellectual's serious consideration, 'a new kind of very lively source material'" (Naquin 1992: 356).

When the findings of the investigation were published in Jing Bao Fu Kan 京报副刊 (Gao 1999: 388) and later edited into a book-sized double issue of the new journal *Folklore* (*Minsu*) (Naquin 1992: 356), its influence in the May Fourth New Culture Movement as an example of learning by "going among the people" was significant (Lü 1980: 617), and ethnographic investigation went on to become a tradition in the field of Chinese folklore studies (Liu 1996: 185).

At the same fair where Gu and his colleagues were out gathering data, sociologist Li Jinghan 李景汉 was also on the scene. In Lü Wei's account, the temple fair at Miaofengshan had come to the attention of Li's associate, Sidney Gamble, in 1924 during the research for his "Beijing: a social survey," and it was apparently Gamble who encouraged Li to accompany him and a couple of Gamble's American friends out to the fair (Lü 1996: 12). In Susan Naquin's account, Gamble had to convince Li to ignore his Chinese intellectual friends who "thought it bizarre to spend effort studying such superstition", and accompany him out to the fair at Miaofeng Shan (Naquin 1992: 356).

In either event, Li published the results of his investigation in August 1925 in *Sociology Magazine* (*Shehuixue zazhi* 社会学杂志) (Gao 1999: 388; Lü 1996: 12) based on his own observations, supplemented by materials from Rong Geng 容庚's earlier textual study of the Bixia Yuanjun temple and its origins (Lü 1996: 12, 26). And Gamble "preserved a record of the investigation in movies and photographs" (Naquin 1992: 356).

In 1926, Beijing University suffered destruction from the troops of the northern armies, and Cai Yuanpei and Jiang Menglin divided up the university, with some scholars fleeing to Xiamen University and others to Zhongshan University, where folklore studies continued to develop (Liu 1996: 185).

Gu Jiegang was among those dispatched to Zhongshan University in Guangzhou where he stayed for two years, and continued to craft a "sophisticated intellectual structure" in which the field of folklore studies might continue to develop. Shortly after Gu's arrival at Zhongshan University, the university's Historical and Philological Research Institute published the first issue of what was to become the folklore movement's most prolific and versatile journal, *Folklore* (*Minsu* 民俗), under the editorship of Zhong Jingwen. Gu Jiegang was given the honor of writing the introductory statement (Schneider 1971: 104, 138, 141).

Schneider has characterized Gu Jiegang as the "Johnny Appleseed" of the folklore studies movement, since in his sojourn south he never stopped proselytizing for the movement, encouraging young folklore students to specialize in the field, seeing to the establishment of a folklore studies society at Zhongshan University, and stimulating the interest of his friend Zhong Jingwen (Liu 1996: 185; Schneider 1971: 104, 137). Zhong carried on the work of promoting folklore studies until his death in 2002 at the age of 100, leaving behind hundreds of professional folklorists and anthropologists who trained at his knee.

Gu became the chief spokesman and publicist for the folklore movement. "Over and over again, without any lapse of eloquence, Gu reminded his readers that they too were essentially 'of the people'" (Schneider 1971: 140–141). His general program was to legitimize the empirical study of folklore, to argue the case for the value of folklore data, and to urge his colleagues to gather that data while circumstances still permitted it by acquiring the scientific tools and the methodology necessary to develop the field of folklore properly, much as his contemporary Franz Boas was promoting scientific empirical research in the field of American anthropology.

In May of 1929, Gu Jiegang returned to Beijing, and together with Wei Jiangong, Bai Dizhou, Luo Xianglin, Zhou Zhenya, Xu Bingyong, Zhu Ziqing, and others (a total of 13 people) organized the Beijing University and Qinghua University "Yiba" 一八 research team (since it was the 18th year of the Republic) to carry out a second investigation of Miaofeng Shan (Lü 1980: 628; 1996: 14). They had funding of ¥110 to conduct an investigation over eight days, and their report was published in the Zhongshan University journal *Folklore* 民俗 numbers 69 and 70 (Gao 1999: 388; Lü 1980: 628). Although the results of the second investigation were not as dramatic as the first, the investigators were a bit more familiar with the ("open country") ethnographic method (Lü 1996: 16).

By 1933, the folklore movement was centered at Zhongshan University, and Zhong Jingwen, who had organized a National Folklore Society with its home office in Guangzhou, was its leader, although Schneider claims that "the fervor of the late twenties" had cooled (Schneider 1971: 138, 142).

Temple fairs surfaced again as an object of folklore investigation when in August 1936 two middle-school teachers, Lin Yongzhong and Zhang Songshou, carried out an investigation of Hangzhou's Dongyue temple fair (Liu 1996: 186). For the authors, the investigation was a "good opportunity to go among the people, to understand their psychology, and investigate their social circumstances" (Lin and Zhang 1936: 3).

Zhong Jingwen, who was teaching in Hangzhou at the time, wrote the introduction to the published report. After a paean to the predecessors at Miaofengshan ten years prior, Zhong wrote:

> In recent years, the collection and study of folklore materials has gradually come to flourish. And while we should be happy about that, we can't avoid feeling that there is still something lacking; that is, that actual empirical investigations are still too few. In the work of folklore, the first step, gathering materials, must involve fieldwork ... Broader, more accurate fieldwork, empirical observation and investigation, is the most hopeful road to travel, even if the work be difficult.
>
> The Dongyue Temple outside of Hangzhou is a center of popular belief in Jiangsu and Zhejiang. Its temple fairs in the spring and autumn

are even grander, with more complex religious activity than Miaofengshan. Participants number no less than 100,000, and the fair extends to more than two weeks ... its customary activities are enough to make us open our eyes wide ... If we want to understand the urgent desires of the people, the enthusiasm with which they put matters in order, their organizational skill, and artistic performances, this is a most complete opportunity; I doubt there is a better one.

(Lin and Zhang 1936: 1–2)

At the end of the 1930s, during the eight years of war with Japan and the three years of revolutionary conflict/civil war, folklore studies practically disappeared. From the 1950s to the 1970s, with leftist ideological policies imposed in the scholarly world, folklore studies was classified as a bourgeois science, and was for all practical purposes halted (Liu 1996: 187).

Not till the implementation of the policies of reform and openness in the 1980s has the field of Chinese folklore studies resurfaced, and resumed the study of temple fairs among other habits and customs of the people. Between the years 1994 and 1997 the journal *Minsu Yanjiu* published numerous discussions of the various dimensions of temple fair activity in many places in China based on ethnographic observations, and several collections of essays, as well as monographs on the subject have been published by Chinese researchers in recent years (Gao ed. 1992; Gao 1999; Wang and Liu 1997; Zhao 2002).

Our study of temple fairs is thus informed by the work of these Chinese colleagues, confirming while hopefully elaborating upon their findings both geographically and substantively. In the following chapter, we proceed to an unraveling of the modern total social phenomenon that is the temple fair.

Part II
Unraveling the strands of the total social phenomenon

Part II

5 Secular fairs
The commercial/economic dimension

In this chapter I begin unraveling the various dimensions intertwined in the total social phenomenon that is the temple fair. My interest in temple fairs was of course first tweaked by repeated encounters with secular market fairs during earlier research in Dongyang county, a manifestation of the loosening controls on rural trade implemented in the course of China's market driven reforms.

But such secular trade fairs were also a feature of the early years of the People's Republic when Communist curtailment of temple activity led to the truncation of temple fairs into secular trade fairs in the 1950s. In Jinhua prefecture in 1952 more than 67 such commodity exchange fairs (*Wuzi Jiaoliuhui* 物资交流会) were held, with a total trade volume of ¥289,000,000,000 (old RMB), of which 65 percent was conducted by supply and marketing cooperatives, and 35 percent by private merchants (*Jinhua Shizhi* 1992: 645; *Yongkang Xianzhi* 1991: 265).

One of those 1952 Jinhua trade fairs was held in Wuning (Dongyang county seat) on lunar 8/13, the date of Wuning's traditional Hugong temple fair (DYSZ 1993: 472; see Chapter 8). Such trade fairs were increasingly common in Jinhua counties and townships throughout the 1950s, but after 1958, due to the restriction on commodity trade resulting from the closing down of standard markets during the Great Leap Forward, and the implementation of a system of rationing of industrial products and goods of everyday use, commodity exchange fairs were held much less frequently (*Yongkang Xianzhi* 1991: 265).

From 1961 to 1965, in the period of recovery from the disasters of the Great Leap, trade fairs made a brief comeback, but with the onset of the Cultural Revolution in 1966, commodity trade fairs were denounced as a manifestation of creeping capitalist restoration and suppressed.

Beginning in 1979, with the implementation of economic reform commodity exchange fairs made another comeback. In 1980, in Yongkang county alone, Tangxian, Shizhu, Zhiying, Fangyan, Gushan, Xiqi, Silu, Qingqi, Xiangzhu, and Baziqiang townships held successive commodity exchange fairs. Thereafter, the larger towns in the county held such fairs every year in the spring and autumn, posting advertisements, publicizing the events, and arranging for entertainment (*Yongkang Xianzhi* 1991: 265).

In 1988 Dongyang county alone played host to 74 commodity exchange fairs at 43 sites (DYSZ 472), a dramatic increase compared with 67 fairs in the entire municipality of Jinhua in 1952.

In contrast to most everything else in China which arises as the result of initiatives by the Communist Party, the revival of contemporary secular trade fairs is characterized proudly by participants as "*zifa*" 自发, that is to say, generated by the spontaneous activity of the people themselves with little or no participation on the part of the state, or its bureaucratic organs.

Surely the secular fairs of the post-liberation period have been and remain much more closely supervised and monitored by the local state bureaucracy than their pre-liberation cousins. The modern secular fairs (*hui chang* 会场 or *wuzi jiaoliu* hui 物资交流会) are overseen by local market regulation offices in the Bureau of Industry and Commerce (*Gongshang Ju* 工商局), which take charge of licensing traders and their wares, collecting taxes on goods sold, and working with the institutions of public security to arrange appropriate policing (Zhou and Wang eds. 1985: 26).

But there is a sense in which even contemporary secular fairs exhibit a high degree of spontaneity. Thus I have been careful in the introduction to respect that initiative by phrasing the revival of secular market fairs as authorized by the party, as opposed to begun at the instigation of the party. So while the fairs may be understood as part of an effort on the part of the state to induce economic change and stimulate commodity circulation in the countryside, the initiative seems to have been begun at the grass roots, with Communist authorities simply authorizing rather than initiating the convening of the secular market fairs of the 1980s.

And finally, secular trade fairs are still sites for entertainment and recreation, where popular cultural performance genres, operatic, theatrical, narrative, divinational, martial, acrobatic, craft, artistic, and musical, as well as a variety of gambling and games of chance are arrayed in great profusion.

In this chapter I present mini-portraits of five communities, and descriptions of the secular market fairs I attended in each. Their choice was governed most by their fairs' occurrence during the latter half of the year when my ethnographic work was conducted, but I also took advantage of the same clustering of fairs that merchants avail themselves of to attend successive fairs in the Lanxi towns of Xiawang and Zhudaishi.

The fairs in these five towns provide the opportunity to observe the operation of the temple-less temple fairs given space to function in the course of China's market-driven economic reforms, the kernel from which, my argument runs, the total social phenomenon of the post-reform temple fair may yet spring forth anew.

Huqi town 湖溪镇

In 1988 Professor Jiang Yinhuo and I were housed in Huqi during our research on the nearby village of Litang, coincidentally just when the annual secular trade fair was being held in Huqi. Fieldnotes from that period provide something of a baseline with which to compare my observations of the fair in 1998 when I returned to Huqi ten years later. It also provided an opportunity to observe the enormous changes that had occurred in the town in the interim.

Huqi town is located in central Dongyang on the banks of the South river (Nanjiang), 26 km southeast from the county town. Due to factors of location, convenience of water transport, and its traditions of craft production, Huqi has been known as one of four large markets in Dongyang county since the Ming dynasty. In October 2003 neighboring Guozhai township was consolidated into Huqi township making for a combined population of 42,121 (Guo 2007a).

Huqi is known as a "town of 100 skills." Both men and women work in a pattern of "*Yinong, Yigong*" (亦农亦工—combining agriculture with sideline craft production). During agricultural busy season everyone is in the fields; during slack seasons they engage in craft production, men as itinerant construction, carpentry and wood carving workers, women as weavers in the home, and in Huqi historically that meant silk.

Silk production in Huqi began in the Tang dynasty (618–907), and during the Ming and Qing dynasties it was an important production center. It boasted its own silk-reeling factory during the Republican period, which supplied domestic weavers in the surrounding villages with thread, and Huqi remains one of the important silk-production centers of Dongyang (HQCZ 1996: 3, 209).

As a silk producing township, mulberry has always been among Huqi's more important agricultural products, apart from grain. Tea, fruit, medicinal herbs, and lumber are also produced, and the township is known for its livestock, pigs, cattle, goats, rabbits, and chickens (HQCZ 1996: 3, 209). There is a cow-breeding station, and a bee-keeping enterprise, and the township's Jitangshan egg farm has won gold medals at the Jinhua Municipality rural products fair (Guo 2007a).

In 1994, the periodic vegetable market that convened on days one, four, and seven of the ten-day market week was replaced by a new vegetable and small commodities market that convenes daily, with hundreds of additional shops and services. The new market was constructed on a 5,000 sq m site, the clearance of which involved moving Huqi Primary School to a new location on the newly constructed North Ring Road (Huancheng Bei Lu) at the cost of ¥750,000 (HQCZ 1996: 3, 8, 209).

On January 1, 1995 the new vehicular Qingji Bridge 清济桥 across the river connecting to the North Ring Road was formally opened with an adjoining park. The Jinhua Yue Opera troupe and the Dongyang and Wuyi Wuju opera troupes performed for nine days and nights in celebration (HQCZ 1996: 8). The Dongyang Wuju opera troupe was formed in the early 1950s by the amalgamation of several local traditional troupes, most of which were actually based in Huqi. Huqi's operatic traditions involve local troupes whose activities and performances date to the late Qing dynasty, and in more recent decades the township cultural center has brought those traditions forward by organizing its own amateur Wuju opera troupe with 37 members. As a result of such efforts, the Huqi cultural center has received several awards for excellence (HQCZ 1996: 211).

One of Huqi's more successful post-reform enterprises is the Yuanlin tool factory. Designated a provincial "backbone" enterprise (HQCZ 1996: 3), it was begun with an initial investment of ¥280,000, and in 1995 exported ¥86,000,000 worth of goods. With Yuanlin as the "dragon head," in the mid-1990s, the township party committee started up a ham-processing factory, and an electro-plating factory. In November 1995 they began construction on a rubber/chemical factory which came online the following year, and produced ¥5,000,000 worth of product (HQCZ 1996: 225).

The impact of the reforms in Huqi is manifest in the enormous expansion of its industrial output. In 1995 industrial APV was ¥210,000,000 (HQCZ 1996: 4). Nine years later in 2004, industrial APV had expanded ten times to ¥2,330,000,000 (Guo 2007b).

In 2003 Huqi township opened its own foreign-export office in Shanghai to directly meet with international merchants, and eight of its companies with direct export rights exported ¥744,000,000 worth of goods, an increase of 20.4 percent over the previous year (Guo 2007a).

In 2006, there were 266 private and collective township and village enterprises in Huqi, 53 of which were located in the new Huqi industrial zone which occupies 135 hectares, and involved a total investment in infrastructure on the part of the township of ¥155,000,000 (Guo 2007a).

This industrial expansion has brought along a doubling of per capita rural income from ¥4180/year in 1995 to ¥8003/year in 2007 (Guo 2007a, 2007b; HQCZ 1996: 4; Jinhua City webpage #10).

And some of that wealth has clearly been deployed in prominently refurbishing and proudly displaying Huqi's many temple sites. Among these is Tianbao Chansi 天宝禅寺, located in a crook of the surrounding hills. It is not an especially ancient temple, constructed in the early 1940s when local notable Zhang Yunsong invited Chan Buddhist master Du Xuecheng 杜学诚 of Guoqing temple 国清寺 to come to Huqi, supervise the building of Tianbao Chansi, and serve as its head monk. The temple ceased functioning during the cultural revolution, a cluster of old buildings on the hillside during my fieldwork in Huqi in 1988. But in 1995, Chan master Shi Guangquan 释光泉, a member of the Shanghai Buddhist Association, came forward to take over Tianbao Si. The principal *pusa* and the offerings table of the temple were carved in wood by Zhang Tianhua, the son of carving master Zhang Zhengxi, now deceased (whose life and times were described in Cooper and Jiang 1998). Although the temple is quite small, in August 1996 the Dongyang City government gave its official approval for Tianbao Chansi to operate as a site of Buddhist activity, with Shi Guangquan as head monk. Every lunar 2/8 and 4/8 (Buddha's birthday), good men and faithful women from as far away as Shanghai and Hangzhou come to participate in the Buddhist rituals,

Secular fairs 69

although in 1998 these activities were not yet coordinated with any market fair (Fieldnotes Huqi 12/8/98; HQCZ 1996: 166).

Huqi also has a fairly active Christian community, one of whose members, Zhang Wanlong, is the proprietor of a woodcarving factory, producing Christian-themed carvings (described in Cooper and Jiang 1998). The congregation is of the government-approved Protestant denomination, its latest meeting hall constructed at the end of 1995 (HQCZ 1996: 167).

The Huqi fair 1988

As mentioned, it was my good fortune to have found myself in the midst of Huqi's secular trade fair on June 14, 1988 (lunar 5/1) while conducting fieldwork in nearby Litang village (see Cooper and Jiang 1998). From the window of our room at the inn, Professor Jiang Yinhuo and I looked down at the road into Huqi jammed with trucks, carts, and pedestrians, loaded down with goods, stopped for inspection and registration of the goods going into the market for tax purposes, reflected in a stamp indicating that they might be sold legitimately at the fair (Fieldnotes 6/14/88 Huqi).

Along all the streets and lanes of town, there was furniture, clothing of all types, shoes, agricultural equipment, tools and prepared foods of all kinds. Vegetables in great profusion, sweet potato shoots for planting, and medicinal herbs were all out on display.

There was a circus troupe that performed out on a field adjacent to the river with performing dogs, a contortionist girl who could let two people stand on her stomach while twisted backward over herself, a snake handler, a performing bear, and a boy who puffed smoke through a mouthful of sand, performing as a circus stunt what had once been part of a ritual to release tormented souls from purgatory, "full sand flaming mouth" (*Misha Fang Yankou* 弥沙放焰口) (Fieldnotes 6/14/88 Huqi).

At the middle school, a variety of games of chance were offered. Ten fen earned a spin of an electric wheel with a chance to win a small trinket, ring, whistle, etc. if the spinner landed on your number. Or shoot five balloons with a rifle, and win a pack of cigarettes. There was also a primitive marble pinball game—get so many points by landing successive marbles in appropriate resting places, and win a prize (Fieldnotes 6/14/88 Huqi).

The broader market was filled with more expensive games of chance too. Lining the footbridge across the river were large numbers of men seated on the edge of the walkway, each with a board behind them explaining what combinations of cards win how much money. One buys five cards from the deck, the host pays on certain combinations, the rest lose. Mixed in with these hucksters was an older gentleman offering the service of reading one's fortune in one's facial features (*kanxiang* 看相) (Fieldnotes 6/14/88 Hu Qi).

On the main street there was a performance by a young Qigong master of nearby Hengdian town who put on quite a show, whooping and hollering, with a constant patter in unintelligible Dongyang dialect, clapping hands and beating his breast, climaxing with the smashing of a brick on his forehead, to the delight of the surrounding crowd. Finally, he distributed envelopes of herbs to be steeped in wine and drunk to heal pains in the bones, in exchange for a "contribution" (Fieldnotes 6/14/88 Huqi).

In this region of Dongyang, where the production of Jinhua ham is ubiquitous, every rural household raises at least one pig per year for slaughter and consumption during New Years, and thus the pig market is an important part of the Huqi fair. Held on the opposite side of the river from the rest of the market for obvious reasons, it was depleted but for some unsold stragglers by early afternoon.

The Huqi fair 1998

Ten years later at the Huqi fair from December 8–10, 1998 [lunar 10/20–10/22], the town had changed dramatically. New housing fronted on all the main streets, concealing the old housing that remained behind, the result of an urban-renewal plan that compensated residents for the razing of their old homes, and rebuilding new ones.

Nevertheless, in 1998, some old landmarks were still present, the old cooperative department store with its internal departments now separately privatized in *chengbao* subcontracts, the old footbridge, the old low dam across which cars, trucks and buses would have to wade to enter town, now replaced by the new vehicular bridge just upriver that connects to the newly constructed North Ring road, Huancheng Bei Lu (Fieldnotes Huqi 12/8/98).

Late in the afternoon of the first day of the fair, goods began arriving, and stalls began going up. On day two, when my escort/colleague Chen Chongren from the Cultural Bureau and I arrived from Dongyang early in the morning, the main street was filled with hawkers' stalls, and the crowds were already starting to form. There was no circus at the 1998 fair, but there was a "freak show" which when one had paid to gain admission turned out to be a series of fetuses (presumably stillborn) with various defects in large jars of formaldehyde on a table, sheer grotesquery.

But somewhat surprisingly, in 1998 there were no opera performances in town. There were the usual shorts, sweaters, underwear, shoes, and children's clothes on sale in great profusion. And for ¥1, one could try one's luck pitching a plastic tub to try to cover one of many toys arrayed on a mat, earning thereby the right to take it home (Fieldnotes Huqi 12/9/98).

As in 1988, there was a Qigong aficionado performing on the street and drawing a crowd. This one broke bricks with his hands, and then caused a brick, stood up on end, to fall by focusing the *qi* in his hand from a distance of eight or nine feet without ever touching the brick. It seemed to me, that in this old parlor trick, he had unobtrusively moved the carpet on which the brick was setting upright with his foot at the crucial moment, and my companion from the City Cultural Bureau agreed it was a fake. Still in all he put on a very good show and had the assembled crowd laughing at his

Figure 5.1 Freaks of nature: Huqi

wisecracks and his whoops and hollers (I used the same terms in Fieldnotes ten years earlier!), after which he passed the hat to great effect.

An itinerant erhu player/singer from Anhui made his rounds of the local fairs in the area, busking for money on the streets, and a gentleman with several Chinese chess boards set up before him in various positions, challenged onlookers to compete with him for a wager. Needless to say, the pieces on the various boards were configured in such a way as to make beating him extremely unlikely (Fieldnotes Huqi 12/9/98).

Down river at the furniture section of the market, there must have been 50 different enterprises represented, each with an array of traditional carved-wood cabinets, tables, chests, and dowry furniture, as well as modern-style coffee tables, sofas, and chairs.

On the way out of the furniture market, a loud quarrel ensued, which quickly escalated into a knockdown drag out fight between two men who really had at each other. The cause of the fray was never made clear as the combatants were finally separated and parted ways. It was one of several fights witnessed at the fairs I attended, all of which seemed to occur toward the end of the day (Fieldnotes Huqi 12/9/98).

Qianxiang town 千祥镇

Qianxiang 千祥镇 is Dongyang's southernmost township, 26 km due south from the county town Wuning, in the central Zhejiang hilly mountain area, bordering Pan An and Yongkang counties on the east and south. Cheng Qi

桂溪 creek flows from east to west across the middle of the township. In 2002 Qianxiang had an area of 42 sq km, and a population of 20,100 (JHSDTC 2003: 190; YCZX n.d.). However, in October, 2003 in a regional administrative adjustment, Qianxiang was merged with Sanlian township, and the territory of the new Qianxiang county expanded to 104 sq km, with twice the population 44,802 in 2007 (Dongyang Government webpage #1; Jinhua City webpage #10).

The township boasts a 270 hectare rice demonstration/experimentation farm. Tea, mat straw, and sugar are also grown, and there are four centers specializing in raising chickens, three in raising goats, and one where pheasant are raised (JHSDTC 2003: 190). But Qianxiang is best known for the cultivation of the six medicinal herbs: Yuanhu 元胡, Baizhu 白术 (rhizome of atractylodes), Baishao 白芍 (peony root), Yuanshen 元参 (Ginseng), Beimu 贝母 (fritillary bulb), and Jiegeng 桔梗 (balloon flower root).

Among these, Qianxiang produces 70 percent of the nation's Yuanhu, more than 6,000 tons per year, with the price fluctuating around ¥16 per kilo. The Yuanhu of Qianxiang is said to have more than twice the active ingredients as that of other provinces (YCZX n.d.). In addition to the 6,000 tons of Yuanhu produced annually, Qianxiang's production of the other medicinal herbs is as follows:

- Baizhu—1450 tons
- Baishao of two varieties:
    - Kang 抗 Baishao—1000 tons
    - Hui 徽 Baishao—4000 tons
- Yuanshen—470 tons
- Beimu—2500 tons
- Jiegeng—200 tons

(YCZX n.d.)

The township's Chongde Tang 崇德堂 apothecary in Shangdongchen village 上东陈村 has been designated a historic protected site, preserving as it does all the original accoutrements and furnishings of a Qing dynasty medicinal herb shop (JHSDTC 2003: 190).

Historically, roughly 80 percent of the land area of Qianxiang was planted in medicinal herbs, but for many years national policy mandated grain production, and medicinal herb production was relegated to private plots. But since the implementation of economic reform and the privatization of the agricultural sector, the production of Chinese medicinal herbs has taken off.

In 1986, the township Industrial and Commercial Bureau with the approval of the local government opened the Qianxiang Chinese medicinal herb market, occupying more than 3400 sq m, with trade service buildings, sales buildings, consignment, storage, and transport facilities, as well as an outdoor covered market. More than 56 firms, state run, collective and private, established permanent offices in the market, with capital investments totaling ¥14,570,000 (YCZX n.d.). Indeed, Qianxiang's market is recognized as one of ten national medicinal herb markets with an annual trade volume exceeding ¥100,000,000 (Dongyang Government webpage #1).

In May 1994, Qianxiang played host to the seventh Conference of National Medicinal Herb Markets which brought the township's Yuanhu to the attention of international merchants from Japan and South Korea, and had the immediate effect of raising the price of Yuanhu to ¥33/kilo (YCZX n.d.).

In the late 1990s, nearly 25,000 people in the Qianxiang area participated in the production and processing of medicinal herbs, roughly 65 percent of the labor force. Between Qianxiang, Sanlian, and Mazhai counties there are more than 400 firms dealing in medicinal herbs, employing more than 3000 people in transport alone. There are companies and factories from more than 20 provincial cities conducting trade in medicinal herbs valued at ¥120,000,000, providing the township with annual tax revenues of ¥260,000 and market administrative fees of ¥170,000 (YCZX n.d.).

The rise of the Qianxiang Chinese medicinal herb market has opened a new road to prosperity for the people of township, summed up in the slogan: "Create a market, raise up an industry, give life to the economy, enrich the people."

Rural per capita income has increased from ¥4,678 in 2003, to ¥5519 in 2004, to ¥6310 in 2007 (Dongyang Government webpage #1; Jinhua City webpage #10), and has even produced a host of medicinal herb millionaire households (YCZX n.d.).

A portion of Qianxiang's economic prosperity must also be attributed to its industrial development. The township's 1350 township and village enterprises produce bamboo products, metal work, wire and electro-plating, cloth spools, shale, leather belts, furniture, arts and crafts items, many of which are exported to some 30 countries. The leather industry is the pillar of the township economy with 90 percent of its product exported, and a foreign trade volume of ¥10,000,000, and the township is also one of the major producers of straw mats for the national market (Dongyang Government webpage #1; Jinhua City webpage #10; JHSDTC 2003: 190).

Industrial APV increased from ¥993,680,000 in 2003 to ¥1,150,300,000 in 2004, slipping somewhat to ¥1,024,000,000 in 2006. Export volume increased from ¥226,539,028 in 2002, to ¥307,640,000 in 2003, to ¥392,530,000 in 2004 (Dongyang Government webpage #1; Dongyang Government webpage #2; Dongyang Government webpage #3).

In the face of the world economic crisis in 2008–9, the township leadership became concerned that enterprises make improvements in the efficiency of their operations and the quality of their products. Among the measures promulgated to achieve these goals was the admonition:

"Four compares, four don't compares" (*sibi, sibubi* 四比四不比):
不比汽车比设备，不比别墅比厂房，不比香烟比管理，不比关系比贡献
Don't compare cars, compare equipment

Don't compare villas, compare factory space
Don't compare cigarettes, compare management
Don't compare *guanxi*, compare contribution
(Dongyang Government webpage #5)

The Qianxiang fair

The Qianxiang fair is first and foremost an occasion for the trade of medicinal herbs, and performs important wholesaling functions in local, national and international markets, providing an opportunity for Chinese pharmacists, hospitals and medical practitioners to replenish their supplies with purchases in bulk.

While in the past, it is said there was a temple fair on this date [lunar 6/11], the old temple just on the outskirts of town has long been destroyed, and the contemporary fair is strictly secular. In 1998, the old temple was being reconstructed, and may well play a role in future fairs (Fieldnotes Qianxiang 8/2/98).

Merchants had come from as far away as Shandong and Henan provinces to attend the fair, and many merchants had arrived in Qianxiang after having attended successive fairs in Ma Zhai the day before, and Pan An several days before that.

It was unbearably hot, but the *huichang* was lively, stalls lining the streets with clothes, shoes, belts, toys, furniture, food, vegetables, chickens, eggs, keys, snakes, winnowing machines, books, medicines, rat poison, etc.

Figure 5.2 Toy vendor: Qianxiang

Figure 5.3 Winnowers for sale: Qianxiang

Streets and lanes were crowded with people, bumping, pushing, making purchases, trying their luck at various games of chance. I had my face read by an old gentleman whose local dialect I could scarcely understand except for his rather unlikely prediction that healthy as I was, I would live to be 80, and have three children (Fieldnotes Qianxiang 8/2/98).

At one gambling stall ¥1 gave the patron the opportunity of drawing from a deck any number of cards up to five. The value of the cards was then added up, after which one found the value on the board, and counted from there to a square which told you if you won or lost, and how much. On my first two draws, I went up ¥6, but on the next three I lost ¥29. Quite a scam, with the odds clearly stacked in favor of the house (Fieldnotes Qianxiang 8/2/98).

Some of the stall keepers, have their own retail shops in the various cities and towns in the municipality, but still do as much as 50 percent of their annual business at the fairs. Others are strictly fair entrepreneurs whose livelihood depends exclusively on the goods sold at successive fairs during the agricultural slack seasons. Renting a stall space at the Qianxiang fair costs ¥5 for the privilege for both days of the fair, plus a ¥1 school fee (Fieldnotes Qianxiang 8/2/98).

Furniture on sale is mostly locally made, but many "fashionable" clothes and shoes on sale were manufactured in Guangdong. A stall keeper I had photographed ten years ago selling wooden tubs at the fair in Huqi town, smiling while holding up a fist full of money, was there in Qianxiang in 1998, still selling tubs. There was no mistaking his distinctive dentition.

On one street a dough artist fashioned little figures of mythic beasts and heroes, operatic characters, birds and flowers, from colored "playdough" prepared himself, mounted on wooden skewers mainly for sale to children.

He learned the skill from a Jiangsu master resident in Jinhua, and has had a number of apprentices of his own, one of whom has immigrated to the US. He works the fairs regularly, selling small pieces for ¥3/piece, and larger ones for ¥10 and up, and generally heads south to Fujian, Shantou, and Guangzhou for the winter where the weather is warmer. His business at the Qianxiang fair has been brisk (Fieldnotes Qianxiang 8/3/98).

Unfortunately, on this particular day his business, not to mention my observations, were cut short by a torrential downpour, which sent many people fleeing for their transportation home. No opera seems to have been performed in Qianxiang during the fair, perhaps rained out.

Luodian town 罗店镇

Luodian town 罗店镇 is located some 4 km to the north of Jinhua's city center, known colloquially as the "northern gate of Jinhua" 婺城北大门. The township covers 72 sq km with a population of 230,000 (18,100 in Luodian town) (JHDTC 1998: 33).

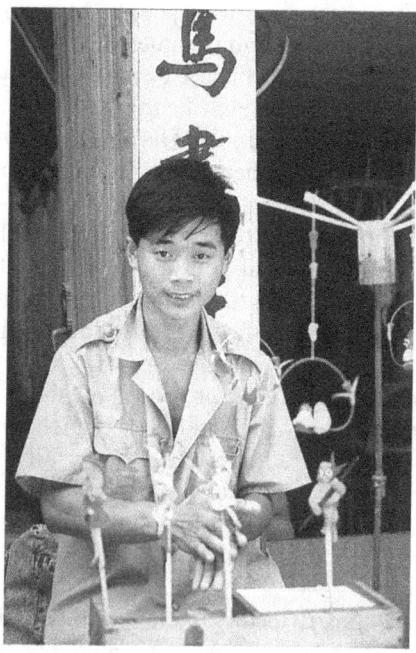

Figure 5.4 Dough artist: Qianxiang

The nationally well-known Shuanglong (Double Dragon) Cave scenic area was within Luodian's borders until 1992 when two administrative village units were hived off into a separately administered Shuanglong Scenic Area. Over the centuries, the two caves on the site, Shuanglong cave and Bing Hu cave 冰壶洞, have inspired many literati to put their impressions of the place in print, and they remain an important tourist attraction of Jinhua municipality (JHDTC 1998: 33; Luodian Township Government n.d.).

The township's cultivated area is about 700 hectares (582 irrigated, 117 dry fields) with 3,267 hectares of hill forest. In addition to irrigated rice, Luodian's location in the Jinhua city suburbs gives it a natural market for locally grown vegetables and fruit, and its *luobo* (daikon) are famous throughout the province. Sugar, oranges, and grapes are also an important constituent of its agricultural output (Luodian Township Government n.d.). The tea of the township's Lutian 鹿田 village is included in the Tea Classic of Tang Luyu 唐陆羽, and the township also produces fresh water pearl clams and fish in the 6.7 hectare Luodian fish pond (JHDTC 1998: 33).

But above all, Luodian is known historically as the "township of flowers and plants" (*huahui zhi xiang* 花卉之乡). During the anti-Japanese war, flower culture ceased, and immediately after liberation, grain production was stressed, so not many flowers were grown or marketed. During the co-operative period of the early 1950s, the township did produce some 2,000 kg of flowers annually, mainly Moli Hua 茉莉花 (Jasmine flowers) and Bailanhua 白兰花 (White orchids) (JHDTC 1998: 33). But since the economic reforms flower production has blossomed (Ooops!), and the township now produces some 130,000 kg of flowers/year—white jade orchids (白玉兰), Jasmine flowers (茉莉花), camellias (茶花), and "Buddha hands" (佛手). At present there is greater demand for ornamental flowers than ever before and the township has moved to meet that demand, as well as moving into the production of miniature trees and rockery (Luodian Township Government n.d.).

With 85 percent of households raising flowers for the market, grain is now generally bought from outside. The rather high degree of commercialization has led to a rise in living standards. Per capita rural income rose from ¥5543 in 2005, to ¥6241 in 2007. As a result there has not been much outmigration from Luodian (Fieldnotes Luodian 12/2/98; Jinhua City webpage #10).

The town of Luodian is the center for production of the distinctive fruit known as "Jinhua Buddha Hands" (*Jinhua Foshou* 金华佛手). The plants blossom in the early summer, and the fruit ripens in early winter, rounded at the base, with projections from the top which give the fruit an uncanny resemblance to the human hand.

It is said that during the Ming dynasty, Jinhua magistrate, Zhou Qin, brought two seedlings from his home in Nanjing, but because they didn't flower for several years, he simply threw them out of the *yamen* garden just as an old peasant from Luodian was passing by. The old peasant took the seedlings back to Luodian and planted them, using water from Shuanglong cave to nurture them. That year the seedlings flowered and bore fruit, and ever since,

Foshou have been grown in Luodian. Indeed they have become a commodity for which the township is known far and wide (Dai ed. 1997: 147).

The skin of the fruit is like that of an orange, and it has a strong fragrance. A few slices put in tea, produces a fragrance that "gladdens the heart and refreshes the mind." Placed in a room the fragrance pervades and remains for a long time. It can be eaten fresh although its flavor is somewhat bitter/sour, so it is more often candied. Its flowers and fruit are also used in medicinal preparations, said to be good for the spleen, the lungs and liver. It cures nausea and vomiting, coughing, and bloating, clears the body of phlegm, and does not affect one's appetite (Dai ed. 1997: 147).

In addition to flower raising, Luodian has also developed its rural industries, the most important products of which are woven goods, pumps, silicon-manganese steel, concrete/cement (two factories), electrical equipment, industrial crucibles and scales (Jinhua City webpage #10). The township's knives and cutlery are marketed internationally, and its tea and crucibles have a large domestic market in both northern and southern China (JHDTC 1998: 33; Luodian Township Government n.d.).

To accommodate its enterprises, Luodian has created a small industrial zone in the vicinity of the Jinhua–Lanxi highway, near which a special "open" zone (*kaifa qu* 开发区) was created to house private enterprises. The township has also constructed a large-scale country villa estate, to accommodate investing merchants and factory entrepreneurs, and provide them with a pleasant living environment. Given its location in suburban Jinhua, the Luodian estate could well prove attractive to urban Jinhua businessmen as well (Luodian Township Government n.d.).

During a stop at a tea house, it came to light that during the war, the Japanese had bombed Luodian with bacterial weapons killing a great many people. Those who buried the dead one day were dead themselves within a few days. Several octogenarians in town who managed to survive are participants in a suit seeking reparations from the Japanese government. At the same teahouse, I met two merchants from Shandong in town for the fair to purchase flowers which they ship back home by truck. Including the fair, they make the trip five to six times per year (Fieldnotes Luodian 12/3/98).

In pre-liberation times, there was a Flower God Temple (*Huashen Miao* 花神庙) in Luodian's Xiwu village 西吴村 with a temple fair on lunar 2/2— the birthday of Huashen. There were opera performances and ceremonies of sacrifice, but since liberation, these practices were classified as superstition and discontinued (Fieldnotes Luodian 12/2/98).

In the past there was a small Confucian temple in Luodian town known as *Konggong zhenren Miao* 孔公真人庙, which hosted a temple fair on lunar 2/28 at which there were Jinhua-style bull fights (in which bull fights bull) and operas and processions of the pusa on tours of inspection around the township. But the old fair has no relation to the present secular fair on lunar 10/15. The temple was destroyed during land reform in December 1950, rebuilt on a small scale in 1993–4, only to be razed again when the government failed to approve its functioning on account of its small size and lack of devotees (Fieldnotes, Luodian 12/3/98).

The Luodian fair

The market fair in Luodian on lunar 10/15 is strictly a post-reform secular phenomenon. There were no temple fairs in Luodian on this date in the past. Agricultural equipment, tools and hardware, and books were all on display. A vendor from distant Wuhan sold microphones. Large stands of lumber (rough hewn trees) were for sale to the south of town (Fieldnotes Luodian 12/2/98).

Two Tibetans, squatted in the street, preparing and selling medicinal herbs, with a constant speech patter as they cut, shaved, grated, and added various herbs, horns and powders to the preparations on sheets of paper, folded up and sold for ¥20/packet (Fieldnotes Luodian 12/2/98).

And there were opera performances. The opera stage at the Luodian fair was a pretty rugged affair, a temporary stage (caotai 草台) erected specifically for the event. Seating was on benches under a huge temporary tent with tea cups set out for the audience on the benches, some of the places on which were reserved, with the names and number of guests taped to the bench. But on this day, because of the rain for the past two days, the floor was a muddy mess, and just navigating the puddles to a seat was no easy task. Still in all, in these adverse conditions, the troupe from Yongkang put on an enthusiastic performance very much in the spirit of "the show must go on" (Fieldnotes Luodian 12/3/98).

The Luodian village of Xiwu is the point of origin of one of Jinhua's local operatic genres Xiwu Gaoqiang 西吴高腔, widespread in Jinhua, Lanxi, and as far as eastern Jiangxi and southern Anhui during the late Ming and early Qing, reaching its peak of popularity in the early ninettenth century (Zhang and Hong 1985: 42). Subsequently its popularity declined, as did the number of troupes specializing in Xiwu Gaoqiang performances. The genre was still performed by so-called "combined" troupes (heban 合班) whose repertoires include operas from several genres (see chapter 7), and Xiwu Gaoqiang has thereby survived into the present (Ding 1990: 163–164).

Given Luodian's tradition of operatic performance, it is not surprising that amateur performance troupes remain a common form of popular entertainment. Both so-called Zuochang Ban (seated singing troupes 坐唱班) and the somewhat more refined semi-professional Taizi Ban (Imperial Prince troupes—太子班) were widespread in Luodian historically. It is reported that in 1946, a single temple fair at Baidu village was entertained by 12 Zuochang troupes. After the establishment of the PRC, some 80 odd amateur troupes were said to have sprung up and been active in Jinhua county, and Luodian township accounted for 13. In more recent years, the Taizi Ban of Xiwu and Houqi He 后溪河 villages have attained a certain local notoriety for the high quality of their performances (Ding 1990: 159–160).

As regards performance genres common at traditional temple fairs, in 1977 Luodian was one of several locales to convene training classes in the narrative performance art of Daoqing (see Chapter 6), under the auspices of Jinhua's cultural center (Zhang 2003: 16), although no Daoqing practitioners were encountered at the fair in 1998.

It was, all in all, two miserable, rainy and cold, dreary days at the Luodian secular fair, and according to locals, participation was down 40 percent on account of the weather.

Xiawang township 下王镇

Xiawang town is located some 20 km to the southwest of Lanxi city in western Jinhua. In 1986 its population of 8,216 people engaged in agriculture growing mainly irrigated rice, with three kinds of wheat and rape seed in rotation (XWXWHZ 1987: 3–4). The township also produces forest products, lumber, and a variety of livestock, and has well-developed fish farms. Local craftsmen practice woodcarving and bamboo basketry as sideline occupations, and most women in the township were capable of embroidery and decorative paper cutting (XWXWHZ 1987: 52).

Specialized households (*zhuanye hu*) engaged in masonry, carpentry, metal work, ornamental flower raising, orchard keeping, tailoring, and hair cutting, as well as raising pigs, cows, ducks, and fish. Rural industrial enterprises include a knitting factory, hosiery factory, plastics factory, a wooden bed-frame factory, a brick and tile factory, and an electrical equipment and machinery repair shop (XWXWHZ 1987: 46).

In 1986, total industrial APV for the township was ¥3,644,500, divided among township administered enterprises—¥958,500; village administered enterprises—¥257,600; private/household run enterprises—¥2,428,400 (XWXWHZ 1987: 3–4).

The township of Xiawang was traditionally one in which opera occupied an important place. Before 1949 nearly every village ancestral hall had an opera stage, although after 1949 most of the ancestral halls and their opera stages fell into disrepair, and by the mid-1980s there were only a few remaining (XWXWHZ 1987: 25).

In traditional times, amateur Zuochang Ban were ubiquitous in the area. They performed in the Wuju 婺剧 (Jinhua opera) genres of Huixi 徽戏, Kunju 昆剧 and Tanhuang 滩簧, at weddings, decanal birthdays over 50, house building, and happy occasions. In the immediate aftermath of the defeat of Japan, Zuochang Ban were everywhere, but the civil war that followed clearly took a toll, and by 1949, for every ten such troupes, there was only one remaining (XWXWHZ 1987: 20; see also Chapter 7).

Among the temples that held fairs traditionally in Xiawang township was Huangbitang Dian 黄碧塘殿 (Temple of the Yellow Jade Pool) originally built during the Ming dynasty in Huangbitang village, later moved to Zhengjia cun 郑家村, about 1 km up the road from Xiawang.

The temple housed altars where one might worship Dizangwang 地藏王 (King of Hell), Guanyin 观音 (Goddess of Mercy), or Weituo 韦陀 (sword-wielding guardian of the dharma), and its upkeep was shared among ten villages—Shangwang, Xiawang, Zhengjia, Huangbitang, Jiangcun 江村, Shangtangwu 上塘坞, Siji 寺基, Maocun 毛村, Hugutou 湖谷头, and Lilang 里郎. The temple fair was held on lunar 9/26, and responsibility for hosting the temple festivities rotated annually among each village. The host village would prepare and slaughter a "Big year pig" for presentation and sacrifice at the temple, decorated with "Zhuangyuan flowers" and lanterns, and a red cloak draped over all, an awesome display.

The host village for the year was also responsible for hiring the opera troupe or troupes to perform on the temple stage to entertain the deity. The last time opera was performed at the Huangbitang Temple fair was in 1947, when Shangwang village served as the host, and hired the well known Zhou Chunju 周春聚 troupe from Longyou to perform. Famed female performer Zhou Yuexian 周越仙 performed the lead in Borrowed Fan 借扇 (XWXWHZ 1987: 86, 91; also see Chapter 7).

The secular fair at Xiawang was held on November 13–14, 1998, none other than the lunar date 9/25–9/26 on which day the Huangbitang temple fair was held traditionally, but as the locals put it, the temple was destroyed during the Cultural Revolution, leaving behind only commercial exchange. The secular commercial fair was brought back as a temple-less temple fair with the implementation of the economic reforms (Fieldnotes Xiawang 11/13/98 (lunar 9/25)), but remarkably (or perhaps not so) the secular fair was still scheduled on lunar 9/26 as the old temple fair at Huangbitang had been traditionally.

Another of the temples of significance to Xiawang townsfolk is Mafu Dian 马夫殿, located in Baitoufan 百头畈 village, built during the Qing dynasty (third year of Guangxu—1878), occupying 996 sq m. The name of the temple derives from the figure to whom it is dedicated, Mashi Tianxian 马氏天仙 or Mafu Niangniang 马夫娘娘, about whom the following story is told.

Many years ago there was a prosperous household surnamed Ma that took in a child daughter-in-law from a poor family. The mother-in-law treated young Mafu like a slave, feeding her food fit for dogs and pigs; forcing her to sleep wrapped only in a straw cape; and requiring that every day she weave three bolts of cloth, lest she suffer vicious beatings. Daughter-in-law bore up the best she could, not daring to oppose, pouring her bitterness into the cloth. Day and night, she sweated at the loom, turning out the most radiant cloth, but she still could not get the old woman's approval.

It went on like this for several years, until overworked and underfed, afflicted with disease, on the verge of death, still sitting at the loom, a compassionate uncle discovered her emaciated body, and went out on the street to publicly humiliate the old the woman, saying: "You had better not mistreat your daughter-in-law in this way, lest she become an immortal."

The mother-in-law laughed in reply: "If this useless bone becomes an immortal, may I become a mother pig, and lick her ass."

The behavior of such a patient and enduring child daughter-in-law finally moved the gods to take pity, and they sent her mother's brother with a *dan* of metal, who instructed her to prepare a *dan* of cotton for her escape by way of the Dao to achieve immortality. Fleeing with her uncle, the two soon came to the edge of a stream and had to get across. Realizing that once in the water, she would be unable to prevent the cotton from taking up the water, and weak as she was would probably sink to the bottom, Mafu gave the cotton to her uncle to carry. And sure enough, it grew heavier and heavier as he waded deeper into the stream, until uncle gradually fell behind. In the end, niece/daughter-in-law spotted a large pine tree with lush branches hanging down close to the stream. As she floated by, she was able to grab hold of a branch and pull herself up, climbing higher and higher up the tree till she ascended to the pavilion of heaven, and became an immortal. What became of uncle we are not told.

Afterwards, as an immortal Mafu took pity on the poor common folk (*laobaixing*), and would quietly provide assistance, bringing some happiness and relief to their bitter lives. The people were grateful for her mercies, and built a temple (*dian* 殿) next to the great pine tree, with a carved *pusa*, and have expressed their reverence over the generations. Since her husband's household was surnamed Ma, the *dian* was called Mafu Dian (The temple of Mrs Ma).

Strangely, the old mother-in-law died suddenly, and changed into an old mother pig. It was suggested that the head of the old mother pig be chopped off and placed below the ass of Mafu's *pusa* in the temple, so as to fulfill the evil mother in law's prophecy of licking her immortal daughter in law's ass. Whether the advice was taken is not revealed in the source (XWXWHZ 1987: 56).

Mafu Dian was divided into a Great Hall where Mafu Tianxian's *pusa* presided, and a side hall where Guanyin was housed. Every year on lunar 7/7, the day on which Mafu Tianxian became an immortal, there was a large-scale temple fair, the high point of the year until 1949 when religious activities at the temple were halted. The Buddhist idols, iron bell, iron incense burner, drums, and sedan chair for the *pusa* did not survive the early liberation period attacks on feudal superstition. During land reform, since the premises were a religious space, no one was willing to take responsibility for their upkeep, and the temple became public property. In 1960, a red-brick school house was built on the site that served students in the area for several years. Finally, during the cultural revolution campaign to destroy the Four Olds, the temple was razed but for a single stele, inscribed at the top with the date of the third year of Guangxu 1878, below which were inscribed the names of those who had made contributions to support the temple's construction with the amounts contributed (XWXWHZ 1987: 92).

The Xiawang fair

As predicted by the street hawkers in Lanxi city many of whom would be attending the fair in Xiawang, the first day of the three-day fair, 11/13/98 (lunar 9/25), was a bit slow getting started. There were several tea stalls on the side street which early in the day were packed with elderly men sipping tea, smoking, gossiping, playing cards and Mahjong.

The District Government Office Head (*Chuzhang*) was just back from Lanxi, and in soldier's uniform. In his company, my escort from the cultural bureau, Mr. Wang, and I went for a walk around Xiawang town. Along the way, we chanced upon a coterie of gamblers, squatting at the street side and shooting the local equivalent of craps, three dice shaken in a tea cup covered by a sauce dish, turned over in the sauce dish, and revealed. Folks put their money on a number between one and six, and if any die shows the number they win. If multiple die show the number they win that many times. Perhaps on account of embarrassment over my observing such behavior, our *Chuzhang* broke up the game, actually stamping and crushing the gamblers' tea cup and saucer with his military boot in the process (Fieldnotes Xiawang 11/13/98).

Later in the day, the goods for tomorrow's big day started rolling in. Furniture made its appearance up the road toward Lanxi, and stalls for clothes, shoes, and knit goods were being raised on both sides. The paving of the road was finished only three weeks prior, in preparation for this year's event. By 4.00 p.m. the road was clogged with stalls making vehicular traffic virtually impossible. By the end of the day one could begin to imagine a rather large-scale market fair despite the rather unimpressive look of things during the morning.

The following day, the stalls stretched down the new road for longer than expected. The crowds were enormous, the atmosphere festive. On the road in, the inevitable tax assessors put their registration stamp on the commodities entering the market. Tax rate was 6 percent on raw materials, 4 percent on finished products. The charge for stall space was ¥20.

Figure 5.5 Street peddler: Xiawang

84 *Unraveling the total social phenomenon*

And the circus was in town today, from Anhui, its huge tent pitched in a fallow field, featuring a host of acrobatic acts, a contortionist girl, two unicycle performers, a dog that could read, a horse riding monkey, a performing goat, a performing bear, etc. (the same circus would be in Zhudaishi the following week) (Fieldnotes 11/14/98 Xiawang). The little contortionist girl was trained at a martial arts school 武术学校 in Hebei province (吴桥县, 杂枝文乡), supported by the central government. She was accompanied in the circus by two family members and was paid the princely sum of ¥2,000/mo. Not bad for a five-year old. Mr. Wang however was somewhat concerned about her education (Fieldnotes 11/19/98 Zhudaishi).

In the afternoon, at the neighboring village of Weijia cun 魏家村, there were opera performances (the first I'd seen during the research), and what an absolutely fabulous spectacle it was. The audience was primarily old timers, including a great group of elderly gentlemen sitting at a long table sipping tea on the right-hand side of the rear "orchestra" section of the audience, clearly the seats of honor. They all wore straw hats to fend off the extremely warm sun.

But the performers themselves were surprisingly youthful, and a trip backstage earned the privilege of watching as the troupe members made up their faces in preparation for a performance of Xue Dingshan 薛丁山, a Tang dynasty tale of love and intrigue.

Also of note during the day was my paying ¥2 to draw a ticket from a huge rotating bin whose number actually entitled me to a two-pilot gascounter stove, which Mr. Wang said he could indeed use. So amidst the crowds we walked off with our prize and Mr. Wang took it home to his sure to be pleased wife (Fieldnotes 11/14/98 Xiawang).

Figure 5.6 Xiawang child contortionist in Zhudaishi

Figure 5.7 Child contortionist performing: Xiawang

The end of the day at the fair was marred somewhat by a knock-down, drag-out brawl just as we were leaving the township government headquarters for our return to Lanxi. A group of folks dragged in a rather large guy for some offense or another, and as they were doing so, a group of guys descended on him, beating him on all sides till his face was a bloody mess. No telling what started it all. The somewhat embarrassed *Chuzhang* explained it as the result of too much alcohol, but it seemed a bit more complex than that.

And then outside the Xiawang cloth-dying factory, two women were having a go at one another, scratching and tearing each other's hair. They were pulled apart, but the argumentation of one hefty battleaxe went on for some time thereafter, entertaining a large group of spectators peering through the fence (Fieldnotes 11/14/98 Xiawang).

Zhudaishi town/village

The town of Zhudaishi 珠带式 lies 27 km to the southwest of Lanxi City. Once the seat of the local government of Shengshan "Shezu" Township, it is well connected by road to Lanxi in the east and Longyou in the west. But in more recent years, in an administrative reorganization, the township government was moved to Shuiting and rechristened Shuiting Shezu Township, and Zhudaishi became an administrative village (Fieldnotes 11/18/98— Zhudaishi; Chen ed. 1987: 3). The new township has had "minority nationality" status since 1986, although the Shezu represent only about a fifth of the otherwise Han Chinese population of 22,755 (Chen ed. 1987: 139).

In 1998, Zhudaishi town/village had a population of about 1000, somewhat more than 200 of whom were She minority people, occupying the northeast quarter of town (Fieldnotes 11/18/98—Zhudaishi). Shezu founding ancestor Lei Jinshan 雷金山 migrated into the area and settled in Kuitangban 奎塘板 village in the fourth year of the Qing dynasty, Tongzhi reign (1866). Initially, the She people had no choice but to settle in marginal, desolate, and out of the way places, in the hills, making their living on reclaimed waste land, laboring and hunting (Chen ed. 1987: 43). The gazetteer of the early period of settlement noted marked cultural characteristics of clothing, custom, and settlement pattern for the She nationality that set them apart from the majority Han (Chen ed. 1987: 139; 3–4).

The contemporary township gazetteer notes that until the mid-1980s the She nationality were matrilineal and matrilocal, with children taking the surname of their mother, and husbands residing in the household of their wife's parents, so marriages of She women to Han men required the latter to move in with their wives' families and assume their wives' surname (Chen ed. 1987: 144). Notwithstanding such inconvenience for a Han Chinese bridegroom, there has been frequent intermarriage during the more than 150 years since the She first settled in the region.

And the She have undergone a process of continuous acculturation/assimilation to Han Chinese culture, until now they are virtually indistinguishable from their Han Chinese neighbors (Chen ed. 1987: 139; 3–4; Fieldnotes 11/18/98–Zhudaishi). They grow the same crops, work in the same factories and enterprises, attend the same market fairs, listen to and perform the same operas, and even worship the same local deities.

Agriculture in the township is dominated by irrigated rice, with three different kinds of wheat, and rape seed (*youcai*) grown in rotation. Tallow, tea, mulberry, sugar cane, peaches, and dates are also grown. Livestock include pigs, poultry, cattle, and rabbits, and aquaculture and bee raising are well developed. There is also a significant lumber and forest products industry (Chen ed. 1987: 4).

Since the institution of economic reform in the late 1970s and 1980s industry has developed to an unprecedented degree. Shuiting township is home to 57 township and village enterprises producing cotton cloth, silk, metal wire, food processing, as well as machine repair factories, and a saw mill. At the end of 1986, industrial APV for the entire township was ¥5,000,000, and average per capita income for the township was ¥519 (Chen ed. 1987: 5). By 2007, per capita income had risen to ¥3,979 (Jinhua City webpage #10). Zhudaishi boasts a towel factory and workshop (*jiagongdian*), the cotton for which is locally grown and ginned (Fieldnotes 11/18/98).

Zhudaishi has had a long relationship with opera in the form of both amateur and professional troupes. It was home to an amateur troupe in the 1920s and 1930s, the Zuochang Ban (seated performance troupe) of Xu

Sanduan Tang 徐三端堂坐唱班, which took its name from the Xu Sanduan ancestral hall and stage in Zhudaishi where it made its home and performed most often. The troupe performed in the Kun genre, and made the transition to semi-professional Taizi Ban involving costumed performance in the early 1930s, subsequently performing in neighboring villages in Shuiting, as well as in Youbu and Longyou counties for several years thereafter (Chen ed. 1987: 26, 28, 34).

After the establishment of the PRC, many amateur troupes morphed into what became known as spare-time opera troupes (Yeyu Jutuan 业余剧团). One such troupe in Zhudaishi was formed in 1952, assembling more than 20 performers who subsequently learned to perform more than 20 different operas. The troupe went on to win a performance prize at the Jinhua Mass Culture Competition in 1957, but disbanded in 1964 (Chen ed. 1987: 25, 31).

In the mid-1980s there were still a handful of practitioners of the narrative performance arts of Daoqing and Shuoshu performing in the tea houses and trade fairs of Shuiting township (LXSZ 1988: 574). In the old society, Daoqing practitioners were typically blind men, whose performances were spoken and sung accompanied by an Yugu bamboo drum, and a set of bamboo clappers (see Chapter 6).

Practitioners of *Shuoshu* 说书 (story telling) in the township performed in two distinct subgenres. The first, *Zhanghui xiaoshuo* 章回小说, is a type of serialized traditional Chinese novel, usually performed in nightly installments, each chapter of which is headed by a couplet, giving the gist of the evening's content. The second, Xiaoluo Shu (小锣书 Small Cymbal Narrative), is a kind of extemporaneously composed poetry, full of wit and often critical humor, in which practitioners beat a small brass cymbal to accompany their narrative (see Chapter 6).

Among the tea houses where such artists perform is Zhudaishi Xu Bogen Cultural tea room 徐柏根文化茶室, begun in 1983 when the Xu family bought a TV set; subscribed to a batch of newspapers and magazines, and opened a tea house in their home. In addition to tea, they sold candy, cigarettes, and wine. Playing cards and chess boards, as well as the TV and magazines could be used free of charge, and business has prospered. During the day, people drop in for tea from surrounding villages, and during the evening, there are recitations of Shuoshu, performances of Daoqing, etc., often performed in nightly installments, guaranteeing repeated patronage. In the mid-1980s, there were three other tea houses in the township, one each in the villages of Kuitangfan 奎塘坂, Liutangzhang 柳塘章, and Shengtanghu 生塘胡 (Chen ed. 1987: 23–24).

Unfortunately, although such performers were reported active in the 1980s in and around Zhudaishi, my path did not cross with practitioners of any of these genres during my visit to the market fair in Zhudaishi in 1998.

Before the establishment of the PRC, almost every village in the township had a temple of some kind, at minimum a shrine honoring the local earth god, Tudi Shen 土地神, who protected the tranquility of the area. His customary birthday was lunar 2/2, a She ri 社日, occasion for a fair in his honor with an opera performance (Shexi 社戏) for his entertainment. In addition there were Buddhist and Daoist temples in the township where Guanyin, Rulai, Zhenwu, Guanyu, and the God of Wealth could be worshiped (Chen ed. 1987: 158).

A measure of the assimilation of the She minority in this locale is their employ of Daoist practitioners to perform rites on their behalf, but most interesting was their worship of a local deity also worshiped by the Han majority in nearby Xiawang, Mashi, or Mafu Niangniang马氏/夫娘娘, or Mashi Tianxian 马氏天仙. For the Shezu Mafu Niangniang provided the raison d'être for their custom of "eating new rice."

According to the Shezu version of the story, Mafu Niangniang was from Lishui, an adopted in child daughter-in-law whose mother-in-law was particularly nasty. Hardly a day went by that she was not beaten. So from a young age she was strengthened, working all day and all night. Only her father-in-law and future husband were a little kinder, but in the household, whatever the mother-in-law said was the law. In the end, her future husband died before adulthood. And from this point her mother-in-law was even more cruel, saying her son's death was the result of Mafu's fate; and even her father-in-law began to often find fault with her.

Mafu was small of stature, and she grew increasingly emaciated with the scraps she was given to eat, but even without much strength, she still had to go up into the hills to gather firewood. There she met the She minority people, and each time she went up to the hills she would steal some wheat cakes from the house and bring them up to the hungry She people and distribute them to the children. Sometimes she would skip a meal herself to supply the She children with food (Chen ed. 1987: 97).

One day during the fifth month period of "green and yellow not connected" (*qinghuang bujie*—青黄不接, i.e. when last year's grain has been consumed but the new grain has not fully ripened), Mafu was at the edge of the field cutting grass. She looked at the early grain in the fields turning yellow. She stared and stared, and finally got an idea. That evening, after her in-laws had gone to bed, she took a hemp bag, quietly left the house and went to the family's rice field where by the starlight she walked here and there in the rice field cutting stalks of new yellow grain. When the village cock crowed (signaling dawn), she quickly put the satchel on her back and went up to the hills, bringing the grain to the She people. Three days passed without event, but on the evening of the fourth day, her mother-in-law, sick since the day Mafu had left, called for her in the house, over and over, but got no response. Finally she went to Mafu's room, and finding it empty, flew into a rage.

Early the next morning, Mafu returned home soaked with dew, and met her mother-in-law at the gate. When the old woman saw her, she scolded her: "Whore, where have you been all these days?"

She grabbed a broom stick and began beating Mashi, and locked her up in the wood shed. After three days, some kind-hearted neighboring She people urged the old woman to release Mafu, but even as she did so she had venomous words for Mafu: "If you want forgiveness, you must take this basket to draw water, and wash this pickle crock clean. Otherwise, you have no one to blame but yourself for my ill temper" (Chen ed. 1987: 98).

Despite the sad condition of the basket, and the persistent smell of pickles that emanated from the crock, Mafu had no choice but to take them to the side of a nearby pool, and do as she was instructed. The She people to whom she had been so good knew of her difficulties, and offered prayers to heaven on her behalf. The smoke from their incense blew to the southern sea, where it entered the temple of Nanhai Guanyin.

Thus, when Mafu got to the pier at the pool, and placed the basket and the crock in the water, strangely neither sank down, but floated on the surface. When she bent over, filled the basket with water and started to pull it back up, the basket didn't lose a drop. When she grabbed the pickle crock, it changed into a pig stomach. She turned it inside out and washed it on the pier. When she pulled it back rightside in again it took its original shape. So she took the water and the cleaned out crock back home, placing them both in front of her mother-in-law. When the old woman saw this, she realized that her daughter-in-law must have had the help of the gods. She knelt in front of her, tightly embracing her daughter-in-law's legs, repenting and begging forgiveness. Unable to move, Mafu looked up to heaven and saw a colored cloud which parted to reveal Guanyin motioning to her to ascend. She felt her body lighten and fly away like a sparrow. After a long while, the old woman finally realized that she was only holding Mafu's human remains.

After Mafu ascended to heaven, the She people especially remembered her kindness, and every year on Bingshen 丙申 day of the fifth month, when early rice has ripened to yellow and the heads of grain begin to droop, the She people would "Eat New Rice" in commemoration. Women prepared zongzi with the new grain on the night before, and on Bingshen day, the She elders would command the youngsters to retrieve Mafu Niangniang's pusa from her temple in Youbu's Lilang village, and carry her back in a sedan chair to Kuitangban village banging cymbals and drums all along the way. In Kuitangban a platform was prepared to receive the *pusa*, and once she was seated in a solemn ceremony, people brought forward their golden colored new grain and offered sacrifices of the three sacrificial animals. Afterwards, several opera troupes competed for audience (*doutai*) on several stages for Mafu's entertainment (Chen ed. 1987: 97, 99, 140).

While the rituals were curtailed after 1949, it is reported that even during the days of the communes and production brigades, notwithstanding the persistent propaganda against religion and superstition, a banquet commemorating Mafu Niangniang was held annually "in which all participated" (Chen ed. 1987: 140).

The story of Mafu Niangniang's special relationship with the Shezu people is still in circulation among the rural folk of Zhudaishi, and she is worshiped by the Han Chinese of Xiawang as well. Given the strength of the indigenous "minjian" religious revival, the cult of Mafu Niangniang may well be ripe for a comeback.

The Zhudaishi fair

The Zhudaishi fair on 11/18–11/20/98 (lunar 9/30–10/2) is strictly commercial, and has only begun since the economic reforms. There is also a spring fair on lunar 5/10, but neither date, lunar 9/30 nor 5/10, was of any ritual or religious significance traditionally, and there was no temple fair on either date in Zhudaishi in the past.

At 8.00 a.m. on the first day, the stall spaces were chalk marked out in anticipation of the arrival of the merchants and hawkers. They corresponded to a map displaying spaces for more than 300 participant sellers, which a township party committee member was consulting out on the road. Lumber merchants (some of whom remembered me from last week's fair at Xiawang) were already present just outside the government warehouse where farmers were bringing in their grain for compulsory sale to the state. Furniture dealers came from Pujiang, hardware dealers from Zhudaishi. Clothing came from Lanxi and Jinhua, several of the hawkers of which were regulars at the night market in Jinhua's central plaza.

For day two of the Zhudaishi fair, the rain of the previous night cleared and the sun broke through in the morning and remained for most of the day. At the livestock market, there must have been 100-plus water buffalos for sale. Young cows sell for ¥700, larger ones for ¥1,000+; a pair of young

Figure 5.8 Road to the fair: Zhudaishi

water buffalo could be had for ¥1,000, older ones trained to the plough for ¥3,000. There were no pigs at the Zhudaishi fair; pigs are sold privately in this area, not at the market fair.

A wild animal show from Henan province was set up with big painted signs advertising the "freaks of nature" inside the tent. These proved to be a series of freak fetuses in large jars of formaldehyde—Siamese twins, a two-headed girl, a two-headed dog, etc. There were also assorted live reptiles in wood and glass display cases and live pheasants and other wild fowl in cages.

Down the main street, a woman gambler with cups and dice set up at the curb proved to be from Xiawang, and several other sellers from the Xiawang fair were also on hand. The Anhui circus (seen in Xiawang) arrived late on account of the rain last night, and anticipated a reduced audience and losses as a result, but they set about unloading their gear and animals, and putting up their tent.

A loud-mouth woman from the night market in Lanxi complained about how poor her business had been all day, but during our 10–15-minute stay with her, she did some ¥40–50 worth of sales in women and children's clothes.

In a small field adjacent the road into town, three capuchin monkeys performed, and then demanded payment from onlookers. It was an impressive show even if unfortunately once their trainer had spotted me, the crew of simians descended upon me and demanded money, doing somersaults literally in my face until I complied.

A bamboo brush maker was engaged in making her brushes at the stall where she sold them. There were shoes for sale in great profusion, as well as T-shirts, underwear, woolen leggings for men and women, nick-nacks and

Figure 5.9 Draft animal market: Zhudaishi

Figure 5.10 Freaks of nature: Zhudaishi

Figure 5.11 Snake handler: Zhudaishi

Figure 5.12 Raising the circus tent: Zhudaishi

Figure 5.13 Trained monkey: Zhudaishi

tools of all kinds. According to the stall keepers, much of their merchandise is purchased at the Yiwu small commodities market (see Chapter 2).

Summary of secular fairs

Each of the above communities within Jinhua municipality is distinctive in its own way, one specialized in silk production, one in the production of medicinal herbs, one in commercial flower raising, one classified as a minority nationality township, and most interesting from our point of view, two (Xiawang and Zhudaishi) sharing worship of a local female deity, Mashi Niangniang, who may yet come to serve as the host deity for revived temple fairs in both communities on lunar 7/7.

At least two (Xiawang and Qianxiang) of these secular fairs were scheduled on the date of a traditional temple fair, even when the temple no longer existed, almost begging for the temple to be rebuilt to complete the total social phenomenon.

There are clearly all sorts of goods on sale, from those specific to rural life (agricultural tools and livestock) to those common to urban residents (clothing, household appliances, medicinal preparations, toys). Not surprisingly, many vendors from the urban street and night markets of Lanxi and Jinhua were present, and several vendors appeared at successive fairs. And the Yiwu small commodities market was noted as a source of goods on sale at one of our fairs, and doubtless played such a role in the others as well.

There were also a great variety of entertainments, some of which were clearly grotesque in a sense Bakhtin (1965) would surely have understood—the circus, the girl contortionist, displays of freaks of nature, trained animal acts (see Chapter 6). Qigong performers, busking street musicians, fortune tellers, craft artists out on the streets; games of chance in great profusion. And the opera was prominent, in performance (Luodian and Xiawang), or as tradition or amateur avocation (Huqi, Luodian, and Zhudaishi), important in the life of these communities.

The revived secular fairs, beyond their role in providing a wide range of goods are clearly sites where popular cultural performance genres and entertainments have proliferated. Absent the temples and deities of the past, they are nonetheless sites where the boundaries of acceptable discourse may be stretched if not breached. And most interesting in this admittedly non-random sample is the near or soon to be revival of the cult of Mafu Niangniang, which seems poised to stretch those boundaries still further.[1]

Let us turn then to an examination of the popular cultural dimension and the relation of its practitioners to the state which is of course the source and enforcer of those boundaries.

Note

1 Not to mention several fist fights. Put that many people together in one place, and conflicts are sure to erupt, or old grudges be rekindled.

6 The popular cultural dimension

As we have seen in the previous chapter, revived secular fairs almost immediately came to serve as venues for practitioners of popular performance genres of all kinds, serving to expand the boundaries of contemporary popular expression. In the crowds of the revived secular fairs, folk artists found ready audiences for whom to perform. And it is in their performances that James Scott's notions of sub-insurrectional or "everyday" forms of resistance (Scott 1985) find some application to the Chinese data.

To his credit, Goossaert appropriately calls attention to these "less spectacular" but often equally effective, passive forms of resistance that Scott's work evokes, rhetorical subversion, hidden transcripts, apparent compliance hiding defiance, and one might add metaphor, allegory, innuendo and indirection, humor and sarcasm (Goossaert 2005: 14–15).

Temple fairs are clearly not "everyday" events, but they are just as clearly sites where many popular cultural performance genres employing such discursive devices have proliferated in the venues offered by the revived fairs. Practitioners of such genres while enjoying some expressive license must nevertheless tread carefully in their performances, lest they cross an ideological threshold and run afoul of public security. It is in this sense that new limits are most often "negotiated", not in cross-table talks but in testing the old limits through practice in performance (see Chapter 9).

Mikhail Bakhtin writes of European carnivals as "islands of time," scattered throughout the year, when "the world was permitted to emerge from the official routine but exclusively under the camouflage of laughter," that expression of "universalism and freedom . . . the people's unofficial truth . . . the victory of laughter over fear . . . over the oppression and guilt related to all that was consecrated and forbidden" (1965: 90). He adds:

> The carnivalesque crowd in the marketplace . . . is the people as a whole . . . outside of and contrary to all existing forms of the coercive socio-economic and political organization . . . This festive organization of the crowd . . . concrete and sensual . . . the pressing throng . . . The individual feels that he is an indissoluble part of the collectivity, a member of the

people's mass body ... the people become aware of their sensual, material bodily unity and community.

(Bakhtin 1965: 255)

He also makes the point: "Carnival is not a spectacle seen by the people; they live in it, and everyone participates because its very idea embraces all the people" (Bakhtin 1965: 7).

C.K. Yang, in his classic work on Chinese religion, echoes Bakhtin, characterizing temple fairs historically as occasions when the regular rules of conventional sociality and morality were temporarily suspended, "removing participants from preoccupation with small-group, convention ridden, routinized daily life", impressing them with a "distinct sense of community consciousness" (Yang 1967: 89).

In Bakhtin's analysis, the display of the grotesque expresses a mockery of the quotidian:

All these jugglers, acrobats, vendors of panaceas, magicians, clowns, trainers of monkeys, had a sharply expressed grotesque bodily character ... most fully preserved in marketplace shows and in the circus ... the important role of the inside out and upside down in the movements and acts of the grotesque body.

(Bakhtin 1965: 353)

He might well have been describing Chinese temple fairs which are replete with jugglers, acrobats, contortionists, circuses, trained monkey and animal acts, snake oil salesmen, herbalists, freaks of nature displays, and houses of horror depicting the tortures awaiting in hell, many clearly grotesque in precisely Bakhtin's sense.

Zhao Shiyu is most explicit in his evocation of Bakhtin and of the carnivalesque character of China's traditional temple fairs. For Zhao, the mass character of the temple fair transgressed the hierarchical class restrictions of Chinese society, asserting a counter-hegemonic egalitarianism. Traditional Chinese society was one of strict class standards. Temple fairs and their performances in entertainment of the deities were one of the few mass activities of traditional Chinese society in which people of different classes, occupations, and sexes could all participate without restriction, thumbing their noses at class regulation as they did so (Zhao 2002: 123). While the fair organizers might include members of the upper classes, most of the important participants and leading role players were people of the lower ranks (Zhao 2002: 130).

Compared with the standards of behavior imposed by everyday life in Chinese civil society, the temple fair was a "wild show" (Flath n.d.: 32), an arena for the expression of the irrational (Zhao 2002: 117). From Zhao's dialectical perspective, the "rational" constraints of traditional Chinese society were to a great extent quite irrational, even to the point of being inhumane, and thus forms of expression involving seemingly irrational behavior and speech often possessed great and humane rationality by contrast (Zhao 2002: 136).

In Zhao's analysis, the carnival spirit of the temple fair is an "irrational" spirit, iconoclastic and subversive, which breaks through regular social standards in the performance of mass cultural activities, often displaying rough and carnal modes of behavior (Zhao 2002: 116). The clothing, equipment and other symbolic goods of temple fair performances often expressed ridicule of the "official symbolic system"; men wearing women's clothes and vice versa implicitly critiquing traditional attitudes toward the sexes and their moral standards, all this for Zhao "a means of borrowing spiritual power to oppose [the heavy weight of] tradition" (Zhao 2002: 131).

For Zhao, the most prominent expression of the heterodox character of the temple fair was the relatively unrestricted participation of women in the activities of "entertaining the deity" (Zhao 2002: 131). In traditional society, the words and actions of women were hedged about with restrictions of all kinds, not to mention their bound feet. But the temple fair gave them a legitimate and "legal" opportunity to participate in a variety of entertainments outside of the home, one of the few situations in traditional society where women could intermingle with men, even to the point of uproarious talk and laughter (Zhao 2002: 196–197, 238).

Not all, or even most, of the performance genres at the contemporary temple fairs of Jinhua are counter-hegemonic in any direct sense. Most are mere entertainment. The more grotesque among them might perhaps be characterized as expressing "mockery of the quotidian" in the Bakhtinian sense—the performances of Qigong aficionados at Huqi, the circuses at Huqi and Xiawang/Zhudaishi, each with a "star" contortionist girl, acrobats and trained animal acts, the performance of "full sand flaming mouth" at the Huqi circus, the one man band at Fotang, trained monkeys at Zhudaishi, snake handler at Zhudaishi, trained bears at Luodian, maker of dough figurines at Qianxiang, houses of horror at Fotang and Luodian, freaks of nature at Huqi and Zhudaishi, the grotesquery of opera make-up and performance voice.

Other performances are simply meant to evoke laughter, that expression of "universalism and freedom." And among these latter, indirection, innuendo, sarcasm, metaphor, allegory, as well as humor may often be the vehicle for implicit critical social commentary. The Chinese expression "Da Bianqiu" 打边球, which means to hit a ping pong ball so as to nick the edge of the table, is indeed a metaphor for making a point through indirection, without putting it on the table so to speak. In the spirit of such performance arts is Xiaoluo Shu (Small Cymbal Narrative), which began life as a clear "weapon of the weak" during the late Qing dynasty, since transformed into a somewhat less subversive medium of entertainment.

Following the discussion of Xiaoluo Shu, I move on to consider some of the less directly counter-hegemonic genres of the Jinhua region—Chang

Daoqing, Huagu, and Taige before moving on to a chapter-length consideration of Wuju (Jinhua opera).

Xiaoluo Shu 小锣书 (Small Cymbal Narrative)

Xiaoluo Shu has the distinction of having been designated one of the "five great folk arts of Zhejiang Province," along with Jinhua Daoqing, Wenzhou Guci 鼓词 (Drum Poems), Ningbo Zoushu 走书 (Walking Narrative), and Shaoxing Lianhua Luo 莲花落 (Drooping Lotus) (Zhang 1990: 181).

Xiaoluo Shu is generally associated with the provincial capital, Hangzhou, where it arose during the late Qing/early Republican period, although there is also a Suzhou branch. It consists of extemporaneously composed poetry, full of wisecracks and humor, and was first called "Cosmic joke telling" (Xingshi Tanxiao 星世谈笑—my translation) (Wu ed. 1987: 524), but was also known as "Sing the Pear Syrup Candy" (Chang Ligao Tang 唱梨膏糖) and "Little Feverish Gibberish" (Xiao Rehun 小热昏) (Zhang 2003: 53).

The genre was developed by purveyors of "pear syrup candy," a kind of medicinal cough drop, during the late Qing dynasty as a means of attracting customers on the streets of the market towns of the region. "Little Feverish Gibberish" was the nickname of early practitioner Du Baolin 杜宝林 of Hangzhou, whose performances were often a pretext for speaking the outrageous, the iconoclastic, the unmentionable, the irrational, the taboo, the unthinkable, all by way of criticizing the decadent Qing dynasty in the early twentieth century. Performed as "feverish gibberish" and thus not to be taken seriously, political criticism might thus be publicly expressed, a true counter-hegemonic "weapon of the weak" (LXSZ 1988: 574; Scott 1985; Zhang 2003: 53).

An apprentice of Du Baolin, He Yifeng 何一峰, is credited with having brought the art from Hangzhou upriver to Lanxi county during the anti-Japanese war of the 1930s (Zhang 2003: 56), and from there it has spread more broadly in Jinhua prefecture in the postwar period. Zhou Jinfa 周锦法 and Luo Suqin 骆素琴 were a husband and wife team of Xiaoluo Shu performers from Hangzhou who also brought the genre to Jinhua at the end of the Republican period (Zhang 2003: 57). Four Xiaoluo Shu practitioners were still active in Lanxi in 1985, among whom Mr. Xiao Hongli 筱红利 had the largest mass following (LXSZ 1988: 574).

Xiaoluo shu is generally a solo performance art in narrative and song, and falls in the shuo-chang (speech-song) category, with only small cymbal and clappers as accompaniment (Wu ed. 1987: 524). Lanxi practitioners developed a two-man version of Xiaoluo Shu known as Shuangdang 双档 (Double Record/File) in which a Qianpeng (前棚 front canopy—a performer of lesser skill and experience) performed first, and a Houpeng (后棚 rear canopy—a more experienced performer) performed once a sizeable crowd had assembled. For this reason Xiaoluoshu is often called Diaopeng 吊棚 (setting up the canopy) (Zhang 2003: 55).

During my attendance at the Fotang fair on lunar 10/10 in 1998, I was lucky enough to have encountered the nationally famous Xiaoluo Shu performer, Jia Youfu 贾有福, on a street corner of his hometown, performing in his inimitable style (and impenetrable dialect), providing the surrounding crowd with numerous opportunities to break into sustained laughter. Like all practitioners of the genre, he dispensed pear syrup medicinal candy at the end of the show, accepting "contributions" in exchange for a small packet of candy (Fieldnotes 11/27/98).

Jia Youfu is known affectionately by Fotang residents as "Very funny Jia" (Jia Haoxiao 贾好笑), but also has been given the not especially euphonious nickname "Fotang's pockmark and dysentery" (Fotang Mali 佛堂麻痢).

In the early 1950s, together with partner Wang Zhengfa 王正法, Jia Youfu 贾有福 learned the art of Xiaoluo Shu while working as a laborer in Lanxi, and later performed with Wang in the townships of Yiwu, selling pear syrup medicinal candy, presumably performing as a Shuangdang team. Over a 30-year period, Jia and Wang tailored their performances in accord with the demands of the contemporary central government line, creating their own jokes and stories, criticizing corruption, propagandizing virtuous behavior, with clever use of words, sarcasm, and humor (Wu ed. 1987: 524).

Figure 6.1 Xiaoluo shu: Fotang

As Jia tells it, when he first heard the sellers of pear syrup candy hawking their wares by reciting humorous tales on the streets of Lanxi, he was immediately enchanted. Didn't ordinary Chinese people endure enough misery and hardship? Couldn't he give them a little simple pleasure in their life? Jia Youfu thus elected to take the difficult career path of professional performer. But the expression, "On the stage for three minutes, off the stage seven years merit" encouraged him to persevere (Li and Yang 1996).

To get his expression just right, Jia would practice every day in front of the mirror until he could move virtually every muscle in his face at will, every limb on his supple body with precise attention to the character being portrayed, male or female. With years of experience, he has evolved his own style, humorous, elegant, educational, entertaining, with an exquisite sense of timing (Li and Yang 1996).

Many folks say if you listen to Mali's performance for five minutes you are hooked. You simply cannot pull yourself away. As illustration, the story is told of a man on his way to market who stopped to listen to Mali's "speech song" narrative, holding back a pee. He listened to one joke after another, thinking he would listen to just one more before finding a public restroom. Finally, he held it for so long, his "lower equipment" 下面的机关 failed and he wet his pants (Li and Yang 1996).

At one point during the Cultural Revolution, Jia Youfu took his gear on his back to perform outside the county. Several rebel Red Guard group members "who couldn't even keep their pants on straight" came along, and as soon as they saw him decided that he wasn't to be trusted, and without a word confiscated his gear, taking his pear syrup candy as an evening snack. The old artist was outraged, but fortunately survived unharmed to tell the tale (Li and Yang 1996).

After the Gang of Four were overthrown, Jia Youfu, like other folk artists, experienced a new spring. He used all his creative powers to write and perform pieces to turn "bitter into sweet" 苦头变甜头 (Li and Yang 1996), respectful of the Communist Party's policy of reform and openness. Jia is not a political critic. He would not survive long as a public performer if he were. Rather, interpersonal conflicts, morality, marriages, market conditions, and the most minor events in people's lives are the subjects of his performances, but they often contain a lesson. "Family deliberations" 家庭商讨会 describes the maltreatment of an elder. "Receive Mother in Law" 接婆婆 describes a good daughter-in-law who respected her mother-in-law. "Burn the red double happiness" 火烧红双喜 is a criticism of excessive marriage expense. And although his jokes in dialect went way over my head, I can nevertheless testify to the fact that he leaves the inevitable crowds that surround him at his street corner performances in persistent fits of laughter. In 1984, Jia Youfu received a prize for performance excellence at the Jinhua Regional Folk Arts Festival (Wu ed. 1987: 524).

When the temple fair convenes for three days in the vicinity of Fotang, you are likely to find Jia Youfu out on the street hawking his pear syrup candy with humorous narratives of contemporary life from early morning till darkness, "spreading his obvious love of the people across his native Fotang and beyond" (Li and Yang 1996), contributing to the red fire of the region's temple fairs.

Jinhua Daoqing 道情

Like Xiaoluo Shu, Jinhua Daoqing 道情 has also been designated one of the five great folk arts of Zhejiang Province. But Daoqing is a genre with much greater historical depth and geographical breadth than Xiaoluo Shu, is more copiously documented, and has produced many more practitioners historically than Xiaoluo Shu, although it faces an uncertain fate in the present.

Daoqing is one of the solo arts of shuochang (说唱—speech song). Singing is the basis, and the sung portions are set in pentatonic scales, with text arranged in seven character lines. Spoken parts include interludes of narration, asides, and dialogue, expressive of the various personalities and emotions of the characters in the story, their happiness, anger, sorrow and joy. A single performer performs all the roles in the narrative: "One man, one opera, perform the literary, perform the military, all myself" 一人一台戏 演文演武 我自己 (Zhang 1990: 181).

The accompanying instrumentation is quite simple—a three-segment-long bamboo tube (qingtong 情筒 or Yugu 渔鼓) with an oiled pigskin attached at one end, which gives off a "peng peng 蓬蓬" sound when beaten, and a set of two-inch-wide foot long bamboo clappers/castanets which produce a "ji ta" 吉嗒 sound (Mao ed. 1996: 92). But the range of sounds the performer is able to create, with just the drum and clapper and his own voice is quite astounding, the sounds of natural phenomena, wind, rain, thunder, and lightning, the roar of the sea, the echoes of the mountain, etc. (Mao ed. 1996: 93; Shi 1997; Wu ed. 1987: 521), as well as the sounds of animals, chickens, dogs, tigers, etc., "making children cry and old women moan." A Daoqing singer is capable of singing across the spectrum of traditional operatic voice roles, both male and female (Zhang 2003: 36, 40).

Folk myths and stories make up much of the content, so Daoqing is also known as "Sing Stories" (chang gushi—唱故事), but local news or anecdotes also constitute a significant part of an artist's repertoire, so Daoqing was often called "Sing the News" (chang xinwen 唱新闻), a kind of minstrelsy, with a communication as well as an entertainment function.

Artists would often "buy" stories from Yamen personnel who had inside information on criminal or civil proceedings in the region, in transactions known as Mai Kougong 买口供 (a Kougong is a statement or confession made by an accused under examination). The artist would invite his inside man out to a meal to talk about the latest case or cases, and subsequently edit the information into a Daoqing narrative (Zhang 2003: 37). Titles of Daoqing composed with such information are usually marked by the character "ji"

(记 meaning "record of"), like Record of the Silver Pouch 银袋记, Record of the Silver Token 银牌记, Record of the [Buddhist] Nun 尼姑记, Record of the Red Snake 红蛇记, etc.

The Daoqing repertoire is divided into Tantou or Duanpian (摊头 or 短篇—short pieces) and Zhengben (正本—Middle and long pieces). Tantou are mostly sung, and are generally performed before the Zhengben to attract and warm up the crowd. Tantou can be divided into two types. One type has no story, as in "Flowers of the Twelve Months" 十二月花名; "Twenty-Four Solar Calendrical Terms" 二十四节气; "Thirty-Six Docks" 三十六码头, etc. These are generally sung with no spoken parts. The other type is narrative in form, generally stories that make people laugh, making fun of foolish people, praising wise people, or just plain vulgar and obscene.

Zhengben are often called "Sing the Libretto" 唱戏文, generally divided into acts, the longest of which, like "Qianlong visits Jiangnan" can last several tens of hours (Zhang 2003: 40). Daoqing was a fixture of entertainment at the teahouses of the Republican period. Some performances like "Strong Young Man" 壮丁记; "Meeting of the Dragon Pair" 双龙会; "Meeting of the Heroes at Wudang" 武当英雄会 might be strung out over more than ten evenings, and one couldn't afford to miss a single installment, thus encouraging patronage (Mao ed. 1996: 92, 94).

Themes are generally didactic, encouraging people to cleave to the righteous path, castigating deception and treachery, criticizing the unprincipled pursuit of wealth, rewarding loyalty and filiality, praising righteous officials, etc. The items of the traditional repertoire with their emotionally moving plots are especially enjoyed by the elderly. In the summers, on bright moonlit evenings, men and women, old and young sit at the village entrance under a great camphor tree, in a pavilion, or threshing ground, or open space, in crowds as large as several hundred straining to hear the performance deep into the night. Others may gather in the teahouses of the town to hear Daoqing performed, or be entertained by Daoqing performers on the streets during temple fairs (Mao ed. 1996: 94).

> When the Yugu sounds, the audience is full;
> No matter the season, the singing goes on.
>
> 渔鼓一响, 听众坐满;
> 春夏秋冬, 唱声不断
>
> (Wu ed. 1987: 521)

Daoqing has its roots in the lower rungs of society. Its performers were most often blind men, who performed on an itinerant basis all over Jinhua (Wu ed. 1987: 520). Their social standing was quite low, and under the circumstances of the old society they had few alternatives to earn a living, although some were lucky enough to find stable employment in urban teahouses, or to be invited to perform on occasion in the homes of the wealthy. But generally, their experience was of a cold unforgiving world (Zhang 2003: 37), given expression in the following ballad:

> The blind do not cultivate the soil,
> Their heaven and earth are planted in their three-sectioned bamboo tube.
> Everyone listens to the flavorful Daoqing,
> Pity the blind man's stomach is (still) empty.

> 盲眼人不种田不种地，
> 天地种在三节竹筒里.
> 大家道情听得真有味，
> 可怜盲眼肚皮饥

(Mao ed. 1996: 93)

Thus even though the various song styles of Daoqing differ in dialect from Jinhua, to Dongyang, to Pujiang, to Wuyi, to Yiwu, they are all marked by a sad, mournful, sorrowful musical style (Zhang 2003: 37, 41–42).

Daoqing is said to have originated with Zhang Guolao, one of the Eight Daoist Immortals, who having gone down to earth to set people back to the Dao, was lacking musical accompaniment. The old man of the south pole provided him with the trunk of an "Immortals" bamboo, from which Zhang Guolao took three sections and fashioned a Qingtong 情筒 (Yugu 渔鼓 drum) to accompanying him in singing Daoqing. Ever since, Zhang Guolao has been depicted with his Yugu slung over his shoulder, riding backwards on his mule. Later generations of Daoqing singers celebrate him as their patron/founder and each year on his supposed birthday, lunar 6/1, they come together to pay respects to their master (Zhang 2003: 167, 232).

It is fairly commonly agreed in the sources that historically Daoqing originated in the Jiuzhen 九真, Chengtian 承天 and other Daoist songs 道曲 of the Tang dynasty (AD 618–907). Indeed Tang Emperor Xuanzong (known posthumously as Tang Minghuang 唐明皇), who ruled from AD 713–756, was said to have been something of an aficionado, and is also worshiped by Daoqing performers as a founding ancestor along with Zhang Guolao (Mao ed. 1996: 93; Wu ed. 1987: 520; Zhang 2003: 233).

However, Chen Chongren (1986: 51–52) has offered a revisionist view, arguing that modern "Daoqing" has little to do with the Daoist songs of the Tang; that the melodies, songs, and stories originate in local rural airs, ballads, and events much less remote in time. And while Chen's view has yet to be widely accepted, it is agreed by most authorities that Daoqing did indeed absorb popular folk influences as it evolved into a form of accompaniment to the preaching of the Dao among the people (Zhang 2003: 233; Wu ed. 1987: 520). In the course of that evolution, the Yugu 渔鼓 drum or Qingtong 情筒 (Daoqing tube) and Jianban 简板 (clappers) were said to have been added as accompaniment during the southern Song dynasty (1127–1280), when literary references to Daoqing also appear. But due to the fact that in the old society there were very few Daoqing performers who were literate, and most of them were blind, the repertoire of Daoqing was generally passed down from master to apprentice by word of mouth, with no written texts left behind (Mao ed. 1996: 93; Wu ed. 1987: 520–521; Zhang 2003: 36–37).

During the Ming and Qing, Daoqing spread more broadly nationwide, and the content also expanded, continuing to combine with and absorb local stories and themes from local events and folk ballads, and leaving its Daoist content (if ever there was any) behind (Mao ed. 1996: 93). While no one knows for certain exactly when and where Daoqing entered the Jinhua region, extant Daoqing pieces set in Jinhua's various counties can be dated from their content to the end of the Ming dynasty which suggests that Daoqing was circulating in Jinhua from at least the early Qing (Zhang 2003: 233).

In one story, which may be apocryphal, Daoqing's arrival in Jinhua occurred as the result of events which transpired at the Ming court. There, an official native to eastern Jinhua, surnamed Zhu 朱, was convicted of treachery, stripped of his position, and thrown in jail. Upon hearing the news, his son, Zhu Fengyi 朱凤益, went to the capital to help his father, but it was already too late. His father had been convicted, and Fengyi had no money to get back to Jinhua. Just at this time, Daoqing performer, Fang Qing 方卿 was gaining fame in the capital, and Daoqing was all the rage. After watching him perform, Fengyi fashioned a Qingtong and clappers for himself, and crafted the tale of his father's misfortune into a Daoqing narrative, which he "sold" on the streets until he had enough money to return to Jinhua, bringing the art with him.

In any event, there seems little question that by the late Ming, Daoqing was a national phenomenon. Down to the present, Daoqing artists have a saying to express its circulation nationwide: "Liang Jin Shiba liang" (两斤十八两—2 Chinese pounds, 18 ounces); a pun on 2 capitals and 18 provinces (两京十八省), which is to say that Daoqing circulated nationwide (Zhang 2003: 233).

During the Qing Qianlong period, composing and performing Daoqing became a diversion for young scholars who had failed the imperial exams to while away their idle hours, but even well-known Qing literati, Deng Banqiao 郑板桥, Xu Dachun 徐大椿, and Jin Nong 金农 composed short Daoqing pieces (Li 1982: 54; Zhang 2003: 36–37, 41).

The Yiwu branch of Daoqing is said to have had its beginnings in the nineteenth century with a Mr. Yan Song 严嵩, and there was a tablet with his image in Yangji theater 养济院 where the Yiwu Folk Artists Association convened its first meeting in 1951 and was subsequently headquartered. Yan was a former court official of the nineteenth century, who having lost his official position in a scandal founded the theater to support the elderly and orphaned of his native Yiwu (Yangji 养济 means support and assistance). He edited many of his past deeds and misdeeds into Daoqing narratives, and performed them both in the theater and on the street outside the theater for passersby (Zhang 2003: 233).

But Daoqing seems also to have arrived in Yiwu via at least one other independent route. According to an investigation carried out by the Cultural Bureau of Panzhai Township in Pujiang County, Dongyang's Zhao Huniang 赵虎娘, known as the "wetnurse" (Lao Mama 老嬷嬷) of Daoqing, had a hand in the process. Born in 1863, she learned the art of Daoqing (from whom it is not clear), and while performing in Pujiang took on an apprentice from Yiwu, Mao Jinxiu 毛锦秀, who is said to have been the first Daoqing performer in Yiwu (Zhang 2003: 40).

At the end of the Qing dynasty (early twentieth century), Daoqing was quite common in Jinhua cities, towns and villages (Zhang 2003: 37), and during the Republican period (1911–1949), Daoqing was second only to local Wuju opera as the most important form of entertainment in Jinhua. The teahouse trade created a great demand. Artists took the important and not so important news of the time and edited it into Daoqing pieces (Zhang 2003: 37). During the early Republic, Luo Zhanglun 骆樟轮 was known in city and town as one of Daoqing's premier performers (Mao ed. 1996: 94; Wu ed. 1987: 521).

During the anti-Japanese war, many Daoqing artists created pieces that reflected the anti-Japanese struggle, among whom Ma Lieshang 马烈商 was especially noteworthy (Zhang 2003: 38). Ma began his career at the age of eight singing the Daoqing "Great Victory at Tai Er Village" (Tai Er Zhuang Dajie—台儿庄大捷). At ten he performed the anti-Japanese Daoqing "Tale of the Wozi (the Japanese)" (Wozi Ji—倭子记), and he has been editing, performing, and promoting Daoqing for more than 60 years in service of the struggles of the common folk, the "first master who opened the road" (开路先师) of the sighted artists (Zhang 2003: 245). In 1982, at the request of fellow artist Wu Rongchun, Ma collaborated with Zhao Shouxing in the creation of 26 new Daoqing pieces, and began a training class to teach Daoqing, giving new life to the art. In 1993, he was designated Zhejiang Provincial Level Folk Artist (浙江省民间艺术家) (Zhang 2003: 42–43).

In the last years of the Republic there were some 200 Daoqing performers still active in Jinhua's various counties, 100 of whom were concentrated in the various villages and towns of Yiwu county, and most of whom were blind or partially blind (Chen ed. 2005: 24; Wu ed. 1987: 521; Zhang 2003: 38). In their repertoires were more than 300 traditional Zhengben and 100 Tantou that survived into the Communist period (Zhang 2003: 37), and there have been some 50 additions to the repertoire of assorted length since (Zhang 2003: 40). Some 20 or so repertoire items still extant memorialize events that actually happened in and around Yiwu. "Double Knives" 双刀记 , "Fire Consumes Xiangshan Temple" 火烧香山寺, "Greet the

Lanterns" 迎灯记, "Four cows" 四牛记, "Borrowed Umbrella" 借伞记, "Chase the Pig" 赶猪记, "Buy grain" 买米记, "Ear" 耳朵记, and "Sandals" 脱鞋记 all tell true stories about real people (Mao ed. 1996: 94; and see Appendix 1).

The official master narrative of the development of Daoqing has Daoqing artists throwing themselves enthusiastically into the great wave of the revolution in the early years of the People's Republic, composing and performing Daoqing narratives and songs for the anti-American struggle during the Korean War, for land reform, for the campaign to crush counter-revolutionaries, etc., and there is plenty of evidence to justify that narrative (Zhang 2003: 42).

But it is also fair to say that when the Yiwu people's government approved the establishment of the Yiwu Folk Artists Association in August 1951, it was seeking not only to put the blind artists to work in a propaganda role, but was also duly concerned for the welfare of these folk to whom no one paid much attention, so that they also have the opportunity to walk the road of civic engagement in the new society.

It was Ye Yingmei, a blind Daoqing performer from Fotang, and seven other practitioners who are credited with organizing the Association from the bottom up, the county's first local folk arts mass organization. 41 practitioners of Daoqing and Huagu attended the first meeting held at the old Yangji Theater 养济院 near Yiwu's west gate, which also became the organization's headquarters (Wu ed. 1987: 521).

Relevant offices in the cultural field helped them record and organize the traditional repertoire, as well as to write and edit new stories, and to participate in the propaganda efforts of the new government (Mao ed. 1996: 94). Among the accomplishments of the association was carrying out a registration of all folk art practitioners in the county in 1956 (Wu ed. 1987: 521), and winning government wages for Yiwu's blind performers in 1959 (Zhang 2003: 40). In 1965 there were 65 member-practitioners of various folk performance arts (Wu ed. 1987: 521).

Ye Yingmei 叶英美 (1925–1964)

Ye Yingmei 叶英美 was a native of Wuqiye village (吴溪叶村) in Fotang township, on a branch tributary of the Yiwu river. Born blind, he lost both his parents early in life, and at the age of 13–14 he was already begging on the streets of Fotang. At the age of 16, he ended up returning to his home village. To reduce the burden on his uncle with whom he resided, he took up the Yugu drum and clappers of the Daoqing profession, and began going from village to village selling songs (Mao ed. 1996: 95; Zhang 2003: 237; Zhang and Fu 1998).

In 1949, when Communist forces proved victorious in the civil war, Ye took the creation of a new society seriously and "fanshen"-ed, becoming a leader in the organization of folk performers. In the early years of the PRC, he embraced the idea that art should serve the people, going out to perform at workplaces, fields, and markets, leaving his footprints throughout Yiwu (Fotang Government 2005: 89). He sang out comparing the old society with the new, using his Daoqing genre to sing the praises of socialism, and the new society (Zhang 2003: 237; Zhang and Fu 1998).

During land reform he sang:

> The landlord eats and plays,
> the peasants are his horses to ride,
> hungry all year round,
> this society is unjust.
>
> 地主吃吃嬉嬉，
> 农民给他当马骑，
> 一年到头饿肚皮，
> 这种社会不合理
> (Mao ed. 1996: 95;
> Zhang and Fu 1998)

In 1953 during cooperativization there was a severe drought in Yiwu. Ye was out singing in the mountain villages and chanced upon a group of rural folk going up the mountain to pray to the Dragon King for rain. When he heard what they were up to, he blocked the way, and composed a *tantou* 摊头 (short piece) on the spot:

> You can't believe in the Dragon King, don't spread superstition.
> To fight the drought we must rely on everyone's cooperation,
> If we unify in our struggle, a bountiful harvest will be guaranteed;
> If you want water, dig a well, human ability beats heavenly power;
> Superstition has hurt people over thousands of years;
> Smart people should not be fooled.
> (Mao ed. 1996: 95; Zhang 2003: 237; Zhang and Fu 1998)

Beginning in 1954, Ye Yingmei was successively selected as representative to the first, second, third, fourth, and fifth annual Yiwu County People's Congress. In 1958, he was elected chairman of the Yiwu County Folk Arts Association (Quyi Xiehui) he helped to found, while also participating in the formation of the Zhejiang Provincial Folk Artists Association which elected him vice chairman. In the same year, he was admitted to membership in the Communist Party, and was invited to Beijing to participate in the First National Folk Arts festival (Fotang Government 2005: 89; Mao ed. 1996: 95).

He took the stage in Beijing's Chang An Opera Theater with his Yugu and clappers and sang his own composition, "Yu Xiaoyu" 虞小玉, celebrating the career of a woman of that name from Yiwu's Huaqi township Binshitou village, who lost a son in the Korean war, but unfazed went on to make great contributions to the construction of socialism. In later years, she served as the party branch secretary at the Ershisan Li feather products factory of Yiwu (feathers for sugar), where she expanded the labor force from ten workers to over 500, and enterprise APV to ¥400,000 (Mao ed. 1996: 95; Zhang and Fu 1998). At the end of Ye's performance, there was continuous applause, and three curtain calls; the crowd refused to quiet down.

In 1963, Ye was named a national "red flag" worker in the rural propaganda effort. At the awards ceremony, a banner declared: "In the north there is Han Qixiang, in the south there is Ye Yingmei" 北有韩启祥，南有叶英美. (Han Qixiang (1915–1989) was a blind story teller, a model modern folk artist who performed in Yanan, the Communist base area during the anti-Japanese and Chinese Civil wars, and a popular singer of socialism) (Mao ed. 1996: 95).

In 1963, Ye went to Beijing again, this time as chair of the National Conference of Outstanding Workers in Education, and at the banquet of leaders sat with Zhou Enlai, who served him his food. Ye was quoted as saying: "Even in my dreams, I never thought such a day would happen, I must keep on singing . . ." Unfortunately, Ye Yingmei would not have much more time to make contributions to Chinese socialism. In 1964, at the age of 39, he died in a Jinhua hospital of kidney disease (Fotang Government 2005: 89; Zhang and Fu 1998).

During the Cultural Revolution, the folk artists organized their own "Mao Zedong Thought Frontline struggle teams" (Wu ed. 1987: 521), but their efforts on behalf of the revolution were ultimately unappreciated. Folk arts organizations were "attacked as rotten." Performances from the traditional repertoire, associated with the Four Olds (old ideas, old habits, old customs, old culture) were prohibited, and many artists were forced to confess to "spreading feudal, capitalist, revisionist propaganda." Many who had sincerely lent their efforts to propagandizing on behalf of the new society were forced to endure public criticism and humiliation, and had their equipment confiscated and destroyed. The Yiwu Folk Arts Association was disbanded altogether, and 38 of its members on state salary were taken off the state payroll and transferred to the countryside (Wu ed. 1987: 521).

To support themselves during this period, artists held "underground performances" where they could, closing up doors and windows, and performing in back rooms. Others simply dropped their paraphernalia and changed from singing Daoqing to telling stories. Even though Daoqing performances were prohibited, it is claimed that Daoqing and other Shuochang genres continued to be performed privately throughout the Cultural Revolution without interruption (Mao ed. 1996: 96; Wu ed. 1987: 521; Zhang 2003: 38).

In any event, once the Gang of Four were repudiated, and reform and openness adopted by the Third Plenum of the Eleventh Central Committee in 1978–9, a "Spring Wind" in the arts ensued, and the folk arts in Jinhua blossomed. Various performance arts, Daoqing, Huagu, Xiaoluo Shu 小锣

书 (Small Cymbal Narrative), Kuaiban 快板 (Clapper Narrative), Xiangsheng 相声 (Comic Dialogue), Shuogushi 说故事 (Storytelling), all came back to life (Chen ed. 2005: 24). A "heat wave of Daoqing" commenced in the late 1970s and 1980s in which the number of sighted performers expanded, and a new level of creativity in the art reached (Mao ed. 1996: 96; Zhang 1990: 184; Zhang 2003: 38;).

Symptomatic of this movement was the appearance of a "new singing method" 新派唱法 of whom Ms. Zou Aiqin 邹爱琴 was the most prominent exponent. She introduced Jinhua folk songs and music from the local Wuju opera genres into Daoqing performance, while adapting the content to make it more compatible with the new times and the contemporary lifestyle. In 1981 she performed in Beijing at the National Rural Cultural Congress of Progressive Workers, performing Zhang Zhulin's "Congratulate the Newlyweds" 贺新房 and "Control the Insects" 治虫 to great acclaim. She became known as the King's Choice of Daoqing 道情王牌 (Zhang 2003: 39).

In June of 1980, the Yiwu Folk Arts Association revived, housed in the Yiwu Cultural Center, and beginning in 1984 sponsored a performance festival each year (Zhang 2003: 40). But despite the post-Cultural Revolution revival of Daoqing and the other folk arts, new challenges lie ahead for their reproduction and continuity. "There's no hiding the facts." Following the nation's economic development, and the expansion and improvement in the cultural life of the masses, the proliferation of movies, TV, CDs and DVDs, and magazines, and various "modern" forms of media and entertainment from Hong Kong and Taiwan, Daoqing has been eclipsed and superseded. Its role as a source of news and information is insignificant, its appeal to youth minimal, its audience much reduced. Many blind performers have sought less anachronistic occupations (Wu ed. 1987: 521), and the genre now faces a crisis to which local cultural offices have tried to respond (Mao ed. 1996: 97).

In an effort to stem the brain drain away from Daoqing, Jinhua city has held Daoqing training classes, in which many younger people have participated, and in which women have been the majority, with performers like Zou Aiqin, as their role model. These youngsters have continued to move away from the sad and mournful tones and rhythms of the traditional genre (Li 1982: 55), to a more upbeat, more optimistic, more contemporary tone, with more complex musical accompaniment and instrumentation (Zhang 1990:184). Their efforts have yielded some results.

If the genre does survive another generation, it will no doubt be as a gentrified, folklorified genre, far removed from the blind beggars for whom it served as means of livelihood in the old society.

In Jinhua villages, if there is someone failing in their responsibilities to the elderly, or with a gambling problem, or otherwise inappropriate or anti-social behavior, they say: "We'll get Zhang Xiaogui (little devil Zhang, i.e. Zhang Zhulin) to write you up in a Daoqing, then where will you show your face?" (Zhang 2003: 249).

To give some flavor for the content of Daoqing performances, I include several plot summaries from the repertoire of Yiwu Daoqing performers in Appendix 1 (after Zhang Zhulin (2003)).

Huagu (flower drum 花鼓)

In Yiwu, blind male Daoqing artists often combined their performances with blind female Huagu (flower drum 花鼓) artists, and historically the genres were known as "husband and wife folk arts" (Fuqi Quyi 夫妻曲艺). "Men sing Daoqing, women sing Huagu," or "husband sings Daoqing, wife sings Huagu." The repertoire is the same, the accoutrements of performance differ (Zhang 2003: 40–41).

Like Daoqing, Huagu is classified in the folk art category of Shuochang 说唱—speech-song, and is usually performed while seated, generally sung, but interspersed with spoken parts. In Huagu performance, the left hand holds a small cymbal and a Yaogu drum; the right hand holds the cymbal hammer and the drum stick. The drum and cymbal keep the rhythm, and accompany the speech-song. Like Daoqing, the singing style is slow and mournful, with the sung text in seven character lines. Its melodies are said to be gentler and softer than Daoqing, its content includes family operettas, love stories, as well as local anecdotes and news (Wu ed. 1987: 520).

At the end of the Qing, Huagu had already followed Daoqing in among the people, circulating in the Jinhua counties of Yiwu, Dongyang, and Pan An, although its practitioners were fewer in number than their male Daoqing counterparts. In Republican times, Zhang (2003) estimates their number in Yiwu and Dongyang to have been about 30 or 40.

Some 30-odd pieces from the traditional Huagu repertoire survived into the 1950s, and another ten modern pieces and short pieces have been composed since the establishment of the PRC. During the Cultural Revolution Huagu was suppressed, and by the end of the 1990s there was scarcely a practitioner anywhere. The art has all but disappeared in Jinhua (Zhang 2003: 48).

Taige

Taige 抬阁 is a form of display in which small children from 5–10 years old are dressed in the costumes of famous historic personages, emperors, generals or opera characters, or famous beauties, strapped onto high platforms, and carried aloft as part of a great procession, accompanied by the gongs and cymbals, drums and banners of the local Luohan Ban martial arts troupe, performed in the hope of coaxing the deity down to have a look (Fotang Township Government 2005: 7). In these contexts they are sometimes known as Luohan sun (罗汉孙—Luohan grandchildren) (Wang ed. 1997: 55; YKXZ 605).

According to Wu, the custom began in Song times, with wooden or metal puppets/effigies mounted on top of long poles carried by people who marched

The popular cultural dimension 111

Figure 6.2 Taige children: Fangyan

Figure 6.3 The author with a Taige child: Fangyan

in procession. The idea of substituting live children, appropriately made up, was apparently an innovation of Ming and Qing times (Wu 1988: 149).

The most elaborate Taige processions are said to be in Zhejiang (Wu 1988: 149), and in Yiwu's Fotang township, Plum Grove village 梅林村 and Jiangnan Street village 江南街村 are noted for the custom (Fotang Township Government 2005: 7). Taige processions are also a feature of Yongkang's Houtang village's grand procession to entertain Hugong Dadi (Wang ed. 1997: 55), and were also common historically in Lanxi (*Lanxi Shizhi* 1988: 575).

In less formal versions of the genre I have observed, a father may dress up his child in Taige costume, and merely carry the child on his shoulders while attending a temple fair.

The next popular cultural genre I wish to discuss, Jinhua Opera Wuju, deserves a chapter unto itself, the next one.

7 More popular culture
Wuju 婺剧 (Jinhua opera)

Historically, although opera served as a diversion for the elites of Chinese society as well as the masses, opera performers were relegated to the lowest rung of the class hierarchy in Chinese society, a veritable outcaste group, with which no respectable commoner family would consider a marriage. With men performing as women, and make-up and costume that transformed ordinary humans into larger than life gargantuan deities, heroes or heroines, Chinese opera provides an excellent example of the Bakhtinian grotesque on display at temple fairs. In the Communist period, the stigma associated with the opera profession was removed, and its members came to occupy a legitimate standing among the masses. Wuju or Jinhua opera was no different in this regard.

In the pre-liberation period, Wuju was performed in entertainment of the deity (yu shen 娱神) during temple fairs in the region. But the opera also became a fixture of the secular commodity trade fairs, the temple-less temple fairs of the early post-liberation period, and of the more recently revived secular fairs of the reform era as a means of entertaining the humans, to attract crowds to the secular market.

The significance of opera to rural Chinese is expressed in the following proverb: "Of all the possible entertainments, None approaches watching opera" (Qixi Baxi, Buru Kanxi 七嬉八嬉, 不如看戏 (Zhang and Hong 1985: 12). And in the following quote from an aficionado:

> In those days, we ordinary folk would hardly know the name of the township or district head, or the provincial governor or county head, but we could tell you at once who the best local opera performers in each of the various singing roles were ... where they came from, and their signature opera pieces.
>
> (Zhang 2005: 34)

Like everything else in China, opera has a long history, and lots of regional variation. Indeed Jinhua has produced its own regional operatic traditions that in part derive from other prominent national genres, but also represent distinct local inflections. Since the establishment of the PRC, these locally inflected traditions of Jinhua have been grouped together under the general heading Wuju 婺剧, Jinhua having been known periodically in dynastic times as Wuzhou 婺州.

Thus, Wuju is not a single local opera genre, but includes six different operatic traditions: Gaoqiang 高腔, Kun Qiang 昆腔, Luantan 乱弹, Huixi 徽戏, Tanhuang 滩簧, and Shidiao 时调 (Zhang and Hong 1985: 1).

In several of these genres, the Jinhua Wuju branch preserves archaic qualities that have long since disappeared in the genres' places of origin. For example, anyone interested in researching the development of southern opera (Nanxi 南戏) during the Song dynasty (960–1279 AD) will find representative operas in the repertoire of modern Wuju Gaoqiang 高腔 troupes, like Tale of the White Rabbit 白兔记, In the Shade of the Scholar's Tree 槐荫树, and Golden Chop 黄金印 (Zhang and Hong 1985: 2).

Nanxi divided into two branches, one of which produced the four Gaoqiang genres of Jinhua Wuju, the repertoires of which consist mostly of anonymous pieces dating from the Ming dynasty, still preserved in the hands of contemporary artists (JHSZ 1992: 995–996). The second branch of Nanxi is represented by Kunshan Qiang 昆山腔 and Haiyan Qiang 海盐腔 and representative genres from both branches were circulating in Jinhua during Ming times. During the Wanli reign (AD 1573–1620) Jinhua already sported its own professional Kun troupe, and a variety of localized genres like Yiwu Qiang also took root and evolved in the Jinhua region (JHSZ 1992: 995).

A Brief overview of Wuju's constituent genres

Gaoqiang 高腔

The Gaoqiang genre of Jinhua is itself divided into four sub-genres: Houyang Gaoqiang 候阳高腔, Songyang Gaoqiang 松阳高腔, Xi An Gaoqiang 西安高腔, Xiwu Gaoqiang 西吴高腔 (Ge et al. eds. 1986: 98), each with a fairly distinct history.

Houyang Gaoqiang 候阳高腔

Houyang Gaoqiang was widespread in Dongyang, Yiwu, Pujiang, Jinhua, Yongkang, Jinyun, Lishui, Wenzhou, Taizhou, and in several counties of neighboring Jiangxi, but it was centered in Dongyang. Some believe Houyang Gaoqiang to be descended from Ming dynasty Yiwu Qiang; others suggest it was descended from Haiyan Qiang. In either event, all agree there occurred a copious mixing of local airs, folk songs, and ballads in the process of its popularization through performance in local Dongyang dialect (Song 1984a: Part 1: 72–73; Zhang and Hong 1985: 43–44), and Houyang Gaoqiang is also said to have absorbed some strong influence from Kun (Wang ed. 1998: 225).

During the Qing Daoguang reign (1821–1851) there were some 60 Houyang Gaoqiang troupes performing around Jinhua, Quzhou, and Yanzhou. It was the golden age of the genre. Later Kun, Luantan, and Hui grew more popular, and the performance of Gaoqiang operas was relegated to combined troupes (Heban 合班) (Zhang and Hong 1985: 43–44; and see below). Sanhe Ban (three in one combined troupes) that perform Houyang Gaoqiang often have the characters Ziyun 紫云 (azure cloud) in their names and are referred to as Ziyun Ban (Ge et al. eds. 1986: 98).

Songyang Gaoqiang 松阳高腔

Songyang Gaoqiang is widespread in Zhejiang's Songyang, Suichang, Lishui, and Longjing, but it is also found in Wenzhou, parts of Fujian, and Jiangxi. Prior to the establishment of the PRC, Songyang Gaoqiang was also performed by puppet troupes of which Songyang had more than ten. The repertoire of the puppet troupes included the often-performed Furen Zhuan (夫人传—Legend of the Wife), one of the more popular operas in the Songyang Gaoqiang repertoire (Zhang and Hong 1985: 50–51, 241).

Xiwu Gaoqiang 西吴高腔

Xiwu Gaoqiang 西吴高腔 gets its name from Xiwu village of Luodian township in Jinhua where it was earliest performed and taught during the Ming dynasty. It reached a pinnacle of popularity just before Qing Daoguang (AD 1821–51), circulating in Jinhua, Lanxi, and as far as eastern Jiangxi and southern Anhui. But after Daoguang, like the other Gaoqiang genres, it declined in popularity with only ten or so troupes performing in the Jinhua region. After the Taiping rebellion of the 1860s, only five or six troupes remained, and at the end of the Qing/early Republic, Guo Pinyu troupe 郭品玉班 and Bao Pinyu troupe 包品玉 were the only two Xiwu Gaoqiang troupes performing, and both had disbanded by the year 1908. Among Guo Pinyu troupe's more distinguished performers was Jiang Heyi 江和义 (see below) who was a youngster at the time (Ding 1990: 162).

Xi An Gaoqiang 西安高腔

Xi An Gaoqiang is widespread in Quzhou and Jinhua, southeastern Jiangxi, and northwestern Fujian. In dynastic times Quzhou was known as Xi An County 西安县, and that is the derivation of the name (Ge et al. eds. 1986: 98). Xi An Gaoqiang, like Xiwu Gaoqiang, was already a distinct genre during the Ming, and reached its height of popularity just before Qing Daoguang (1821–51), after which its performance was relegated to combined troupes (Zhang and Hong 1985: 40). Sanheban combined troupes that perform Xi An Gaoqiang often have the characters Wen Jin 文锦 (scholarly brocade) in their names and are referred to as Wenjin Ban (Ge et al. eds. 1986: 98).

Kun Qiang 昆腔

Kun Qiang originated in the latter part of the Yuan dynasty, as Nanxi spread through the Kun Shan region of Jiangsu, and underwent revision at the hands of that region's musical master Gu Jian 顾坚 at the beginning of the Ming (Zhang and Hong 1985: 271–272).

At the end of the Ming Wanli period (1573–1620), Kun Qiang spread north and south, and for a century from the beginning of the Ming Tianqi period (1621–1628) to the final years of the Qing Kangxi reign (1662–1723) Kun Qiang enjoyed wide popularity (Zhang and Hong 1985: 14–15). During the subsequent Qianlong period, a Suzhou Kun troupe is said to have toured from Hangzhou up the Qiantang River, stopping first in Lanxi, before moving on to Jinhua, performing Kun opera as they went. The people of Lanxi and Jinhua enjoyed the opera, and some even went so far as to endure the five years of training necessary to gain entry to the Suzhou troupe, later returning to Jinhua to organize a troupe of their own. Kun became especially popular in Jinhua during the Jiaqing (1796–1821) and Daoguang (1821–51) periods (Zhang and Hong 1985: 15).

In the history of Chinese opera, the influence of Lanxi native Li Yu 李渔 (1611–79) has been profound, both as an author of operas and as a theorist. Born in Xialicun 夏李村 in Lanxi, he headed up the local village amateur Kun opera troupe, preparing and editing libretto and serving as director. In later years he moved to Hangzhou where during a decade of creative work, he wrote operas after the famous Tang dynasty story "Errors caused by the Kite" (风筝误 Fengzhengwu), and the Song dynasty story "The Dawn will Come" (奈何天 Naihe Tian), the two most popular of his ten operas, performed most often by Jinhua Kun opera troupes. His Wusheng Xi (无声戏 Silent Opera) explored issues of same-sex love, and he also authored the collection of short stories Shi Er Lou (十二楼 Twelve Towers), as well as the theoretical work Xianqing Ouji (闲情偶寄 Random Posts in a Leisurely and Carefree Spirit) (Zhang and Hong 1985: 27–28).

Kun Qiang troupes experienced another wave of popularity at the end of the Qing and early Republic, when there were some 28 such troupes in Jinhua (Ding 1990: 164). After several generations of localization as to dialect in its spoken and sung parts, the Sukun 苏昆 genre gradually became vernacularized in Jinhua, into what is known as Caokun 草昆 (grass [roots] Kun), somewhat freer in performance style than classical Sukun (Ge et al. eds. 1986: 98; Wang ed. 1998: 189). But even so, many Jinhua Kun troupes perform operas of the ancient repertoire of Su Kun that have been lost to the mother genre, such as Hua Feilong (花飞龙 Flower Flying Dragon), Fei Longfeng (飞龙风 Flying Dragon Wind), Jinqi Pan (金棋盘 Gold Chess Cup), Ji Pin (济贫 Aid the Poor; also known as Ya Bei Feng 哑背疯 Mute Carries the Crazy One) (Zhang and Hong 1985: 2).

Since liberation professional Kun Qiang troupes of either Su or Cao variety have become less common in Jinhua (Ge et al. eds. 1986: 98; Wang ed. 1998:

189), although both the Sanhe Ban and Erheban Ban combined troupes of Jinhua all perform some operas in the Kun genre, and nowadays there are also quite a few amateur Kun opera troupes in Jinhua, Lanxi, Dongyang, and Yiwu (Wang ed. 1998: 189; Zhang and Hong 1985: 2, 16).

Huixi 徽戏

Huixi is of course the opera genre that has gained national prominence as the immediate ancestor of Beijing opera, originating in the Huizhou and Cizhou regions of Anhui in the late Ming–early Qing periods (Zhang and Hong 1985: 17). Since 1949, Huixi troupes have become Jinhua's most important, most numerous troupes and all professional Wuju troupes can sing at least some numbers in the Huixi style (Ding 1990: 164).

In 1959, Beijing opera star Mei Lanfang called attention to the Qing dynasty origins of Beijing opera as the result of four prominent Hui troupes entering the capital and creating the basis for what would become Beijing opera. But when work began on the revival of Hui opera in its native Anhui, the provincial cultural bureau had no choice but to come to Jinhua to recruit nine artists to teach Hui opera in Anhui (Zhang and Hong 1985: 18). The Huixi of Jinhua Wuju preserved the archaic flavor and primitive simplicity of its Anhui operatic ancestor, whereas practitioners of traditional Huixi in Anhui were difficult to find (Ge et al. eds. 1986: 99; Zhang and Hong 1985: 2 and 273).

During Qianlong (1736–96) Huixi spread from its home in Anhui to Jiangsu and Jiangxi, and by the end of Qianlong had made its way to Jinhua in Zhejiang where some four or five Huixi troupes were already performing. Huixi troupes followed the trail of Anhui merchants who came to the Jinhua/Quzhou region to do business along the Xin An river through Jiande, Lanxi, Jinhua, Longyou, and Quzhou. (See Map 2.4.)

Once Huixi appeared in Jinhua and Quzhou, it was warmly embraced by the rural folk, being both easier to understand and learn than Gaoqiang or Kun Qiang (Zhang and Hong 1985: 17). In the Jiaqing reign period (1796–1821) there were more than ten professional Huixi troupes in Jinhua; in the Daoguang period (1821–1851) more than 20; and in the Tongzhi period (1862–1875) the genre reached a high tide of popularity with some 30 troupes performing. Later their numbers gradually declined, only 15 remaining during Guangxu (1875–1908), and by the end of the dynasty only 12 troupes remained. During the Republican period the genre experienced a revival, and there were some 20 troupes active in Jinhua. But the anti-Japanese war and the civil war further depleted that number until on the eve of liberation there were only 11 Huixi troupes still performing (Zhang and Hong 1985: 71).

The Republican period revival may well have been the result of the appearance in Jinhua of Huixi women's troupes which gave new vitality to Hui opera. The earliest, Minsheng Wutai 民生舞台, was organized in 1935 by the proprietor of Changli Theater in Jinhua, Mr. Xu Shoukang 徐寿康

with ten supporters. They posted a notice to recruit teenage girls, and hired the famous performers Fang Huaquan 方华泉, Fang Yonglin 方永林, and Lin Chunhua 林春华 to instruct them. The students endured many hardships but after three months, the new troupe had its first performance, after which, they were hailed wherever they went, greatly increasing the popularity and audience for Hui opera (Ding 1990: 166, 174), and the troupe became a training center for many future artists in the Wuju world (Zhang and Hong 1985: 84–85).

Luantan 乱弹 *(chaotic playing)*

The Luantan genre gets its name from its deviations from strict Kun standards of performance, as it combined with local folk-song styles in the Tongcheng region of Anhui during the late Ming dynasty, to produce a distinct genre, while retaining a very strong flavor of Kun Qiang. The genre arrived in Jinhua during the Ming-Qing transition (Zhang and Hong 1985: 272–273), where four branch genres developed: Pujiang Luantan, Dongyang Luantan, Jinhua Luantan, and Lishui Luantan. Repertoire items include Yu Qingting (玉蜻蜓 Jade Dragonfly) in the Pujiang branch; Tieling Guan (铁灵关 Tieling Pass) in the Dongyang branch; Biyu Zan (碧玉簪 Jade Hairpin) in the Jinhua branch; and Sangyuan Hui (桑园会 Rendezvous in the Mulberry Garden) in the Lishui branch (Zhang and Hong 1985: 248).

Tanhuang 滩簧 *(shoals reed)*

The Tanhuang of Wuju originated as a kind of popularized version of Kun Qiang, with subgenres in Lanxi and Jinhua, and was performed in the counties of both Jinhua and Quzhou prefectures (Ge et al. eds. 1986: 99; Shen 1997: 95). It originated in Suzhou, and it is sometimes called Su Tan 苏滩. At the end of the Ming and early Qing it spread across southern China, and is thus often referred to as Nanci (南词 Southern Tunes). Nanci Tanhuang 南词滩簧 spread into Jinhua during the Qing, said to have been taught to locals in Lanxi by a magistrate from Suzhou during the Qianlong reign period. At the beginning it was only a form of personal entertainment for the magistrate and his peers. But later, after the defeat of the Taiping rebellion, a group of merchants got together to study Tanhuang, and the genre gradually spread to their employees, whom the shopowners supported in competitions, to the point where it suffused among all classes (Zhang 2003: 46–49).

After Daoguang (1821–51), Kun Qiang declined in popularity, but amateur Tanhuang Zuochang Ban (seated singing troupes) continued to perform selected songs from Kun operas. And during Guangxu (1875–1908), Tanhuang migrated from Lanxi onto Jinhua stages, after which many troupes could sing at least some Tanhuang numbers (Zhang and Hong 1985: 273).

Sanhe Ban combined troupes also perform Tanhuang operas, the most popular of which are: The Little Nun Descends the Mountain (Xiao Nigu

Xia Shan 小尼姑下山); Twice Empty the Kiln/coal pit (Shuang Bie Yao 双别窑); and Jade Screen Mountain (Cuiping Shan 翠屏山). Nowadays, the Tanhuang genre is being carried forward by a new generation of aficionados in Lanxi (Shen 1997: 95–96).

Shidiao 时调

Shidiao 时调 is a term used to refer to rural airs and folk songs. There are only a few operas which evolved in the Wuju Shidiao style, and these were for the most part derived from the repertoires of Tanhuang amateur Zuochang Ban, having absorbed some local folk melodies and rural singing styles in the process.

Shidiao is relatively easy to learn and fun to sing, as well as pleasant to listen to. It is an operatic form very dear to the hearts of the laboring people, since its content is often expressive of their life circumstances. As a result Shidiao minor operas were very popular during the Republican period (Zhang and Hong 1985: 274), and remain so today in the hands of mainly amateur troupes (Ge et al. eds. 1986: 99).

There are no Shidiao troupes per se, but the minor operas of the genre are often found in the repertoire of Huixi troupes, as well as Sanhe Ban combined troupes and many amateur troupes (Ge et al. eds. 1986: 190; Zhang and Hong 1985: 253).

Heban 合班 *(combined troupes)*

Sanhe Ban 三合班 (3 in 1 troupes) and Erheban Ban 二合半班 (2½ in 1 troupes) are combined troupes which perform more than a single genre of opera, and made their appearance in Jinhua during the Qing Daoguang period (1821–1851). So called Sanhe Ban (3 in 1 troupes) performed Gaoqiang, Kun, and Luantan operas; Erheban Ban (2½ in 1 troupes) performed Kun, Luantan, and Hui operas (Hong 1988: 45; Lanxi Shizhi 1988: 567; Zhang and Hong 1985: 244).

Given the various local genres of Gaoqiang that circulated in Jinhua, Sanhe Ban troupes varied as to which of the Gaoqiang genres they performed. Dongyang Sanhe Ban sang Houyang Gaoqiang; Jinhua Sanhe Ban sang Xiwu Gaoqiang; and Quzhou Sanhe Ban sang Xi An Gaoqiang (*Jinhua Shizhi* 1992: 996).

Because of the growing popularity of Huixi among nineteenth-century audiences, and the decline in popularity of Gaoqiang, many Sanhe Ban troupes expanded their repertoire to include Huixi, and dropped their Gaoqiang repertoire altogether, becoming so-called Erheban Ban troupes, singing Kunqiang, Luantan, and Hui operas (Wang ed. 1998: 189; Zhang and Hong 1985: 251, 66).

Some veteran performers say that the name "Erheban" (2½) derives from the fact that troupes generally performed 18 Kun operas, 18 Luantan operas,

Table 7.1 The genres of Wuju

Genre	Sub-genre	Place of circulation	Representative opera
高腔 Gaoqiang	西安高腔 Xi An Gaoqiang	衢州 Quzhou	槐荫树 Huaiyin Shu
	西吴高腔 Xiwu Gaoqiang	金华 Jinhua	白兔记 Baitu Ji
	侯阳高腔 Houyang Gaoqiang	东阳 Dongyang	合珠记 Hezhu Ji
	松阳高腔 Songyang Gaoqiang	松阳 Songyang	夫人传 Furen zhuan
昆腔 Kun Qiang	金华昆腔 Jinhua Kun	金华 Jinhua	十五贯 Shiwu Guan
	兰溪昆腔 Lanxi Kun	兰溪 Lanxi	风筝误 Feng Zhengwu
	东阳昆腔 Dongyang Kun	东阳 Dongyang	长生殿 Changsheng dian
	衢州昆腔 Quzhou Kun	衢州 Quzhou	火焰山 Huoyan Shan
乱弹 Luantan	浦江乱弹 Pujiang Luantan	浦江 Pujiang	玉蜻蜓 Yu Qingting
	东阳乱弹 Dongyang Luantan	东阳 Dongyang	铁灵关 Tieling Guan
	金华乱弹 Jinhua Luantan	金华 Jinhua	碧玉簪 Biyu Zan
	处州乱弹 Chuzhou Luantan	丽水 Lishui	桑园会 Sangyuan Hui
徽戏 Hui Xi	单一性的剧种 single genre		二度梅 Erdu Mei
滩簧 Tanhuang	金华滩簧 Jinhua Tanhuang	金华 Jinhua	酒楼醉归 Jiulou Zuigui
	兰溪滩簧 Lanxi Tanhuang	兰溪 Lanxi	僧尼会 Sang Ni Hui
	衢州滩簧 Quzhou Tanhuang	衢州 Quzhou	貂蝉拜月 Diao Chan baiyue
	浦江滩簧词调 Pujiang Tanhuang Cidiao	浦江 Pujiang	读书赠米 Dushu Zengmi
	东阳滩簧 Dongyang Tanhuang	东阳 Dongyang	卖草囤 Mai caodun
时调 Shidiao	单一性的剧种 single genre		走广东 Zou Guangdong

Source: Zhang and Hong 1985

More popular culture: Wuju (Jinhua opera) 121

and nine Huixi operas (Zhang and Hong 1985: 66). But another version of the derivation of the name "2½" suggests that the history of Huixi was not as long as that of Kun and Luantan, and thus Huixi constituted only half a genre so to speak (Song 1984a: Part 1: 84).

Erheban troupes were most numerous during the 1860s when there were some 20 troupes performing in Jinhua. By the Guangxu period (1875–1908) their numbers had dropped to ten or so, declining to seven during Xuantong (1908–1911). By the end of the Republican period on the eve of liberation in 1949, only two remained (Zhang and Hong 1985: 66), the activities of one of which, Zhouchunju Ban, are discussed later in this chapter.

Whenever an Erheban troupe performs at a temple fair, they will always perform a Kun opera on the first night. The first night's performance is for the temple deity (*pusa* 菩萨), and legend has it that *pusa* are partial to Kun opera. The second and third nights' performances are for the people, and thus Luantan and Huixi dominate the program (Song 1983a: 88).

Organization of troupes

Professional performance troupes are generally composed of at least 24 members, "13½" of whom are singers, corresponding to the 13 voice divisions of Wuju, divided into three role categories called "tang" or halls:

- five members of Dan tang 旦堂 (hall of female roles): Zuo Dan 作旦, Hua Dan 花旦, Zheng Dan 正旦, Wu Dan 武旦, Lao Dan 老旦;
- four members of Huamian tang 花面堂 (hall of painted faces): Da Hualian 大花脸 (or Zheng 净), Er Hualian 二花脸 (or Fuzheng 副净); Xiao Hualian 小花脸 (or Chou 丑); Si Hualian 四花脸 (or Wuzheng 武净);
- four members of Baimian tang 白面堂 (hall of plain faces): Zhengsheng 正生 (or Laosheng 老生), Xiaosheng 小生, Laowai 老外, Fumo 副末

(Zhang and Hong 1985: 36–38)

Altogether this is 13, with the "½" referring to the Sanxiang, one of three prop men who is sometimes called upon to perform minor roles (Ding 1990: 162; Zhang and Hong 1985: 31).

Thus the costumes of the troupe are said to have 13½ nettings (Wangjin 网巾), the netting being one of the make-up articles used by the performers, fashioned of horse tail, and worn on the head, to receive whatever decoration or headgear the performer might be called upon to wear. Every performer has one. Thus, "13½ nettings" refers to the full complement of the troupe's 13½ performers (Zhang and Hong 1985: 31).

The Zhengsheng role is the young male lead, courageous and resourceful, who often ends up marrying the female lead Hua Dan role character. Xiaosheng is often the male protagonist's nephew, or his good friend or old acquaintance. Xiaosheng is usually also skilled in acrobatics and martial arts. The Laodan is an older female role. Laowai is the role of an older official.

Fumo is a lower-class male role. Da Hua are bold and unconstrained characters for good or evil, skilled in martial arts. Er Hua are generally villains. Si Hua are clowns, agents of comic relief (Shen 2003: 226, 232).

And the five different tones of the Pentatonic scale—Jin 金 Metal, Mu 木 Wood, Shui 水 Water, Huo 火 Fire, Tu 土 Earth—each correspond to particular role singers. The female Dan 旦 roles sing the metal 金 tone. For the male roles Laosheng 老生 sings the wood 木 tone, Xiaosheng 小生 sings the water 水 tone, Da Hualian 大花脸 sings the fire 火 tone, Xiao Hualian 小花脸 (Chou 丑) sings the earth 土 tone (Shen 1997: 95).

In addition to the 13½ performers, there is generally also a band of five or six musicians: Zhengcui 正吹 first wind, Fucui 副吹 second wind, Guban 鼓板 drums, San Xian 三弦 three string (banjo), Da luo 大锣 big cymbal, Xiaoluo 小锣 small cymbal (who doubles as a stage hand) (Song 1983a: 84; 1984a: Part 1: 75).

The care and arrangement of costumes is extremely complicated, and requires precise management. Three costume keepers, the touxiang 头箱 responsible for the clothing, the Kuixiang 盔箱 for head gear, and the sanxiang 三箱 for the weapons, require a system, and must be very familiar with the operas: which character wears what costume, and when, what they need to change into when they come off the stage at what point; and all must be carefully prepared and arranged in advance (Song Bo 1983a: 84; Zhang and Hong 1985: 147). Because of this, the important performers are especially respectful of the three costume keepers, and at every festival performance, will send a small gift to express appreciation for their efforts. The three must also be versatile, able to step in as "half performers," creeping like a tiger, or doing somersaults, sometimes even directing (Zhang and Hong 1985: 147).

The troupe's Dingtou 定头 makes arrangements for the stage, draws up contracts, and collects the performance fees from the sponsors. The Lingxiu 领袖 leader is often a performer himself and is in charge of organization, recruiting performers and musicians and assigning tasks. The Hangtou 行头, occasionally a performer himself, is assistant to the lingxiu, and keeper of the ledger (Song 1984a: Part 1: 75), and there is also a cook, an errand boy, and a preparer of tea.

Facial make-up and its symbolism

I don't think it an exaggeration to say that the facial make-up in Wuju (as well as in Chinese opera in general) genuinely qualifies as grotesque, transforming ordinary humans into larger than life imposing figures with symbolically distorted facial features. As in other Chinese opera genres, the make-up of the face in Wuju may be in one of three modes: representational/patterned design (Tu An Hua 图案化), metaphoric/implied meaning design (Yuyi Hua 寓意化), and personality design (Xingge Hua 性格化) *(Jinhua Shizhi* 1992: 999; Zhang and Hong 1985: 151).

Figure 7.1 Putting on make-up: Xiawang

In representational/patterned make-up, the patterns may be those of animals, weapons, or natural phenomena, the "Feng Hua Lei Yue" (风花雪月 wind, flowers, snow, and moon—the subject matter of traditional literary works). Or they may take the form of Chinese characters to represent the traits of the opera character.

In metaphorical make-up (Yuyi Hua 寓意化), the patterns and lines have an implied meaning designed to evoke particular traits of the character (Zhang and Hong 1985: 151, 153, 155).

In personality make-up, Xingge Hua 性格化, different colors depict different personality traits:

- red face represents loyalty and bravery;
- black face represents upright and outspoken;
- white face represents craftiness and treachery;
- green face represents violence and ferociousness;
- purple face represents wisdom and bravery;
- gold face represents otherworldliness;
- blue face represents evil and fraudulence.

The Yin Yang symbol represents ghosts and monsters, forces of evil (*Jinhua Shizhi* 1992: 999; Zhang and Hong 1985: 152–153)

It is said that in the distant past, opera performers wore masks, but in later times came to feel that the masks interfered with the expression of emotion, so they took the likeness of the masks and painted them directly on the performers' faces, and in this way all the performers attained their distinctive make-up. Later still Dan role and Baimian role performers in the Wuju genres came to feel that the elaborately painted face was not good looking and interfered with the performance, and thus no longer paint their faces except for perhaps a small amount of red color (Zhang and Hong 1985: 150).

Structure of performance: the Nine Gates (九关)

When a Wuju troupe is hired, it is often to entertain the deity (and the people) at a temple fair which normally lasts for three days. Thus a troupe is usually expected to perform what is known as Yipiao xi 一票戏 (one play bill), which consists of performances over two days and three nights, a total of five performances. When the troupe arrives on the scene, they will normally consult with the host of the fair or its committee to select the operas, and do their best to meet their host's requests (Ding 1990: 162).

Each day's program consists of Nine Gates or passes, during the course of which one complete grand opera (Zhengben 正本) and three minor operas/operettas (Zhezi 折子) (yiben sanzhe 一本三折) are performed, lasting for more than five hours. The final night's performance may also involve a Tianliang Xi 天亮戏 (morning light opera), beginning after dinner on the third night and lasting until the cock crows the following morning. The Tianliang performance consists of two complete grand operas and three minor operas, and generally involves an additional payment to the troupe (Song 1984a: 76; Wang ed. 1998: 219).

The Nine Gates are as follows.

Figure 7.2 Opera performance: Luodian

More popular culture: Wuju (Jinhua opera) 125

Figure 7.3 Opera performance: Fotang

Figure 7.4 Opera performance: Luodian

Gate 1: Nao Toutai 闹头台 (First Harassing the Stage)

Nao Toutai 闹头台 (First Harassing the Stage), or Nao Huatai 闹花台 (harassing the flower stage), is a musical introduction with four parts. In the first part the bamboo flutes are principal; in the second the small "hu"; in the third the small suona; in the fourth the large suona. The sections are divided clearly, and function to let people know that the performance is beginning, to attract and entertain, while demonstrating the performance skills of the musicians of the troupe (Song 1984a: Part 1: 76; Wang ed. 1998: 219).

Gate 2: Da Tai 打台 (Hit the Stage)

Da Tai (打台) is a demonstration of the martial arts skills of the troupe's performers.

Gate 3: Ta Baxian 踏八仙 (Dance the Eight Immortals)

Ta Baxian is an obligatory prelude whenever a Jinhua Wuju troupe performs (Chen Chongren 1997: 87). The Guangxu period (1875–1908) gazetteer of Jinhua Prefecture records that Ta Baxian was always performed at temple fairs to "welcome/entertain the deity, and at "eye opening" ceremonies celebrating the opening of new temples, or the refurbishing of old ones. But it was also often performed by amateur troupes at celebrations of longevity, or for fulfilling vows made to the deity for granting the safe birth of a child (Hong 1990: 142–144).

The stage is set in the style of the Tang dynasty, and the assembly of eight immortals emerges, with dance and song in praise of the sages, requesting protection from calamity, seeking timely rains, plentiful harvests, and peace in the realm, good luck, prosperity, and wealth. The dance movements are lively, and expressive of happy feelings, seeking auspicious results. The performance also displays the opera troupe members in all their finery to the audience. The troupe members who will later perform as Kuixing, Jiaguan, and Caishen bang drums and cymbals to enliven the prayers for protection and health, adding a little red fire (*honghuo*) to the occasion (Chen 1997: 87; Wang ed. 1998: 220).

When the performance of Ta Baxian is concluded, the host offers a gift to the head of the troupe in the form of a red paper envelope, in the old days containing five or six silver dollars. Members of the audience may also give red envelopes to their favorite performers. And then the audience members vie with one another to retrieve peaches of immortality (mantou hung from trees), and thus come away from the performance with a guarantee of good fortune (Chen Chongren 1997: 87; Hong 1990: 146; Song 1984a: Part 1: 76).

Chen Chongren claims that since the founding of the PRC the custom of performing Ta Baxian continued uninterrupted (Chen Chingren 1997: 87). But according to Hong in the early years of the PRC, Ta Baxian was classified as a manifestation of feudal superstition, suppressed and prohibited, and only after the Gang of Four were toppled has the dance revived. In either event, the dance is part of the performance package that Wuju troupes offer to their employing patrons (Hong 1990: 143).

Gate 4: San Tiao 三跳 (Three Dances)

Tiao Kuixing 跳魁星

Kuixing 魁星 (also known as 奎星—originally one of 28 celestial houses) has evolved into the goddess in charge of fate. It is Kuixing who selects the Zhuangyuan, the top scorers on the imperial examinations, by placing a celestial dot from her red brush on their papers. She has also been enshrined as the goddess of luck for the literati who often established Kuixing Pavilions (Kuixing Ge 魁星阁) to worship her, and as the "goddess of literature" (Hong 1990: 145; 1997: 80).

Tiao Kuixing 跳魁星 is generally performed by the troupe's xiao hualian/xiaochou (小花脸 / 小丑). He comes out dressed in Kuixing costume, half male, half female, wearing a green mask with a red dot at the top. The mask has a moveable mouth, and eyes. In his left hand, he holds a grain measure, or carpenter's ink line, in his right hand a brush pen, as he performs Kuixing Luo 魁星锣 with small cymbal accompaniment, pronouncing four verses:

> Kuixing comes out of the flower hall,
> Raises her brush to write an essay.
> The Qilin gives birth to a precious son,
> Who will certainly attain Zhuangyuan status.

> 魁星出华堂，
> 提笔做文章，
> 麒麟生贵子，
> 必中状元郎
> (Hong, Aiqin 1990: 145; Hong, Bo 1997: 80;
> Song 1984a: 76–77; Wang ed. 1998: 219)

As regards Kuixing's origins, it is said that a certain emperor's daughter was especially ugly, but very clever in classical learning, having achieved Zhuangyuan rank. Later a young imperial son in law was found for her, but when he lifted the veil and saw her face, he dropped dead on the spot, and thus humiliated, she took her own life. The emperor was remorseful, and buried them together, making a vow to heaven: "A girl is not born to be a Zhuangyuan; after her death I decree that all Zhuangyuan be marked/designated with her pen."

In another version, Kuixing was the daughter of a certain official, again very ugly, but reasonably bright, honest, and unselfish. She took the imperial exams and passed the Jinshi-level exam. But during the palace exam (for the Juren degree), when the emperor saw such an ugly person engaged in taking the exam, he kicked her out of the examination hall on the spot, and in a fit of imperial anger, beat her to death on the dragon column outside the palace, so that blood flowed on the jade steps. The presiding test official was curious, and went to retrieve her examination paper. After examining it, he found it quite impressive, and took it to the emperor, who upon reading it was overcome with regret. Pointing down at the dead woman, he declared, "When this talented woman was alive, I couldn't make her a Zhuangyuan. After her death, let all Zhuangyuan be graded with her red pen."

Afterwards, she was given a state burial. And when her soul ascended to heaven, she was invested by the Jade emperor as the goddess Kuixing. As such, she became very beautiful, and resided in heaven's northern palace, in charge of Zhuangyuan examinations and of the heavenly constellations. However, if she were to return to the human world, she would again take on her original ugly appearance (Hong 1997: 80).

In Dance Kuixing, young people are encouraged to study hard, to achieve the Zhuangyuan status that Kuixing's exams merited, and thereby bring glory to their lineage and ancestors (Hong 1997: 80; Song 1984a: 76–77). During the dance, there are no words spoken or sung, but the performance is the concern of all the opera troupe performers, since whether the Kuixing is performed well or not reflects on the success of the whole opera performance (Hong 1990: 145; Song 1984a: 76–77).

Dance Kuixing is divided into two parts, Wen and Wu. The Wen Kuixing 文魁星 selects the civil Zhuangyuan. The Wu Kuixing 武魁星 selects the military Zhuangyuan (Hong 1990: 145; Song 1984a: 76–77; Wang ed. 1998: 219).

Tiao Jia Guan 跳加官

Tiao Jia Guan 跳加官 is performed by the troupe's Laosheng (老生), portraying an older man in a white faced head mask, official's robes, cap, and court tablet. His movements are low and quick as he boldly proclaims "Heavenly officials grant prosperity", or "Peace and tranquility in the realm" (Hong 1997: 81).

Historically "Jia Guan" was the worthy official of the early Tang dynasty, Wei Zheng 魏征 (580–643 AD), a prominent politician, prime minister, and one time Daoist priest. He encouraged Tang Taizong (who reigned from 627–650) to take the decline of the previous Sui dynasty seriously, with the sage wisdom that "water can carry a boat, but water can also capsize a boat". Under his guidance, the Tang dynasty attained peace in the realm, and Wei has been praised by later generations as a model official, respected by the laobaixing. The idea of the dance is thus to encourage righteous behavior (Hong 1990: 145).

Tang emperor Xuanzong (Tang Minghuang) who succeeded to the throne in 713 AD, was especially enamored of the opera, and even performed on occasion himself. Once in preparing to perform, the emperor tapped empress Yang Guifei to sing the female lead (Huadan 花旦), while the emperor himself would perform the Xiaosheng 小生 role, but they lacked an older Laosheng 老生 singer. Thus they especially invited Wei Zheng to perform (even though he had been dead for 60 years!). When Wei Zheng saw the invitation, it was difficult to decline, and he was fearful of being criticized were he to refuse. So he donned his white mask, and took the stage. When the performance was over and he removed his mask, the audience discovered that the artist was indeed Wei Zheng. Tang Minghuang raised an eyebrow and smiled, and raised the rank of all in attendance one level. Tiao Jiaguan commemorates this event, and the peace of the realm with which Wei is associated (Hong 1997: 81; Hong 1990: 145; Song 1984a: Part 1: 77; Wang ed. 1998: 219).

Tiao Caishen 跳财神 (the God of Wealth)

Tiao Caishen 跳财神 (sometimes also referred to as Peng Yuanbao 捧元宝 Hold High the Ingot/Tael) is performed by a Da Hualian 大花脸, dressed as the God of Wealth, wearing a golden mask with a thick beard, a black robe, and a metal helmet or crown. In his hand he wields a gold ingot as he enters the stage, so that all those who seek wealth can attain their desire, declaring on behalf of merchants:

[May] business prosper throughout the four seas,
sources of wealth luxuriate in three rivers

生意兴隆通四海，
财源茂盛达三江

Shengyi xinglong tong sihai,
caiyuan maosheng da sanjiang.[1]

According to myth, Caishen, the God of Wealth, was Zhao Gongming 赵公明, who later became known as Zhao Gong Yuanshi (赵公元帅 Count Zhao First Master) after the jade emperor invested him as Zhengyi Xuantan Yuanshi (正一玄坛元师 Orthodox Unity First Master of the Dark Altar). He was thus also sometimes referred to as Zhao Xuantan 赵玄坛 (Zhao of the Dark Altar). He is said to have taken to the mountains as a hermit during the Qin dynasty, attained the Dao through cultivation, and become an immortal. He is often depicted holding a metal whip and riding a black tiger which is said to control thunder and lightning, and to expel disease and avert calamities (Hong 1997: 81; Song 1984a: Part 1: 77; Wang ed. 1998: 219; Zhang and Hong 1985: 31).

The origin of the custom is attributed to an opera company boss who had the misfortune of falling into a river when the boat in which he was riding capsized. After he was saved by a fisherwoman, he went to Caishen's temple, kowtowing for three days and three nights, in thanks for saving his life.

When he returned home, he discovered that the water crock was emitting light. When he looked more closely, he saw that it was full of large and small ingots. Afterwards, he used them to purchase three sets of the best opera costumes for his troupe, and before every performance, he performed Tiao Caishen in a black mask, to thank Zhao Gong Yuanshi and to express the hope that all under heaven might become wealthy and prosperous (Hong 1997: 81).

In general, Naotoutai lasts about half an hour, and Ta Baxian, Tiao Kuixing, Tiao Jiaguan, and Tiao Caishen take about 40 minutes combined. The main performance begins when they are concluded (Song 1984a: Part 1: 77).

Gates 5–8

The actual performance of the evening's featured opera begins with three minor operas: San Zhe 三折 to warm up the crowd (Gate 5), followed by a second harassing of the stage (NaoErtai 闹二台) to warm up the musicians (Gate 6), followed in turn by the main attraction (Gate 7). After the major opera (Zhengben Xi 正本戏), the troupe will perform yet another minor concluding opera, or Houxi 后戏 (Gate 8) as their last hurrah to the audience.

Gate 9: Zhuangyuan pays respects 状元拜堂

At the conclusion of the evening's performances, the artists come out to perform Zhuangyuan pays respects 状元拜堂, giving members of the audience a chance to engage in a custom known as Zhuangyuan Flowers 状元花. They buy the flowers from the troupe head or prop man, cheap ones, 20 to 50 cents, more expensive ones as much as one dollar. They then insert the flowers in the hat or wig of the performer they like best. The performer with the most flowers is deemed the Zhuangyuan, the best performer of the evening (Zhang and Hong 1985: 314).

Amateur troupes

Amateur village opera troupes are ubiquitous in Jinhua. Almost every village in the Jinhua Quzhou region has such a troupe, and larger villages sometimes more than one. Amateur troupes in the Jinhua region are variously referred to as Shixiang Ban 十响班 (Ten Tone Troupe), Zuochang Ban 坐唱班 (Seated Singing Troupe), Luogu Ban 锣鼓班 (Cymbal and Drum Troupe), or Taizi Ban 太子班 (Prince's Troupe).

The so-called Ten Tones refer to ten musical instruments: the vanguard 先锋 (trumpet), bamboo flute 笛子, pear flower 梨花 (large suona 唢呐), jizi 吉子 (small suona), Huihu 徽胡, banjo 月琴, big cymbals 大钹, little cymbals 小钹, big gongs 大锣, and little gongs 小锣 (Shi 1997b: 78; Zhang and Hong 1985: 102).

Zuochang, as the name suggests, refers to the fact that the singers perform seated, without costume, usually around an Eight Immortals table with a cloth draped over it bearing the troupe's name, equipped with drinking water, and some snacks, for consumption between numbers (Ding 1990: 159–160). The activities of later nineteenth-century amateur seated opera troupes are documented in a painting by the artist Li Weixian 李维贤 (1825–1907), entitled "Zuochang Tu" (坐唱图 Picture of Seated Amateur Opera Troupe) (Hong 1997a: 97).

Amateur troupes perform songs from the repertoire of Wuju, and divide singing roles in the same way as professional troupes, although they generally have far fewer members than professional troupes (Shi 1997: 78), and some members may divide time between singing and instrumental accompaniment. Performing at festive occasions, troupe members will also usually get a seat at the banquet (Zhang and Hong 1985: 102).

The minor leagues of Wuju

In addition to the entertainment they provide, amateur troupes are talent pools for recruitment to professional troupes, the basis for the reproduction of the Wuju genres. Occasionally amateur troupes may even develop on their own into semi-professional or professional troupes. In the history of Wuju, the role of amateur troupes as a kind of minor leagues of the profession has been extremely important to the continuity of the genre (Zhang and Hong 1985: 106).

If a professional troupe has a performer take ill, they will hire a performer from an amateur troupe to fill in temporarily for one or two performances (Ding 1990: 159). The finer amateur performers are continuously recruited into professional troupes (Zhang and Hong 1985: 11), and some of them have become quite famous (Ding 1990: 161). Renowned performer of female Huadan roles Li Baojian 李宝剑 of Yongkang got his start in the opera profession in exactly this way in an amateur Taizi Ban (Zhang and Hong 1985: 12).

Taizi Ban 太子班 (Triple A Ball)

If amateur troupes constitute the minor leagues of Wuju, then Taizi Ban are the Triple A teams of the minor leagues. The organization of Taizi Ban is more like that of professional troupes, with a formal head, a person in charge of costumes, a regular instructor/director, etc. In general Taizi Ban require a higher level of commitment and seriousness of purpose in the performers than ordinary amateur troupes, but essentially they are still part-timers. Troupe members are most often younger, more active folk who sing and perform with greater energy, and thus they are favored by rural audiences over other amateur troupes (Ding 1990: 161; Zhang and Hong 1985: 105).

Unlike their Zuochang, Shixiang, and Luogu Ban colleagues, Taizi Ban perform in costume, mainly old costumes discarded by professional troupes, perhaps supplemented by some newly bought. Some Taizi Ban are supported by a wealthy patron family or an association, known as the costume host (xingtou zhu 行头主), whose support may also go toward purchase of string and percussion instruments, or to pay the wages of the master/teacher/director, and provide him with a celebratory banquet upon hiring. The contract with a master/teacher is generally for a period of three years, and sealed with a deposit 押金 as bond lest the employed master renege on its terms (Ding 1990: 161; Hong 1997a: 97).

What they do, where they play

The most active time for amateur troupes to perform is during New Year, and the lunar first and second months, agricultural slack season. In many places in Jinhua New Year was the time when ancestral portraits were taken out and hung for all male descendants to pay their respects. During the hanging of the portrait, amateur troupes would perform Dance the Eight Immortals or other lucky opera selections in front of the portrait, to entertain the ancestor, receiving red envelopes as token payment from the host family for their service. The entertainment of the ancestor continued until 1/18, Yuanxiao (the lantern festival), before concluding.

During the Greet the Dragon Lantern procession of Yuanxiao, one or more amateur troupes would escort the dragon lantern on its itinerary through the surrounding villages, to "blow and bang," dispersing unfavorable influences, increasing the desirable commotion/red fire (*honghuo*) of the event (Fotang Township Government 2005: 94).

In addition to New Year celebrations, the principal performance venues for local amateur troupes were rural temple fairs, welcoming and entertaining the deity, but they also performed at festivals celebrating good harvests, at "eye openings" at newly constructed temples, at happy events, rites of passage like weddings or the birth of a son, at decanal birthdays of 60 years and above, so-called "celebrations of longevity," and also at funerals. And of course, the troupes meet to play and sing for their own entertainment and enjoyment. Those who join a troupe but fail in their attempts to sing adequately may still take up a useful role with percussion, gongs and drums (Ding 1990: 159; Mao ed. 1996: 78; Shi 1997: 78–79; Zhang and Hong 1985: 103).

Like the professional troupes, amateur troupes tend to specialize in the performance of one of the several different genres of Wuju—Gao, Kun, Hui, Luantan, or Tanhuang—and there are even amateur Sanhe Ban 三合班, which perform several different genres. Amateur Huixi troupes are the most numerous in the Jinhua region. But there are also amateur troupes which perform Beijing opera and Shaoxing Yueju, since these are genres with national followings (Hong 1997a: 97), libretti and recordings of which are readily available for study and emulation.

Nowadays, some private entrepreneurs, or shop owners will hire an amateur troupe to entertain their employees, or sponsor their own employees' troupe (Shi 1997: 79).

Jinhua opera custom

Patron founder Tang Minghuang 唐明皇

The patron founder of the operatic profession, the object of worship by its practitioners, is Tang emperor Tang Xuanzong, who reigned during AD 713–741, commonly referred to as Tang Minghuang or Laolang Shi (老郎师) (Song 1983a: 89). He is usually depicted as white faced and beardless, wearing a king's crown and yellow robe (Zhang and Hong 1985: 310).

Tang Minghuang took great pleasure in song, dance, and opera. He is said to have dispatched several hundred men and women of the palace to the imperial Pear Garden to learn opera arias and dances, and within the palace they became known as the Sons and Little Brothers of the Emperor's Pear Garden. Because of this, the opera profession is colloquially referred to as the Pear Garden, and its performers are known as sons and brothers of the Pear Garden (Song 1983a: 89).

Tang Minghuang is also said to have compiled the texts/libretti of the operas of his time, and to have been especially enamored of the humorous roles portrayed by Xiaohualian (Xiaochou). On several occasions, he even performed as a Xiaohualian himself, stepping in to sing the role during performances in his Pear Garden. It has thus become the duty of the Xiaohualian to care for and carry Tang Minghuang's carved wood image at the head of the troupe, taking the lead to open the road when the troupe moves to a new performance venue (Hong 1997: 99; Song 1983a: 89).

When the troupe arrives at a new site, the Xiaohualian takes Tang Minghuang inside to have a look around, to dispel any evil influences in the arena, before other troupe members may enter. Once the new site has been "cleaned" of evil influences, Tang Minghuang is placed in the wings of the stage on a costume chest, and three incense sticks offered, to protect the troupe from calamities and illness, and to insure that their performances will be successful (Song 1983a: 89; Song 1984a: 77; Wang ed. 1998: 220–221).

If a quarrel should occur between members of the troupe, the troupe's head would not scold or hit, but quietly take out the small statue of Tang Minghuang and place it on one of the trunks, whereupon both sides would immediately become silent, the opponents peaceful. Out of respect for the deity the quarrel would cease (Song 1983a: 89).

Professional association

The professional association of Wuju artists was known as Laolang Guan 老郎馆. Its headquarters in Jinhua was equipped with an altar bearing a statue of Tang Minghuang (Laolang Shi 老郎师), as well as a library of libretti, and its own opera stage. Each year on Tang Minghuang's birthday, lunar 4/16, the artists would present candles, incense, and sacrifices at the altar in celebration, and perform operas for the entertainment of their founding patron (Zhang and Hong 1985: 310).

The leaders of the organization were usually two or three distinguished elderly artists, who were available to adjudicate disputes and contradictions that arose among performers, and for whatever reason had not been settled to everyone's satisfaction within the troupe (Zhang and Hong 1985: 310–311).

After the establishment of the PRC, the Jinhua Laolang Guan morphed into the Wuju Improvement committee 婺剧改进委员会 and subsequently into the Opera Federation 戏曲联合会 (Zhang and Hong 1985: 310).

Jitai (祭台 – sacrifice/consecrate the stage)

Whenever a new opera stage is built, before it can be used, a solemn ceremony of Ji Tai "sacrifice the stage" must be held, and a troupe invited to entertain the deity for two days and three nights to insure good luck in its use. Ji Tai is usually held in the mornings, at about 7:00 or 8:00, before the first performances are scheduled to begin. The ritual is presided over by a lineage head or an elder of the village with standing/prestige.

A large eight immortals table is set in front of the new stage to serve as an incense altar, on which are placed two red candles, five sticks of incense, an offering of a cooked pig's head, white uncooked rice, bean curd, and eight bowls of dried fruit from each of the four seasons, a pewter decanter full to the brim with rice wine, three wine cups and three pairs of bamboo chopsticks on the side. Below the incense burner is placed a white winged rooster with its legs bound, all as sacrifice to the stage (Lei 1997: 89–90).

After all is in place, those present come forward to present incense, paper offerings and candles, seeking health for their families, and all wishes fulfilled. The host reads aloud a "sacrifice the stage text" 祭台文, written on a two-foot square sheet of red paper (Lei 1997: 89–90).

> Year, month, day, _____ village is opening a Ten thousand year opera stage 万年戏台. We beseech heavenly emperor to instruct master immortal Lu Ban to descend and expel the evil spirits and demons, and give protection for 10,000 years; and offer good fortune and peace in all things to the workers, farmers, soldiers, students, merchants, performers and the audience.
>
> (Lei 1997: 89–90)

In the lower left-hand corner of the Ji Tai Wen, in small characters, are the day, time and corresponding constellation of the completion of the stage, together with the names of possibly offending evil spirits, expressing the desire to avoid their influence. After the recitation, the paper is pasted on a corner of the stage. The host at the table/altar below the stage grabs up the rooster and a knife, and passes them to the presiding elder, who cuts off its head, and its blood and wine are poured on the four corners of the stage to expel the 100 ghosts; after which the chicken is thrown under the stage, and three sticks of incense are lit, and offered to the audience three times as a sign of respect: once for heaven, once for earth; and once with their back to the audience, in honor of master patron saint of carpentry, Lu Ban (Lei 1997: 89–90).

The band from behind the stage begins to beat gongs and drums, and intone their wind instruments. Members of the troupe emerge dressed as Guan Gong 关公, Wei Tuo 韦陀, the Four Warrior Attendants of Buddha (Si Da Jingang 四大金刚), Bingyong Shending 兵勇神丁 among others. They all march around the stage in form of an eight trigram 八卦 symbol, shouting "Ke Ruo!" so loud as to shake heaven and earth.

When these military figures have finished, two actors dressed in white ragged mourning clothes, with their faces painted in black and white, the heaven demon and the earth demon prance onto the stage. The heaven demon is dressed as a man, his head and waist wrapped in rice grass rope, wielding a false bloody head in his hand; the earth demon is dressed as a woman, with a grass robe, carrying a vegetable knife in her hand. They dance in front of the stage.

But then, the drums and cymbals begin again and the heaven and earth demons retreat to a corner of the stage. Guan Gong and the other military deities return. Guan Gong lights a stream of firecrackers suspended from his sword, and he and the others pursue the demons off the stage and out of the grounds. The audience at first shouts at the demons as they pass, and then takes up the pursuit behind Guan Gong et al. The demons run to the village earth god shrine where they stop and remove their costumes, grass robes and sashes, which are then burned by Guan Gong et al. The heaven and earth demons remove their make-up and resume their human identities, returning to the village with the others. But they are careful to take a route different from the one on which they came, and to pass the main door of the village temple or Citang, to escort the deity or the apical ancestor (Taigong Daren 太公大人) back to the village to see the opera. At this point, the band begins to play on the stage, the Ji Tai ritual is complete, and the performances on the new stage may begin (Lei 1997: 89–90).

Doutai 斗台 *(Competition for the Stage)*

Doutai (Competition for the Stage) is actually a competition for audience, and is a common occurrence at temple fairs and eye opening ceremonies. A small competition might involve two or three troupes competing; a large competition 15–16 troupes. Depending on the occasion, or the resources of the host, Doutai competitions may involve either amateur or professional troupes. The more troupes the greater the red fire (*honghuo* 红火), and the overall success of the ritual event (Chau 2006: 155; Hong 1997: 81; Zhang and Hong 1985: 295).

The beginning of the competition is signaled by the setting off of a canon, or the firing of a gun, and the troupes perform simultaneously throughout the day and through the night. Doutai can last for a single day and night, or as many as seven days and nights. The victor is determined by the crowing of a rooster at daybreak, at which moment, the troupe with the largest audience is the "winner." The more wins a troupe accumulates the greater its reputation, and the larger the price it can command for future performances. Particularly memorable Doutai involving close competition between famous artists of well-known troupes may be discussed or argued over by aficionados for years thereafter (Hong 1997: 81; Zhang and Hong 1985: 296).

In the spring of 1947, at a Doutai held at the Yiwu Merchant's Huiguan in Lanxi, Zhouchunju Ban was pitted against Minsheng Wutai, both performing the Luantan opera "Huiyinyuan" (悔姻缘 Regret the Fated Marriage). Zhouchunju Ban's female Xiaosheng Zhou Yuegui 周月桂 and Minsheng Wutai's female Xiaosheng Wu Yezhi 吴叶枝 both performed the role of Cai Wende 蔡文德 in an evenly matched contest. The capacity crowd of Huiguan members and audience let out persistent cheers, and the Zhouchunju troupe prevailed in the end by a narrow margin (Song 1983c: 59; Zhang and Hong 1985: 302).

Zhou Chunju's troupe was a frequent winner of the Doutai in which they participated. Each of their many well-known singers had established repertoire items that repeatedly won Doutai competitions for the troupe, Zhou Yuexian's Hongmei Ge (红梅阁 Red plum pavilion), Zhou Yuegui's Fa Zidu (伐子都 Attack Zidu), and Ye Agou's Jiujian Yi (九件衣 Nine articles of clothing) (Song 1983a: 88; and see below).

Amateur troupes, like their professional cousins, may also participate in Doutai competitions. The saying has it: "Generals get merit on the battlefield, amateur opera troupes gain fame in Doutai competitions" (Shi 1997: 79).

Doutai is said to be a quite ancient custom, and to be quite useful for all troupes, both professional and amateur, to evaluate their strengths and weaknesses, while bettering themselves through artistic competition, and encouraging the development of the art (Shi 1997: 79; Zhang and Hong 1985: 296).

Venues and occasions

Opera houses/theaters in Jinhua are essentially a Republican period, urban, twentieth-century phenomenon. Professional troupes usually performed on temple stages, stages in ancestral halls, or in the open air on temporary stages, typically making the rounds from village to village. Remuneration was generally in accord with the reputation of the troupe. For temple fairs, or eye openings, involving performances over several days, a place to unroll the troupe members' bedrolls on the floor of the temple was also included (Ding 1990: 162; *Lanxi Shizhi* 1988: 570; Wang ed. 1998: 205).

Temple stages 庙台 were permanent structures, often known as Wannian Tai (万年 10,000 Year Stages), built into the temple for the purpose of entertaining its resident deity (Zhang and Hong 1985: 299). Temporary stages, called Grass Stages 草台 or Rain Stages Yutai 雨台, were often erected in front of the temple or out in a field, especially when multiple troupes were invited to Doutai (compete for audience). At such times, as many as ten to 15 such stages might be constructed for the event, of simple bamboo frame, wood plank construction. When Doutai concludes, the stages are dismantled (Zhang and Hong 1985: 300–301).

In the early twentieth century opera theaters began appearing in cities and towns. In Jinhua, one of the more influential was Changle Opera House 长乐戏院, constructed in 1925. According to one authority its opening marked the first time Jinhua opera troupes performed for those who had bought tickets (Ding 1990: 162). For the price of admission the patron got a stool, and could also drink tea and nibble on sunflower seeds. On the eve of liberation, Changle was undergoing renovation into an 800–900 seat theater (Zhang and Hong 1985: 302).

Temple fairs are always mentioned first as the venue for opera performances, associated of course with rituals for entertaining the temple deity. From the invitation of the deity to watch the opera (Jiefo kanxi) delivered by the Xiao Hualian and Da Hualian together with the local host, to the carrying of the deity's pusa out of the temple to assume an honored seat in the audience, through the "Nine Gates" of which each performance is composed, the entertainment is a mass activity enjoyed by all.

By some estimates, during the Ming and Qing dynasties, the number of deities for whom temple fairs were convened during the year numbered more than 100, but Zhao suspects this number to be far too small (Zhao 2002: 193). And apart from the temple fairs, there were quite a few other occasions when operas were and are regularly performed.

Figure 7.5 Opera audience: Fotang

So-called Shexi 社戏 are performed on the two days during the year on which Tudi shen 土地神 (the earth deity) is worshipped, known as She days (社日 She Ri). The Spring She 春社 is the fifth 戊 "wu" day after Lichun 立春 (the first solar term of the year). On this day, the people pray to Tudishen for a bountiful harvest. The fifth 戊 "wu" day after the solar term Liqiu 立秋 is Autumn She 秋社. On that day, the people express thanks to Tudishen for having bestowed the bountiful harvest they previously prayed for at the Spring She (*Jinhua Shizhi* 1085; Liu and Sun eds. 1991: 372; Zhou and Wang eds. 1985: 111–112). The spring She rites roughly coincide with spring planting, so it is also a kind of welcoming spring ritual (Wang ed. 1998: 218).

But performances at temple fairs during other times of the year are also often colloquially referred to as Shexi (see, e.g., Lu 1922).

Kaiguang Xi 开光戏 are performed at "eye opening ceremonies," held when a new temple was consecrated or an old temple refurbished. The temple's *pusa* has its eyes covered until the final moment just before the new or newly refurbished temple doors are opened, when its eyes are uncovered, its pupils painted in, so that it might be entertained by the performing opera troupe or troupes, the greater the commotion/red fire the better. Kaiguang festivals are often held at ten-year intervals at any given temple to refresh its idols and replenish the temple's efficacy.

Huanyuan Xi 还愿戏 (Honor a Vow) takes its name from when, in their prayers to deities, supplicants often make a vow to reciprocate if the deity proves efficacious. This reciprocation may take the form of a donation of money to the temple in question, or, often as not, putting on an opera for the deity's (and community's) entertainment.

Fa Xi 罚戏 are operas in which the cost has been imposed as a fine or punishment, often by a lineage tribunal for breaking a lineage regulation; generally performed in the ancestral hall (*ci tang*).

Lingpu Xi 领谱戏 or Zuopu Xi 做谱戏 is performed when the updating of the lineage genealogy is completed and the document dedicated; generally performed in the ancestral hall (*ci tang*).

Taigong Xi 太公戏 is performed for the benefit of the ancestors in the *ci tang*.

Ping An Xi 平安戏 are performed in villages during New Years to bring good luck during the coming year.

Huichang Xi 会场戏 or Xingshi Xi 兴市戏 is performed at secular commodity exchange fairs, to bring in the crowds.

Huoxiao Xi 火烧戏 is an opera offered to a deity when the individual or community finds itself in an urgent or desperate situation, drought, flood, famine, etc.

Youqiao Xi 游桥戏 or Yuanqiao Xi 圆桥戏 is performed at the completion of bridge construction, usually for three days and three nights; sometimes seven days and nights; with many troupes invited to doutai.

Fengshan Xi 封山戏 or Jinshan xi 禁山戏 is performed at the ritual closing off of a mountain from gathering wood, or grazing animals.

Zhushou xi 祝寿戏 is performed in celebration of the "longevity birthdays," the decanal birthdays of 60, 70, or 80 years old.

De Zi xi 得子戏 is performed at the behest of a wealthy family celebrating the birth of a son.

Gengniu Xi 耕牛戏 is to express respect for the draft animal; performances can go on for as long as a month, as in Dongyang's Weishan town.

Judu Xi 聚赌戏 is to attract gamblers to a temporary casino, usually convened in a large tent for from two weeks to a month during agricultural slack season; although prohibited by authorities, the custom was often in the hands of organized criminal gangs which were difficult to suppress, or able to bribe local officials. (Information culled from Hong 1997: 99; *Jinhua Shizhi* 1992: 1085; Wang ed. 1998: 218–219.)

Opera troupes generally perform for seven months during the year, beginning in the first lunar month and continuing to the third month. The fourth, fifth, and sixth lunar months usually coincide with the agricultural busy season, and in general there are few if any performances. Most performers return home to help out with back to back summer harvest/summer planting. Performances begin again in the seventh, eighth, and ninth months. The tenth and eleventh are agricultural busy seasons again, harvesting late rice. In the twelfth month, performances begin again and continue into the first two months of the year, the golden season for performers when their services are in great demand (Ding 1990: 162; Song 1984a: Part 1: 78; Wang ed. 1998: 221; Zhang and Hong 1985: 68).

In recent decades subscriptions for the opera are generally taken from various village households door to door. Smaller villages will sometimes arrange to share the expense of bringing an opera troupe to perform among several such villages. And more recently, village-run factories have become an important sponsor for opera performances, financed by entrepreneurs as a holiday "benefit" for their workers on festival days like Duan Wu and Chongyang, sometimes taking over a local temple stage for the purpose, with the whole village community invited to enjoy the largesse (Liu 1996: 211).

Thus the venues and occasions for performance of Wuju are many and varied, giving rural folks many occasions during the year to attend, watch and listen. In an environment without electronic media, Wuju performances occupied a place in traditional culture somewhere between our own society's Marvel comic books and BBC TV's historical melodramas.

The repertoire and its didactic content

As regards the content of Wuju, the Cultural Revolution critique of the repertoire complained of its promulgating the values of feudal morality, superstition, and sexuality. And even Zhang and Hong, writing in the post-Cultural Revolution period, suggest that to continue the traditions of Wuju, the repertoire required some work to separate the gold from the sand, the genuine, good, and beautiful from the false, ugly, and evil; "weeding through the old to bring forth the new" in the Wuju repertoire (Zhang and Hong 1985: 255, 260).

The contrasting view is expressed by Zhang Bengao in his paean to Wuju opera. Zhang's position is that there are certain themes that are universal in literature and art, the contradiction between good and evil, loyalty and betrayal, *junzi* and *xiaoren* (gentleman and rogue), and of course romantic love (Zhang 2005: 36). He concedes that there is much scheming, violence, and evil in the plots of many operas. But for Zhang, the operas of Wuju ultimately renounce evil, and propagate the idea that good is rewarded with good, evil with evil. In most of the operas, although the good and loyal always find themselves in difficult straights, and suffer in their struggle with evil people, in the end the forces of good do prevail, and virtue is rewarded (Zhang 2005: 36).

There are operas with stories set in virtually every dynasty in Chinese history, from the Xia dynasty (ca. 2000 BC) clear on through to the Qing (1644–1911) (Zhang and Hong 1985: 255), and among the illiterate or partially literate, the stories of the operas were the way they learned about history, the heroes and villains of the past, and the endless series of wars, calamities, conquests, triumphs, betrayals, and defeats of which Chinese history is composed. Through opera, Zhang asserts, he himself, although quite literate, learned much about Chinese history, and came to understand society and the many kinds of people that inhabit it (Zhang 2005: 35).

In the past, the stories were widely known, and expressed the values of the common people as regards righteousness and punishment. Characters from the operas were and are used as metaphors for the personality types one encounters in life. One who is constantly seeking retribution is a Lü Gu 吕鼓, one who is hot tempered is a Zhang Fei 张飞, one who hides his true feelings beneath a veneer of honesty is a Cao Cao 曹操, one who is treacherous and crafty is a Pan Hong 潘洪. And the humorous fool characters (傻子 shazi) performed by the Xiao Hualian artists, in such operas as Beggar [Immortal Cao] Guojiu (Taofan Guojiu 讨饭国舅), or Medicine and Tea One After the Other (Qianhou Yaocha 前后药茶) alert us to our own shortcomings (Zhang 2005: 36).

For rural folk and their children, the opera was thus an important educational institution. The proverb "Rich people read books, poor people watch opera" expresses this idea quite nicely (Hong 1997a: 97).

The concept of Wuju

While the constituent genres of Wuju were in place in Jinhua by the Qing Daoguang (1821–1851) period, prior to the anti-Japanese war of the 1930s, the name Wuju simply does not appear (Hong 1988: 45). Its first use may well have been in 1939, when in order to help out with anti-Japanese propaganda, the head of the Guomindang (GMD) #22 rearguard hospital,

Wang Shoucheng 王守诚, together with his staff, organized an Amateur Wuju Troupe (Yeyu Wujutuan 业余婺剧团), since Jinhua had periodically been known as Wuzhou in dynastic times. This seems to be the earliest documented use of the term, although on the basis of his own participation in the events of the period, Tan (1988) suggests that the first use of the term only came much later in 1949, when a group of Jinhua Middle School students who had used the term informally among themselves for several years established an amateur troupe called Jinhua Middle School Wuju Study Group (Jinzhong Wuju Yanjiushe 金中婺剧研究社) with Tan Dehui 潭德慧 as instructor (Hong 1988: 46). According to Tan (1988: 60), this would have been the first use of the term Wuju to refer to Jinhua opera.

To get a sense of the Republican-period operatic world and its transformation in the early years of the PRC and thereafter, I propose here to present an account of an opera troupe with Republican-period roots, Longyou's Zhouchunju Ban, and of the life and career of its lead female performer, Zhou Yuexian, who played a central role in effecting that transformation.

Zhouchunju Ban

Zhou Yuexian and her sisters

In 1928, Mr. Zhou Chunsheng 周春生 purchased an Erheban troupe (二合半班—2½ in 1 combined opera troupe) for 200 silver dollars from local landlord Chen Chunju 陈春聚, who had inherited the troupe from his father. The younger Mr. Chen was not particularly enamored of opera, didn't manage the troupe very well, and was happy to unburden himself (Song 1983a: 85).

The troupe had originally been a Sanhe Ban (3 in 1 combined troupe) and performed Kun, Luantan, and Gaoqiang operas, but when Gaoqiang lost popularity, it dropped its Gaoqiang repertoire and adopted Huixi to become an Erheban Ban (2½ in 1 troupe), performing Kun, Luantan, and Huixi, with Luantan most important (Song 1983a: 84).

When Zhou Chunsheng took over the troupe he incorporated the "ju" 聚 character from the original owner's name into his own name, becoming Zhou Chunju, and called the troupe Zhouchunju troupe 周春聚班 or Chunju Wutai 春聚舞台. The troupe came to acquire a reputation for excellence performing in and around the temple fairs and villages of Longyou's southern townships.

Zhou Chunju's wife Wang Juying gave birth to three daughters: Yuexian 越仙 in 1929, Yuegui 越桂 in 1932, and Yuexiang 越芗 in 1935. Owing to the growing popularity of Yueju/Shaoju, the only genre in which women performed, in 1937 Zhou Chunju decided to incorporate a separate Yueju track into his troupe to create a niche in which his daughters could learn and perform opera. Chunju subcontracted (承包) the management of the original Erheban troupe to Ye Agou, the troupe's distinguished Laosheng, the pillar of the troupe. Ye established his reputation at the age of 28 with his performance in *Jiujian Yi* (九件衣 Nine Articles of Clothing), and also helped to establish the fame of the Zhou Chunju troupe (Song 1983a: 90).

Zhou Chunju then prepared to open a Yueju class for girls, and his wife Wang Juying hosted an audition at Jinhua's Changle Opera House 长乐戏院 at which she recruited 18 girls, who together with a group from the Longyou area made a total of 40, all girls of rural families from seven to 14 years old. Among them was an orphaned nine- year-old girl, Lou Dongmei 楼冬梅, who once accepted in the class, grew up in the company of Zhou's three daughters, Yuexian, Yuegui, and Yuexiang as a sister. They learned Yueju together in class, and subsequently performed together professionally (Song 1983a: 90; 1983c: 64).

The plan was to have the group of 40 debut in 50 days. Those in the group who could not make the grade in the assigned time were sent home, but in the end 28 students made it through. Because Yuexian's performance in the Yue opera *Luanfeng Shuangxiao* (鸾凤双箫 Husband and Wife Perfectly Matched) was so distinguished, her delighted parents named the new Yueju troupe "Yuexian Wutai" (Song 1983a: 90–91).

The troupe's debut as Yuexian Wutai was a great success, but in the fall of 1938, when they arrived in Xuanping for a performance, one after another the young performers fell sick. Some of their parents, who came to take them home, complained that the girls were being worked too hard. At the same time, conditions in the countryside were increasingly insecure, as Japanese and KMT planes were alternately dropping bombs here and there. So many of the parents lost their nerve, and withdrew their daughters from the troupe. As a result, Zhou Chunju and his wife had no choice but to disband the Yueju troupe temporarily (Song 1983a: 91), and assigned Yuexian and Yuegui to help out in the original Erheban troupe being managed by Ye Agou. But after a brief hiatus, the Yueju troupe was revived, and once younger sister Yuexiang started learning to sing opera, the three sisters and Lou Dongmei sang together in the Yuexian Wutai Yueju troupe till 1942 when the Japanese invaded Jinhua (Song 1983a: 91).

Zhou Yuexian 周越仙 (1929–1982)

From the moment she was born, Zhou Yuexian went with the Zhouchunju troupe from village to village, carried on her mother's back, sleeping in temples with the ground as their bed. At the age of two, she awoke one night with a nasty headache, and cried continuously. Thinking she had caught a cold, her parents went out to gather some herbs for her to take, but in the morning there was an unsightly lump on the side of her neck.

They consulted a doctor, who prescribed all kinds of Chinese medicine, but there was no improvement. The condition stayed with her until she was six years old, when one member of the troupe suggested that he cut the lump from her neck. Without antibiotics or anesthesia, he used Baijiu (white whiskey) as an antiseptic, and cut out the lump on the side of her neck, but the problem tissue apparently was not completely removed, and a second operation was necessary. Finally, and remarkably, Yuexian regained full movement of her head without any pain, and emerged from her sick bed (Song 1983a: 91).

Zhou Chunju and his wife saw that Yuexian enjoyed learning opera, but when she was eight years old and enrolled in the new Yueju class, several of the masters expressed concern about her scars, and even though she was the boss's daughter, they complained that she didn't have the talent and should try a different profession. But Zhou Chunju insisted that his daughter had a passion for opera and urged them to give her another chance. The masters had no choice. She was after all the boss's daughter (Song 1983a: 91).

In the Yueju class, Yuexian did not participate but merely watched from the side. Where others made mistakes, she was able to perform, and her teachers took note. She became familiar with the songs, movements, and places of each opera, and when any of her classmates was sick or had a problem, she would often stand in, following the master's instructions very carefully with a little of her own creativity mixed in. The master was often pleased and her fellow classmates often applauded.

Yuexian sang Huadan roles primarily, but she was also able to perform Dahualian, Laodan, Xiaosheng, and Xiaohualian roles. Because of her excellent skills, at the end of 50 days of training she was deemed to be ready to perform. On stage, whether it was a major opera or operetta, a Huadan role or a Xiaosheng role, or even a non-singing role, Yuexian was assiduous in her performances. She took every opportunity to "steal" the skills of the other troupe members by observing closely all facets of their behavior and performance, bearing, stage steps, expression, and make-up.

In 1942, when the Japanese invaded Jinhua, Quzhou and Yanzhou, Yuexian and the family went into hiding in the hills for the duration of the war (Song 1983a: 91; Zhang and Hong 1985: 320).

Traditionally, all the parts in the Erheban troupe were performed by men. Yueju troupes were the only troupes in which women performed. Nevertheless, Zhou Chunju and his wife decided to disband the Yueju troupe "Yuexian Wutai," and have their three daughters and Dongmei perform in Ye Agou's Erheban troupe. This was quite an unprecedented move since the Erheban troupe performed Kun, Luan, and Hui, but the three Zhou sisters and Lou Dongmei were trained in Yueju. And ... they were girls! "Fire and water don't mix, as incompatible as ice and hot coals." What to do?

In the fall of 1946, despite the lack of precedent for women performing in an Erheban troupe, or for an Erheban troupe to perform Yueju, the troupe began first performing one or two short Yueju pieces (Zhezi xi 折子戏), followed on the program by the usual repertoire of Erheban, Kun, Luantan, and Hui operas (Song 1983b: 55). Before long, the three sisters (Yuexian, Yuegui, and Yuexiang) together with Lou Dongmei all made the transition from Yueju to Wuju, and became the first women *huadan*, *xiaosheng*, *xiaohualian*, and *laosheng* in an Erheban troupe, greatly contributing to the troupe's success (Song 1983a: 85; Song 1983b: 55; Zhang and Hong 1985: 68).

In 1947, at the age of 18, with some ten years of performance behind her, Yuexian was already well known around Longyou, and people referred to her as the "Wantou Huadan" (弯头花旦—flexible Huadan). Wherever she performed people strained to see and hear this young phenomenon. Among the most popular of her performances was "Little Shepherd" 小放牛, in which she performed as the shepherd boy, true to life, lively and loveable (Song 1983a: 91).

Zhou Yuexian and Jiang Heyi 江和义 (1881–1964)

In October 1949, the Zhouchunju troupe was performing in Lanxi. After a performance they were eating dinner when an old beggar dressed in rags approached Yuexian asking for something to eat. Yuexian went to get him some food, and in talking to the old man discovered that his name was Jiang Heyi 江和义, that he had been an opera performer of Laosheng and Xiaosheng roles in the Gaoqiang genre, but had not worked in some ten years, and could no longer sing. He was nevertheless a mine of information, able to recite the entire texts of Gaoqiang operas *Huaiyin Ji* 槐荫记, *Hezhu Ji* 合珠记, *San Xiaozi* 三孝子, *Baiying Ge* 白鹦哥, and *Hongmei Ge* 红梅阁 among others (Song 1983b: 59).

Yuexian was delighted. The old man was a thoroughly talented old master, and she forthwith offered the old man a place in the Zhouchunju troupe, sending two troupe members to the old man's village with a sedan chair to fetch him. She bought him some new padded clothes for the winter, and discussed the situation with her parents, agreeing to give half her monthly salary to the old man. And she herself paid for a pen, ink, stone and paper for Jiang Heyi to begin putting the texts of the operas in his head to paper. Jiang Heyi was so moved by Yuexian's generosity that every night he continuously wrote out more and more of the Gaoqiang repertoire. First he "spit out" 18 Xi An Gaoqiang grand operas, before moving on to operas in the Xiwu Gaoqiang genre, and the present known repertoire of these genres is largely the result of Jiang Heyi's writing. His texts were later compiled and edited by opera scholars, with appropriate musical scoring (Song 1983b: 59–60).

During the 1950s, Zhou Yuexian kept Jiang Heyi by her side. When as Director of the Quzhou Experimental Wuju troupe in 1952, she was allocated a wage of ¥30/month, the highest wage grade of the time, she saw to it that Jiang Heyi was allocated the same wage. During this period, Jiang Heyi continued his work of recording from memory additional repertoire items. Under his guidance, Yuexian and younger sister Yuegui performed together in two of the pieces he had set down from memory, "Huaiyin Ji" and "Hezhu Ji," and won awards at several provincial performance festivals (Song 1983b: 61).

Jiang Heyi died of illness in 1964 at the age of 83. His contribution to the Wuju genre is inestimable, and Zhou Yuexian was clever enough to have perceived his potential (Song 1983b: 62).

Zhou Yuexian, the transition to PRC and the name "Wuju"

Shortly after the establishment of the PRC, on August 8, 1950, Zhou Yuexian represented her father's troupe at the Huadong Opera Reform Work cadres' meeting convened in Shanghai. Its participants included Xinxin Wutai 新新舞台 troupe's Laosheng performer and scholar Xu Xigui 徐锡贵, known in Jinhua opera circles as the "the imperial scholar Laosheng performer" (Xiucai Laosheng 秀才老生), having written a history of Jinhua Huixi (Zhang and Hong 1985: 71–2). Also present were Lanxi's Shen Ruilan 沈瑞兰, Longyou's Su Zhiyan 肃志岩 and Chen Pinlun 陈品仑, and Quzhou's Yan Shaoliang 焉绍良. Xu Xigui put forward the suggestion that Jinhua's various opera genres ought to be called "Wuju" 婺剧, and the representatives from Jinhua and Quzhou all agreed (Hong 1988: 46).

On November 19, 1950, in recognition of the meeting's consensus, Zhou Yuexian changed the name of Zhouchunju Ban 周春聚班 to Quzhou Experimental Wujutuan 衢州试验婺剧团 (Hong 1988: 46). In April 1951 Xu Xigui, following Zhou Yuexian's example, changed the name of Xinxin Wutai 新新舞 to Jinhua Prefecture Experimental Wujutuan 金华专署试验婺剧团 after which other troupes followed suit, and the name Wuju was thereby formally adopted into the lexicon of Jinhua opera troupes (Hong 1988: 46; Zhang and Hong 80–81).

Yuexian and the early years of the PRC

After more than ten years of warfare and civil war, many performance troupes had disbanded, costumes lost or destroyed, artists taken up other professions (Ge et al. eds. 1986: 101; Wang ed. 1998: 188). Many temple and Citang stages had been destroyed or converted to other functions, and rural folk often had to travel many km. to see an opera (Zhang and Hong 1985: 313).

But peace, and a modicum of stability encouraged a revival of opera, and amateur troupes began to appear, performing anti-imperialist and anti-feudal modern operas like *San Shi Chou* (三世仇 Three Generations Revenge), *Baimao Nu* (白毛女 White Haired Girl), *Qiongren Hen* (穷人恨 The Hatred of the Poor), *Li Ersao Gaijia* (李二嫂改嫁 Auntie Li Changes the Marriage Arrangements), and *Xiao Erhei Jiehun* (小二黑结婚 *Little Erhei Gets Married*) (Wang ed. 1998: 188). During this period, Dongyang county alone is reported to have had as many as 300 rural amateur troops (Zhang and Hong 1985: 12).

Jinhua had more professional opera troupes than anywhere else in the province (*Jinhua Shizhi* 1992: 996), and after the establishment of the PRC the association of professional Jinhua opera performers, the Laolang Guan, was first transformed into the Wuju Improvement Committee 婺剧改进委

员会, as the result of the Jinhua prefectural government's implementation of the Central government's "Instructions on Operatic Reform Work" promulgated in May 1951. The Wuju Improvement Committee was formally established in 1953, and despite prefectural government involvement, the Committee actually seems to have been something of a "grass-roots" organization in which the artists themselves had a good deal of control.

The Committee subsequently embarked on a systematic investigation of the repertoire of Wuju, in which Zhou Yuexian played a leading role, along with He Zhanbai 何占白, Xu Dongfu 徐东福, Chen Ping 陈平, and Nie Mei 聂梅. They saw to the collection, organization, and editing more than 860 operas and 120 individual arias into Wuju Jumu 婺剧剧目 (Wuju Repertoire) and Wuju Qupaiming 婺剧曲牌名 (Melodies of Wuju), establishing the basis for further study of the genre. In 1959, the Improvement Committee changed its name to the Jinhua Regional Opera Federation 金华地区戏曲联合会 (Zhang and Hong 1985: 310–312).

The Quzhou Experimental Wujutuan which Zhou Yuexian organized in 1950 lasted only till October 1952 when it broke up. In 1953, the three sisters (Yuexian, Yuegui, and Yuexiang) together with Jiang Heyi and others moved to Hangzhou to join the Wuju team of the Zhejiang Provincial Cultural Work Team (Wengong Tuan 文工团) (Song 1983b: 61; Zhang and Hong 1985: 167).

In February 1953 the Provincial Cultural bureau took the initiative, and with state subsidies amalgamated the new Wuju team with artists from Darongchun troupe 大荣春舞台 into the Zhejiang Province Wuju Experimental Troupe, with Zhou Yuexian as director, and Xu Dongfu 徐东福, a noted comic Xiao Hualian performer, as second in command (Zhang and Hong 1985: 167). In 1954 Yuexian and Xu Dongfu established a provincial Wuju training class to bring along a new generation of artists (Ge et al. eds. 1986: 101; Song 1983b: 64).

In August, 1954 Yuexian participated in the Zhejiang Province First Opera Festival and took a first place prize (Zhang and Hong 1985: 219). In September, 1954 she participated in the Huadong Opera "performance before fellow artists for the purpose of discussion and emulation" 观摩演出, and took a first place prize (Zhang and Hong 1985: 219). In June 1956, she became a member of the Communist Party, and from June to August of the following year went to Shanghai to study in a central-government-organized training class directed by Mei Lanfang 梅兰芳 (Song 1983b: 64).

In 1960, Chairman Mao attended a performance by the Zhejiang Wujutuan of Mudan Duike 牡丹对课 in Hangzhou, receiving several troupe members after the show and offering warm encouragement. In the fall of 1962 the Zhejiang Wujutuan performed in Beijing, winning high praise in the capital's cultural circles, and 18 performers were invited by Zhou Enlai to Zhongnanhai for extended discussions.

In 1964 the troupe's newly composed modern-themed piece *Shuang Honglian* (双红莲 Double Red Lotus) won praise at the Huadong Modern Opera Performance Festival (Ge et al. eds. 1986: 101).

During the Cultural Revolution (1966–1976), Wuju suffered a serious blow. Performances from the traditional repertoire were halted, criticized as decadent and feudal, classic specimens of the "Four Olds" needing to be "smashed." Costumes and paraphernalia were burned, the artists submitted to struggle sessions, troupes disbanded, and replaced by Mao Zedong thought propaganda teams, performing the eight revolutionary operas approved by (Mao's wife) Jiang Qing (*Jinhua Shizhi* 1992: 996; Wang ed. 1998: 188, 203).

It can only be inferred that members of the Zhou family took little or no active part in the performances or class struggle activities of the Cultural Revolution, since the sources at my disposal do not discuss the family's circumstances during the period. But after the demise of the Gang of Four, Wuju troupes revived, and by 1980 there were 11 professional county-based troupes once again performing in the province. Repertoire items that had been suppressed for ten years began to reappear. Many county cultural bureaus took measures to attract and train a new generation of Wuju performers, and at the Provincial Opera Youth Performance Festival in Hangzhou in August 1980, which included performers from Zhejiang's many local opera genres, there were more than 80 youthful Wuju performers among the prize winners. By 1982, more than 550 amateur troupes had sprung up in Jinhua (Ge et al. eds. 1986: 101).

In April 1980, in deteriorating health, Yuexian called the Zhejiang Wujutuan then performing in Hangzhou's Victory Opera House (胜利戏院 Shengli Xiyuan), saying her time was short, and if she couldn't pass on the art of her signature piece *Xueli Mei* (雪里梅 Plum in the Snow), she could never rest in peace. The troupe leaders responded immediately and sent young performer Han Jianying 韩建英 to study with her in daily sessions at Yuexian's home in Hangzhou. Yuexian survived long enough to take on two additional pupils, Wang Shiju 王世菊 from the Zhejiang provincial Kunju troupe, and 14-year-old Zhang Xiaoying 张小英 of the Yiwu Wujutuan (Song 1983b: 66–67), to whom to pass on her legacy.

Zhou Yuexian rewrites *Ya Bei Feng* (哑背疯 Mute Carries the Crazy One) as *Xueli Mei* (雪里梅 Plum in the Snow)

In 1947, when Zhou Yuexian was just 18, Zhouchunju troupe hired master Jin You 金友 from Lanxi to teach some opera favorites (Caixi 彩戏) to its performers. Master Jin recognized that Zhou Yuexian was bright, and taught her many Kun arias and pieces, including *Ya Bei Feng* (哑背疯 Mute Carries the Crazy One) which became Yuexian's signature piece.

Ya Bei Feng is said to have been present in the "hundred plays" 百戏 of the Han dynasty (206 BC–AD 220) (Zhang and Hong 1985: 5–6). It endured as a folk song and dance called *Jipin* (济贫 Come to the Aid of the Poor), and later was integrated as a short piece into the Ming dynasty Kun opera *Yiwen Qian* (一文钱 One Penny) (Song 1983b: 62).

In performance, one performer plays both roles, an old mute man carrying his young crazy wife on his back. The performer's actual face is made up as a woman, wearing the costume of the crazy wife on the upper portion of the body, and that of a mute old man on the lower portion. The upper portion of the old man's body on which she appears to be riding is composed of a false head and torso affixed to and protruding from the performer's stomach. The legs of the crazy woman are also false and similarly protrude from the performer's stomach as if attached to the woman's upper torso. Looking at the single performer, it appears as if the old man is carrying a woman on his back.

The couple (played by the single actor) begs for a living, and on the road meets a fisherman, a peasant farmer, and a Confucian scholar. None of them feel any compassion for the couple, refusing to give them any money, and each also ridicules and scolds them. Finally, the couple comes to a landlord's house, and the landlord and his servant are moved deeply, giving them ten liang of silver. The couple, with tears of joy, thanks the landlord profusely, and takes leave.

The opera's content was clearly "reactionary" from the new Communist perspective, making the ruling class look benevolent, ignoring class oppression, while painting the working classes and intellectuals in a bad light. At the time that Yuexian learned the piece from Jin You, she was not really happy with the plot, but she enjoyed performing as two people, and gave a notable performance of the piece in 1948 when the Lanxi merchants' association held a performance festival in Lanxi's Chenghuang temple (Song 1983b: 62).

After liberation in 1950, she thought that she ought to do something about the piece's dreadful content if she were going to continue to perform it in the new society. So she experimented, and first changed the relation between the two from husband/wife to father/daughter, the male from old servant-slave to hired laborer, the female from crazy wife to farm laborer's daughter. Later she changed the scene at the landlord's house to one in which the landlord gives them nothing, scolds them and shoos them away, bringing out the class contradiction. She also rechristened the opera *Xueli Mei* (雪里梅 Plum in the Snow). Audiences loved it and everywhere the troupe performed it the rural folk responded with enthusiasm (Song 1983b: 63).

During the early 1950s when she was posted to the Zhejiang Cultural Work Group, she worked with director Qian Zhangping 钱章平 making additional changes, from the original Kun style to the more accessible Luantan, and worked with members of the National Academy of Arts (Meishu Xueyuan) in Hangzhou to devise a more realistic false head and body for the father character. In April 1954, she took the piece to Beijing, and participated in the central Cultural Bureau's first National Folk Music and Dance Festival as well as several other festivals thereafter, whereupon it became known nationwide (Song 1983b: 64). In later years she continually refined *Xueli Mei*, and it has become a "jewel of the Chinese operatic world" (Song 1983b: 63–65).

It has also become a fixture performance at the Hugong temple fair, where it is performed by the Ying An troupe of Zhiying town among others as a short performance piece in entertainment of the deity rather than a full-fledged opera (Song 1983b: 62–63; Ying 1991: 48; *Yongkang Xianzhi* 1991: 604; and see Chapter 8)).

The present circumstance of Wuju

After the demise of the Gang of Four, Wuju troupes, both professional and amateur revived, and many places took measures to attract and train a new generation of Wuju performers (Ge et al. eds. 1986: 101). But the post-reform "golden age" of traditional Wuju would not be long lived, as new challenges arose. Beginning in the late 1980s with the spread of movies, cable TV, video cassettes, CDs, and DVDs of popular songs and dances, domestic as well as from Hong Kong and Taiwan and the US, the space occupied by opera in the entertainment market began to shrink in both relative and absolute terms. While tape recordings, CDs, and DVDs initially helped spread Wuju into the homes and TVs of its aficionados, the broad availability and popularity of Hong Kong and Taiwan pop music and the modern cinema have overwhelmed Wuju as a share of the entertainment market, greatly marginalizing the genre.

While there are still many talented younger performers on stage, it is becoming more and more difficult to recruit new talent. Many of the profession's backbone performers have abandoned the profession, and taken up more lucrative opportunities in commerce. Opera troupes are in decline, rural amateur troupes have become fewer in number, and according to some the quality of performances has experienced a serious slide. Nor is this crisis confined to Jinhua Wuju. The decline in audience for traditional opera is a nationwide phenomenon.

But even while the number of troupes in the Jinhua countryside is down, the opera is still a favorite of temple deities who find it entertaining, and still a factor in attracting the human crowds to rural market and temple fairs, thereby contributing to the red fire of the event (Wang ed. 1998: 188, 203; Zhang and Hong 1985: 313).

A possible hopeful sign for the future was the recent launch of a Wuju webpage (www.zj.xinhua.org/wuopera), with links to pages on famous performers, the various genres of Wuju, explanations of the verbal expressions and colloquialisms of the operatic profession, etc., although not all the links were active in 2010.

Note

1 The text of the duilian on the doorway of the carved wood furniture factory in which I did my original dissertation fieldwork in the 1970s, from which the factory took its name, Maosheng company 茂盛公司.

8 The religious dimension
The temple fair of Hugong Dadi 胡公大帝

In Chapter 3 we met the Three Buddhas and Five Marquises of Jinhua (Jinhua de san fo wu hou 金华的三佛五侯), among the latter of whom is this chapter's Hugong Dadi. The temple fair in Hugong's honor at Fangyan during the month surrounding his "birthday" on lunar 8/13 is one of the grandest in the region, and noteworthy for the popular religious dimension associated with it from the very inception of its revival, marking it as the definitive contemporary total social phenomenon.

In this chapter I first present a brief introduction of Yongkang city, and Fangyan township, the setting of the main Hugong temple and its fair. Then, I present an account of the northern Song dynasty official, Hu Ze, around whom the cult materialized, his career as an official, the process by which a posthumous demonstration of his power earned him the imperial designation "Youshun Hou" (佑顺侯 Marquis [who] Protects with Success), and ultimately his deification as Hugong Dadi. The chapter also presents a history of his temple site at Fangyan, the popular cultural performances and activities that have become associated with his temple fair centered around lunar 8/13, the geographic extent of the cult, and something of its history and contemporary circumstances/development.

In the following chapter, we will encounter Hugong again examining how he became the object of political machinations on the part of communities eager to establish themselves as stops along the pilgrimage route to worship him.

To situate the reader geographically, I first provide some background on the county/city of Yongkang, and the district of Fangyan, the central site of the annual Hugong temple fair.

Yongkang

Yongkang county/city is located in Jinhua's southeast corner about 150 km south from the provincial capital Hangzhou. It occupies an area of 1049 sq km. of the Yongkang plain bordering Wuyi county on the west, Yiwu county on the north, Dongyang and Pan An counties on the northeast, and Jinyun county on the southeast. Historically Yongkang and its fellow eastern counties of Jinhua were relatively poor in comparison to the western counties which were the more agriculturally fertile, productive and prosperous. But, as pointed out in Chapter 2, the implementation of market-driven economic reforms has been transformative. The historically, relatively backward eastern counties of Jinhua (Yongkang, Yiwu, and Dongyang) have witnessed the greatest economic dynamism and growth, far outpacing their historically more prosperous western neighbors (Lanxi, Jinhua, and Wuyi).

Yongkang county now boasts a thriving modern industrial sector in which traditional craft skills in metal work and the network of ties its residents established in their pre-revolutionary perambulations nationwide served as an important foundation. Metal work occupies a particularly prominent place in the county's economy, accounting for about 70 percent of county industrial APV which reached ¥65,700,000,000 in 2006. There are established industrial lines in machinery, metals, excavation, construction materials, chemicals, woven textiles, electrical meters and other electrical products, leather goods, umbrellas, arts and crafts products, food, and drink. The county tractor factory, electrical tools factory, machine tools factory, piston factory, and automotive electrical components factory have been designated national "key point" factories, and licensed to export (Yongkang city webpage).

No small measure of the recent economic dynamism of the Yongkang economy can be attributed to the construction in the 1990s of a branch rail line from the city of Yiwu through Yongkang and on to Wenzhou, greatly enhancing Yongkang's accessibility and transport facility.

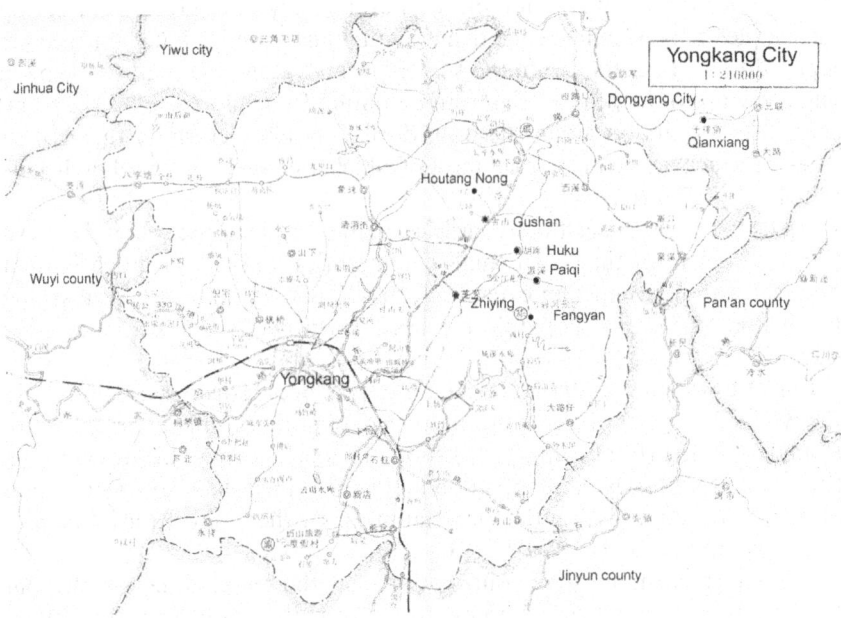

Map 8.1 Yongkang

Fangyan

Fangyan 方岩, the "first mountain of East Zhejiang," is perhaps Yongkang's most scenically stunning area, with dramatic rock formations, and many historically significant sites. Since 1984, 36 sq km surrounding the mountain have been designated a province level scenic area (风景区 fengjing qu), and its administration taken over by a bureau (管理处 guanlichu), autonomous of the township government.

Outside the scenic area, Fangyan township has experienced a certain level of industrial development, and the products of its 475 township and village factories include metal tools, hammers, saws, stainless steel tools and kitchen utensils, brass and aluminum *"huoguo"* (hot pots), knives, chains, and fencing. Export commodities include slicing machines, sand castings, and air pumps. Industrial APV surpassed ¥500,000,000 at the turn of the century, and by 2007, Fangyan's population of 25,371 had a rural per capita income of ¥4,749 (Jinhua City webpage #10).

Notwithstanding its recent industrial development, the Fangyan economy has been described as "deformed" or "distorted" by its reliance mainly on provisioning supplicants of the Hugong temple with "superstitious commodities". Nearly every establishment on Yanxia Street 岩下街, the commercial center of Fangyan, sells incense, paper, and candles, and some even rent out sacrificial articles, pig's heads and goose carcasses for temporary use and return. In addition, Fangyan boasts some 150 practitioners of the occupation of explaining and interpreting bamboo divination slip texts, who perform their service for a contribution of "whatever you wish to give." And during the temple fair season in the eighth and ninth lunar months, Fangyan becomes a paradise for beggars. From the Wufeng bridge along the road to the main entryway up to the peak of Fangyan mountain for four or five "li" (2.5 km) there are beggars all along the way, displaying one deformity or another, some of which are genuine, but "most of which are false or even self inflicted" (Hu 1991: 217–220).

Apart from the "superstitious" articles, most everything else sold in Fangyan shops comes from the Yiwu small commodities market, so much so that Fangyan can be seen as an extension of the Yiwu market. The local saying has it that "Fangyan people do business, Yiwu people collect the money" (Hu 1991: 218).

For Hu Guojun, "a distorted economy produces a distorted culture". In the whole 36 sq km of the Fangyan scenic area, he complains, there is not a single Shuhua (书画 calligraphy) shop. This area known historically as a site of great scholarly contemplation and achievement has been turned into a tourist attraction with little appreciation or further cultivation of its past scholarly traditions (Hu 1991: 218).

For Hu, the one positive contribution that the temple fair complex has brought to the Fangyan economy apart from the cultivation of popular cultural performance genres (which we will address below) is the paper flowers industry which has existed as a female sideline occupation in the area since the Qianlong period (1736–1796) of the Qing dynasty. The annual market for the flowers is always good since most of the several hundred thousand supplicants who visit Fangyan each year for Hugong's temple fair will want to take a couple home with them (Hu 1991: 220).

Wufeng Shuyuan (五峰书院 Academy of the Five Peaks)

Among the most significant historical sites of the Fangyan scenic area associated with the great scholarly tradition whose decline Hu Guojun regrets is Wufeng Shuyuan (五峰书院 Academy of the Five Peaks). Local historiography associates its establishment (c. 1180) with the southern Song dynasty scholar-politician Chen Liang 陈亮 (1143–1194), founder of the Yongkang school of neo-Confucian philosophy (Yongkang Xuepai 永康学派). Chen, a native of Yongkang, attained Zhuangyuan status (highest honors) in his performance on the imperial exams, and later became known for his espousal of a kind of utilitarianism, learning derived from deeds or practice 事功之学, in which "the Dao is in things, the Dao is in affairs" 道在物中，道在事中. He was also an accomplished poet of the Haofang (bold and unconstrained 豪放) school of the Song Ci 宋词 poetry genre (Wang ed. 1997: 8).

As local sources tell it, during the southern Song dynasty, Chen's academy, known as Wen Hui Tang 文会堂 (Literary meeting hall), attracted the foremost thinkers of his day, notable Song dynasty scholars Zhu Xi 朱熹, Lü Zuqian 吕祖谦, and Ye Shi 叶适 who came successively to visit and lecture (Hu 1997c: 281). The site assumed the name Wufeng Shuyuan during the Ming dynasty, some three centuries later, renamed by the local prefect after the five peaks (wufeng 五峰) that can be seen from its entrance: Jiming feng (鸡鸣峰 Cock's crow peak); Taohua feng (桃花峰 Peach Blossom peak); Fufu feng (覆釜峰 Overturned cauldron peak); Pubu feng (瀑布峰 Waterfall peak); and Guhou feng (固后峰 Behind the fortification peak) (Wang ed. 1997: 66).

The Academy structure was built into a cave at the base of Peach Blossom Peak, sometimes also referred to as Longevity Mountain Hollow (Shoushankeng 寿山坑), on the very spot where a century before Hu Ze had studied for the imperial examinations as a youth (Hu 1997c: 281). The "back" road up to the peak at Fangyan begins nearby, a somewhat more rugged ascent than at the main entryway.

According to local historiography, during the Zheng De reign period (1506–1521) of the Ming dynasty, local scholar Ying Shimen 应石门 (from Yongkang's Zhi Ying township) came to visit the site and, inspired by its three worthies (sanxian 三贤), Zhu 朱, Lü 吕, and Chen 陈, saw to the construction of Lize Ci (丽泽祠 Shrine of the Beautiful Pool) in the western corner of a cave, beside the water fall that drops from Pubu Feng 瀑布峰, to commemorate the three worthies, and to serve as a lecture room and accommodation for visitors. Once completed, Ying Shimen convened his contemporaries to discuss the theories of Wang Yangming, and the prefect of Jinhua, Yao Wenzhao (姚文照), kept a record of the proceedings (Wang ed. 1997: 73).

However, the story seems to have been somewhat more complicated, as Lee (2007) makes clear. According to Lee, the creation of Wufeng Academy during the Ming was undertaken in an attempt to establish the legitimacy of Wang Yangming's challenge to the orthodox neo-Confucian interpretations of Zhu Xi. Wang's emphasis on unmediated access to an inner moral source appealed to newly emerging families who were willing to challenge the cultural hegemony of established literati lineages and seize their own local cultural authority. For Lee, Ying Shimen's leadership role in establishing the Wufeng Academy was an extension of his family's cultural ambitions, since once these families had established their prestigious status locally, they sought to confirm their prestige by creating institutions of scholarly cultivation that legitimated their new ideology (Lee 2007: 70–71).

Chen Liang's designation as one of the three worthies commemorated at Lize Ci was, however, somewhat problematic. Chen Liang was something of an outlyer in the company of Zhu Xi and Lü Zuqian. Indeed, Zhu Xi had criticized Chen for his utilitarianism, and "ever since Yongkang had never been free of its label as 'a home of utilitarianism.'" Nor was Chen associated in any way with Wang Yangming's views. Those who observed the array of the spirit tablets of Zhu Xi, Lü Zuqian, and Chen Liang would surely find it incoherent, and would hardly be able to determine the academy's intellectual orientation, let alone the identity of its founders as advocates of Wang Yangming learning. Chen's elevation as a worthy thus "risked publicly misrepresenting the intellectual identity of the Academy's founders" (Lee 2007: 55).

However he did prove useful in providing the Wufeng Academy founders with a crucial historical link between Yongkang and the neo-Confucian Daoxue legacy of Zhu Xi and Lü Zuqian. No matter how problematic Chen Liang was in Daoxue terms, it was a widely known historical fact that a meeting had been held somewhere in Yongkang in which Zhu Xi, Lü Zuqian, and Chen Liang participated, even if no valid sources specify the exact location where the meeting was held, let alone establish any connection to the cave at Longevity Mountain Hollow, the actual location of Chen's Academy. Thus, in Lee's estimation, the Ming dynasty Wufeng academy's founders grafted the historical fact that the meeting had been held somewhere in Yongkang during the Song dynasty onto a "new history" of the Wufeng site (Lee 2007: 54–55).

Lee's analysis raises some doubts about the local historiography which uncritically portrays Chen Liang being enshrined as a worthy in an academy to which his own philosophy was largely irrelevant. But in any case, some time later in the fall of 1553 (Ming, Jiajing period), Prefect Yao Wenzhao returned to the site with the county magistrate, Hong Yuan 洪垣, and after inspecting the academy's premises and observing the calligraphic inscriptions of the famous scholars Zhu Xi, Lü Zuqian, and Chen Liang, ordered the construction of a two-story structure at the base of Guhou Feng 固厚峰, to commemorate four scholars of later repute, the Four sons (Si Zi 四子): Wang Yangming 王阳明, Ying Shimen 应石门, Cheng Fangfeng 程方峰, and Lu Yisong 卢一松, and named it "Fine Accommodation of the Beautiful Pool at Peach Bluff" (Tao Yan Lize Jing She 桃岩丽泽精舍). A subsequent prefect Chen Shouquan 陈受泉 provided the inscription "Wufeng Shuyuan," and the complex of buildings has been known by that name down to the present (Wang ed. 1997: 73).

From Ming times onward, Wufeng Shuyuan and its associated structures came to serve as a kind of academic temple of scholars. Every year at Chongyang festival (lunar 9/9), the Three Worthies were commemorated; on the following day, the Four Sons; and on the third day all the Confucians (诸儒). Celebrants came from far and near to attend, and Wufeng earned the nickname Jiangnan's "Little Home of Confucius" (Xiao Zou Lu 小邹鲁) (Wang ed. 1997: 73).

Due to the action of the elements over 450 years, the external appearance of the Academy is nothing like what it might have been during the Ming let alone the Song dynasty, despite its designation as a county-level historically significant site as early as 1952. During the Cultural Revolution, it also suffered vandalism at the hands of red guards (Hu 1997c: 281).

In the 1980s, a four-star hotel, the Wufeng Binguan was added to the site, an impressive string of rooms that run up the mountain slope alongside Guhou Feng, capable of accommodating several hundred guests. High-ranking notables and foreigners are generally accommodated there in their visits to the Hugong temple complex atop Fangyan. The hotel's guests take their meals in a dining room located in Luohan cave, just adjacent to and below Fine Accommodation of the Beautiful Pool, where the hotel staff is now billeted.

The saga of Hugong Dadi (Great Emperor Uncle/Count Hu; aka Hu Hou—Marquis Hu)

Hu Ze the person

Hu Ze 胡则 (963–1039), literary name Zizheng 子正, was a historic official of the northern Song dynasty (960–1126). As such, his life and career are well documented. The family home was in Yongkang's Huku town 胡库镇. His great grandfather was Hu Peng 胡彭; his grandfather was Hu Yangu 胡彦毂; and his father was Hu Chengshi 胡承师. His mother was surnamed Ying 应 (Wu 1993: 242).

The home into which Hu was born was a humble one, and his was a genuine rags to riches success story. As a youth he worked in the fields, studied crafts, and enjoyed martial arts. Growing up close to the rural people, he never lost his deep feeling and appreciation for their suffering. Thus, in his later career as an official, he was inspired to do good works on their behalf (Hu 1991: 187; Wu 1993: 242).

In AD 984, he began his studies at Fangyan, in Longevity Mountain Hollow (Shoushankeng 寿山坑), on the very site where Chen Liang would later establish his Wen Hui Tang 文会堂. In the spring of 988, Hu Ze continued his studies at Da Bei Si (大悲寺 Temple of Great Mercy) on the peak at Fangyan in the monks' residence under the tutelage of Chen Shengyu 陈生寓, a monk from Hunan. In the eighth month he qualified to go to Kaifeng to participate in the Jinshi examinations (Ying and Hu 1990: 85–86), and in AD 989, at the age of 27, he attained the Jinshi degree, the best performance by a Yongkang exam candidate since the second century AD (Hu 1991: 195). His success opened the gates to an ensuing flood of Jinshi degree holders from the Jinhua region during the Song dynasty (Hu 1997e: 284; Wang, ed. 1997: 44).

During the northern Song, the peasantry was increasingly burdened with heavy taxation, in part the result of having to finance defenses against the Jurchen/Jin who threatened from the north. Eventually the court was forced to retreat from Kaifeng to Hangzhou, inaugurating the southern Song dynasty (1127–1278). As an official during the northern Song period, Hu Ze was a reformer whose goal was to carry out benevolent government by implementing the principles of Confucius and Mencius (Hu, ed. 1987: 6). Kind and magnanimous, he spared no effort on behalf of the masses, was always honest and assiduous in the performance of his duties, and worked to bring stability to the nation (Hu 1997e: 284; Wu 1993: 244).

Hu Ze's official career during the Song dynasty

After attaining the Jinshi degree, Hu Ze served the Song emperors Taizong (AD 976–997), Zhenzong (AD 998–1022), and Renzong (1023–1064) as magistrate in ten different prefectures (jun 郡) and six different districts (lu 路), including two stints as Magistrate of Hangzhou (1026 and again in 1033) (Hu 1997e: 284). He also served in a variety of high-level administrative posts in central ministries and government boards.

In 1031, he was dispatched to Chenzhou 陈州, where he had occasion to meet renown scholar, politician, reformer Fan Zhongyan 范仲淹, who was serving as assistant prefect. Fan was 26 years younger than Hu Ze, but mutual admiration and respect had led the two to correspond before actually having met face to face. In 1021, Hu Ze sent a poem to Fan Zhongyan, who was then in an official position in Taizhou. Fan added notation for musical accompaniment and returned the poem. When they finally met in person in 1031, Fan was under censure for his attempts to implement reforms in his Chenzhou post. But notwithstanding his political difficulties, Hu Ze entertained him with the courtesies due a leading national scholar 国士, and deepened their pre-existing acquaintance into a firm friendship (Jiang n.d.a.; Ying and Hu 1990: 85–86).

In the eighth month of 1032, Hu Ze was ordered back to the capital in Kaifeng to serve in the Ministry of Public Works, and assume the rank of Scholar at the Academy of Assembled Worthies 集贤院. Fan Zhongyan was sorely disappointed that after only little more than a year, the two would be separated again, and sent his friend off with heavy heart (Jiang n.d.a). However, when in the following year Hu Ze was dispatched to Hangzhou, Fan Zhongyan was also there, and the two were reunited. Fan wrote a poem to memorialize the occasion:

> The honest and upright one once again rises to be prefect of the beautiful place in the southeast [i.e. Hangzhou], I so honor and respect him, and now we are together
> 青风又振东南美，好梦多亲咫尺颜
> Qing feng you zhen dong nan mei, hao meng duo qin zhi chi yan
> (Jiang n.d.a.)

In the first month of 1034, Fan Zhongyan was dispatched to Mu Zhou (modern-day Jian De county in Zhejiang) as a prefect, and to send him off Hu Ze accorded him lavish hospitality. The two took a boat ride on West Lake, and drank to each other's honor and mutual admiration (Jiang n.d.a.).

It was in 1032, during the reign of Song emperor Renzong, that the famous memorial to the emperor to commute the head tax (身丁税 shending shui) on Jinhua and Quzhou prefectures during a serious drought is recorded in the Song dynastic history (Wang, ed. 1997: 44). This event of Hu Ze's official career is always highlighted as a symbol of his righteousness, and the basis for the construction of a shrine in his honor at Fangyan, and his later deification as Hugong Dadi (Hu 1997e: 284; Wu 1993: 244).

However, writing skeptically in 1929, Cao Songye allows that the people of Jinhua and Quzhou may well have honored a beneficent official by constructing a shrine at Fangyan, but refers to the head tax story as a myth most likely fabricated by the populace and added to Hu's legacy after his death, in the years following the shrine's construction (Cao 1929a: 26).

Perhaps addressing this very claim, Hu Guojun has actually made an attempt to verify the head tax story by examining the records of the period in search of such a memorial. He concluded only that there was a "distinct possibility" that the conditions of the time might have prompted an official like Hu Ze to have made such a petition to the emperor (Hu 1991: 187–189), but he finds no smoking gun.

In a similar effort to find some basis for the story, the modern Yongkang county gazetteer (1991: 714) suggests that the memorial in question referred to a drought in the Huai River region more broadly, and requested that the entire Jiangnan region be forever exempt from the head tax. If that were indeed the case, then the fact that the inhabitants of Jinhua and Quzhou built a shrine in Hu's honor at Fangyan, may well have been a paean to the hometown boy whose petition was aimed to relieve the suffering of the broader populace of Jiangnan, not just the specific suffering of the people of Jinhua and Quzhou.

However, the citation of the Song History (Notes of the Renzong period 仁宗本纪 cited in Wang, ed. 1997: 44) is explicit in its reference to Wuzhou (Jinhua) and Quzhou which would seem to make Cao's skepticism and Hu's equivocation over the existence of the memorial, as well as the gazetteer's speculations as to its target, moot. There does in fact seem to be historical evidence for the memorial in question addressed specifically to the sufferings of Jinhua and Quzhou.

In 1033, in the fourth month, Hu was promoted to Vice Director of the Ministry of Punishments, and Magistrate for Hangzhou prefecture for the second time. In that position, he invited Fan Zhongyan to membership in the register of Hangzhou notable scholars (奏乞余杭州 学名额表) (Ying and Hu 1990: 85–86).

In 1037, Hu was promoted to Vice Director of the Military Board and served there till his retirement a year later at the end of a career of more than 40 years. He took up residence in Hangzhou where he died in 1039, and was buried at the foot of Lion Cliff mountain (Shifeng Shan 狮峰山) in nearby Longjing. Fan Zhongyan wrote the memorial inscription on his grave. (Wang, ed. 1997: 44; Wu 1993: 242; YKXZ 1991: 714).

> Entered [service] with merit, retired with longevity, righteousness worthy of recording, a rock against corruption, his 100 years of deeds, ah, will last for 1,000.
> 进以功，退以寿，义可书，石不朽，百年之为，兮，千载后.
> (Wu 1993: 244)[1]

The Fang La uprising and Hugong's deification

Some time during the decade after Hu Ze's death in 1039, a shrine was constructed in his honor alongside Da Bei Si 大悲寺 (Temple of Great Mercy) on the peak at Fangyan where he studied as a youth, perhaps in appreciation of his beneficence in office as exemplified in the head tax memorial (Hu 1995: 2). In 1065 (during the reign of northern Song emperor Yingzong), Da Bei Si burnt down and was rebuilt and renamed Guang Ci Si 广慈寺 (Temple of Broad Compassion) (Hu 1991: 185; Hu 1997d: 283; Wu 1993: 245).

Some decades thereafter Hugong's spirit is said to have played a role in the suppression of the Fang La peasant uprising which broke out in 1120 toward the end of the Northern Song dynasty (960–1126). The local manifestation of the uprising in the Yongkang area was the peasant rebellion led by Mdm. Chen Shisi (陈十四娘娘; sometimes also known as Chen Yisi 陈一四), who used Fangyan as a mountain stronghold.

While holed up in Fangyan, Mdm. Chen is said to have had a dream in which Hu Ze appears, and foretells her defeat. In the dream Mdm. Chen observed a sage (Hu Ze) watering horses at Tian Chi (Heaven Pool) on the peak at Fangyan. The horses drank and drank till there was no water left. Tian Chi was a pool one mu in area, a beautiful site supposedly created by the goddess Queen Mother of the West (Xi Wangmu) during a visit to Fangyan. One of its remarkable characteristics was that it never ran dry and never flooded, regardless of the weather. Chen Shisi's troops relied on the pond for sustenance and relief, day and night. When she awoke from the dream, she went to inspect the pond and found that it had indeed dried up. Her followers were shocked and panicked, and in subsequent days defeated (Hu 1997e: 284).

Thus is Hu Ze said to have had a supernatural hand in the final defeat of Chen Shisi. When the broader Fang La uprising was ultimately suppressed some years thereafter in 1123, "local officials" requested that emperor Song Huizong (1101–1125) recognize Hu Ze's supernatural assistance. Song Huizong complied by conferring on him the title of Youshun Hou 佑顺侯 Marquis [who] Protects with Success) (Wu 1993: 244), "Assisting the emperor to destroy the great threat" 助王师殄灭巨关, simultaneously recognizing Hu Ze as "Deity of Fangyan" 方岩神, (Hu 1997a: 156), and ordering the construction of an entirely new shrine at Fangyan in his honor (Wang, ed. 1997: 40; Wu 1993: 245; Ying and Hu 1990: 78).

In 1161 (during the reign of Southern Song emperor Song Gaozong), Hu Ze's fourth-generation descendant Hu Yanzhi was appointed magistrate of Jian An county, and petitioned the court to renew its recognition of the shrine at Fangyan where his ancestor was worshipped. In the second month of the next year (1162), Song Gaozong complied, making a gift of a plaque/screen inscribed with the characters He Ling (赫灵 conspicuous efficacy) in his own hand, and ordered the repair and refurbishing of the shrine. The investiture documents read in part: "excellent in responding with good fortune and bounty; efficacy manifest everywhere" (嘉应福泽，灵显极于) (Wang ed. 1997: 28; 40).

In the ensuing years, however, He Ling Ci deteriorated, and Hu Ze's *pusa* was moved into Guang Ci Si, and placed in front of Da Xiong 大雄 in the rear hall. He Ling Ci continued to decay until it had disappeared entirely, and Hugong turned from "guest to host" in Guang Ci Si, gradually replacing Da Xiong as principle deity in the rear hall (Wang ed. 1997: 40).

During the reign of Southern Song emperor Lizong (Chun You period 1241–1252), Hu Ze was accorded further posthumous nobility with the addition of the honorific "gong" (公 – Count) to his name. And it was also in this period that the title "xian ying" (显应 "manifesting response") was conferred on him, a clear reference back to characters in the investiture documents of Song Gaozong (Wang ed. 1997: 28). The temple at his gravesite in Longjing on the outskirts of Hangzhou was renamed "Xianying" Miao at the time (Hu 1995: 3). Later during emperor Lizong's reign (Baoyou period 1253–1258) Hu Ze was accorded the further posthumous honorific "zhong you" (忠佑 loyal protector) (Wang ed. 1997: 28).

The final steps by which he came to acquire the title Dadi (Great Emperor), reserved for only the most powerful deities, are obscure, though the designation does not seem to have involved any further imperial recognition, but rather to have been a product of popular adoration. In any event, this final step in his deification was surely completed by the Tongzhi reign period (1862–1875) of the Qing dynasty when Ying Baoshi (1821–1890), a Yongkang native posted to Jiangsu province, wrote of him in his "Notes on the repair of the Hugong temple."

> The fragrance of longevity incense, ah, [has lasted for] 800 years,
> He attained the status of Count and Marquis, and is called Emperor".
>
> 寿馨香兮八百载，
> 进公侯而称帝
>
> Shou xinxiang xi babai zai,
> jin gong hou er cheng di
>
> (Wang ed. 1997: 28)

The Hugong temple at Fangyan: the cult center

From Wufeng Shuyuan to the "main gateway" up Fangyan mountain is about a 3 km walk. There is also a "back" way up the mountain that begins just behind the Shuyuan, somewhat steeper in ascent, which meets up with the "front way" just before the final ascent up to Heaven's Gate (Tian Men) via Flying Bridge (Fei Qiao).

The main gateway at the foot of Fangyan is at the end of a long recently constructed plaza, on the southern end of which there towers a great green stone screen/wall, He Ling Zhaobi (赫灵照壁 screen of conspicuous efficacy), 12.7 m. wide and 7.28 meters high. On the screen is a re-creation in huge gold characters of the inscription He Ling (conspicuous efficacy) in the hand of Song emperor Gaozong. There are stairs and railings up to a platform just in front of the inscription, a popular place for visitors to take souvenir photos (Wang ed. 1997: 28).

Through the entrance gate, on the way up the mountain, the first landmark one encounters is the flower market at "Dismount spring" (Xiama quan 下马泉). Constructed in 1986, the covered market is some 60 m long on a site with a spring that traditionally was a stopping point for watering horses, for those lucky enough to ride (Wang ed. 1997: 29).

Further on, about half way up the mountain trail to the peak, is Luohan ancient cave, surrounded by a grove of maples. Near the western wall of the cave is an ancient well, called "Flood Dragon Spring" (Jiao Long Quan 蛟龙泉), the water of which is sweet and deep. It is said that when Chan Buddhist master Zheng De first climbed Fangyan in the ninth century, it was at Luohan ancient cave that he first rested, and later established an altar in the cave for the presentation of offerings to the 18 Luohan (Wang ed. 1997: 30–33).

From the cave's entrance up to "Flying Bridge" (Fei Qiao 飞桥) there are more than 100 stone steps, called Bai Bu Jun (百步峻 100 step mountain).

At the top of the stairs is the four sided "Step on the Cloud pavilion" (步云亭 Buyun Ting) where supplicants can stop and take a breather, rest their legs, look into the distance, and admire the lovely scenery. The Pavilion bears the inscription "Mingshan Huofo" (名山活佛 famous mountain living Buddha), and a painting of the Eight Immortals crossing the sea decorates the ceiling (Wang ed. 1997: 32).

From Buyun Ting on up a very steep road about 100 m or so one arrives at Fei Qiao (飞桥 Flying Bridge), one of the most scenically beautiful spots in Fang Yan. It was originally a tortuous plank path of stone and wood, one meter wide, built along the face of a cliff, a deep gully dropping off to the west. From the foot of the mountain, Fei Qiao is said to have the appearance of the sash of a female immortal. Before liberation in 1949, because of many years of neglect, the bridge was blocked and cut off and the site considerably deteriorated. In 1962 the Yongkang county government raised funds to rebuild Feiqiao, widening the pathway to 2.5 m, and reinforcing it with steel and concrete, making the temple on the peak at Fangyan once again more widely accessible. But the inscription commemorating the bridge's original construction by a trust of the Lü family, Lü Liugeng Tang 吕留耕堂 is now difficult to locate (Wang ed. 1997: 34).

Heaven's Gate (Tian Men 天门)

At the upper end of Fei Qiao at the end of a 180 degree turn on its final ascent are two huge boulders, between which one "passes through" (tou guan 透关) in a northerly direction, proceeding up through an octagonal stone Ting on which the characters "Heaven's Gate" (Tian Men 天门) are inscribed (Wang ed. 1997: 33–34).

The Palace of the Four Heaven Kings 天王殿

The Palace of the Four Heaven Kings 天王殿 is located just behind the narrow passage at Heaven's Gate (Tian Men 天门). It is a double-eaved structure in the form of a covered corridor (lang 廊), some six meters high, through which the path passes, and on either side of which are giant sculptures of the Four Heavenly Kings, two on each side. They are known colloquially as the Four Great Jin Gang (金刚 Buddhist Warrior Attendants), or the Four Celestial Kings who Protect the World (Hu Shi Si Tianwang 护世四天王), but before their "conversion" to Buddhism, and integration into the Chinese Buddhist pantheon, they were said to have been Daoist evil demons, or in another version four brothers who guarded the "pass of beautiful dreams" 佳梦关, known as Moli Qing 魔礼青, Moli Hong 魔礼红, Moli Hai 魔礼海, and Moli Shou 魔礼寿 (Wang ed. 1997: 35).

Each has charge of a particular direction, and is associated with a particular color, and a particular "weapon." When Chan Buddhist master Zheng De began construction of the temple Da Bei Si, the four great heavenly kings came to Fangyan to demand that he build a palace for them at Tian Men so that they could have a place to reside and feast.

Zheng De saw the weapons that the four kings carried with them and insisted in turn that:

> Eastern "support the nation" heaven king 东方持国天王, whose armor was white, remove the strings from his Pipa lest he play it without restraint and release wind and fire;
>
> Southern heaven king "of increase" 南方增长天王, whose armor was blue, discard the scabbard of his precious sword so as to conveniently have its magic power at hand to punish evil doers, and turn them to dust;
>
> Western "wide eyes" heaven king 西方广目天王, whose armor was red, remove the scales from his snake, lest it escape and do harm to the people;
>
> Northern "all hearing" heaven king 北方多闻天王, whose armor was green, remove the ribs from his umbrella so that it would not cover the heavens and blacken the sky.

Down to this day, the four weapons of the heaven kings of Fangyan are a pipa without strings, a sword without a scabbard, a snake without scales, an umbrella without ribs, and thus they are referred to as the "Four Withouts" (Si wu 四无) (Wang ed. 1997: 35).

There is an associated tale of one Ji Gong 济公, who came along to Fangyan from Hangzhou's Lingyin Temple. When he had passed through Tian Men, he noticed that the Palace of the Four Heaven Kings was full of garbage, so he got a broom and began to sweep it up. When he got to the feet of the Four Heaven Kings, they ignored him and continued to sit.

Ji Gong got angry: "With all these eight feet blocking the way, who can sweep up around here." The Four Heaven Kings thought no harm in complying, and ultimately realizing they were in the presence of a living Buddha, obediently each lifted a leg. When Jigong was finished sweeping and left, he forgot to tell them to put down their feet, and to this day, each still sits with one leg raised (Hu 1997d: 283; Wang ed. 1997: 35–36; Ying and Hu, eds. 1990: 87).

Heaven Street 天街

One emerges from Heaven's Gate and the Palace of the Heavenly Kings out onto Heaven Street 天街, and on festival days one is greeted by the tones of a Suona (Chinese oboe), played by a welcoming gate keeper posted just outside. The walk along Heaven Street is some 250 m to the temple entrance. Along the left, the mountain slopes down, but along the right (mountain side) of the street there are a series of shops selling religious articles, incense, candles, joss paper, ceramic figures of the Buddha, etc.; other shops dispensing food and drink, mainly Yongkang delicacies—doufu hua 豆腐花, meat stuffed pastry 肉麦饼 (said to have been a favorite of Hu Ze's), fried rice noodle 粉干, etc.; and still others dealing in tourist items—mainly children's toys, stuffed animals, pecking roosters, frog whistles, somersaulting monkeys, bamboo flutes, wooden "precious" swords, colorful paper flowers to give to the children of friends and neighbors upon return home, so-called "Fangyan Goods" (Fangyan Huo 方岩货) (Eberhard 1970: 38; Wang ed. 1997: 37; Wu Gangji 1993: 249).

The Hugong temple complex

After a brief walk along Heaven Street, one arrives at the Hugong temple complex of Fangyan, occupying some 4000 sq m. The complex consists of four primary structures, the first of which, the entry pavilion (Guoting 过厅), is decorated with the characters "Hugong Shrine" (Hugong Ci 胡公祠) (Hu 1997e: 284).

Passing through the entry hall, one arrives at the main palace, Da Dian 大殿 which is divided into front, middle and back "jin" (sections), each separated by a courtyard (heaven well "tianjing" 天井). In the front hall, Mi Le 弥勒 (Maitreya) is the host Buddha, and one can also make offerings there to Weituo 韦陀, guardian of the dharma. Guanyin Pusa (观音菩萨, the Goddess of Mercy) is the host of the middle hall. Historically, the rear hall was the Palace of Da Xiong (大雄宝殿 Da Xiong Bao Dian), Buddhist sovereign of the western paradise, on each side of whom were nine honored Luohan, 18 in all, each sculpted in a distinctive pose (Hu 1997d: 283; Wang, ed. 1997: 49). But over the years, and in the post-Cultural Revolution reconstruction of the temple, Hugong came to replace Da Xiong as the principle deity of the rear hall, in the center of which now stands a colorful statue of Hu Ze, five meters tall, and on the east and west walls of which are eight murals depicting events from Hu Ze's life (Hu 1997d: 283; Wang, ed. 1997: 41).

Figure 8.1 Hugong temple: Fangyan

164 *Unraveling the total social phenomenon*

To the right (east) of the entry hall as one faces the entrance to the complex, there is a sutra tower, a Chan 禅 room of contemplation, a small dormitory, a kitchen, and other structures (Hu 1997d: 283). And directly to the left of the main palace bordering on its west wall is an open square surrounded in part by a connected pavilion housing noodle shops, souvenir shops and sheltered eating areas. The square is the site where an unending stream of Ying An troupes perform martial arts, and dances and songs to entertain Hugong during his temple fair in the eighth and ninth lunar months.

The rear hall of the main palace is situated some ten meters in front of a substantial cave, about 19 m wide and 11 m deep, known colloquially as the "Lion's mouth." Built right into the cave is the Screen Pavilion (Pingfeng Ge 屏风阁), in which the primary altar to Hugong, the Hugong Palace (胡公殿) is located, with a carved camphor wood statue of a seated Hugong Dadi—square head, large ears, red face, and long beard.

Behind the seated statue there was originally a very deep well, known colloquially as the "opening of the Lion's throat" (Hu 1997e: 284; Wang, ed. 1997: 40). The Hugong palace in Pingfeng Ge is where the incense and fire is most intense, and was the only "religious" shrine on the site to escape the vandalism of the cultural revolution (Wang ed. 1997: 41).

The present Hugong Ci on Fangyan peak is built on the site of the early Buddhist temple, Da Bei Si 大悲寺 (Temple of Great Mercy), constructed in AD 850 during the Tang dynasty (fourth year of Xuanzong), associated

Figure 8.2 Hugong Dadi: Fangyan

The religious dimension: Hugong Dadi temple fair 165

with the Zhejiang-centered Tiantai Guoqing Buddhist sect (天台 国清) (Wang ed. 1997: 49). In 1065 (during the reign of the northern Song emperor Yingzong), Temple of Great Mercy (Da Bei Si) burnt down and was rebuilt and renamed Guang Ci Si 广慈寺 (Temple of Broad Compassion). The temple enjoyed its most prosperous time during the Ming dynasty (1368–1644), when there were more than 500 resident monks, but during the late Qing, the number of resident monks at Guang Ci Si gradually declined (Hu 1991: 185; Hu 1997e: 284; Hu 1997d: 283; Wang ed. 1997: 49; Wu 1993: 245).

Hugong and the Guomindang

During the anti-Japanese war, the Zhejiang Nationalist provincial government was forced to flee a soon to be occupied Hangzhou, and ultimately located its headquarters in exile at Fangyan in January 1938, more remote from possible Japanese attack. Headquarters were set up at Fine Accommodation of the Beautiful Pool near to the Wufeng Academy at the base of the mountain.

But even before that, some prominent Guomindang personalities became acquainted with Hugong and his powers, and maintained relations with his temple. It is said that on December 12, 1936 on the evening before the Xi An incident, Chiang Kaishek's first wife Mao Fumei had a nightmare in which Chiang Kaishek was kidnapped in a forest by more than ten armed soldiers. In her dream there suddenly descended from heaven a red faced, bearded and robed deity/immortal whom she vowed to reward if her husband were freed. After the Xi An incident occurred, and Chiang was indeed kidnapped and ultimately freed unharmed, it was determined that the deity in her dream was none other than Hugong. So on Chiang's next birthday in February 1937, Ms. Mao traveled from Ningbo to Fangyan to fulfill her vow.

Escorted by the *laoban* of the inn on Yanxia street where she stayed, she rode a sedan chair up the mountain, kowtowed to Hugong, and draped a dragon cloak on the *pusa* of Hugong. She hung two great Buddha curtains in front of Hugong Dian on which the image of a dragon chasing a pearl was embroidered in gold thread, and donated a huge sum of money to Guang Ci Si. The great Buddha curtain and the dragon cloak were later stored at the inn where she had stayed, but were confiscated by red guards during the Cultural Revolution and destroyed (Wang ed. 1997: 44).

In another version of the story, just as Ms. Mao was preparing to leave Ningbo to deliver the cloak to Hugong in person, she was killed in a Japanese bomb attack. So it fell to her son Jiang Jingguo to return from Russia to fulfill his mother's vow, delivering the cloak to Fangyan's Hugong temple (Ying and Hu, eds. 1990: 133).

Hugong and the People's Republic

Since the founding of the People's Republic in 1949, worship of Hugong was subject to all the administrative and legal measures adopted to wipe out "superstition." While the effect of such measures on people's belief and devotion is said to have been minimal, such characterizations are usually made in the context of the broad revival of his worship in the present. It is my impression that worship of Hugong Dadi was not at its greatest strength, even before the onset of the cultural revolution in the mid-1960s.

However, one significant event contributed to Hugong being treated differently than other deities by Communist authorities before, and by Red Guards during, the Cultural Revolution. It occurred on August 21, 1959, after the conclusion of the Communist Party conference at Lushan. For reasons known only to himself, Chairman Mao Zedong took advantage of the fact that his train back to Beijing passed through Jinhua, to stop and call a meeting of local officials. Lushan of course was the meeting at which the Chairman was forced to endure criticism for the failure of the Great Leap Forward from Marshall Peng Dehuai, so he must not have been in very good humor. In any case, upon hearing that agricultural production in the Jinhua region had recovered, that markets had made a come back, that cigarettes, soap, and other daily use commodities were once again available, he relaxed considerably.

He turned to Yongkang county party secretary Ma Yunsheng, and asked: "What is the most famous thing in Yongkang?"

Secretary Ma answered without hesitation: "The ginger of Wuzhi Yan."

Mao Zedong nodded but replied: "Nah! It's not the ginger of Wuzhi Yan. Don't you [guys] have a Fangyan mountain? And on Fangyan mountain there is a Hugong Dadi, for whom the incense and fire are never ending. Now that's the most famous thing in Yongkang."

He continued: "Actually, Hugong was not a Buddha, nor a deity. He was a man, an enlightened official of the northern Song. He did many good things for the people, and thus the people commemorate him.". Finally, Mao Zedong earnestly and sincerely encouraged those assembled to remember Hugong as a model for their own performance:

> 为官一任，造福一方 (when an official is appointed, he should bring benefits).

Apparently, there was no irony intended, even given the disasters of the Great Leap Forward for which he had just been taken to task. In any event the quotation is engraved on a wall to the west of the entryway to the Hugong temple at Fangyan, 4 × 6 m, constructed and installed in 1996 (Wang ed. 1997: 48).

Hugong and the Cultural Revolution

I had always puzzled over conflicting reports regarding the fate of Fangyan's Hugong temple during the Cultural Revolution. On the one hand I had heard that it had been leveled, and its timbers used in the construction of housing for county officials (Fieldnotes 10/4/98). On the other, I had heard that the Hugong temple was spared vandalism because of the high regard in which he was held by the broad masses (repeated in Hu 1997d: 283). Chairman Mao's evocation of Hugong as an exemplary official gave the latter version some additional credibility.

It now seems to me that the leveling of the "Hugong" temple which occurred at Fangyan referred to Guang Ci Si, the Buddhist temple on the peak at Fangyan, in the rear hall of which Hugong had indeed replaced Da Xiong as principle deity. Hu Guojun has written that in the wake of the Cultural Revolution the peak at Fangyan was just "one great empty space" (Hu ed. 1987: 6–7), so it seems clear that the Hugong hall of Guang Ci Si was indeed leveled, whereas the principal altar to Hugong in the cave behind the temple might well have escaped vandalism, for reasons other than the simple difficulty of tearing down a cave.

The present temple at Fangyan with its entryway and three halls was rebuilt on the leveled remains of Guang Ci Si, beginning in 1984 when Fangyan was designated a province level scenic area. Construction was completed and the temple opened to the public in October 1988, grand in scale, and classical in style (Hu 1997d: 283; Wang, ed. 1997: 41).

More than likely due to the praise of Hu Ze by Chairman Mao, the Hugong temple fair at Fangyan was one of the earliest fairs with religious content to revive under the policies which gave secular market fairs license to operate. Once the rebuilding of the temple at Fangyan had been completed in 1988 with a dominant Hugong theme, towns throughout Jinhua set about restoring their community's Hugong temples, and reinstituting their annual temple fairs on Hugong's birthday, with the usual expanded market and popular cultural performance genres, and the attendant ritual observances and processions of spiritual renewal to the cult center in Fangyan.

Rituals of worship and performance at the Fangyan Hugong Miaohui

Supplicants of course come to Fangyan to worship Hugong, and perhaps make a vow (xuyuan 许愿), or fulfill a vow (huan yuan 还愿) previously made, to reciprocate a favor from the deity with a donation to the temple, the sponsoring of an opera performance, or some other act of charity.

Some supplicants may come prepared to sleep a night in the presence of Hugong so as to prompt a dream (Kaoshan Sumeng 靠山宿梦 or Kaomiao 靠庙). Every year during the temple fair the entire grounds on the peak of Fangyan is crowded with "kaoshan" supplicants, almost exclusively women, from Yongkang, Dongyang, Wuyi, Yiwu, and Jinhua (Hu 1991: 211). For three days prior, supplicants eat only vegetarian food, refrain from sex, and bathe to cleanse themselves before departure. Supplicants must arrive at the peak during the daylight hours, and return home at day break of the next day. They generally carry their own sleeping mats from home, but these can also be rented from the monks of the temple. They also carry gongs and drums, flutes and stringed instruments, Hugong banners and yellow parasols, firecrackers, crowns for Hugong and his wife, candles and incense, sacrificial goods, cakes and fruits. As they walk, they strike the 'wood fish' (*muyu*), or a chime, chanting the Hugong sutra, in groups of as many as 300 (Wu 1993: 251).

They camp out on the peak with the goal of evoking a dream in which Hugong might appear, so that they might communicate with him, tell him of their hardships, seek his assistance in overcoming them, or simply in insuring good luck, prosperity and long life, favorable winds and timely rains, the birth of a son, etc.

Upon awakening in the morning, the cakes and fruits the Kaoshan supplicants have brought along are divided among their companions to form ties of affection and friendship. The practice is called jieyuan (结缘 assemble the fate; same yuan as in yuanfen 缘分—fate that brings people together). Or one may divide the Jieyuan cakes and fruits among the children "spreading the fortune and fate around" (fuyuan puji 福缘普及). After returning home, any left over paper or incense is used to make offerings to the stove god, or the god of wealth, called "return home incense" (huitou xiang 回头香) (Hu 1991: 211; JHFSZ 1984: 147; Wu 1993: 250).

Kaoshan Sumeng may also be performed throughout the year, on the first and fifteenth day of each lunar month, either at a Hugong temple or at the temples of other deities as well (Fieldnotes 10/2/98 Huku).

Historically, Confucian commentators railed against such practices largely because they involved large numbers of unsupervised women out in the wilds in the dead of night (Zhao n.d.). In condemning similar practices in other parts of China, such commentators complained "that almost all the women who went to the temple were those who had failed to produce a child after marriage." In addition to burning incense and silent prayer . . . they would "wear bright and eye-catching dresses, and display themselves without restraint," looking for a man with whom to make love. "They would not exchange names and would say good by when the night was over . . ." (Zhao n.d.: 3, 15).

While I have no evidence of such practices taking place during Kaoshan at Hugong's temple fair, the custom of passing the night in the presence of the deity would seem nevertheless to have been common enough in China historically to draw criticism from orthodox Confucian commentators.

Other supplicants come to seek the protection of the deity for sons and grandsons (tuobi zisun 托庇子孙). In Yongkang and neighboring counties those who attend the Hugong temple fair will always bring young children along. On the evening before departure, the child is bathed and informs Hugong of his impending arrival in Fangyan to pay respects and present incense. On the road, should the child utter any disrespectful or unlucky words, then his or her mouth must immediately be wiped with a tissue, in imitation of wiping his behind, so as to confound the one emission with the other. After entering the Hugong temple the child must once again wash his face and hands, before it can accompany an adult to present incense, address Hugong as "qinye" (亲爷—grandpa), and attain Hugong's protection in growing up quickly, studying well, and insuring a happy future (Hu 1991: 214).

Local boys in the Yiwu area, having gone through the capping ceremony at the age of 20, would go to Fangyan where Hugong studied as a youth to pay respects to (bai 拜) Hugong, while seeking his blessing (YWFSZ 142–143).

Nearly everyone who goes to the Fangyan temple will take the time to divine their fate using bamboo slips (Qiujian Wenyun 求签问运). After paying their respects to Hugong, a cup full of divination slips is shaken continuously until one slip emerges and drops to the ground. The supplicant takes the slip to the divination tables against the back wall of the rear palace, facing the mouth of the cave, where it is exchanged for a corresponding printed text, which may then be interpreted by an attendant for a fee (Hu 1991: 215). During my visit to the Fangyan temple fair in 1998, one divination table among six or so collected ¥1,300 during one day of operation, all of which goes to support the temple (Fieldnotes 10/3/98 Fangyan).

The divination poems/texts of the Hugong temple at Fangyan are said to have been composed by none other than southern Song dynasty philosopher/scholar, Chen Liang. There are about 100 different interpretive poems, each consisting of four seven-character lines. An accompanying explanation follows a pattern characteristic of Buddhist scripture, four-character lines in four line stanzas (Hu 1991: 215; 1993).

Each poem falls into one of seven categories of favorableness and is marked as such:

> double high, high, middle high, middle, middle low, low, and double low.
> 上上, 上, 中上, 中, 中下, 下, 下下
> shangshang, shang, zhongshang, zhong, zhongxia, xia, xiaxia

While one can judge one's fate in general from the category to which one's poem belongs, the texts themselves are often obscure, and hard for most people to understand. Thus, one seeks out the assistance of the attendants at the divination tables in interpreting the more detailed significance of the text in regard to one's fate.

Yet another reason people attend the Hugong temple fair is to seek his assistance in bringing rain. In theory one should ask the Dragon King for rain, but in the Yongkang area when the common folk encounter drought, they most often turn to Hugong (Hu 1991: 216).

Many of these ritual activities can also be accomplished outside the temple fair period. Indeed, there is hardly a day when Fangyan's Hugong temple grounds are empty (Hu 1991: 216). But the most elaborate and highly organized activity at the Fangyan temple, exclusive to the Hugong temple fair period, are the performances of Ying An (greet/welcome the deity) troupes, with martial arts (Luohan Ban) and cultural arts (song and dance) components. Sponsored by local village Hugong Associations, they perform in the square adjacent to the Hugong temple on the peak of Fangyan.

Greet/welcome the Deity (Ying An 迎案) performances are the raison d'être for the Hugong temple fair, the very heart of the fair (Hu 1991: 202). The performances in entertainment of the deity (Yu Shen 娱神) commence on lunar 8/1, when the Ying An troupe from Hu Ze's native village of Huku ceremonially opens Heaven's Gate to begin the temple fair at Fangyan, and the performances continue daily through two high tides, lunar 8/13 (Hugong's birthday) and lunar 9/9 (Chongyang festival).

Ying An troupes are composed of three parts:

- the deity niche (shen kan 神龛) or dragon pavilion (longting 龙庭), in which a statue (pusa 菩萨) of Hugong is carried on the shoulders of a single individual;
- a martial (wu 武) escort of Luohan Ban composed of strong young men, to serve as protectors of the deity (Wuhu Shen 武护神) and carry the flags and weapons up the mountain to perform for Hugong;
- a cultural (wen 文) escort of song and dance troupes composed of men and women who perform in their colorful costumes to "culturally entertain the deity." (Wenyu shen 文娱神)

Altogether, a Ying An troupe might include 200 people or more, old and young, male and female (Hu 1997a: 156).

Figure 8.3 Pusa visiting: Fangyan

The limitations of space on the peak, and the narrowness of the trail up the mountain require some restriction on the numbers of people the site can accommodate on any given day. So there is a schedule for the troupes of the various villages to climb the mountain and perform for Hugong which has gradually become formalized over the years through customary practice. During the Republican period in the 1920s that schedule was already being printed in a handbook for the benefit of supplicants (Hu 1991: 197).

Nowadays, there are many Hugong Associations wanting to come to Fangyan on lunar 8/13, Hugong's supposed birthday, but only a privileged 72 are so scheduled, among them Houtang Nong village for whom Hugong is known as Gu Ye 姑爷 (husband of a woman of my lineage; in-law) (Hu 1991: 216). The others must be satisfied with coming to perform on other days of the eighth and ninth months, through to Chongyang Festival, lunar 9/9. On Chongyang the number of Luohan Ban and song and dance troupes performing once again reaches a high tide, with as many as 50 different villages represented. In the days between 8/1 and 9/9, some 10 or so troupes per day get their chance to "entertain the deity" (Hu 1991: 196; 1997a: 157).

Hu Gong Associations (Hu Gong Hui 胡公会)

The activities of Ying An troupes are generally organized by village Hugong Associations (Hugong Hui 胡公会) which take charge of the entire cycle of preparations and pilgrimage to Fangyan. An excellent account of the activities of the Hugong Association of Houtang Nong village 后塘弄村 and its preparations for participation in the Hugong temple fair in 1947 is provided in Hu (1991: 200ff) and Wu (1993: 254–258). Its activities are exemplary of the more than 1,000 such associations in Yongkang and the surrounding region which came back to life in the 1980s (Wu 1993: 258).

Houtang Nong, lies some 20 km northeast of the Yongkang county town. It was founded during the Song dynasty in the year 1257, and in 1993 had a population of some 750 households and 3500 people. Its Hugong Association was first organized during the Wanli period (1573–1619) of the Ming dynasty, from which time it has enjoyed a privileged position among other Hugong Associations (Wu 1993: 255), perhaps as the result of its claim to be an inlaw of Hugong, or its possession of several items of ceremonial paraphernalia donated to the association by a retired official of the Cheng family, Mr. Cheng Zhengyi.

After his stint in office, Mr. Cheng brought back with him to the village two bronze gongs, the navels of which were said to have been cast of gold, and three iron cannons, which he donated to the Houtang village Hugong Association. They became known as the "Hugong gongs" and "Hugong cannons," irreplaceable heirlooms of the village, something that no other Hugong Association could claim. During the Cultural Revolution, the two gongs were sold for scrap by the rebel Red Guards, but the three cannons are still preserved. And now they have been put to use again at every stage of the preparation and performance of the rituals of the Hugong temple fair. They are fired three times on the morning of lunar 8/1 when the gates to the local Hugong temple are opened; and on the evening of 8/1 when the Hugong operas begin. On 8/13 they are fired off again, in greeting/welcoming Hugong, in exchanging incense and fire at the Hugong temple on the peak at Fangyan, and prior to the performances of the village Ying An troupes there (Wu 1993: 255).

In Houtang Nong, the preparatory work for the Hugong temple fair on lunar 8/13 always began in the last third of the seventh month, after the "rush harvest, rush planting" of the fall known as the "double scramble" (Shuang qiang 双 抢) had been concluded (Hu 1997a: 156). Eight masters of affairs, appointed by the Association, known as Longtou Ren 拢头人, took charge of organizing the song and dance Ying An troupes and martial arts Luohan ban troupes, arranging for the performance of the Hugong operas, and preparing for the procession through the neighboring countryside, the ascent up to the peak at Fangyan to worship Hugong, the exchange of incense/fire, and the performances entertaining the deity.

In the seventh month the Longtou Ren set out to raise money, going door to door, and hosting a Longtou banquet. They would bring in a master to arrange and choreograph the performances of the martial arts Luohan Ban 罗汉班 and its percussion accompaniment, and to teach performance skills to the young and inexperienced—boxing, big knives, trident, battle axe, etc. Every evening the sounds of the gongs and drums could be heard into the night as they practiced their routines for greeting/welcoming and entertaining Hugong (Wu 1993: 255).

On lunar 8/1 the Association would formally commence the rituals of worship. The door of the village Hugong temple was opened (Kai Dian men 开殿门) with great solemnity, the three cannons were fired off in front of the temple, and a great pig was brought to the front of the temple and sacrificially slaughtered. In the temple, red candles were lit, incense presented, and gold and silver paper burned, while the Hugong sutra (胡公经 Hugong Jing) was recited, and all knelt and prayed (Wu 1993: 256).

On the evenings of 8/1 through 8/3, "Hugong Operas" were performed. On 8/1, before the show began, the costumed opera performers would go to the village Hugong temple accompanied by a cacophony of gongs and drums to "invite Hugong to the opera." They would retrieve his *pusa* from the temple in its dragon pavilion (longting 龙庭) or deity niche (shen kan 神龛), and carry it to a seat of honor just in front of the stage (Hu 1991: 200; Wu 1993: 256). The niche is handcarved and painted, in the shape of a grand pagoda, and a miniature pusa of Hugong sits within. On 8/13, at the time of Ying An (迎案—"greet/welcome the deity") the niche will be carried in procession by one of the Association members on his shoulders, escorted by a Luohan troupe in great solemnity, all the way to Fangyan peak, to carry out the ritual exchange of incense and fire (Wu 1993: 247).

Once prelude performances of "harassing the stage" and "Dance of the Eight Immortals" were completed, the three cannon were fired off again, firecrackers set off, and the opera performances begun. On the first night, lunar 8/1, "lucky" operas 吉利戏 would be performed such as Heavenly Officials Grant Good Fortune 天官赐福; Kuixing Selects the Zhuangyuan 魁星点状元; or Portrait of a Hundred Longevities 百寿图, etc.

The evening of 8/2 was devoted to "Hugong" Operas, although apart from being for his entertainment the contents of the operas in question have nothing to do with Hugong. They were most often secular operas from the Jinhua Wuju repertoire like "Fire consumes Zidu" (Huoxiao Zi Du 火烧子都), and "Thrice Invite Lihua" (Sanqing Lihua 三请梨花).

The operas of the third night, lunar 8/3, were "fulfilling vow operas" (Huan Yuan Xi 还原戏). Anyone for whom Hugong had successfully interceded in the previous year and had made a vow to reciprocate would place offerings of the three sacrificial animals on the opera stage as a vow fulfillment before the gong sounded signaling the beginning of the performance (Hu 1991: 200; Wu 1993: 256).

Each year, responsibility for funding and arranging the two days and three nights of opera performances would rotate among village lineage segments along with the responsibility for organizing the Association's other activities. But if the responsible segment during a given year should fail to secure an opera troupe to perform it was ridiculed as the host of "dumb" opera. Who could stand the shame? (Wu 1993: 256).

On the morning of 8/2, one of the eight Longtou Ren masters of affairs together with his various assistants would assemble to conduct the ritual Ji Cha (sacrifice the trident 祭叉).[2] To the sound of gongs and drums, Hugong's deity niche was taken out of the temple to an open drying ground in the village. A "Descend the spirit servant" (Jiangshen Tong 降神僮) danced as Hugong, with the goal of being possessed by Hugong himself, and onlookers filled with deep veneration, prostrated themselves in worship (Hu 1991: 200; Wu 1993: 256).

The Luohan Ban troupe members with their various "weapons" in display—banners, swords, tridents, clubs, shields, etc.—all assembled in front of the altar table, over which a tent was erected. On the altar table in front of Hugong's deity niche sacrificial offerings were presented: a pig's head, goose, chicken, eggs, cakes, fruit, old wine. Texts expressing respect for Hugong Dadi were read by village notables or prestigious members of the senior generation, and his protection sought for a bountiful harvest of grain and livestock, avoidance of catastrophe and hardship, peace and tranquility, after which the villagers would present incense, kneel and kowtow. Amidst the din of firecrackers, drums and gongs, the Luohan troupe performed the routines it had worked up for the occasion, dressed in white tops with red trousers in a kind of dress rehearsal for their performances during the grand procession (You An 游案) on 8/11, and during Welcome the Deity on 8/13 at Fangyan and enroute (Hu 1991: 200; Wu 1993: 256; Chen 1997: 170).

Once the opera performances ended on lunar 8/3, everyone began busying themselves with preparations for the grand procession on lunar 8/11, and rehearsals for greeting and entertaining the deity at the Hugong temple fair on 8/13. Early in the morning of 8/11 the Longtou Ren would call together the martial arts Luohan Ban and the song and dance performance troupes of Houtang and neighboring villages to commence the Grand Procession, You An 游案. Beginning in Houtang village, the procession was led by a group of blunderbusses, with gongs and drums opening a path at the head of the troupe, followed by a banner brigade with several score leading flags (touqi 头旗) or centipede flags (wugong qi 蜈蚣旗). These were followed by the martial arts troupe (Luohan Ban) in formation—wielding knives, swords, spears, tridents, shields, maces and clubs, with a group of Luohan sun (罗汉孙 Luohan grandchildren) in Tai Ge 抬阁 display (Hu 1991: 202; Hu 1997a: 156; Wang ed. 1997: 55; YKXZ 605).

Next in procession were the song and dance performance troupes with a variety of themes (36 professions, ten character lotus, 18 foxes, 18 butterflies, nine strung pearls, long legged deer—stilt walkers, see below). And bringing up the rear was the Hugong deity niche escorted by four goose down flags, a command flag, two incense porters, four gongs, four tablets of authority (Zhishi Pai 执事牌), four flower and bamboo porters, ten incense bearers, two "open the way" knife and trident bearers, and one longevity tablet bearer. Surrounding the Hugong deity niche were fan bearers, a protective yellow parasol bearer, and the "Descend the deity servant" (Jiangshen Tong 降神僮) in attendance (Hu 1991: 201; Wu 1993: 247).

On a fixed itinerary, the Houtang procession would pass through 16 natural villages in three townships before returning to Houtang, covering more than 25 km (Hu 1991: 200; Wu 1993: 257). At each village along the procession route, the Luohan Ban and the song and dance troupes performed. Villagers came out to worship, setting off firecrackers, setting out pigs' heads, geese, pork or a rooster and other sacrificial goods, lighting incense and burning paper to seek Hugong's protection, the good fortune of the family, and a good harvest for the whole village.

However, in former times when the Houtang village procession passed the village of Gu Shan 古山, they would not stop to perform at all. There was apparently a long-running enmity between the ancestors of Houtang village and Gu Shan as the result of a dispute over land to be used for graves, in which Houtang village came up on the short end. Thus, there was an old saying: "If you have a daughter don't marry her to Gu Shan; in You An procession, don't stop at Gu Shan."

In the past Houtang village was not well equipped to compete with Gu Shan, but they are said to have used the organization of Hugong activities by their village Hugong Association to strategically strengthen their alliances with surrounding villages. Combined with the united front they were able to present with their affines in Pai Qi, this greatly strengthened their political position vis a vis Gushan. The account is interesting because it demonstrates that in addition to shared belief, there is also a political dimension to the machinations of the Association in its organization of temple fair activities (Wu 1993: 257–258).

After liberation, the administration of Houtang village was moved out of You Xian township 游仙乡 and interactions with residents of Gushan were much less frequent. But in 1958 Houtang villagers were incorporated into Gushan commune together with their former enemies. As the result of efforts on the part of commune "ideological workers," the two enemy families finally settled their differences and have even intermarried. Whether the latter was an instrument in bringing about the former is left unanswered in the sources. But the old saying has been changed to: "If you have a daughter marry her to Gu Shan, in You An procession be sure to stop at Gu Shan" (Wu 1993: 258).

In any event, on the day following You An, lunar 8/12, the troupes rested a day in preparation for the activities to follow early in the morning of 8/13 when the procession would march to Fangyan for a ritual exchange of incense and fire, and a performance welcoming and entertaining Hugong.

For three days prior to climbing Fangyan, participants refrained from eating meat or engaging in sex. Before departure they washed their bodies clean and donned new or clean clothes. On the road they dared not utter any foul language, letting only auspicious and lucky sentiments escape their mouths. This they accomplished by continuously reciting the Hugong sutra as they walked (Hu 1991: 201; Jiang n.d.a.; Wu 1993: 258). While the pilgrims were underway, those who remained at home lit candles, burned incense and sacrificial paper and prayed in the direction of Fangyan (Eberhard 1940: 38).

Before dawn on 8/13, the troupe members from Houtang would gather at Huku mountain ridge (about 3 km from Fangyan) to await daybreak. When the sun came up, they made up their faces, took up their paraphernalia, and gathered together with the groups from the other villages, preparing to march in the same formation as they did in You An to the town of Huku, the native village of Hugong, to perform their routines. After the performances in Huku, the procession continued, followed by crowds of supplicants (xiangke 香客) on their way to worship Hugong at the temple on the peak at Fangyan (Wu 1993: 247). The procession passed through the villages and towns of Qian Keng 前坑, Pai Qi 派溪, and Wen Lou 文楼, on the way to Chengli village 橙丽村 at the foot of Fangyan (Hu 1991: 201).

At each village along the way the Luohan Ban and the song and dance troupes would perform, and because of the long history of intermarriage Houtang residents have with Pai Qi villagers, the martial arts and cultural performances there were performed with special care. When the procession reached Yanxia Street in Fangyan town, the troupes would trade places; the cultural song and dance troupes taking the lead, the martial arts Luohan Ban troupes behind (Wu 1993: 257).

After the somewhat grueling climb to the peak, the group would assemble the last of the stragglers, and fire off its three canons. The Hugong deity niche carried from the local temple was placed in front of the temple on the peak, and amidst the great din of gongs, drums, and firecrackers, the Luohan troupes circled around the temple three times and back, "dancing the Luohan" (Tiao Luohan 跳罗汉). The Descend the deity servant (Jiangshen Tong 降神僮) would then jump up on the large incense burner in front of the Hugong Dian, removing some embers and ash from the burner and placing them in the little burner of the Hugong throne/deity niche. This exchange of incense and fire (huan xianghuo 换香火) was the most important activity of the entire day's rituals, an act of renewal that is the main purpose of the procession to Fangyan (Wu 1993: 258).

Meanwhile the accompanying supplicants present their offerings to Hugong and worship or make a vow. They kneel and present incense. When Houtang's designated time comes up, the Luohan troupe and the song and dance troupe parade onto the square to the west of the temple to begin their performances for Hugong's benefit, entertaining the deity.

When the performances are finished, the troupes leave the Hugong temple area to make way for the next of the hundreds of groups who have made similar preparations during the eighth and ninth lunar months to march to Fangyan to perform. Troupe members may stop to grab a bite to eat, or to purchase some souvenirs on Heaven Street, or to take photographs in front of the temple buildings, but they then proceed down by the same path they came up, back through Heaven's Gate, down the mountain, back to the village, carrying and escorting Hugong's deity niche back to its original place in the local village temple (Gui Dianmen 归殿门), bringing this once a year observance to a close (Hu 1991: 201; Wu 1993: 247; 257).

After liberation, the activities of the Houtang Hugong Association were halted. Many Hugong temples in other villages were either knocked down for or transformed into factories or government offices, or simply allowed to deteriorate as a result of vandalism or neglect, and for many years none of these rituals and performances were carried out. But the Hugong temple of Hou Tang village somehow survived, and even during the Cultural Revolution was spared any damage. Since the advent of economic reform, the Hugong Association has been reestablished, and is thriving (Hu 1991: 202; Wu 1993: 258).

In recent years the Ying An activities of most villages have been simplified, and the period of time consumed in ritual preparations has shrunk from 13 to two or three days. Thus contemporary sources conclude approvingly that much energy, money and resources are saved, the "superstitious" dimension has been reduced, and the entertainment and recreational aspects have become more prominent (Hu 1991: 202; 1997a: 158).

Luohanban 罗汉班 martial arts troupes

On the martial side of Ying An performances are the Luohan troupes (Luohan Ban 罗汉班). They are regarded as the cornerstone of the Fangyan temple fair, so the fair is also referred to colloquially as "greet the Luohan" 迎罗汉 or "perform/hit the Luohan" 打罗汉 (Wang ed. 1997: 55).

Historically, most large villages in the Jinhua area maintained Luohan ban. Young men studied martial arts from a young age to toughen themselves for a future life of hard labor, and the troupes also played a role in village defense. A Luohan troupe with many strong young men might serve as a deterrent against the depredations of bandits, or encroachments on village lands or water (Mao ed. 1996: 81–82). The occasion of the Hugong temple fair gave them a chance to publicly display their skills, while observing the troupes of their near and more distant neighbors. It was not uncommon for such agonistic displays to lead to violent confrontations in competition for right of way, or the simple desire to prove one's dominance. On the narrow mountain paths of Fangyan, such contestations often led to death in precipitous falls.

Luohan troupes are said to have originated with the active promotion of Hu Ze himself, during the northern Song dynasty. As he spent some time during his official career as magistrate in Fuzhou, it is altogether believable that he "called on citizens to cultivate martial arts so as to defend against incursions by Japanese pirates." The troupes were organized with the then newly instituted units of the baojia 保甲 administrative security system as the basis (Chen 1997: 169).

After liberation in 1949, Luohan troupes were suppressed by the new Communist government as a danger to public security (Fieldnotes 8/10/98). But in the late 1990s, as the Communist Party continued to loosen its grip on local daily activity, Luohan Ban were begun again as recreational and ceremonial groups, often centered in village Senior Centers (Laonian Xiehui 老年协会). Many villages have Luohan Societies 罗汉协会 with endowments of land, the income from which supports the troupe's activities, costumes and paraphernalia, and the hiring of a martial arts master to instruct in the various arts of boxing, cudgel, sword, knife, spear, shield, etc. The performance at the Hugong temple at Fangyan is likened to undergoing inspection by Hugong himself, and is thus taken very seriously (Chen 1997: 169; Hu 1997a: 156; JHSZ 1085; YKXZ 605).

The popularity of such troupes and the cultivation of martial arts in general among contemporary young men is inseparable from a form of Chinese "machismo" expressed in part in Gong Fu flicks, but also reflective of the growing individualism of contemporary market oriented daily life.

On their way to Fangyan, the villages en route all invite the troupe to perform, and serve them with tea, wine, cakes, fruit and dianxin (Chen 1997: 170; YKXZ 605). On the temple grounds at Fangyan their performances are known as "canzhen" (参阵 display of formations). The banners come first, leading the performers through their various formations—circles, squares, dragon's gate, the eight trigrams, plum blossoms, long snake, one transforming into another—to the accompaniment of a cacophony of drums and gongs, and the sounds of the Suona (oboes). The performers may divide into small groups and fill the square performing their special skills with swords, tridents, clubs, and shields (Chen 1997: 170; Wang ed. 1997: 55).

Some troupes specialize in "Pile up" the Luohan (Die Luohan 叠罗汉), which combines the skills of martial arts and acrobatics in displays of elaborate structures composed of the performers' bodies. Pile up the Luohan performances are said to have originated in neighboring Yiwu during the Ming dynasty, Wanli period (1573–1620), as a means of recruiting members into a local militia. The practice gradually spread more broadly as a form of recreation, until by late Qing, there were several score such troupes in Yiwu county alone. At present, some 23 towns in Yiwu host such troupes, many of which perform each year at the Hugong temple fair (JHSZ 1085; Mao ed. 1996: 81–82).

Ritual song and dance repertoire

The ritual song and dance troupes are a kind of cultural complement to the martial Luohan Ban. While their purpose is to entertain Hugong, they also function to entertain the people (Hu 1991: 211). Among the performances that have become associated with entertaining the deity at the Hugong temple fair in particular are the following.

Sanshiliu Hang (三十六行 36 Professions)

Sanshiliu Hang (三十六行 36 Professions) is a group parade performance in costume of the adage "36 professions, each produces a Zhuangyuan" (winner of first place in the imperial exams). It is a folk performance that celebrates the division of labor in society, reflecting the mutual respect of practitioners of the various professions. The movements are spontaneous and performed without musical accompaniment. There are gongs and cymbals in the lead, followed by the bearer of the great red triangular flag emblazoned with the characters Hugong Dadi.

Behind the flag are the lead performers of the parade—two clowns, one in the guise of a leper, the other with a festering leg, white powder on their noses, wearing plaited grass crowns on their heads, bare footed and bare chested, with rice straw rope holding up rice straw skirts. They alternately bang large gongs and perform humorous movements and funny faces that provoke laughter in the crowd. They are said to represent the fate of the lazy and idle, unwilling to work in any profession, nothing to eat or wear, reduced to vagrancy, a laughing stock.

The clowns are followed directly by 36 people made up as officials, farmers, craftsmen, and merchants ("shi, nong, gong, shang"), the five crafts, and people of various trades. Each carries a tool representing their profession; the carpenter holds an axe and saw, the fortune teller holds a small gong, etc., and each performs movements associated with the work of that profession (Hu 1991: 205; Hu 1997b: 172; YKXZ 604; Zhang 2003: 61).

The religious dimension: Hugong Dadi temple fair 179

Figure 8.4 36 professions: Fangyan

Ten Character Lotus (十字莲花)

The *Ten Character Lotus* dance is said to have very ancient origins. After Shang dynasty emperor to be, Tang 商汤 conquered the Xia, he is supposed to have ordered the compilation of ritual dances and songs that later became known as "Mulberry grove" (Sang Lin 桑林), after the site where the ancestral altar, the She 社, of the ruling house was located. A *Ten Character Lotus* dance is said to have been in the corpus of Mulberry grove (Hu 1991: 203–204; Ma 1997: 173; YKXZ 604; Zhang 2003: 46–48, 60–62).

The dance is performed regularly at the Hugong temple fair, said to have migrated into Yongkang from Shandong province. It is also performed at rituals seeking timely rains, and at the temple fairs in honor of other deities. In the Republican period, nearly every village in Yongkang, Dongyang, Pan An, and Jinyun counties had a *Ten Character Lotus* troupe.

Zhang Zhulin invokes the grades of bridal dowries, from wealthy to beggar, to mark the distinction made traditionally between "rich man's" (富人 furen) and "beggar's" (讨饭 taofan) versions of the *Ten Character Lotus* performance. The song form of both is of ten character lines. Since the establishment of the People's Republic, the "beggar's" version has disappeared, but the "rich man's" version has attained the status of a folk art form, performed with grace and dignity. The singing, dancing and percussion rhythm accompaniment are coordinated by a "lotus leader" (Lianhua Tou 莲花头), the soul of the troupe. Just before the performance commences, he will comically clear a space for the dancers, pushing this way and pulling that way against the

180 *Unraveling the total social phenomenon*

crowd of onlookers, jumping up and back forcing the crowd to "take pleasure in yielding the way" (Le yu rang dao 乐于让道) (Zhang 2003: 60, 63).

18 Foxes (十八狐狸)

18 Foxes is also called "18 big girls" 十八大姑娘 or "big faced girls" 大面姑娘 because of the masks that the dancers wear in performance that cover the whole head. It is always one of the most popular dances associated with the Ying An performances of the Hugong temple fair in Fangyan (Wang and Liu 1997: 70–71).

According to the resident monk at Guang Ci Si, *18 Foxes* was performed at Da Bei Si temple in Fangyan as early as the reign of emperor Tang Xuanzong (AD 847–860), at which time the 18 foxes were said to be demons of Fangyan vanquished by the Buddha (Hu 1991: 206).

Figure 8.5 18 foxes: Fangyan

In another version of the dance's origin, it is said to portray the tale of an official of the Tang dynasty who had four sons and 18 grandsons. On account of official corruption, the family fell into disrepute and 17 of the grandsons died young, leaving behind 17 widows. The youngest grandson took his 17 sisters-in-law, together with his wife, and established a house of prostitution. The dance performed at Fangyan was composed according to this version by residents of Rutang Tou village 儒堂头村 in Yongkang. It is performed by 20 men, 18 of whom perform as women, wearing big headed women's masks over their heads, and brightly colored flappy women's blouses, with black pleated skirts, and embroidered shoes. Each carries a paper fan in one hand and a silk handkerchief in the other.

Of the remaining two dancers, one performs as the madam of the house of prostitution, with a wig and mask, wearing a red flowered smock, a colored belt, and flowery pants. In one hand she grasps a water pipe, in the other a wheat straw fan. The other performs as a male customer with a long tan robe, a purple and black mandarin jacket, black cloth boots, with a long cigarette holder in his hand.

With drums and band in front, the customer, the "foxes" and the madam march one after the other, dancing to the band's accompaniment. The foxes dance in drunken steps, sometimes criss-crossing in formation. The customer tries to decide which of the foxes to select, while the foxes alternately oppose him and try to sell him their favors (Hu 1991: 207; Wang and Liu 1997: 70–71). The modern county gazetteer describes the customer as cutting a contemptible figure, and characterizes the dance as displaying and satirizing the corruption and decadence of the official class of the old feudal society (YKXZ 603).

Ya Bei Feng (哑背疯 Mute Carries the Crazy One)

Ya Bei Feng (哑背疯 Mute Carries the Crazy One), also called *Xueli Mei* (雪里梅 Plum in the Snow), or 老背少 (Old Carries Young) is a song and dance piece performed by one performer who simultaneously plays the roles of the mute old man and the crazy woman riding on his back, none other than the Ya Bei Feng that became the signature piece of opera performer Zhou Yuexian 周越先 in the 1940s and 1950s (discussed in Chapter 7). It has become a fixture performance at the Hugong temple fair, where it is performed by the Ying An troupe of Zhiying town among others as a short performance piece rather than a full-fledged opera (Song Bo 1983: 62–63; Ying 1991: 48; YKZX 604).

Again, the performer wears the costume of a crazy woman on the upper portion of the body, and that of a mute old man on the lower portion. The performer's real legs are made to seem to be the old man's legs, with the old man's false head and torso protruding from the performer's stomach. Thus the woman appears to be riding on the old man's back, with false legs which appear to be hers, also protruding from the front of the performer's body.

Looking at the single performer, it appears as if the old man is carrying a woman on his back. Four to eight additional performers dance and sing in accompaniment.

In addition there are the song and dance arrangements of 18 butterflies, 18 carp, the clam shell dance, and long-legged deer (长脚鹿 changjiao lu), the latter a stilt-walking performance that is the specialty of Yongkang's Chaochuan village 朝川村 of Qiancang Township 前仓乡 said to have a several-hundred-year tradition of performing on stilts. Some of the villagers are even said to make the climb up the mountain at Fangyan to the Hugong temple on stilts (Hu 1991: 208–209; YKXZ 603–605).

The performances of Ying An troupes at Fangyan continue daily, according to schedule through to lunar 9/9, Chong Yang 重阳 festival, the second high tide of the fair when some 50 troupes are scheduled to perform.

According to incomplete statistics, in the ten years between 1985 and 1994, the scenic area of Fangyan averaged about 600,000 visitors per year, and by some estimates the numbers range up to 700,000–800,000 per year, of whom 60–70 percent were supplicants (xiangke 香客). During the more than month long temple fair period, those visiting range from 7,000 up to 20,000–30,000 per day at the high tides (Hu 1991: 196–197). A survey of visitors to Fangyan conducted in the 1990s showed that the fair attracted supplicants from as far away as Jiangsu, Anhui, Jiangxi, Fujian, Shanghai, Guangxi, and Guangdong provinces (Hu 1995: 4).

Hugong temples and fairs in local market towns historically and in the present

For those not making the pilgrimage to Fangyan, lunar 8/13 may still be an occasion for celebration at locally sponsored temple fairs organized around the many Hugong temples scattered throughout the market towns of the region. These are held in conjunction with the usual three days of expanded commercial activity characteristic of secular fairs, and the proximity of Hu Ze's date of birth, lunar 8/13, to the Mid-Autumn Festival on lunar 8/15 makes the commercial activity of the Hugong temple fairs in the local market towns of the region especially lively. Stalls selling clothing, shoes, agricultural equipment, furniture, livestock, medicinal herbs, tools, and food of all kinds line the streets of the market towns on the fair days, and the multiplicity of performance and entertainment genres typical of all fairs are well represented. By one Qing dynasty estimate, in the eight counties of Jinhua prefecture, there were perhaps as many as 100 Hugong temples (Hu 1995: 2–3).

A search through the local gazetteers of the prefectures (fuzhi 府志) of Zhejiang during the Tongzhi period (1862–1875), recorded eight counties in Hangzhou prefecture with Hugong temples; six counties in Yanzhou prefecture; two counties in Huzhou; eight counties in Jinhua; five counties in Quzhou; six in Taizhou; five in Wenzhou; ten in Chuzhou; eight in Shaoxing; three in Ningbo (Hu 1995: 3); altogether 61 counties in ten prefectures covering an area of 90,000 sq km (the whole province had 12 prefectures and 76 counties at the time), with an estimated 10,000,000 Hugong believers (Hu 1991: 216; 1995: 4).

Ying Baoshi's (应宝时 1821–1890) previously cited "Notes on the repair of the Hugong temple" of the Qing dynasty Tongzhi period, records that hardly a place in eastern Zhejiang existed without a Hugong temple, numbering more than 1,100 "scattered like stars in the skies" (Hu 1995: 3).

Coffee-house gossip, commercialization and the deity niche with no ticket

In the fall of 1998, the coffee-house gossip in Yongkang was critical of the commercialization and bureaucratization of the Hugong temple fair at Fangyan, where Luohan and Ying An troupes must register in advance with the Fangyan Office of Tourism, and pay a fee to obtain a permit to enter the grounds of the scenic area, climb the mountain, and entertain Hugong. The overall feel of the place, they claim, is more and more like that of a theme park.

About a month later, I was given some partial confirmation of this analysis, when on the main road from Paiqi town to the main gate at the foot of Fangyan I chanced to cross paths with a group of about 20 people from Hong Tang 洪塘 village of Xiqi township 西溪镇, beating gongs escorting their *pusa*'s deity niche to the Hugong temple. I walked with them up to the main entry gate to get a picture of their *pusa* in its deity niche which I did, but then the fun started. Why? It seems they hadn't completed the necessary procedures to allow them entry up the hill. The gatekeeper refused to let them pass until they had marched all the way back to the Office of Tourism (Luyou Ju) to get a permit. They had come all the way from their village by foot and there was no motor vehicle in the vicinity to escort them the several kilometers to the Luyou Ju. An argument and scuffle ensued, as the old timer with the deity niche on his shoulders refused to be denied and tried to crash the gate. He was turned away by an unyielding gatekeeper, highly incensed at the nerve of this old man. I went up to the gatekeeper and tried to reason with him. "C'mon," I said, "they shlepped all the way here on foot to worship Hugong; Hugong don't need no stinking procedures; why don't you just let them pass?" Apparently embarrassed by the additional attention the intervention of the foreigner had attracted, he finally let them pass, and I felt I had done a good thing. I'm sure Hugong agreed. But the incident does suggest that there might indeed be something to be said on behalf of the coffee-house gossip in Yongkang.

I also heard from at least one Luohan troupe member at Fangyan that their troupe had stopped coming to Fangyan every year on account of the gate-entry fee being so high. Instead, they go each year to the new Hugong temple in Huku (see Chapter 9) where entry fees are much lower. In 1998, the Fangyan authorities dropped the price to an affordable ¥2/person, so the group made the trip (Fieldnotes 10/28/98 on the story of the deity niche with no ticket).

Those who share such impressions of the Fangyan fair may find the newly constructed temple complexes at Lower and Upper Huku a suitable alternative, discussed in the following chapter.

Notes

1 Interestingly, Hu Ze's gravesite in Longjing was linked to the origin of Longjing's most important product—tea. At the edges of his grave, six tea plants were planted, and cultivated to provide imperial tribute tea (贡茶) to the court. The tea plants thrived, and the cultivation of tea spread more broadly throughout the area, and that is how Longjing tea got its start (Fieldnotes 10/7/98 Yongkang, Hu Guojun personal communication).
2 Sometimes also referred to as Ji Cha 祭插 (sacrifice of insertion), Ji Chai (sacrifice the hairpin 祭钗) or Ji Chan (sacrifice the hoe weapon 祭铲)—chan 铲 an agricultural tool transformed into a weapon, head in the shape of an (upside down) shan character 山 with a long wooden handle.

9 The political dimension
Macro and micro

This chapter explores how practitioners of popular religion are positioned with respect to the secular Communist state, but also considers evidence of the local machinations of rural communities in pursuit of political advantage vis-à-vis one another as centers of pilgrimage and worship.

We have already discussed at some length the Ming-Qing state's somewhat ambivalent attitude toward organized and popular religious traditions, beginning with first Ming emperor Zhu Yuanzhang's regulations. Symptomatic of that ambivalence, Brook has noted three main postures in the state–religion relationship: patronage, prohibition, and regulation. For Brook, the gentry vacillated in attitudes between permitting and even patronizing Buddhism and Daoism, and the desire to prohibit their practice so as to establish a monopoly of Confucian norms that underwrote their own authority (Brook 2009: 23).

But most Confucian compilers of gazetteers adopted a more practical stance: "Religion might well be suspect, but regulation was all that could reasonably be hoped for." And some went so far as to allow that "popular religion, with its zeal to promote the good and punish the evil might well complement Confucianism" (Brook 2009: 34).

The prospect of winning imperial patronage ended with the establishment of the "modern secular" Republican state in 1911, and since that time Chinese government policies (whether Republican or Communist) have alternated between outright prohibition and regulation.

In Chapter 3 we reviewed Vincent Goossaert's "paradigms" for understanding modern Chinese religion, but reserved consideration of his "repression and resistance paradigm" for this chapter on politics. Obviously this paradigm is most useful in analyzing state policies in their prohibition phase, or when religious movements turn insurrectional and threaten dynastic power, but the boundary between regulation and repression is often ambiguous, and resistance may well be sub-insurrectional.

The "repression and resistance paradigm" sees the state as acting predatorily toward popular religious institutions either as a result of anti-religious ideology, or the desire to "seize social, economic, and political resources that form the basis for local power and cultural/political autonomy in the towns and countryside." The reaction of religious institutions to this predation, both historically and in the present, is understood as resistance in the broadest sense (Goossaert 2005: 14).

Gates for example has argued that Chinese folk religion, including non-sectarian Daoism, has historically been the ideology of an anti-tributary petty capitalism, which despite its "syncretic" inclusion of many values consistent with Confucian orthodoxy, by its very existence represented a kind of resistance to the hegemonic, hierarchical, centralizing, Confucian system. With the introduction of global capitalism into the picture in contemporary times, she argues, this petty capitalism had the effect of "facilitating the embrace with [global] capitalism while making that intercourse less like rape" (Gates 1995: 226).

In either event, for Gates, "The capacity of Chinese folk religion to soak up and circulate capital that might otherwise fall into the hands of the state or the multinationals is an important element in the petty capitalists' resistance to the hegemony of these other modes of production" (1995: 236).

As regards the role of temple fairs as institutions of potential resistance, Zhao argues that in relatively settled times, the fairs gave people the opportunity to let off steam, expressing ridicule of the traditional orthodox restrictions in a legally approved arena, performing something of a "safety valve" function. But at times when social relations were tense, the fairs also provided an opportunity to assemble large numbers in insurrection, while submerging the instigators and participants in the anonymity of the crowd. Indeed some religious rebellions of the late Qing dynasty began during temple fairs (Zhao 2002: 134–135).

The crowd and its potential for riot or insurrection made temple fairs an object of suspicion and periodic suppression by the Guomindang Nationalist government. And indeed, Communist agents of the time took advantage of the crowds at the fairs to spread propaganda and foment anti-Guomindang and anti-Japanese resistance. In the summer of 1935 the Communist Party of Dongyang county prepared to provoke an armed rebellion with the goal of overthrowing the local Guomindang Nationalist authorities and establishing a "soviet" government, and the revolt was to begin on lunar 8/13 at the Hugong temple fair in the county town, Wuning, taking advantage of the huge crowds that descended on the town during the fair. However, the plot was discovered before the appointed day, and the Zhejiang GMD provincial government sent seven "reconnaissance" brigades to impose martial law county-wide. The party organization of Dongyang was effectively destroyed, and it took two years before the Shanghai party branch was able to reestablish the Communist Party organization in Dongyang (Wang, ed. DYSZ 1993: 533). But the incident is significant in showing the political volatility of the temple fair, and the Communist Party's awareness of its potential for mobilizing the masses to rebel.

However, the policy that has prevailed in China in the 1990s and 2000s is now recognized by most scholars as one of toleration/regulation of religious institutions by the state rather than outright prohibition, suppression, or predation (Goossaert 2005: 16).

Goldman (1986: 149–150) has contended that the post-Mao state's more tolerant attitude toward the practice of religion, and its willingness to approve the establishment of new and refurbishing of old temples, is due to the fact that the Cultural Revolution had driven religion underground. Giving it space to revive in the reform period has merely been a ploy by the post Mao state to draw religious practices back out into the open so as to more effectively reestablish regulation and control.

Potter attributes the post-Mao regime's more tolerant perspective on religion to its concern to build regime legitimacy. The state accepted a trade-off of broader autonomy for religion in exchange for continued political loyalty on the part of religion's practitioners (Potter 2003: 317–318).

Less inclined to see ulterior motives, Brook attributes the more tolerant attitude toward religion to the state's abandonment after 1979 of the teleological assumption that "the people would give up their opiate once the social relations of production had been revolutionized" (Brook 2009: 22).

In any event, it is apparent that the state has for all practical purposes accepted the revival of popular religion as a reality and a relatively harmless expression of "folk culture" (*minjian wenhua* 民间文化) and is willing to assume a regulatory rather than suppressive role (Chau 2006a: 248; see also Brook 2009: 23).

This shift has prompted Goossaert to suggest that the relation between state and religious institutions might nowadays be better "analyzed as a negotiation" (Goossaert 2005: 16), what might be called a "circumscribed toleration—negotiation paradigm." That circumscription has certainly been loosened in recent years, but as Chau notes, much of popular religion "hovers in the huge gray area between legitimate religion and illegitimate superstition" (Chau 2009: 218) to some extent encompassed by the ambiguous category of *minjian xinyang* (民间信仰—literally "beliefs among the people") or *minjian wenhua* (民间文化—"folk culture"). What is legitimate religion and what is feudal superstition within the category *minjian xinyang* often ends up subject to interpretation and negotiation, and the representatives of the local state are the primary agents of that interpretation, and partner/opponent in that negotiation.

While the criteria the local state has to work with in distinguishing between legitimate religion and illegitimate feudal superstition have not changed since the Maoist era, there has most assuredly been a shift in the interpretation of those criteria by the local state away from radical anti-traditionalism to regulatory paternalism (Chau 2009: 219). And the category *minjian xinyang* by which these practices are characterized may even provide the local state some room for flexibility in its interpretations. The representatives of the local state in all the Jinhua townships where I investigated fairs ignore the presence of practitioners of divination, fortune telling, face reading, and other such manifestations of "feudal superstition" among the people.

Popular religion has also been portrayed as something of an instrument by means of which local communities express their autonomy vis-à-vis the state. In Dean's analysis, for example, the ritual events of popular religious practice in present-day Fujian are characterized as moments in the formation of "temporary autonomous zones" expressive of "fluid emergent community." For Dean, "each ritual is a gamble requiring negotiation with local government and Party officials and complex mobilization of community desires and resources... Every communal ritual performance is therefore both a potential disaster, and at the same time a step in the construction of a temporary autonomous zone" (Dean 2003: 357–358).

From a slightly different perspective, but getting at the same circumstance, Potter describes a "zone of indifference" regarding religious practice, in which the state chooses not to intervene (Potter 2003: 317–318).

Autonomous zones and zones of indifference both express the circumstances of which our temple fairs are a manifestation, providing the space in which practitioners of popular religion and popular cultural genres have enjoyed the license to expand the boundaries of contemporary acceptable expression.

This notion that rural communities are reasserting their autonomy vis-à-vis the state is often also associated with an "emphasis on the collective, community based, if not egalitarian, dimensions of popular religion" (Chau 2006: 69).

Zhao Shiyu (2002) articulates this view in his characterization of temple fairs as asserting a counter-hegemonic egalitarianism that ran against the grain of class-based social regulations. And Flath (n.d.: 31–32) and Wu (1988) have emphasized the community based character of temple fair activity.

But Chau is uncomfortable with the idea of "communal resistance" because "the political implications of the revival of popular religion are often more complex than the resistance perspective can fully capture" (Chau 2006: 8–9). "In the local world, state and society are complexly imbricated," and too much emphasis on communal resistance "diverts attention from other important aspects of popular religious revival such as the actions of the local state and the power claims of local elites" (ibid.). And Dean makes a similar point, arguing that the state-religion relationship is "immensely complex and locally differentiated" (2009: 203).

Finally, Chau points out the undoubted fact that the predominant values of which resurgent popular religious practice is a manifestation are less collective and egalitarian in nature and more selfish, familial-individualistic, and amoral (Chau 2006: 69). And Zhao (2002: 86), among others, has also stressed the pragmatism and utilitarianism of Chinese popular religious belief.

Nevertheless, it seems to me that by its mere existence popular religious expression in the doctrinally atheist Communist state constitutes a way of thinking alternative to/resistant to state discourse. Thus while I agree with Chau (2006) and Dean (2003) that the relation between popular religious institutions and the local state is a complex one, I still consider, contra Chau, that the "temporary autonomous zones" created by ritual events like temple fairs may indeed be understood as manifestations of collective popular "resistance" insofar as they involve the organized expression of sentiments and ideas disapproved of by the modernist, secular, Communist state, and notwithstanding the often self-interested, familistic motivations of the devotees.

In any event, I feel safe concluding this section with the following surmise from Timothy Brook:

> The history of Chinese religion after the 1970s . . . suggests that communities and individuals will continue to create networks of religious activity beyond the framework of state regulation, regardless of the laws of the state or the activism of prohibitionist state elites.
>
> (Brook 2009: 40)

The micro-politics of temple fairs and pilgrimage: the Huku temple(s)

At the micro level, I observed in Chapter 3 that the "functional expansiveness" of Chinese popular religion had led Dean to characterize the networks of local temple and lineage halls in Fujian as a kind of "second government" (Dean 2009: 184), and Chau to conclude that temples are important elements of the local "cultural nexus of power" (Chau 2009: 214).

Flath has noted that the temple fair was an occasion for "symbolic display and observation of social and economic [and one might add, political] capital" (n.d. 31). One of the more important mechanisms by which that display was effected was in the performances of the village Luohanban 罗汉班 martial arts troupes. I noted in Chapter 8 how such a troupe might serve as a deterrent against the depredations of bandits, or encroachments on village lands or water (Mao ed. 1996: 81–82), that the occasion of the temple fair provided an opportunity not only to publicly display their prowess in processions and in entertaining the deity, but also to observe the troupes of their near and more distant neighbors.

In Chapter 8, the machinations of the Hugong Temple Fair Association of Houtang village were instrumental in forging political alliances with surrounding villages that helped strengthen its position vis-à-vis its rival, Gushan. The account bears noting here because it demonstrates that in addition to shared belief, the machinations of the Association in its organization of temple fair activities also had a significant political dimension (Wu 1993: 257–258).

The most dramatic example of the micro-politics of temple fairs involves competition between towns for the privilege of becoming a stop on the pilgrimage to worship Hugong. It is not the politics of religion vs the state, but rather an intercommunity politics in which common worship ends up dividing rather than uniting communities.

Interestingly, in recent years Hu Ze's native town of Huku 胡库镇 (7 km to the north of Fangyan) has mounted a challenge to the Hugong Temple at Fangyan, as a competing center for worship of Hugong. A new temple honoring Hugong was built in "Lower" Huku (Huku Xia 胡库下) in obvious competition with the cult center in Fangyan.

It may be said that the new temple offers a less commercialized, more intimate setting in which to pay one's respects to Hugong. And the citizens of "Lower" Huku succeeded in giving their temple great legitimacy by securing provincial approval for Hu Ze's remains to be moved from their previous burial site outside Xianying temple in the Hangzhou suburb of Longjing, to a shrine just outside the newly constructed temple, Huaizhong Ge (怀忠阁 Pavilion of Cherishing Loyalty), in "Lower" Huku.

In a visit to the new Hugong temple, the caretaker/fortune teller Mr. Hu Weidan 胡维丹 recounted that, in pre-Communist days, on Qing Ming festival Huku residents would make the long trip to Longjing to worship their ancestor Hugong at the Xianying temple and the nearby tomb. When more recently, Huku villagers tried to get the remains of Hugong and his wife moved back to Huku, they met with resistance from provincial authorities in Hangzhou in the office of cemetery affairs, the office of parks and forests, and the office of historic sites who argued that Hugong was a national hero, not just a Huku ancestor. Furthermore they doubted the veracity of Huku residents' claim that Hugong was indeed their ancestor. They suggested that the residents cooperate with Hangzhou authorities in providing funds to restore the temple in Longjing, but the residents were unwilling. The townsfolk finally brought their genealogy to Hangzhou to prove their claim, and eventually, in May 1992, they prevailed. The remains were moved to Huku where a great welcoming ceremony was mounted.[1]

Figure 9.1 Hugong temple: Huku

Residents of lower Huku 胡库下村 had expended great effort in selecting and preparing the site, for which a small hill was leveled preparatory to the construction of the tomb, and the final interring of the remains. The tomb was built near the entrance to Huku town, facing south, with Fangyan's Lion ridge opposite in the distance. In the front of the tomb is a stone lion keeping guard; to the right is Fan Zhongyan's inscription from Hugong's original tomb in Longjing; to the left is a stele with the inscription reproduced; and behind is the tomb of Hu's father Hu Chengshi. The surrounding tomb garden, Hugong Lingyuan (胡公陵园), with its grand temple, Huaizhong Ge 怀忠阁 (Pavilion of Cherishing Loyalty), in which a majestic statue of Hugong sits, was added in 1993 with subscriptions from local residents of more than ¥120,000. It took half a year to build, after which the incense and fire (*xianghuo* 香火) has been continuous (Fieldnotes 10/2/98 Huku).

Since its completion in 1993 local villagers "in the know" come to the Huku temple in preference to Fangyan to pay their respects to Hugong, and the square in front of Huaizhong Ge plays host to scores of Luohan Ban and song and dance troupes in an unending stream (Wang ed. 1997: 147). In the late 1990s, a pavilion with a zigzag bridge over the pool out in front of Huaizhong Ge was added, as well as a main gate and *paifang* (memorial arch) inscribed with Chairman Mao's evocation of the good works of Hu Ze, each at a cost of some ¥60,000 (Fieldnotes 10/2/98 Hu Ku).

The temple fair in Huku also hosts a secular market convened during three days of expanded commercial activity which overlap with lunar 8/13 and 8/14, the day before mid-Autumn festival 中秋节 on lunar 8/15. On lunar 8/14 in 1998, I was escorted on a walk around the Huku fair by Mr. Cheng Nanshan of the township government of Lower Huku (Huku Xia), beginning at government headquarters, where the township government was taking advantage of the temple fair to conduct its registration of the present birth control method being used by township women, and their status with regard to family planning. Registration continued through to the afternoon (Fieldnotes 10/4/98 Huku).

Mr. Cheng and I began our walk up Main Street passing vendors of clothing, shoes, fruit, vegetables, pork, tools, wool, tape cassettes and CDs, the usual run of stuff one sees at the fairs, somewhat smaller in scale than the fair in Qianxiang. Off the side street there were tea, eggs, wooden tubs, and then out in the open square, furniture, wooden couches and chairs, mattresses, wooden boxes, etc.

En route, we met an elderly farmer who wanted to take us to his home, and also show us the temples at Huamei Yan 画眉岩 in "Upper Huku" (Huku Shang 胡库上). It was a fortuitous meeting for had it not been for this farmer's request a delightful paradox would not have come to light regarding the development of Hugong's cult. And fortunately, Mr. Cheng proved flexible enough to arrange for the excursion 2 km out of town by car to Huamei Yan, and return by three-wheel taxi. Huamei Yan is the site of several temples, of which the original Hugong Family Temple (Jiamiao

家庙) gives legitimacy to Huku Shang's aspirations to pilgrimage site status. Reconfigured during the Ming, Yong Le reign (1403–1425), the Hugong Family temple was restored and expanded during the Qing, Kang Xi reign (1662–1723) to commemorate Hugong's accomplishments. Destroyed during the Cultural Revolution, restoration began again in March 1993.

In addition the site boasts a Guanyin Pavilion 观音阁, containing images of Songzi Guanyin (送子观音 Bring sons Guanyin), Dishui Guanyin (滴水观音 Water drip Guanyin), and Song Nü Guanyin (送女观音 Bring daughters Guanyin). Further along there is a temple in honor of Rulai Buddha 如来佛, and a shrine honoring the Jade Emperor 玉皇大帝楼. Finally there is a small area housing images of Dimu Niangniang 地母娘娘 (Daoist goddess of the soil) and Dizhi Huang 地芷皇 or Dong Yue 东岳—deity of the eastern peak (Fieldnotes 10/4/98).

A new *paifang* and a new temple to honor Mdm. Chen Shisi 陈十四娘娘 were under construction in 1998, the innards of the latter still being worked on. Upper Huku's plans for the area included a new road up to the foot of the hill as well as a hotel to house its anticipated visitors. They were eager to attract foreign investment, and hoped (in vain) that I could be of some assistance (Fieldnotes 10/4/98 Huku).

The restoration of this Hugong temple, and the other temples in Huamei Yan was in part stimulated by the construction of the Hugong temple down in lower Huku. The work at Huamei Yan was undertaken by residents of upper Huku. And here is where the paradox lies, since "Lower" and "Upper" Huku are arbitrary administrative divisions imposed on a single "natural" town (*zhen*) and lineage community by Communist authorities after 1949. That those divisions have emerged as the basis for competing temple centers in a non-governmental context would seem to suggest, counter-intuitively, that these two administratively and presumably revenue distinct communities do not share in the proceeds that the new temple down in lower Huku has brought its residents. Thus, the incentive for upper Huku to get in on the act, and vie with lower Huku in a scramble to attract supplicants and pilgrims during the fair commemorating Hugong's birth on lunar 8/13. Rather than unifying kin communities in common belief, it would seem that the cult of Hugong Dadi and its temple fair have merely provided another medium in which the expression of local parochialism is reproduced, albeit in the new administrative categories of the PRC. The machinations of lower Huku in competition with Fangyan, and then the machinations of upper Huku in competition with both, in pursuit of popular patronage as pilgrimage sites reveal a political dimension to the total social phenomenon that is the temple fair.

It is here that I would proclaim to "rest my case" as to the totality of the temple fair as a social phenomenon. The Hugong temple fair represents most forcefully in the contemporary setting the functionally complete traditional temple fair, combining religious worship with popular expressive cultural and operatic performance, three days of expanded commercial activity in the hinterland market towns with Hugong temples, and even serving as a context for the crafting of political alliances, and machinations in pursuit of pilgrimage site status. The Hugong temple fair is the total social phenomenon par excellence.

Its ability to weather the secularization of society imposed by Communist authorities for 40 years was due in no small measure to Chairman Mao's invocation of Hu Ze as a genuinely righteous official, worthy of emulation by modern Communist cadres. But the temple fair surrounding him has provided a model to the towns where the temples of other deities were located historically as to what a total temple fair "ought" to be like, and has therefore served as an additional stimulus to an already vigorous religious revival in the Chinese countryside. Many of the secular fairs, the temple-less temple fairs authorized for the sake of commodity circulation, were already scheduled on the dates of traditional temple fairs, and have become sites where the religious revival finds a congenial arena in which its activities reverberate sympathetically with traditional practice, and help to complete in the present the multifunctional totality of which temple fairs were an expression. The following chapter provides just such an example.

Note

1 Professor Peter Bol says he heard they stole the remains and brought them back in the dead of night.

10 Fotang town
The resacralization of a commercial fair

The saga of Fotang town provides the opportunity of observing how newly refurbished temples have recently "opened [their deity's] eyes," to resume providing the appropriate popular religious context to fairs authorized by the state for the sake of commerce. Thus the narrative runs: reviving the commercial fairs has provided a setting in which popular religious rituals and symbols that were part of the traditional context in which the fairs were imbedded have reemerged, resacralizing the fair, and adding fuel to the revival of popular religion and the recycling of popular religious symbols which the Communist state seems prepared to tolerate.

The Temples Duqing Si 渡罄寺 and Shuanglin Si 双林寺 and Fotang's Origins

The name Fotang dates to the Northern and Southern dynasties (AD 420–581), and the Liang dynasty (AD 502–557) in particular. There are several versions of the story of the origin of the name, each of which involves the creation of the temple Duqing Si.

In the first, Buddhist monk Song Toutuo 嵩头陀 (or Tianzhuseng Damo 天竺僧达摩) (AD 502–557) came to Yiwu from India to spread the teachings of Buddha. He arrived in Fotang on lunar 10/10, when there was a great flood in the Yiwu river. He threw his prayer bowl into the river and it changed into a boat, saving many people who were able to escape to a place on the bank where present-day Zhuyuan village is located. To commemorate Damo's deed, the people built a small temple named Du Qing Si 渡罄寺, fashioned an image of him, and placed it in the temple. Thereafter, the incense was continuous. Merchants and peddlers assembled, the community expanded, and developed into a market town.

The *duilian* couplets hanging at the doors of the temple read:

> 佛光透彩传万代 Buddha's light penetrates through 10,000 generations
> 堂烛生辉照八方 The brightness of the hall's candles illuminates the eight directions

The first of the couplets begins with the character "Fo," the second with the character "tang," and so it came to be known as the old "Fotang" (佛堂—Buddhist Hall) as did the surrounding town. Ever since, lunar 10/10 has been celebrated with a temple fair in Fotang (Fotang Township Government 2005: 1; Fotang Fieldnotes 11/27/98).

In the second version, Duqing Si's origin is attributed to Damo's fellow student, Fu Xi 傅翕 from Jiting 稽亭 village in the Fotang area, who is said to have achieved enlightenment with Damo's assistance. It is said of Fu Xi and Damo that they shared a single master. When the master died, two pellets were fashioned from his ashes and thrown asunder. One landed in India, the other in Fotang, the homes of Damo and Fu Xi (Fotang fieldnotes 11/27/98).

When Fu Xi returned to the place of Damo's transformation at Songshan 松山 in AD 520, he planted two pine trees, constructed a road and established a convent, called Mi Le An 弥勒庵. 24 years later, on Damo's birthday, Fu Xi took two disciples to the place on the bank where Damo's bowl "boat" had landed, and constructed a small Buddhist Hall (Fotang). He convened a great Buddhist fair, lasting three days, to promulgate Buddha's teachings. Later, to commemorate the event, a permanent temple was built on the site where the small Fotang had been constructed, and called Duqing Si 渡磬寺, or Gu Fotang 古佛堂 (the old Buddhist Hall) (Fotang Township Government 2005: 1).

In still another version of the origin of Duqing Si, it was built on the site of Buddha's footprint, Fotang's Da Fo Jiaoyin 大佛脚印. It is said that the founder of Buddhism, Sakyamuni himself, came to China to spread the faith, and passing through Fotang found no way to cross the river. Using his godly power, he leapt across, leaving a footprint on the bank. When the people became aware of it, they built a temple on the spot to commemorate the Buddhist founder, and gave it the name Fotang. Because the spot was a thoroughfare, and an important transport intersection, over the years it gradually prospered, attracted merchants in large numbers and became a commercial center. The name Fotang continued down to the present (Mao ed. 1996: 98).

In the course of history, Duqing Si has seen many changes, fallen down and risen up several times. During the Cultural Revolution it was seriously damaged, and the present Duqing Si was reconstructed by the common folk on their own initiative, on its original site in the 1980s. But its scale, records, uniqueness, and cultural details are considered of minor importance in the history of Buddhism, when compared to its suburban neighbor Shuanglin Si 双林寺 (Fotang Township Government 2005: 103), also known as Shuanglin Chansi 禅寺 and Baolin Chanyuan 宝林禅院.

The origin of Shuanglin Si 双林寺 is also associated with Fu Xi, who is said to have seen to its construction in AD 534 at the foot of Cloud Yellow Mountain (Yunhuang shan 云黄山), some 5 km to the northeast of Fotang town (Mao ed. 1996: 38).

Some years later, in 540, Fu Xi sent his younger son Fu Ren 傅荏 to the capital to study. In making the arrangements, Fu Xi respectfully referred to emperor Liang Wudi as "Guozhu Jiushi Pusa" (国主救世菩萨—savior Buddha head of state). Before long, Fu Xi was invited to the capital to expound on the Jingang 金刚 sutra in an audience with emperor Liang Wudi, and to teach Buddhism at the court, the first of three such audiences he was granted. Liang Wudi had all his officials and relatives attend his lectures (Fotang Township Government 2005: 102; Wu ed. 1987: 598). The emperor awarded Fu Xi the title Dashi (大士), and later provided assistance in expanding Shuanglin temple on a grand scale (Mao ed. 1996: 38).

After attaining the title Dashi, Fu Dashi went on to build the Convent of the Seven Buddhas (七佛庵 Qifo An), with seven pavilions, and three seven-story pagodas on Cloud Yellow Mountain (Yunhuangshan 云黄山) (Fotang Township Government 2005: 103). During the Ming, it came to be known as Cloud Yellow Convent (Yunhuang An 云黄庵), but on the night of 27 August, 1677 during the Qing Kangxi period, the three towers were blown over in a windstorm (Wu ed. 1987: 598). Nowadays the site is occupied by a recently refurbished Cloud Yellow Temple (Yunhuang Si 云黄寺).

Fuxi referred to himself as the "good and wise master who attained salvation under the trees at Shuanglin" (Shuanglin Shuxia Danglai Jietuo Shanhui Dashi—双林树下当来解脱善慧大士). He was one of the early purveyors of Mahayana Buddhism in China, propounding a philosophy of "natural wisdom, deep understanding of the Great Vehicle (Mahayana)" (ziran zhihui, shenjie dacheng—自然智慧, 深解大乘). He established one of the first libraries of Chinese Buddhism, and was the first to emphasize combining the teachings of Buddhism, Daoism, and Confucianism (Fotang Township Government 2005: 86).

Among Buddhist disciples, Fu Dashi is known as Dongfang Shengren (东方圣人—Sage of the East), and recognized by followers of the Tiantai 天台 school of Buddhism as one of its two founding ancestors. He is also #131 of the group of 500 Buddhist Luohan (Arhat), in whose company he is known as "venerable wise one" (Shanhui Jun 善慧尊).

According to historical records Fu Dashi died in 569 and his ashes were said to have been divided into two parts; one part placed in Grave Mountain Pagoda (Zhongshan Ta—冢山塔), the other part in Mountain Peak Pagoda (Shanding Ta—山顶塔), both sites on Cloud Yellow Mountain. Nowadays the ruins of Grave Mountain Pagoda are difficult to locate with certainty, but Mountain Peak Pagoda has been restored several times over more than 1000 years, and still stands (Wu ed. 1987: 598).

And, at an undetermined date he became one of Jinhua's "Three Buddhas" in the ensemble of "Three Buddhas and Five Marquises" (Jinhua de Sanfo Wuhou 金华的三佛五侯). In Jinhua city the temple fair of Fu Dashi is held on lunar 1/18, on which day each year supplicants go to Black Cloud Temple 黑云寺 in Jinhua to greet/welcome Fu Dashi with amateur opera performances, dances and songs, and Taige displays (Cao 1929: 20).

Because of Fu Dashi's place in the history of Buddhism, Shuanglin Si became a center of Buddhist activity and a sacred site, with international influence that continued long after his death. In the Northern Song (AD 960–1126) there were more than 1,200 resident monks at Shuanglin Si, and in the subsequent Southern Song the numbers expanded to several thousand, with 1000 nuns in its associated convent, one of the more important temples in all of Jiangnan (Fotang Township Government 2005: 103).

In 1066, Song emperor Yingzong provided the inscription "Baolin Chansi" (Chan temple of the Precious Forest—宝林禅寺), and in 1108 Song emperor Huizong published a compilation of notable mountains (five) and temples (ten) in the empire. Of the ten temples, Shuanglin was #8 (Wu ed. 1987: 599). Song Huizong also donated more than 1000 mu of land to the temple (Mao ed. 1996: 39).

Throughout the Tang, Song, and Yuan dynasties, for some seven centuries Shuanglin Si maintained close connections with Japanese Buddhist communities. The best known of the sojourners to Japan was a Yuan dynasty monk known by his monastic name "Ming Ji Chu Jun" (明极楚俊—"Extreme clarity, keen refinement") who was invited to Japan in 1329, where he lived for an extended period, visiting Japanese temple sites, proselytizing Chinese style Chan teachings, and organizing the construction of the temple Rendeng Dasi 仁等大寺 in Japan. His poetry had great influence in Japanese literary circles, and many of his poems are still in circulation (Fotang Township Government 2005: 103; Wu ed. 1987: 599).

Throughout the Yuan, Ming, and Qing dynasties, the temple had its ups and downs, and was destroyed and rebuilt several times, for the last time during Qing Jiaqing times (1796–1821) (Wu ed. 1987: 599; Fotang fieldnotes 11/27/98). During the Qing dynasty, Shuanglin Si was referred to as "#3 in all the world, #1 in the Jiangzhe region" (天下第三，江浙第一) (Fotang Township Government 2005: 103).

But it met its match during the Great Leap Forward in 1958 when a reservoir was constructed, its environs inundated, and Shuanglin Si destroyed. The temple was thus not around to suffer vandalism or destruction during the Cultural Revolution (Fotang Fieldnotes 11/27/98).

The present Shuanglin Si was rebuilt in the 1980s in the same style as the original, near the shore of the reservoir. The famous iron pagoda, cast during the Five Dynasties (AD 952), 2.15 m high, elaborately decorated with mountains and seas, dragons fighting for a pearl, and images of various deities, rescued from the original site, is now housed in the Float on the Clouds Pavilion (Fuyun Ting 浮云亭) adjacent the rebuilt temple (Mao ed. 1996: 39). From the pavilion one can look out over the reservoir under which the original Shuanglin Si was submerged.

At the end of 1985, the Yiwu county government moved to protect nine sites where temples existed as religious and tourist spots among which Shuanglin temple and Yunhuang Si were included (Wu ed. 1987: 599).

Fotang town 佛堂镇

I had the privilege of visiting Fotang in 1998 during its lunar 10/10 temple fair, and again during a visit in 2006, when the town was scarcely recognizable, its built-up area dramatically expanded, with paved streets, corner bus stops, boutique shops, evidence of its growth and prosperity under the economic reforms.

Fotang is located on the upper reaches of the Dongyang River (called the Yiwu River in Yiwu) which feeds the Qiantang River. Boats could reach Dongyang upstream, and Jinhua, Lanxi, Quzhou, and Hangzhou downstream. In periods of high water, goods took a little more than two days to reach Hangzhou. When water transport was primary during the Qing dynasty and Republican periods, merchants, passengers, and cargo passed through the town in large numbers, and Fotang became a collection and dispersal point for the sideline products of neighboring counties. Every market day, held on days one, four, seven of the ten-day market week, red sugar, ham, dates, wine, and other goods were collected and loaded on boats, and shipped to the coast. Before liberation, the taxes collected from Fotang township amounted to half of all the taxes collected in the entire county of Yiwu (Fotang Township Government 2005: 41, 43, 51).

For one li on the banks up and downstream of the bridge, Fuqiao 浮桥, as many as 500 boats might be docked at any one time at a variety of specialized piers, salt pier, dog market pier, pig market pier, bamboo garden pier, etc., and Fotang had its own boat construction and repair factory (Fotang Township Government 2005: 41, 78). The piers connected up with the streets and lanes of the town, whose residents depended on the town's commerce and trade for their livelihood.

The main market was at the north end of Straight Street. "New Market" was opened at the south end of Straight Street in 1936 by the Merchants Association. The new market handled red sugar, draft animals, wood and charcoal; the old market mainly handled grain (Fotang Township Government 2005: 51). Between the new and old markets the entire length of Straight Street was lined with some 400 shops, in two-story wood structures, shop on the lower floor, living quarters above—teahouses, bars, traditional banks, pawn shops, agricultural goods, and dry goods shops (Fotang Township Government 2005: 73).

According to one account, there were 14 cloth shops, six cloth factories, eight hosiery knitting factories, 18 shops handling or specializing in agricultural tools, 12 Chinese medicine shops, four private hospitals, 13 lumber companies, ten ham shops, ten oil pressing workshops, more than 20 iron and metals shops, three gold and silver jewelry shops, one salt shop, one pawn shop, three banks, 23 teahouses, 40 bars, and 22 shops handling "goods from south of the mountains" 山南货 (dried preserved fruits shipped primarily from Guangdong, lychee 荔枝, guiyuan 桂圆 (Long An), Nanzao 南枣 (dates), etc. (Fotang Township Government 2005: 44).

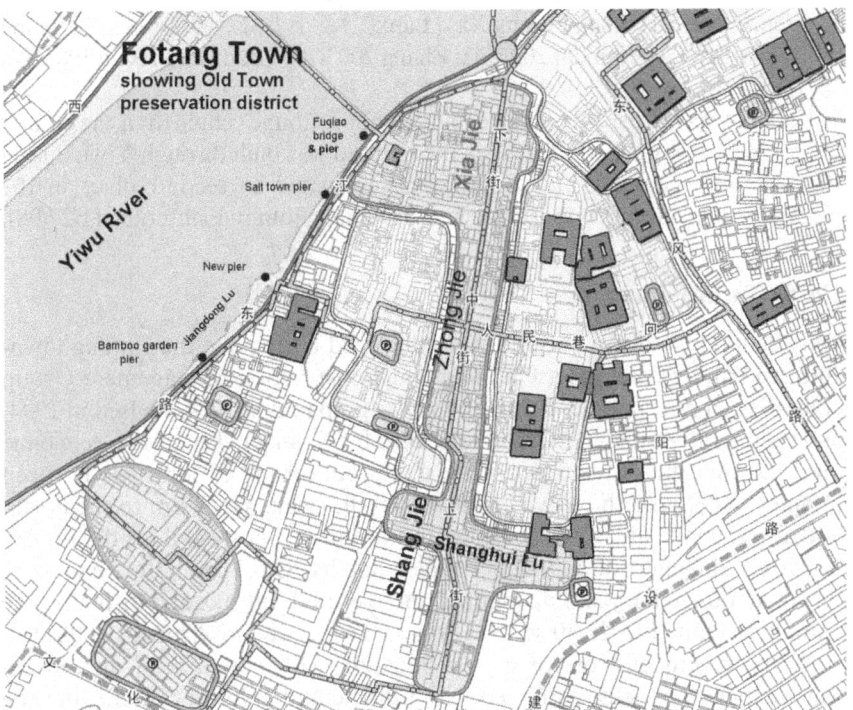

Map 10.1 Fotang with historic preservation area
Source: Fotang Township government, private communication

In 1936, the Bai He Chao Feng (百鹤朝凤 Hundred Cranes face the Wind) opera stage was constructed at the new market end of Straight Street under two old sheltering camphor trees, arrayed with tea tables so that one could sit and enjoy tea while watching the opera. The opera stage has long since disappeared, replaced by an indoor opera house, the Xinhua Juyuan 新华剧院 constructed in 1955 on the Central Street segment of Straight Street, but the south end of Straight Street is still marked by the sheltering camphor trees (Fotang Township Government 2005: 73).

The merchants attracted by Fotang's flourishing commerce established their own commercial associations (Huiguan 会馆) according to their native place, the Shaoxing Huiguan, Anhui Huiguan, etc. There was also a general Chamber of Commerce or Shanghui 商会 whose headquarters was formally inaugurated in 1910, the earliest merchants' association in Yiwu county. It regulated trade in, and resolved disputes among all of the businesses in Fotang, and within its constituent occupational associations/guilds 同行工会 (Fotang Township Government 2005: 43–44).

In Republican times Fotang was known as Little Lanxi 小兰溪 another thriving riverine commercial port, that was in turn known as Little Shanghai:

Lanxi xiao Shanghai, Fotang Xiao Lanxi 兰溪小上海，佛堂小兰溪 (Fotang Township Government 2005: 41; Zhang 2003: 46; Zhang and Hong 1985: 24)

Fotang was historically a more important economic center than the county seat of Yiwu, only superseded when the railroad was built through Yiwu during the twentieth century, and Fotang was relegated to second place in the hierarchy of economic importance in the county (Fotang Fieldnotes 11/27/98).

Post-reform Fotang

Once economic reform became the watchword nationally, the Fotang township government created a Planning and Construction Management Group consisting of nine people. Its first plan was prepared in 1984, revised in 1994, and again in 1999, and in its essentials called for Fotang to become an economic and cultural center of southwest Yiwu, a producer of "cultural goods" (wen huapin 文化品) for the Yiwu small commodities market, 8 km to the north, and also to make use of the considerable resources it possessed for developing tourism—Shuanglin and Duqing temples, and its "Old Town." In the process, its population in the year 2020 should not to exceed 230,000, and its built space should be limited to 22.30 sq km (Fotang Township Government 2005: 15).

The northern end of town is residential, with commercial and urban functions as the focus, equipped with athletic and cultural centers, and the Yiwu–Fotang road/now highway as the axis. The southern end of town is the administrative and commercial hub, the political and economic center, and also the location of the newly constructed Fotang Industrial Zone. Both sides of the river are slated to be urbanized, except for the core historic preservation area of Old Town (see below).

After 1982, when the Yiwu Small Commodities Market began its expansion, Fotang was able to take advantage of its neighbor's development. With land in Yiwu at a premium, Fotang was attractive as a small commodity production center supplying Yiwu-based entrepreneurs, and an ideal bedroom community for the employees and merchants of the Yiwu market center (Fotang Township Government 2005: 33). Already a suburb of Yiwu, Fotang is poised to be absorbed into the expanding city before too long.

Fotang has always been a center for the production of agricultural goods, grain, sugar, pigs and goats, fruit, sugar cane, mandarin oranges and Hongqumi 红曲米 (a red coloring agent for food, also used in Chinese medicine). In 1980, Fotang also witnessed developments in fish breeding and pearl raising (Fotang Township Government 2005: 18).

In the 800-year history of Jinhua Ham (Huotui 火腿) production, Fotang has played an active role. In 1983 Fotang's Tianxin 田心 village started the first modern rural ham processing factory in the township, producing 4,613 hams, and a variety of sausage and preserved meats in its first year, soon becoming an important center of processing and production of Jinhua Hams (Fotang Township Government 2005: 33).

Yanli 燕里 village in Fotang is the point of origin of the Yiwu sugar industry, beginning in 1662, when Jia Weicheng 贾惟承 brought back some sugar seedlings from Fujian and the processing of red sugar began as an industry. In 1986 there were 10,831 mu planted in sugar, producing 49,155 tons (Fotang Township Government 2005: 22).

Mandarin oranges are another important local product. A mandarin orange research center was established in 2000 to devise new breeds, promulgate new techniques, and provide education. The center started its work with less than 3000 mu of trees, but by 2003 had more than 26,000 mu planted. In 2002, the center was named a national level Agricultural Technical Educational Center, the only such project in the country to receive United Nations UNDP sponsorship (Fotang Township Government 2005: 22, 29; *Zhejiang Ribao* June 14, 2006).

In 1984, the Township and Village Enterprises (TVEs) of Fotang surpassed ¥10,000,000 in production value, and in 1985 they surpassed ¥25,000,000, more than ten times the figure for 1980. Township enterprises produced clothing of all kinds, food products, leather and other goods for the Yiwu small commodities market, as well as machinery, electrical supplies and construction materials (Fotang Township Government 2005: 34).

In 1990 Fotang's industrial production broke through the ¥100,000,000 mark for the first time, and with the opening of the South Yiwu Industrial Park in Fotang in 1992, industrial production expanded tenfold in the ensuing years. By 1994 Fotang boasted 1268 industrial enterprises, with a production value of ¥1,006,000,000. At the end of 2004, as its Industrial Zone matured Fotang had more than 2000 enterprises of various kinds, 1598 of which were industrial, with a fixed capital investment of ¥992,000,000 and more than 26,470 workers, producing goods valued at ¥4,516,000,000 (Fotang Township Government 2005: 34).

In 2004, rural per capita income was ¥5,548, reaching ¥6,067 in 2005, and ¥9,024 in 2007 (Fotang Township Government 2005: 18; *Zhejiang Ribao* June 14, 2006; Jinhua City webpage #10).

In 2005, the township government allocated ¥4,000,000 to deliver running water to 33 villages in the township, and construction began on an 80 mu, ¥150,000,000 water treatment plant. In 2006, ¥150,000,000 was allocated for the construction of Fotang Central Primary School, and for the construction of a dormitory and classroom building for Fotang Middle School (*Zhejiang Ribao* June 14, 2006).

The new town is bubbling (如火如荼 Like fire, like tea). The area of the town has expanded, from the original 3 sq km to 5 sq km. New streets have a new modern look, and the town has been cleaned up and greened up. Township Party secretary Luo Huayong 骆华勇 has emphasized environmental beautification, giving people pride in their surroundings, and the township has spent ¥120,000,000 on control of industrial pollution and emissions. It has also achieved an average per capita green space of 11 sq m (*Zhejiang Ribao* June 14, 2006).

As the result of these efforts, Fotang has received repeated awards and citations, designated a national "environmentally beautiful rural town," a national and provincial level "civilized town," a national and provincial-level "progressive work in sports and recreation town," a nationally designated "town of 1000 strengths," a provincial-level "strength in education town," "sanitary town," etc. (*Zhejiang Ribao* June 14, 2006).

Historic preservation of Old Town

One of the Fotang town government's more noteworthy areas of achievement has been in its efforts on behalf of historic preservation. This is quite remarkable in view of the relative indifference to the subject on the part of local township planning authorities in the other counties of Jinhua. Development is a good thing, and the old homes, shops, and architectural landmarks like city walls are old and ugly, shameful even.

The historic preservation consciousness in Fotang dates to November 1989, when the Yiwu City Architecture Study Association convened a national study meeting on the subject of the architecture of Yiwu's traditional dwellings. The specialists attending were extremely interested in the large number of such dwellings in Fotang, and in particular emphasized the potential for preservation represented by Fotang's Old Town, with so many Qing dynasty and Republican period structures still intact (Fotang Township Government 2005: 82).

Another contributing factor was the leveling for development of Yiwu county town's Chaoyangmen 朝阳门 city gate which inspired some knowledgeable people to call attention to the contradiction between urban construction and the preservation of classical architecture (Township Government 2005: 82).

In July 2000, a half-month of study activities were convened in Fotang on the subject of the "Preservation of Old Town," with site visits, seminars, discussions, textual research, etc. In March 2001, with the support of Yiwu city and Zhejiang province leaders, a group of six scholars, specialists, and professors from Beijing and Shanghai were invited to Fotang for an investigation and seminar. All agreed that Fotang's Old Town was notable for its layout of streets, bridges, and piers, as well as for the many specimens of traditional architecture (Fotang Township Government 2005).

In June 2001 the township government formally issued documents establishing the Office of Fotang Old Town Preservation, and later in the month established a leadership group of 13 members, headed by the Vice Chairman of the Yiwu City Communist Party Standing Committee, Mr. Song Yinghao. The Yiwu City government raised ¥1,000,000 for the project, an expression of the fact that this was not only a Fotang matter, but one in which all of Yiwu county had an interest (Fotang Township Government 2005: 83).

The group's work included holding seminars, collecting and organizing historical materials, folk stories and myths, texts, pictures, etc. with the goal of creating an overall plan for the preservation work. Fotang's "Old Town" district stretches for some 2000 m along the river with a total area of 30,000 sq m (Fotang Township Government 2005: 73). Straight Street 直街 was the commercial center of old Fotang, and stretches for 510 meters parallel to the river, divided into Upper Street 上街, Central Street 中街, and Lower Street 下街, from south to north.[1]

According to the plan, the historic preservation area would compose 43 hectares, and a central core area of 23 hectares which would include the east and west banks of the Dongyang/Yiwu river south to New Market, east to Li Ji 利记 mansion and north to Jiexiao ancestral hall 节孝祠, encompassing the Xinhua opera theater on Central Street, and the Quancong Library founded by Republican period entrepreneur Mr. Zhu Guancong 朱灌聪[2] (Fotang Township Government 2005: 84; Zhang and Hong 81).

The market/temple fair of Fotang town

The Fotang Market/Temple Fair on lunar 10/10 is one of the largest in the eight counties of Jinhua, coinciding with the storing up of grain after the harvest, and the onset of the agricultural slack season (Mao ed. 1996: 98–99). Lunar 10/10 celebrates Damo's rescue of the common folk during the flood nearly 1500 years ago (Fotang Township Government 2005: 53), but it is unclear exactly when an annual temple fair began to be held. Shuanglin Temple was already an important Buddhist center during the Yuan and Ming, by which time it seems likely an annual temple fair in Fotang was a fixture of the annual calendar.

During the twentieth century, the scope of the 10/10 fair has continuously expanded. According to the official narrative of Fotang's temple fair, in the early days, the goods sold were mainly religious goods, incense and candles for worship; and later the merchants moved in to take advantage of the crowds, and the secular market became its dominant function (Fotang Fieldnotes 11/27/98). "Seeking out the gods and praying to Buddha *which have no utility* were gradually replaced by the useful trade in goods" (Mao ed. 1996: 99).

Whether the secularization of the fairs was a natural development of the pre-Communist period or not, once the Communists seized power, secularization became the watchword, temples were closed down, and the secular fairs became government run and organized operations. The local authorities saw to the layout of the market place, the coordination of transportation, security and safety arrangements, creating a good environment for the masses to participate in trade. Oddly enough, the secular fair in Fotang during these early days of the PRC was scheduled on the lunar date 10/10 when the traditional temple fair had been held (Mao ed. 1996: 99).

The secular fair in Fotang was not held during the Cultural Revolution period and most popular cultural performance genres were considered representatives of the Four Olds, and not performed in public, if at all

(Fieldnotes 11/27/98; Fotang Township Government 2005: 53). But in the 1980s with the implementation of economic reform and openness, traditional folk cultural activities were encouraged by the convening of a series of cultural and folk art festivals in Yiwu and Jinhua, giving their practitioners the opportunity to begin honing their chops for public performance once again (Fotang Township Government 2005: 59).

The reform-era secular fair in Fotang on lunar 10/10 reached a high point in 1984. At that fair, firms from as far away as Hangzhou, Shaoxing, and Lishui engaged in commodity trade for three days. And there were continuous opera performances by four Wuju opera troupes in the Fotang opera house, the Jinhua City troupe, the Yiwu City troupe, the Tianxin village troupe, and the Peilei village troupe (Zhang and Hong 1985: 313), as well as scores of individual street performers. And the red fire of the Fotang lunar 10/10 fair is said to have become even hotter in the late 1980s and 1990s (Fotang Township Government 2005: 59).

It was my good fortune to have attended the Fotang fair in 1998, after this process of heating up had been going on for some time, and indeed the Fotang fair was the largest and "hottest" of all the fairs I visited in the course of my fieldwork. In 1998, there were at least ten huge tents set up in the center of town, three of which offered night-club entertainment, something I had not seen before, singers and scantily clad dancing girls paraded on a stage outside to entice onlookers in.

In another tent, there was a troupe of performing animals from Anhui, including a monkey, a bear, a goat, a group of dogs, and a real live lion!

Figure 10.1 Dancing girls: Fotang

Exhibits of freaks of nature preserved in formaldehyde, motorized children's carnival rides, a house of horrors with dioramas and automata of the 18 levels of hell, each with its distinctive form of torture, and incredibly grotesque pictures outside to lure prospective customers in.

Along the streets hundreds of temporary stalls were erected, selling clothing of all kinds, basketry, and food.

Furniture stretched out in one direction almost as far as the eye could see.

I was lucky enough to have encountered the nationally famous Xiaoluo Shu (small cymbal narrative) performer Jia Youfu 贾有福 on a street corner, performing in his inimitable style (in impenetrable dialect) (described in Chapter 6).

At least two Tibetans squatted on different street corners making medicinal preparations for small crowds, alternately slicing herbs and fungi, sawing antelope horns, etc. into packets for which they charged ¥20, and couldn't make them fast enough.

On one street a one-man band performed, pumping a drum and cymbal while simultaneously playing the flute and erhu to a small crowd surrounding him.

In 1998, the opera performances were provided by a troupe from Pan An county, which had been performing the week before at a fair in Heng Dian. Their schedule of performances for the Fotang fair included 12 operas over three days, and the audience in the open square just in front of the stage was packed at every performance.

Significantly, by 1998 a rebuilt Shuanglin Temple had already begun receiving supplicants once more, and thus, by this time, the religious element

Figure 10.2 House of horror: Fotang

206 *Unraveling the total social phenomenon*

Figure 10.3 Goods on sale: Fotang

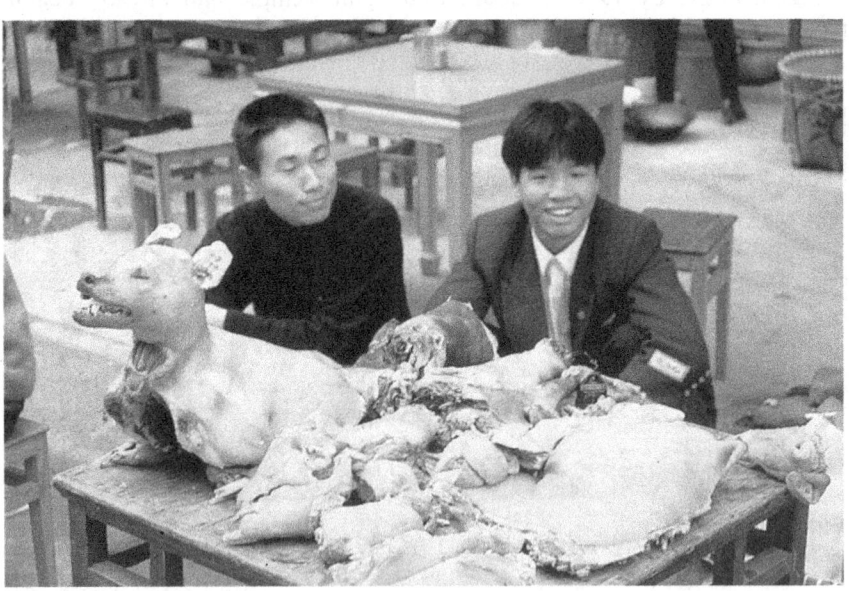

Figure 10.4 Street vendor: Fotang

Figure 10.5 Medicinal herbs for sale: Fotang

Figure 10.6 One-man band: Fotang

had begun to recover some space and functional significance in the Fotang fair that had been absent since the Great Leap Forward when Shuanglin Temple was destroyed by the reservoir. In effect, the secular fair of Fotang has provided a space in which the revival of popular religious practice found a congenial and familiar home, having been the raison d'être for the convening of the fair historically. The rebuilding of Shuanglin Temple has given Fotang back the temple of its temple fair, and restored the fair to its full multi-functionality.

Some years later, in 2003 the heating up of the Fotang market/temple fair climaxed with between 200,000–300,000 attendees from surrounding counties and cities (Fotang Township Government 2005: 60). The streets and lanes of Fotang were filled with people. There were nearly 10,000 temporary market stalls selling clothing, cloth, shoes, hats, wood products, metal products, furniture, agricultural equipment, small commodities, etc. Some 20–30 performance troupes from various neighboring townships, entertained at 12 designated performance venues in village squares throughout the township, where movies were also shown (Fotang Township Government 2005: 53). The Fotang Wuju Consolidated Association had been organized in the same year, and was active in recruiting amateur troupes to perform at the various fair venues (Fotang Township Government 2005: 60).

By now, burning incense at Shuanglin or Duqing temples, praying to Buddha, making a vow, chanting scripture, having one's fate divined have reasserted themselves as the essence of the temple fair, and doubtless many thousands of pilgrims who attended the fair in 2003 came with the goal of visiting Fotang's Buddhist temples and shrines, worshipping and celebrating the feats of Fu Dashi.

Notwithstanding its resacralization, in 2008 the lunar 10/10 Fotang temple fair was rechristened with the very secular sounding title of Fotang Folk Cultural Festival 佛堂民俗文化节 (Wang Chunping 王春平 personal communication 8/09). And for most of the "mountains and seas of people" who attend, the temple fair is a time of relaxation and recreation, a leisure activity, a vacation, a release from the drudgery of agricultural labor. People come for diversion and pleasure, and thus the temple fair is also a golden moment for the practitioners of the various folk arts who in turn contribute to the "red hot" excitement of the fair (Mao ed. 1996: 99). Two of those folk arts native to Fotang, Xiaoluo Shu (小锣书 Small Cymbal Narrative) and Chang Daoqing 唱道情, were discussed in Chapter 6.

So the new designation, "Folk Cultural Festival," is not without some justification in terms of why one goes to the fair, and what one does when one gets there, but it does speak to the government's attitude of stressing the recreational rather than the religious elements of contemporary temple fairs.

Still it seems to me that the resacralization of the Fotang fair constitutes the proof of the pudding for the argument that the totality of the temple fair phenomenon has played a role in expanding the boundaries of popular cultural and popular religious expression in the present.

Notes

1 This is somewhat counterintuitive since the river along which it developed flows from north to south. One would expect that Upper Street would be upriver, but in fact it is downriver, perhaps reflecting the orientation of the businesses in the region to the larger centers with which they traded down river. The stopping point for upstream-bound ships was Lower Street Xiajie to the north; for downstream ships it was Upper Street Shangjie to the south.
2 Mr. Zhu also founded the Fotang Electric Light Co., a roof-tile factory, and the Xinxin Wutai 新新舞台 opera troupe.

11 Conclusions

This has been a multi-sited, regional, ethnographic study of market and temple fairs in the inland municipality of Jinhua, a middle-rung city on the prosperous east coast of China, presented through the experience of a group of its constituent counties and townships. Throughout I have attempted to provide the historical background necessary to make sense of the phenomena observed in the ethnographic present—be they geographic locales, deities, temple sites, or popular cultural genres. And I hope I have succeeded in communicating something of the spirit of the municipality in the process.

While relatively late in attracting foreign investment, modernizing forces have nevertheless placed Jinhua squarely within the circuits of global capital. But notwithstanding such forces, the market and temple fairs of the rural areas remain sites where the multi-functional totality of rural social life is on public display, arenas where popular expressive culture, folk religion, and political economy are simultaneously salient, a quintessential "total social phenomenon" in the Maussian sense.

My observations of the fairs discovered what might be described as several degrees of totality, from the strictly secular commercial fairs of Huqi, Luodian, Qianxiang, Xiawang, and Zhudaishi to the fully fledged "total" religious fair of Fangyan (the Hugong temple fair), with several communities occupying intermediate levels by virtue of potent religious traditions pregnant to revive.

In the town of Huqi a newly reopened and government approved Buddhist temple thus far had not yet begun sponsoring a temple fair, leaving Huqi's present fair a strictly secular affair for the moment. In Luodian a newly reconstructed temple failed to achieve government approval and was subsequently closed down and dismantled. There were plans to reconstruct the old temple in Qianxiang, and in Xiawang and Zhudaishi, the cult of Mashi Niangniang, after many years of neglect, was poised to make a comeback, possibly to serve as the focal point for a revived and total temple fair at some point in the not too distant future. And finally the fulfillment of the process of the secular clearing a space for the religious was manifest in the experience of the Fotang fair and the reemergence of the cult of Fu Dashi.

The fairs represent a high point in the annual round of social, economic, popular cultural, and religious activity in the Chinese countryside, a moment of red fire and excitement in an otherwise daily routine of agricultural and nowadays industrial labor. The sources of that red fire were revealed in the unraveling of the total social phenomenon.

The economic dimension

The economic dynamism of the fairs is surely one contributor to that red fire. From my investigation of the five secular fairs in Chapter 5, it is clear that the fairs have been quite successful in enhancing commodity circulation in rural China. Each of the five communities was distinctive as regards their material endowments and historical traditions, and their experience of economic development. But in each of the secular fairs, the intensity and fluidity of circulation represented a considerable quantum leap over that of the weekly "standard" market. And in each, we observed that even where the religious dimension was absent, the expanded market, the secular popular cultural performance genres, the opera, the games of chance, and the range of entertainments on display, many bordering on the grotesque, all lent heat to the red fire of the event.

The popular cultural dimension

As regards the popular cultural dimension of the fairs, the performances of Qigong aficionados at Huqi, the circuses at Huqi and Xiawang/Zhudaishi each with a "star" contortionist girl, acrobats and trained animal acts, the performance of "full sand flaming mouth" at the Huqi circus, the one-man band at Fotang, trained monkeys and the snake handler at Zhudaishi, trained bears at Luodian, performing animals in Fotang, Houses of Horror at Fotang and Luodian, displays of freaks of nature at Huqi and Zhudaishi, the grotesquery of opera make-up and performance voice in Luodian, Xiawang, and Fotang might all be martialed in support of Zhao's argument for a Bakhtinian understanding of Chinese temple fair entertainment (2002), and Yang's argument for the overall relaxation of the rules of conventional sociality (1967). Such performances and displays all attract crowds of onlookers, creating the heat one experiences and contributes to by one's own presence at the fair sites, partaking of the egalitarian spirit that Zhao (2002) argues characterized the fairs historically.

Two popular cultural performance genres loomed large, in which the rhetorical devices of metaphor, allegory, innuendo and indirection, sarcasm and humor, typical of sub-insurrectional "everyday" forms of resistance, were significant in evoking laughter, that expression of "universalism and freedom" and "the people's unofficial truth."

Xiaoluo Shu provided an example of the evolution of what had historically been a true weapon of the weak, under the constraints of the socialist state in the hands of practitioner Jia Youfu, on the streets of contemporary Fotang.

Daoqing, a genre with greater historical depth, required a lengthier discussion to recount its development since the Tang dynasty (AD 618–907), and the circumstances of its overwhelmingly blind performers in Jinhua since the Ming dynasty (1368–1644). Daoqing also provided the opportunity to chart the path of the folk performance arts in the early Communist period by tracing the career of one of the genre's prominent practitioners, Ye Yingmei. The post-Cultural Revolution revival of the art succeeded in breathing some new life into the genre, but as a folklorified form of entertainment for young people, as singing folksongs was for teenagers in the US in the 1960s.

The local operatic traditions of Jinhua known collectively as Wuju were far and away the most important source of red fire at the temple fairs of Jinhua historically, and remain so in the present, in both their professional and amateur manifestations. Amateur troops are regularly hired to "blow and bang" to enhance the red fire of rituals conducted during the New Year. But the opera made its greatest contribution to the heat of the fairs in the custom of *doutai*, in which several troupes performed simultaneously competing to attract the largest audience, and the red fire that resulted simply could not be matched. And further, the grotesquery of opera costume, make-up and voice lend additional support to Zhao's Bakhtinian interpretation of temple fair entertainment.

The influential career of Ms. Zhou Yuexian provided a window on developments in the Jinhua operatic profession during the Republican and early Communist transition periods, although Jinhua's local operatic genres face an uncertain future. After enjoying a post-Cultural Revolution renaissance, and a period of greater accessibility through new media, tape recordings, CDs, and DVDs, Wuju has been overwhelmed and marginalized in its share of the entertainment market by the broad availability and popularity of Hong Kong and Taiwan pop music and the modern cinema. Whether the recent launching of a Wuju webpage will turn out to be the last gasp of a dying genre, or a sign of its reinvigoration, only time will tell.

All these popular cultural performance genres on display at the fairs attract the crowds that generate the excitement and commotion of which red fire consists.

The popular religious dimension

In the historical survey of the religious terrain of Jinhua, we encountered the municipality's Three Buddhas and Five Marquises who have reemerged as objects of worship in the present.

The contemporary temple fair of one of those Marquises, Hugong Dadi, served to introduce the religious dimension of contemporary fairs. Somewhat improbably/counterintuitively, a few off-the-cuff remarks by Chairman Mao about the deity's human origins served to justify Hugong's revival as an object of religious worship, and thereby imbue the fair on his birthday with a religious dimension from the very inception of its reappearance. This provided the uncommon opportunity to observe the total social phenomenon in full splendor, with its ritual processions, divination customs, martial arts, and popular cultural performances in entertainment of the deity.

The processions to the Hugong temple at Fangyan and the performances of martial arts and cultural performance troupes in entertainment of the deity, escorted by drums and gongs, cannons and fireworks to enhance their red fire, were another outlet for popular cultural creativity and expression as the performances of "36 professions," "18 foxes," "10 character lotus," "Mute carries crazy one," etc. made clear.

The cult of one of Jinhua's Three Buddhas, Fu Dashi, formed the basis for the resacralization of the secular fair at Fotang, and provided the final evidence for the argument that secular commercial fairs have served as incubation sites for popular religious activity. Convened on lunar 10/10, the date of the historical temple fair, the secular fair of the early 1980s helped provide a context for the rebuilding of Shuanglin temple, putting the temple back in this temple-less temple fair, reintroducing the religious dimension into Fotang's previously secular fair, and reestablishing the fair's totality—a clear example of the fair's providing a venue in which the boundaries of acceptable popular religious expression were stretched. And into the 1990s and 2000s all agreed that the red heat of the Fotang fair continued to intensify, notwithstanding its recasting as a folk cultural festival.

The somewhat less than successful attempt to revive the cult of Jinhua native, Daoist deity Huang Daxian, in his native village, orchestrated by Lanxi city officials anxious to promote tourism, served as a kind of negative example of the religious revival carried out from the top down, lacking the grass-roots support and participation of the local population which might have made the revival a success.

The political dimension

I have argued that the fairs are a kind of temporary autonomous zone (after Dean 2003) in which the rules of conventional hierarchical sociality are relaxed (after Yang 1967 and Zhao 2002), and that performers both secular and religious have taken advantage of that license to expand the limits on acceptable discourse.

On the secular side, the fairs' performers are not unaware of the fact that even in such a zone the organs of state power, while in apparent abeyance, are never totally absent. While performers in their practice have considerable license in negotiating new limits as they improvise new ways of entertaining their audiences, they do not have carte blanche, and must tread with caution. However, the rhetorical devices of metaphor, allegory, innuendo and indirection, humor and sarcasm do provide opportunities for occasional sub-insurrectional critical social commentary.

On the religious side, temple fairs may be understood as manifestations of an "ongoing negotiation with the forces of modernity," either in the form of the authoritarian atheist state or global capitalism (Dean 2009: 202). I have argued that temple fairs are a kind of collective popular "resistance" insofar as they involve the organized expression of sentiments and ideas disapproved of by the modernist, secular, Communist state. By its mere existence popular religious expression constitutes a way of thinking alternative to/resistant to state discourse.

And surely Gates has it right that, by soaking up and circulating capital that might otherwise fall into the hands of the state or multinationals, popular religious practice represents an important form of resistance to the hegemony of the state and broader global forces (Gates 1995: 236). But then again arguments like Dean's that, rather than being an obstacle to the movement of capital, ritual events constitute "a different kind of movement altogether," are also quite compelling and go a long way to explaining why it is that popular religion is able to coexist with capital and resist the secularization of society (Dean 2009: 202).

In any event, it seems clear that "communities and individuals will continue to create networks of religious activity beyond the framework of state regulation, regardless of the laws of the state or the activism of prohibitionist state elites" (Brook 2009: 40).

The huge crowds attracted by temple fairs, often in a counter-hegemonic mood, were recognized as politically volatile by successive dynasties historically, and in the 1930s the fairs were indeed put to use by the Communist Party as sites from which to foment rebellion against their nationalist adversaries. So once the Communist government had been established in 1949, the Party must clearly have been vigilant with regard to even the secular fairs' potential as sites for counter-revolutionary mobilization.

In the present, the more confident post-Mao state has retreated from its stance of prohibition–repression toward popular religion characteristic of the cultural revolution period, to one of circumscribed toleration, providing greater metaphorical space in which red fire might find fuel. While the loosening of political constraints and surveillance is not a source of red fire in and of itself, such loosening does provide the environment (the oxygen, if you will) in which red fire may burn.

At the micro level, there were a number of examples in which temple fair activities could be understood to have political significance. Luohan Ban martial arts troupe performances are surely a part of the popular expressive cultural dimension of contemporary fairs, but historically were also a form of ritualized political display of a village's ability to defend itself. And the activities organized by Hugong associations like that of Houtang village in its preparations for the temple fair procession were reportedly instrumental in crafting political alliances with its neighboring villages in defense of its secular interests.

But the most dramatic example of the politics of temple fair activity was discovered as a result of that chance encounter with a farmer on the streets of Huku, which provided an opportunity to observe the local political machinations of Hugong worshiping communities in competition with the cult center at Fangyan and with each other for status as pilgrimage sites during the annual temple fair period. Somewhat paradoxically, the communities competing in this way in the religious sphere were the artificial administrative units created by the Communist state when it divided a "natural" town into two revenue distinct entities, lower and upper Huku; a clear case of local political parochialism trumping the unity of spiritual belief.

These examples of the political dimension of temple fair activity marked a climax in the argument that the temple fair is the total social phenomenon par excellence, combining the economic/commercial, with the popular cultural, popular religious and political dimensions of social life. With significance at all these levels, one might be inclined to say that market/temple fairs are among the more potent enactments of Chinese culture in the contemporary landscape,[1] sites from which it is possible to visualize and theorize the multi-functional totality of rural social life, sites from which Yang's characterization of Chinese religion as "diffused" makes eminent sense.

The fairs' revival was one embodiment of the implementation of China's market-driven economic reforms, and the dismantling of Communist Party controls on rural trade. The secular trade fairs of the reform era have given vent to a grass-roots economic dynamism revealed in the display and sale of enormous quantities of producer and consumer goods in the countryside. And the broader expressive freedom provided by these venues in a climate of loosened political surveillance on the rural citizenry was seized upon by popular cultural performance artists of all kinds, and by practitioners of popular religious ritual given a historically appropriate site in which to perform, all the while improvising/negotiating new political limits on acceptable contemporary discourse and expression.

The fairs may not necessarily be the prime movers in the revival of popular religion in the countryside, but their resacralization and the reestablishment of their "totality" (in the Maussian sense), has certainly been both a contributing factor and a consequence of that revival.

There are signs that temple fairs may well be superseded in their commodity distribution function by modern contemporary industrial and commodity trade exhibitions, so-called bolanhui 博览会, which have become increasingly common in the cities and towns of Jinhua in recent years. At the same time, with a greater variety of goods on sale all year round in a more developed commodity economy, with new daily marketing centers replacing the three market days per week in Huqi, and other similarly situated towns, people may be less inclined to postpone their purchases in anticipation of the annual market fairs.

On the other hand, the fairs remain an important source of recreation, and have had a hand in driving the religious revival. Towns which have reestablished their fair's totality with new or refurbished temples will probably go on hosting temple fairs, but the commodity distribution and circulation function of the future fairs may well be reduced. Fotang's fair, now cast as an annual folk cultural festival 民俗文化节, could well presage the fate of market and temple fairs of the future.

But even as they recede into the past, evolving into something new and different in the future, confronting "the ever-new in the always the same" (Dean 2003: 356), there is no denying that as Chinese rural folk have moved to fill in the ideological interstices left by the delegitimization of Communist orthodoxy and the dismantling of collectivist institutions, the fairs have emerged as temporary autonomous zones, sites where the improvisation of a new habitus proceeds in the hands of popular cultural performance artists, popular religious practitioners, their patrons and audiences, where the boundaries of acceptable contemporary discourse are stretched, in the "struggle to control the concepts and symbols by which current experience is evaluated" (Scott 1985: 27).

The struggle is a metaphoric one to be sure. But by going out and performing, on the street, on the opera stage, in procession, at the temple, these people are staking out a territory that was previously off limits, forbidden. They may not be calling for the overthrow of the Communist state, but they are clearly taking license in expressing themselves in new and different ways, and in their practice they have succeeded in enlarging the universe of acceptable contemporary discourse, while improvising a new habitus in the process (Bourdieu 1977: 8, 11).

May the red fire continue to burn.

Note

1 I am indebted to an anonymous reviewer of the MS at Routledge for this formulation.

Appendix 1
Selected Daoqing repertoire items

To give some flavor for the content of Daoqing performances, I include several plot summaries from the repertoire of Yiwu Daoqing performers, recorded by Zhang (2003).

Shuang Shizi 双狮子 (The Lion Pair)

This is a traditional Daoqing (medium length), current in Jinhua, Lanxi, Yiwu, and Quzhou, put together from local news and performed by Shi Xiaorong 施小荣.

During the Guangxu reign period (1875–1908) there was a young man named Fang Youlin 方有林 who lost his father at six and his mother at 12. He made his living singing Lianhua from Jinhua to Lanxi to Quzhou.

One day in Quzhou, a girl Chen Jinhua 陈金花 sent her maid out to buy some rouge, when she chanced on Youlin singing Lianhua at the door. She thought it so beautiful that she called her mistress out to listen. Chen Jinhua saw the talent of this young man and fell in love. So that her father would not discover, she hid Youlin in the rear garden under the window to continue singing. As she listened she carelessly knocked two jade stone lions off the window sill and they fell at Youlin's feet. He picked them up, and was escorted into Jinhua's room by her servant girl who had gone to fetch them.

When old man Chen returned home he discovered Youlin in his daughter's room and ran with him to the magistrate for punishment. But when the magistrate heard the full story he adopted Youlin as his son, changing his name to Wang Youlin.

When Wang Youlin was 20, Magistrate Wang sent a *meiren* to Chen village. When old man Chen heard it was the magistrate's son, he agreed immediately. Wouldn't you know, Chen Jinhua opposed the match, wanting to marry Fang Youlin. She refused to marry anyone from the Wang family. The father persisted, but his daughter would have none of it. At this point Wang Youlin sent a *meiren* with the small jadestone lions to report that he was none other than Fang Youlin. When Chen Jinhua heard this, she let out a yelp. On her wedding night she finally saw Fang Youlin; her loved one had become her husband. (See Zhang 2003: 72.)

Huiqin Ji 悔亲记 (Regret the Marriage)

This was composed by folk artists from events that transpired at the end of the Ming in Jinhua city and Fotang town. It circulated in many Jinhua cities and towns during the Qing dynasty. At present performed by Zhu Shungen 朱顺根 after his master Xia Yundeng's 夏云登 version; can take as much as 15 hours to perform.

The Liu and Pan families arranged a *gubiaoqin* 姑表亲 (FZD) marriage. The Lius lived in Jinhua City, the Pans outside the city in Xianjiayuan village.

To start, Liu Huaben wanted to betroth his daughter Liu Caifeng to his wife's younger brother's son Pan Xiaoliang. Afterward, Pan Jiguan returned from a business trip having lost some money, got sick and passed away ten days later, leaving an orphan and his mother in great difficulty. Liu Huaben determined to marry his daughter off to a different family, the Wangs of Yiwu Fotang.

On lunar 1/16, the Lantern Festival, Pan Xiaoliang went to seek refuge with his relatives in the Liu family. When Liu Huaben saw him, he immediately assembled 50 *liang* of silver as incentive for Xiaoliang to repudiate the marriage. But Xiaoliang got angry and scolded his uncle for being so concerned with money. Liu Huaben got angry in turn and accusing Xiaoliang of thievery, ordered his servant to tie him up and take him to the magistrate. Xiaoliang knocked over the servant and fled. Liu Huaben sent more servants out to find him, but in fear of the night they didn't return, pressing on to Yiwu Fotang where the Wang family was preparing to greet the bridal procession from the Lius. The bride, Liu Caifeng, was happy with the new arrangement, and that night dressed in men's clothes she snuck out of the Liu house and went to the Pan house to marry Xiaoliang, uniting the pair.

But a villager had already informed Liu Huaben, who bribed the county magistrate to send men to arrest Pan Xiaoliang and imprison him.

However, all the villagers of Xiang Jiayuan village joined together and went to the district Yamen in Jinhua, and when all the facts were known, the District magistrate ordered the County magistrate to release Xiaoliang, and for Xiaoliang and Caifeng to be reunited. (See Zhang 2003: 81–82.)

Shuangdao Ji 双刀记 (Tale of the Pair of Knives)

This is an Yiwu Daoqing traditional piece, according to actual events in Yiwu, circulating in the various counties of Jinhua; it is performed by Wu Huasheng 吴华生.

During Qing Xianfeng period there were three brothers in Yiwu's Xiaowu Village surnamed Lou. The oldest was Lou Yongjian, next Lou Yonggang, and youngest Lou Yongguang. When their parents died, they divided the estate.

Yongjian had three sons and three daughters, the oldest son Xiangwang joined the Qing army, later retiring and returning home with no savings and no land. Through the efforts of an uncle, he was allotted a portion of the lineage land (*gongchang tian*) of his uncle Yongguang. Yongguang had occupied the land for a long time, and hired 18 toughs to try to kill Xiangwang. Xiangwang's youngest son Xueqin said to his mother: "When I grow up I will avenge my father, cut off Yongguang's head and shove it up his ass."

Yongguang, taking no chances, assembled his 18 toughs again and locked up Xiangwang's family hoping to burn them to death. But Xiangqin and Xueqin escaped through the latrine. On the road they met a man from Fengyang who changed their names to Dapei and Xiaopei. After three years, Dapei entered the army and Xiaopei studied martial arts. At the end of their terms they returned together to Yiwu, on the road purchasing a pair of swords with which to avenge their father and kill Yongguang. In the end, through the intervention of an elder, they obtained use of the *gongchang tian*. But after three years of peace and quiet, Yongguang descended upon them again. He assembled a group of local bullies, bribed the magistrate, and was about to have the two brothers arrested. They fled again, and on the road managed to kill one of the 18 toughs that had killed their parents.

In the end Xueqin fled to Yanzhou and went into the dry goods (nail and bowl) business, changing his name to Xiaoniu ("little cow"). He returned to the village with a pair of swords to kill Yongguang's family, but was captured by the Hangzhou police and sentenced to death. Just prior to his execution, he cried out: "I still want to kill someone." The executioner asked him: "Who?" He replied "I want to kill my big brother Daniu." With these words, he saved his brother's life. (See Zhang 2003: 83–4.)

借伞记 (Borrowed Umbrella)

This is a traditional Yiwu Daoqing piece, of moderate length; it belongs to the genre of Daoqing pieces edited from legal cases and performed by Ye Yingsheng, in circulation in Yiwu, Dongyang, Jinhua, and Lanxi.

During the Ming Wanli reign, the daughter of Liu Tianbao, Liu Cuifeng, was studying embroidery at the home of her master in Qianzhai Village. On the way home there was a great rainstorm, and she sought shelter under the eaves of Liu Wenchun's home, and borrowed an umbrella from him to walk the rest of the way home. But her parents were not home, only a worker Chen Baoxi, all by himself. He took advantage of the rain and darkness, and after raping and murdering Cuifeng, buried her stealthily in the village outskirts.

When the case came to court, the magistrate, with Liu Wenchun's name on the borrowed umbrella as evidence, convicted Liu of the killing and sentenced him. Liu's uncle, Wu Legui knew his nephew well, and implored the magistrate to investigate more closely, but the magistrate declined. Wu requested two days during which to find the truth, and begged the magistrate to postpone the punishment; if after two days he had not found Cuifeng's killer, then he offered his own head in place of Liu Wenchun. Wu's son saw the situation and committed suicide for his father. Wu could only take his son's head and present it to the magistrate, who now realized the case was more complicated, and investigated further, finally finding Chen Baoxi and bringing him to justice. (See Zhang 2003: 84.)

Sanshi Chou 三世仇 (Triple Revenge)

This is a modern Huagu piece. It tells the story of Wang Laowu who is beset upon by Wang Longpan over a peach tree. Laowu dies in jail as a result. His wife, who is forced to sell her daughter to make the funeral expenses for Laowu, is hounded to death by Longpan, leaving behind a son Xiaohu, who flees with the aid of #4 uncle from Longpan's efforts to cut off any threat by its roots by burning the child to death. The child crosses the river and joins up with the Communist Party. Thus, while liberating his native county, he gets to take revenge on Wang Longpan, avenging his father's and mother's deaths, getting three worlds' revenge. (See Zhang 2003: 96.)

Appendix 2
Selected Wuju repertoire items

To give some idea of the plot line of some of the operas in the Wuju repertoire, I include a handful of plot summaries as illustration.

Quan Shi Yi 全十义 *(Ten Times Righteous)* (Houyang Gaoqiang genre); also called *Shi Yi Ji* 拾义记

Quan Shi Yi tells the story of Xiucai degree holder Han Peng and his wife who leave town to conduct sacrifices at the altar of a nearby temple. On the road they encounter Wang Peng 王朋 beating a pig. When Wang sees that Han's wife is as "beautiful as an immortal", he wants to take her as his concubine, and after returning to the yamen, he sends an official go between to discuss the marriage. When Han Peng hears of this, he is uncontrollably angry, and chases the go between away.

When Wang Peng discovers what has happened, he gets angry and declares Han Peng a rebel, sending soldiers to capture him. But just on this day, Zheng Tian 郑天 is visiting the Han household, and sees the soldiers coming to arrest Han Peng and his wife, so he goes out and identifies himself as Han Peng, leading the soldiers to wrongly arrest him.

The next day, Wang Peng tries to force Han Peng's wife to marry him by offering her silver candles. But she refuses, and Wang uses a silver hair pin to scar her face, and locks her away in prison. After several months she gives birth to a son, given the name Kunying 困英. Wang Peng's sworn brother Li Changguo, having just returned from a business trip, hears of the previous circumstances and takes Kunying to his own home to raise. Han Peng's wife in a fit of anger and hate, hangs herself from a rafter.

After a while, Wang Peng discovers that Han Peng is still alive, and sends a general to kill him. But the general sees that Han Peng is a good and honest man, and rather than arrest him, he slits his own throat with his sword and lets Han Peng go free. From this moment, Han Peng wanders the streets begging for a living.

Eighteen years pass, and Kunying, raised by Li Changguo attains Zhuangyuan status in the imperial exams. But by now of course he is member of the Li household named Li Tai, and on returning home, he petitions the court to have his "father", Li Changguo, promoted to Dafu. At the ceremonial banquet, Li Changguo thinks of Han Peng and lowers his head and cries. Li Tai sees his father is unhappy, and goes out on the street to call in a Daoqing singer to help cheer him up. As it happens, the Daoqing singer in raggedy clothes is none other than Han Peng. Li Changguo tells Li Tai of the circumstances of his adoption, 18 years before. Li Tai recognizes his birth father, and the two are reunited. Li Tai petitions the throne to have Wang Peng removed from his official position. Li Changguo ends up as Quanshiyi 全十义 (Ten times righteous) (Wang ed. 1998: 209–10).

Pingzheng Dong 平征东 *(Pacification Campaign East)* (Houyang Gaoqiang genre)

During the Tang dynasty, Xue Rengui 薛仁贵 decides to volunteer in the call up of troops to rid the central plain of the Liao clique, and encounters recruiter Zhang Shigui 张士贵.

Xue can draw the iron bow that no one else can, and is well versed in strategy. Zhang sees his talent, but fears that after using him, he (Zhang) won't look so good. Thus he assigns Xue to look after the horses, but uses the plans and strategy Xue has devised to destroy the Liao soldiers, taking all the credit himself.

Yuchi Jingde 尉迟敬德 doubts him, and investigates more carefully. On a moonlit night, Xue Rengui, offended by Zhang's behavior is overheard by Yuchi who rushes to embrace him. Xue thinking he is being kidnapped, throws him to the side of the road and leaps free. When Yuchi sets out to find this amazing talent, he is repeatedly prevented from doing so by Zhang Shigui. In the end, Xue Rengui's talent is recognized and a memorial is sent to the emperor. Xue is promoted and Zhang punished (Wang ed. 1998: 210).

Hezhu Ji 合珠记 *(Bringing Together of the Pearl)* (Houyang Gaoqiang genre); also known as *Zhenzhu Ji* 珍珠记 *(Tale of the Pearl)*

Hezhu Ji tells the story of Gao Wenju 高文举, poor and in dire straits, who went to live in the household of Wang Baiwan as a son in law, taking Wang's daughter Wang Jinzhen 王金贞 as his wife. [Such a matrilocal marriage was the last resort of poor families who could not afford the expense of a legitimate patrilocal marriage]. Despite his unfortunate position in society, he and his wife developed a deep love for one another.

Gao Wenju set out to Beijing to take part in the imperial examinations, and his loving wife Wang Jinzhen escorted him to the bridge. There she broke a pearl in two, giving one half to her husband as a token of her love, and keeping the other half herself.

Gao Wenju attained Zhuangyuan status, the highest marks on the exam. But the official Wen Ge 温阁 forced him into his own home as a son in law, and changed his documents to reflect his new domicile. When Jinzhen saw the documents, she suspected foul play, and set out to Beijing to find her husband. Unfortunately, she was discovered by Wen Ge, who cut off her hair, and after seriously beating her, confined her to his back garden as a slave girl. Fortunately, the old maid servant Du Niang felt pity for the poor girl and ultimately helped Jinzhen out of her fix.

At Mid autumn festival, Gao Wenju returned from instructing the prince, and instructed Du Niang to prepare some congee. Jinzhen took her half pearl and put it in the congee; when Gao Wenju discovered it, he remembered his first wife and their love. Wang Jinzhen, under the guidance of Old Du Niang knocked on the window and although having endured such bitterness she was scarcely recognizable, she was able to prove to her husband that she was his wife by reciting his eight trigrams of birth. In the end, they poured out their mutual feelings, set aside their resentments, and together went to the magistrate to report. The magistrate was righteous, and punished Wen Ge by shaving his hair, making him a servant. Finally, relying on Wang Baiwan's testimony, the two Wenju and Jinzhen were reunited (Wang ed. 1998: 208).

Geng Lishan 耕历山 *(Cultivating Li Mountain)*
(Songyang Gaoqiang genre)

Shun's father, Gusou, doted on his second wife's son, and wished harm to Shun, but Shun kept to the filial Dao. Emperor Yao inquired of Shun's virtue, and sent his two daughters to be his wives, E Huang and Nu Ying. Shun tilled the fields below Mt. Li, and the other tillers followed his example. Emperor Yao gifted Shun with fine linen clothes, cows and goats and the construction of a granary. Shun's father, Gusou was jealous, and ordered Shun to climb into the granary. Once Shun was inside, Gusou secretly removed the ladder, and set fire to the granary. Thanks to wives E Huang and Nu Ying Shun was able to open an umbrella and jump down to safety. Then Gusou ordered Shun to descend a well, and used earth to stop it up, but Shun escaped through a different well. Then Gusou planned to seize his wives and his grain, but Shun returned in time to intervene. Shun went on to serve both his father and brother for a long time, and the two finally realized their error. In the end of course, on the basis of his virtuous filiality, Shun is selected to succeed Emperor Yao as emperor of the Xia dynasty (Zhang and Hong 1985: 254).

Luhua Xu 芦花絮 (Reed Catkin Padding)
(Xi An Gaoqiang genre)

Luhua Xu tells the story of one Min Hui 闵辉 whose first wife died, leaving a son, Min Sun 闵损. Min Hui married again to a woman surnamed Zhang who gave birth to two sons, Min Hua 闵华 and Min Asan 闵阿三. The second wife treated her own sons kindly, leaving the son by the previous marriage hungry and cold. One day she sent Min Sun a great distance pushing a cart to retrieve his father, giving him only a reed catkin padded jacket to wear. Snow fell and the wind blew, and the cold was hard to resist. Min Sun fainted in the snow, but luckily was discovered by his father, who was so angry at his wife that he summoned her parents to his home with the intention of repudiating his marriage. But Min Sun urged his father not to do so, and finally prevailed on him not to send his wife/mother back to her parents. This deeply moved his step mother, and the family lived together happily thereafter (Wang ed. 1998: 208–9).

Tieling Guan 铁灵关
(Luantan genre)

Mei Boqing insults/humiliates general Bai Rong's daughter Bai Ying, when after her mother's death, she follows her father on the road. This is observed by Liu Dingyuan's adopted son Wang Qing who happens by and is angered by the unfairness of the fight. He rescues Bai Ying from Mei Boqing, but both Wang and Mei are drafted into the army to defend Tieling Pass.

Bai Ying admires the martial skill of Wang Qing, and respect turns to love. Mei Boqing conspires with the enemy to get Wang Qing. In the midst of the battle he aims at Wang Qing but mistakenly shoots Bai Rong. When Bai Ying hears her father is dead, she musters her woman soldiers away from the pass to avenge his death, destroys the enemy, retakes the pass, and saves Wang Qing. The plot of Mei and the enemy is exposed and Mei punished for his crimes (Wang ed. 1998: 212).

Zhenzhu Ta 珍珠塔 *(Pearl Pagoda)*
(Luan Tan genre)

Zhenzhu Ta tells the story of Xiucai, Fang Qing 方卿 whose father, an official at court was wrongly disgraced by a wicked official, leaving mother and son in dire straits. In order to take the imperial exams, Fang Qing goes to borrow money from his father's sister. Her husband welcomes him warmly, but she treats him with no respect, and Fang Qing gets angry and storms out. When his biaojie Chen Chui'e (daughter of father's sister) hears of all this, she sends along some dianxin with a pearl pagoda secreted in a dumpling, to serve as travel expenses. Mr. Chen scolds his wife for her treatment of their nephew. When Fang Qing eats the dumpling and discovers the pearl pagoda, he is eternally grateful, but unfortunately the pagoda is stolen. Fang Qing, hungry and cold, collapses in the snow; rescued by the Nanchang magistrate Hua Yunxian who happened to pass by.

When Chen Chui'e discovers the pagoda she gave to Fang Qing in a pawn shop, she understood that something awful must have happened to her cousin, and takes ill.

Fang Qing returns home after succeeding in the exams, disguised as a folk artist, goes to his father's sister's house to perform Daoqing. He threatens to flog her, leaving her no choice but to agree to his marriage to her daughter Chen Chui'e (Wang ed. 1998: 214).

Shuang Xueyi 双血衣 (A Pair of Bloody Garments)
(Luan Tan genre)

Li Ruchun is wrongly convicted of murder as a result of magistrate Hu Shoucheng's relentless prosecution. But Li Ruchun proclaims that an injustice has been done, and gets a message out to his family to produce his weapons and bloody clothes. His sister, in order to help him redress the wrong cuts her own arm to fabricate the bloody garment. On the next day however, the court sends down the real bloody garment, and thus there are a pair.

Before long, a new magistrate replaces the old and appoints the young and energetic Shen Zhiwen, fair to a fault, to investigate. After listening to the claims of the mother and daughter, Shen Zhiwen investigated further despite the efforts of the Hu family and his own mother's obstruction. He discovered that most of the evidence pointed to Zhao Shen, wife's younger brother to Magistrate Hu. And so he had the body exhumed. In the throat of the Miss Wang was a joint of the finger of Zhao Shen . . . who was arrested, and Li Ruchun freed (Wang ed. 1998: 214–15).

Guojiang Sha Xiang 过江杀相 (Cross the River for Murderous Revenge)
(Huixi genre)

The number 2 son of Bai Yingyong of Liangshan, named Bai Shao'en took his daughter Guiying to live temporarily in secret in Taichao, making a living as a fisherman. He came upon his enemy Li Junxie 李俊携 and his visiting friend Ni Rong, drinking on a boat.

Local bully Ding Zixie ordered Ding Lang to collect the fish tax from Li and Ni but the two merely scolded him and sent him packing. Ding Lang reported back to his superior. Ding Zixie sent him out again but this time to the Bai family to collect the fish tax from them, but Shao'en beat him up and chased him away.

Shao'en reported the incident to the county yamen, but was flogged by the magistrate Lu Ziqiu, who forced him to cross the river to the Ding homestead to make restitution. Shao'en was so angry that he took his daughter Guiying to cross the river in the dead of night. Offering a false name at the main gate, he gained access to the Ding homestead, and slaughtered the whole family.

Represents the adage "官逼民反" [the people oppose the official orders]. (Zhang and Hong 1985: 255).

Bibliography

Abu-Lughod, Janet. 1989. *Before European Hegemony: the world system* A.D. *1250–1350*. New York: Oxford University Press.

Bakhtin, Mikhail. 1965. *Rabelais and his World*. Bloomington: Indiana University Press (1984).

Beijing Dongyue Miao Miaohui 北京东岳庙庙会 (The Beijing Dongyue Temple Fair). 2006. *Beijing Minsu Bowuguan Niankan* 2006: 35–39.

Bourdieu, Pierre. 1977. *Outline of a Theory of Practice*. Cambridge: Cambridge University Press.

Brook, Timothy. 2009. "The Politics of Religion: Late Imperial Origins of the Regulatory State." In Yoshiko Ashiwa and David Wank, eds., *Making Religion, Making the State: the politics of religion in modern China*. Stanford: Stanford University Press.

Cai, Fengming 蔡丰明 1995. *Jiangnan Minjian Shexi* 江南民间社戏 (The Popular Operas of Jiangnan). Shanghai: Baijia Publishers.

Cao, Jinqing. 2005. *China Along the Yellow River: Reflections on Rural Society*. Translated by Nicky Harmon and Huang Ruhua. London: Routledge Curzon Studies on the Chinese Economy #12.

Cao, Songye 曹松葉 1929a. "Jinhua de San Fo Wu Hou" 金华的三佛五侯 (The Three Buddhas and Five Marquises of Jinhua). *Minsu* (Folklore). Nos 86, 87, 88, 89 (combined issue).

Cao, Songye 曹松葉1929b. "Jinhua yibufen Shenmiao, yige jiandande tongji" (Basic statistics of some Jinhua temples). *Minsu* (Folklore). Nos 86, 87, 88, 89 (combined issue).

Chan, Selina Ching and Graeme S. Lang. 2007. "Temple Construction and the Revival of Popular Religion in Jinhua" *China Information* 21: 43.

Chau, Adam Yuet. 2006a. *Miraculous Response: doing popular religion in contemporary China*. Stanford: Stanford University. Press.

Chau, Adam Yuet. 2006b "Superstitious Specialist Households? The Household Idiom in Chinese Religious Practices." *Minsu Quyi* 民俗曲艺 153 (9): 157–202.

Chau, Adam Yuet. 2009. "Expanding the Space of Popular Religion: Local Temple Activism and the Politics of Legitimation in Contemporary Rural China." In Yoshiko Ashiwa and David Wank, eds., *Making Religion, Making the State: the politics of religion in modern China*. Stanford: Stanford University Press.

Chen, Chongren 陈崇仁 1986. "Daoqing Yinyue Gaige Qiantan" 道情音乐改革浅谈 (A brief discussion of the reform in the music of Daoqing). *Wu Xing* 婺星 1: 51–2.

Chen, Chongren 陈崇仁 1994. "Wutai zhong de 'Jiaguan' Hexu ren ye?" 舞台中的"加官"何许人也 (Just who is this Jiaguan of the opera stage?) *Dongyang Wenhua* 8: 2.
Chen, Chongren 陈崇仁 1997. "Ta Baxian" (踏八仙 Step the eight immortals). In Qihua Shu 舒启华, Zhu Peiyue 朱佩(王乐) and Shi Huaide 施怀德, eds., *A Broad View of Wuzhou Folklore*, Xining: Qinghai People's Publishers, 87.
Chen, Ming 陈明 ed. 2005. *Yiwu Tong: Zonghe Ban.* 义乌通：综合版 (Generalist of Yiwu: comprehensive edition). Hong Kong: Hengjia Publishers.
Chen, Qiaoyi 陈桥驿 ed. 1991 *Zhejiang Gujin Diming Cidian.* 浙江古今地名词典 (A Dictionary of Zhejiang Ancient and Modern Place Names). Hangzhou: Zhejiang Educational Publishers.
Chen, Qirong 陈崎嵘, ed. 1994. *Zhongguo Xiaoshangpin Cheng Congguan* 中国小商品城纵观 *China's Small Commodity City from top to bottom.* Beijing: Red Flag Publishers.
Chen, Xiuxian, ed. 2003. *Kaifangde Yiwu* (Open Yiwu). Yiwu: City Propaganda Office.
Chen, Yongyuan 陈永源, ed. 1987. *Lanxi Shi Shengshan Shezu Xiang Wenhua* 兰溪市 圣山畲族乡 文化志 (Lanxi city, Shengshan township "She" minority Culture).
Chen, Yunhua 陈云华. 1997. "Da Luohan" 打罗汉. In Qihua Shu 舒启华, Zhu Peiyue 朱佩(王乐) and Shi Huaide 施怀德, eds., *A Broad View of Wuzhou folklore*, Xining: Qinghai People's Publishers,169–170.
Cohen, Alvin P. 1977. "A Chinese Temple Keeper Talks about Chinese Folk Religion" *Asian Folklore Studies* 36: 1:1–17.
Cohen, Myron. 2005. *Kinship, Contract, Community and State.* Stanford: Stanford University Press.
Cooper, Eugene. 1999. "Company town: Chinawood" [Hengdian]. *Hollywood Reporter* (International Edition). August 17–23.
Cooper, Eugene and Yinhuo Jiang. 1998. *The Artisans and Entrepreneurs of Dongyang County: Economic Reform and Flexible Production in China.* Armonk, NY: M.E. Sharpe.
Cooper, Gene. 2000. *Adventures in Chinese Bureaucracy: a meta-anthropological saga.* New York: Nova Science Publishers.
Cooper, Gene. 2005. Review of Cao Jinqing, *China Along the Yellow River: Reflections on Rural Society*, *China Review International* 11 (Fall): 1.
Cui, Xueli 崔学礼 1994. "The mule/horse fair of Lin Yi" 临沂骡马大会 *Minsu Yanjiu* 29 (1): 74–76.
Dagong Bao 大公报 1998a. "Chuangzao Dongfang Meiguiyuan de Nongmin Qiyejia: Xu Wenrong" (创造东方玫瑰园的农民企业家: 徐文荣 The Peasant Entrepreneur Creator of the Oriental Rose Garden: Xu Wenrong). March 10: 1.
Dagong Bao 大公报 1998b. "Hengdian Moshi – Nongcun Shetuan Jingji Qiji" (横店模式 – 农村社团经济奇迹 Hengdian Model – The Economic Miracle of the Mass Organization). March 10: 1.
Dai, Rucai 戴汝才, ed. 1997. Lishi Wenhua Mingcheng – Jinhua (历史文化名城 – 金华 The historically and culturally famous city – Jinhua). Jinhua: Xinhua Printing Factory.
DDZGZJ 1989. Shang, Jingcai, ed. 1989. *Dang Dai Zhongguo de Zhejiang* (Contemporary China's Zhejiang Province), 2 volumes. Beijing: China Social Science Publishers.
Dean, Kenneth. 2003. "Local Communal Religion in Contemporary South-east China." *China Quarterly* 174: 338–358.

Dean, Kenneth. 2009. "Further Partings of the Way: The Chinese State and Daoist Ritual Traditions in Contemporary China." In Yoshiko Ashiwa and David Wank, eds., *Making Religion, Making the State: the politics of religion in modern China.* Stanford: Stanford University Press.

Ding, Yibin 丁毅斌 1990. "Jinhua Wuju Opera Troupes" (Jinhua Wuju Banshe 金华婺剧班社) In Jinhua Xian Wenshi Ziliao 金华县文史资料 3: 159–169.

Dong, Tianze. 1981. "Miscellaneous Notes on Temple Fairs" (*Miao Hui Za Tan* 庙会杂谈). *Zhejiang Minsu* 4 (November): 10–11.

Dongyang Government webpage #1 *Qianxiang zhen*: www.dongyang.gov.cn/dongyang/dysq/dynj/2003/jdzx/19879.shtml.

Dongyang Government webpage #2 *Qianxiang zhen*: www.dongyang.gov.cn/dongyang/dysq/dynj/2004/cx/19335.shtml.

Dongyang Government webpage #3 *Dongyang Daily News* 2007-05-14 东阳日报: www.dongyang.gov.cn/dongyang/zwgk/dydt/xzdt/11362.shtml.

Dongyang Government webpage #4 *Dongyang Daily News* 2007-07-11 东阳日报: www.dongyang.gov.cn/dongyang/zwgk/dydt/xzdt/11362.shtml.

Dongyang Government webpage #5: www.dongyang.gov.cn/dongyang/zwgk/dydt/xzdt/52686.shtml.

Dongyang City Government webpage #6 (Guo, Xinghua 2007a). *Huqi Zhen* 湖溪镇: www.dongyang.gov.cn/dongyang/dysq/dynj/2003/jdzx/19882.shtml.

Dongyang City Government webpage #7 (Guo, Xinghua 郭星华) 2007b. *Huqi Zhen* 湖溪镇: www.dongyang.gov.cn/dongyang/dysq/dynj/2004/cx/19338.shtml.

Dongyang County Cultural Bureau. 1985. *Dongyang Fengsu Zhi* (Habits and Customs of Dongyang) Dongyang: Dongyang Cultural Palace.

Duara, Prasenjit. 1988. Culture, Power, and the State. Stanford: Stanford University Press.

DYFSZ (Zhou Yaoming 周耀明 and Wang Yonghua 王庸华), eds. 1985. Dongyang Fengsu Zhi (Habits and Customs of Dongyang). Dongyang: Dongyang Cultural Palace.

DYSZ 1993. Dongyang Shi Di Fang Zhi Editorial Committee. *Dongyang Shi Zhi.* (Records of Dongyang City). Shanghai: Hanyu Da Zidian Publishers.

DYXXLJS 1910. *Dongyang Xian Xiangtu Lishi Jiaoke Shu.* (anon.) (Textbook of Dongyang County Local History). 4 parts. Dongyang: County Government.

Eberhard, Wolfram. 1970. *Studies in Chinese Folklore and Related Essays.* Indiana University Folklore Institute Monograph Series Vol. 23. The Hague: Mouton.

Evans-Pritchard, E.E. 1962. "Anthropology and History." In *Essays in Social Anthropology,* E.E. Evans-Pritchard, ed. London: Faber and Faber.

Fan, Lizhu. 2003. "Popular Religion in Contemporary China." *Social Compass* 50 (4): 449–457.

Fangyan brochure: "Hugong: buddha? god? person?"

Faure, Bernard 1987. "Space and Place in Chinese Religious Traditions." *History of Religions* 26 (4): 337–356.

Feng, Naixi. n.d. *Field Report on Investigation of Wuju (Jinhua Opera).* Unpublished report.

Fieldnotes 8/6/86 Hengdian.

Fieldnotes 5/31/88 Hengdian.

Fieldnotes 6/2/88 Hengdian.

Fieldnotes Huqi 6/14–6/15/88 [lunar 5/1–5/2].

Fieldnotes Huqi 12/8–12/10/98 [lunar 10/20–10/22].

Fieldnotes Qianxiang 8/2–8/3/98 [lunar 6/11–6/12].
Fieldnotes 8/8/98 Dongyang.
Fieldnotes 8/10/98 Dongyang.
Fieldnotes 10/1/98 brochure on Fangyan.
Fieldnotes 10/2/98 Huku.
Fieldnotes 10/3/98 Yongkang.
Fieldnotes 10/4/98 Huku.
Fieldnotes 10/6/98 Huku.
Fieldnotes 10/7/98 Yongkang.
Fieldnotes 10/27/98 Fangyan.
Fieldnotes 10/28/98 Fangyan.
Fieldnotes Xiawang 11/13–11/14/98 (lunar 9/25–9/26).
Fieldnotes 11/18–11/19/98—Zhudaishi (lunar 9/30–10/1)
Fieldnotes Fotang 11/27/98.
Fieldnotes Luodian 12/2–12/3/98.
Fieldnotes Huqi 12/8–12/10/98 (lunar 10/20–10/22).
Fieldnotes Lanxi 12/11/98 (translation of Huang Da Xian Yuanyuan Yuan temple leaflet).
Flath, James. n.d. "This Wild Show: Temple-fairs in Republican North China."
Forster, Keith. 1998. *Zhejiang in Reform.* Provincial Economic Handbooks of China Series No. 1. Sydney: Wild Peony Ltd.
Fotang Township Government. 2005. *Yiwu Shizi, Fotangzhen Pian* 义乌市志,佛堂镇篇 (Fotang section of the Yiwu City Annals).
Fu, Jian 傅健 1995. *Yiwu Hongtang Shihua* 义乌红糖史话 (A History of Yiwu "Red" Sugar). Yiwu Museum, excerpt from *Yiwu RiBao* (Yiwu Daily) 7/31.
Gao, Youpeng 高有鹏 1999. *Zhongguo Miaohui Wenhua* 中国庙会文化 (The Culture of China's Temple Fairs). Shanghai: Wenyi Publishers.
Gao, Youpeng 高有鹏 and Meng Fang 孟芳 1996. "A brief discussion of the folk culture of the temple fairs of the central plains." 中原民间庙会文化简论 Zhongguo Minjian Miaohui Wenhua Jianlun. *Minsu Yanjiu* 38 (2): 46–51.
Gao, Zhanxiang 高占祥, ed. 1992. *Lun Miaohui Wenhua* 论庙会文化 (A Discussion of the Culture of Temple Fairs). Beijing: Xinhua Shudian.
Gates, Hill. 1995. *China's Motor: a thousand years of petty capitalism.* Ithaca: Cornell University Press.
Ge, Fenglan 葛凤兰, Wang Zhizhong 王志忠 and Zhang Changxian 张昌贤 eds. 1986. *Jinhua Shihua* 金华史话 *Speaking of Jinhua History.* Jinhua: Zhejiang People's Publishers.
Goodrich, Anne S. 1998. "Miao Feng Shan." *Asian Folklore Studies* 57 (1): 87–97.
Goossaert, Vincent. 2005. "State and Religion in Modern China: Religious Policies and Scholarly Paradigms." Paper presented at the Conference "Rethinking Modern Chinese History", Taipei, June 29–July 1.
Gu, Jiegang. 1928. *Miao Feng Shan.* Beijing: Folklore Studies Association.
Guo, Qitao. 2005. *Ritual Opera and Mercantile Lineage: the Confucian transformation of popular culture in late imperial Huizhou.* Stanford: Stanford University Press.
Guo, Xinghua 郭星华 (Dongyang City Government webpage #6). 2007a. *Huqi Zhen* 湖溪镇 www.dongyang.gov.cn/dongyang/dysq/dynj/2003/jdzx/19882.shtml.
Guo, Xinghua 郭星华 (Dongyang City Government webpage #7). 2007b. *Huqi Zhen* 湖溪镇 www.dongyang.gov.cn/dongyang/dysq/dynj/2004/cx/19338.shtml.
He, Huan and Jin Tianshu. 1983. "Miao Hui Fengsu yu Qunzhong Wenhua" 庙会风俗与群众文化 (The Habits and Customs of Temple Fairs and Mass Culture). *Zhejiang Minsu* 9: (March): 2–9.

Hengdian Industrial Company. 1988. *Hengdian Xiangzhen Qiye Jianjie* (横店乡镇企业简介 Brief Introduction to Hengdian Township and Village Enterprises). Heng Dian: GYGS.

Hengdian Jituan Bao 横店集团报 1997. "Dongfang Haolaiwu" (东方好莱坞 Eastern Hollywood). June 9: 1–4.

Hong, Aiqin 洪爱琴 1990. "Ta Baxian, Ying Huashu ji qita" (踏八仙，迎花树及其他 Step the Eight Immortals, welcome the flower tree and others). *Jinhua Xian Wenshi Ziliao* 金华县文史资料 3: 140–147.

Hong, Bo 洪波 1988. "A Casual Discussion of the Origin of the Name Wuju" 漫话婺剧之名由来 Wuxing 婺星 2: 45–6.

Hong, Bo 洪波 1997. "Wuju Xisu" 婺剧戏俗 Wuju Opera Custom. In Shu et al. eds. A Broad View of Wuzhou Folklore 80.

Hong, Yirui 洪以瑞 1997a. "Zuochang Ban" 坐唱班. In Shu, Qihua 舒启华, Zhu Peiyue 朱佩(王乐) and Shi Huaide 施怀德, eds. 1997. *Wuzhou Minsu Daguan* 婺州民俗大观 (A Broad View of Wuzhou Folklore). Xining: Qinghai People's Publishers, 97.

Hong, Yirui 洪以瑞 1997b. Luantan Xiban 乱弹戏班. In Shu, Qihua 舒启华, Zhu Peiyue 朱佩(王乐) and Shi Huaide 施怀德, eds. 1997. *Wuzhou Minsu Daguan* 婺州民俗大观 (A Broad View of Wuzhou Folklore). Xining: Qinghai People's Publishers, 99.

HQCZ (Huqi Cunzhi Editorial Committee) 1996. *Huqi Cunzhi* 湖溪村志 (Annals of Huqi Village). Dongyang: City Printers.

Hu, Guojun 胡国钧, ed. 1987. *Fangyan Hugong Chuanqi* 方岩胡公传奇 (Stories of Fangyan and Hugong). Bao Wen Tang Bookstore.

Hu, Guojun 胡国钧. 1991. "Hugong Dadi Xinyang yu Fangyan Miao Hui" 胡公大帝信仰与方岩庙会 (The Belief in Great Emperor Hugong and the Temple Fair at Fangyan). *Zhongguo Minjian Wenhua* (Chinese Popular Culture) 4: 184–221.

Hu, Guojun 胡国钧. 1993. *Fangyan Qianshi Jieshuo* 方岩签诗解说 (Explanation of Fangyan Divination Slip Poems). Hong Kong: Tianma Publishers.

Hu, Guojun 胡国钧. 1995. "Fushexing de Tongxinyuan: Hugong Dadi xinyangquan gaishu" 辐射性的同心圆：胡公大帝信仰圈概述 (Radiating concentric circles: An outline of the religious sphere of the Great Emperor Hugong). *Zhongguo Minjian Wenhua* (Chinese Popular Culture), "Difangshen xinyang" issue 18: 1–7.

Hu, Guojun 胡国钧 1997a. "Fangyan Hugong Miaohui". In Qihua Shu 舒启华, Zhu Peiyue 朱佩(王乐) and Shi Huaide 施怀德, eds., *A Broad View of Wuzhou Folklore*, Xining: Qinghai People's Publishers, 156.

Hu, Guojun 胡国钧 1997b. "36 Professions". In Qihua Shu 舒启华, Zhu Peiyue 朱佩(王乐) and Shi Huaide 施怀德, eds., *A Broad View of Wuzhou Folklore*, Xining: Qinghai People's Publishers, 172.

Hu, Guojun 胡国钧 1997c. "Wufeng Shuyuan" 五峰书院. In Qihua Shu 舒启华, Zhu Peiyue 朱佩(王乐) and Shi Huaide 施怀德, eds., *A Broad View of Wuzhou Folklore*, Xining: Qinghai People's Publishers, 281.

Hu, Guojun 胡国钧 1997d. "Fangyan Guang Ci Si" 方岩广慈寺. In Qihua Shu 舒启华, Zhu Peiyue 朱佩(王乐) and Shi Huaide 施怀德, eds., *A Broad View of Wuzhou Folklore*, Xining: Qinghai People's Publishers, 283.

Hu, Guojun 胡国钧 1997e. "Fangyan Hugong Ci" 方岩胡公祠. In Qihua Shu 舒启华, Zhu Peiyue 朱佩(王乐) and Shi Huaide 施怀德, eds., *A Broad View of Wuzhou Folklore*, Xining: Qinghai People's Publishers, 284.

Hua, Tianji 滑天稽 1994. "Miaohui, Miaoshi, Ganhui" 庙会 庙市 赶会 (Temple Fairs, Temple Markets, and Going to the Fair). *Minsu Yanjiu* 29 (1): 88.

Hui, Xicheng 惠西成 and Shi Zi 石子, eds. 1997. *Zhongguo Minsu Da Guan (shang)* 中国民俗达观 (上) (A Broad View of Chinese Folklore Vol. 1). Guangzhou: Guangdong Tourism Publishers.

JHDTC (Jinhua City Local Names Committee Office), ed. 1998. Jinhua Shi Wucheng Qu Ditu Ce 金华市婺城区地图册 (A collection of maps of Jinhua city's Wucheng district) Harbin: Harbin Map Publishers.

JHFSZ (Jinhua Prefecture Cultural Bureau) 1984. *Jinhua Difang Fengsu Zhi* 金华地方风俗志 (The Local Habits and Customs of Jinhua). Jinhua: Arts Palace of the Masses.

JHSDTC (Jinhua City Local Names Committee Office), ed. 2003. Jinhua Shi Ditu Ce (金华市地图册 Handbook of Maps of Jinhua Municipality). Changsha: Hunan Map Publishers.

JHSZ (Jinhua Historical Annals Committee), ed. 1992. *Jinhua Shizhi* (金华市志 Gazetteer of Jinhua City). Hangzhou: Zhejiang People's Publishers.

Ji, Fahan 吉发涵 1994. "Miao Hui de Youlai ji qi Fazhang Yanbian" 庙会的由来及其发展演变 (The Origins and Developmental Changes of Temple Fairs). *Minsu Yanjiu* 29 (1): 48–54.

Jian, Jun 剑君 1994. "Qufu Linmen Guhui" 曲阜林门古会 (The Ancient Fair of Qufu's Linmen Gate) *Minsu Yanjiu* 29 (1): 63–65.

Jiang, Yinhuo 蒋银火. n.d.a. "Hu Gong zai Dongyang minsu wenhua zhong de diwei he yingxiang" 胡公在东阳民俗文化的地位和影响 (Hu Gong's Place and Influence in the Folk Culture of Dongyang) Unpublished notes.

Jiang, Yinhuo. n.d.b. "Dongyang Cunzhuang, Shichang he Huichang" (Dongyang Villages, Markets and Fairs). Unpublished notes.

Jinhua Album Committee, ed. 1995. *Jinhua China* Jinhua: Jinhua City Gov't.

Jinhua Daily News (11/12/98) "Yongkang's Industrial Economy Develops Rapidly."

Jinhua City webpage #1 (Jinhua basic data): www.jhstats.gov.cn/jhfzgl/2006/index.aspx.

Jinhua City webpage #2 (Jinhua City description): www.zhejiang.gov.cn/node2/node1619/node1622/node1810/userobject13ai702.html.

Jinhua City webpage #3 (Jinhua social and economic development 2003): www.jhstats.gov.cn/jhfzgl/2004/2004shiqu.aspx.

Jinhua City webpage #4 (Jinhua economic construction): www.jinhua.gov.cn/jhgk/jjjs/gy.htm.

Jinhua City webpage #5 (Jinhua export economy): www.jinhua.gov.cn/jhgk/jjjs/dwjj.htm.

Jinhua City webpage #7 (Jinhua GDP1978–2007 by county): www.jhstats.gov.cn/tjnj/nj2008/2008nj1-7.htm.

Jinhua City webpage #9 (Jinhua foreign capital use 1990–2007): www.jhstats.gov.cn/tjnj/nj2008/2008nj7-12.htm.

Jinhua City webpage #10 (Jinhua townships basic situation 2007): www.jhstats.gov.cn/tjnj/nj2008/2008nj14-1.htm.

Jinhua City webpage #11 (Jinhua industry): www.jinhua.gov.cn/english/gaikuang/industry.htm.

Jinhua City webpage #12 (Hendian movie and television city): www.jinhua.gov.cn/english/lvyou/hd.htm.

Jinhua East Government webpage (East Jinua overview): www.jindong.gov.cn/news/ZRJG_9140/200411128970.aspx.

Jinhua Wenshi Ziliao Committee, ed. 1988. Jinhua Mingsheng Guji 金华名声古迹 (Famous Historic Sites of Jinhua) Hangzhou: Zhejiang People's Publishers.

Johnson, David. 1989. "Actions Speak Louder than Words: The Cultural Significance of Chinese Ritual Opera." In David Johnson, ed. *Ritual Opera, Operatic Ritual*. Berkeley: University of California Press.

Johnson, David. 1997. "Confucian Elements in the Great Temple Festivals of Southeastern Shansi in Late Imperial Times." *Toung Pao* 83: 126–161.

Johnson, David. 2009. *Spectacle and Sacrifice: the ritual foundations of village life in North China*. Cambridge: Harvard University Press.

Kang, Xiaofei. 2006. *The Cult of the Fox: Power, Gender and Popular religion in Late Imperial and Modern China*. New York: Columbia University Press.

Katz, Paul R. 1995. *Demon Hordes and Burning Boats: The Cult of Marshal Wen in Late Imperial Chekiang*. Albany, NY: State University of New York Press.

Katz, Paul R. 1999. *Images of the Immortal: the cult of Lü Dongbin at the Palace of Eternal Joy*. Honolulu: University of Hawaii Press.

Katz, Paul. n.d. "Recent Developments in the Study of Chinese Ritual Dramas: an Assessment of Xu Hongtu's Research on Zhejiang." Review of the books from the *Minsu Quyi Congshu* (Studies in Chinese Ritual Theatre and Folklore Series) 21–25, 55, 59, Xu Hongtu et al. eds.

Lagerwey, John. 1987. *Taoist Ritual in Chinese Society and History*. New York: Macmillan.

Lee, Junghwan. 2007. "Wang Yangming thought as Cultural Capital: the Case of Yongkang County." *Late Imperial China* 28 (2) (December): 41–80.

Lei, Guoqiang 雷国强 1997. Ji Tai 祭台 (Sacrifice to the stage). In Qihua Shu 舒启华, Zhu Peiyue 朱佩(王乐) and Shi Huaide 施怀德, eds., *A Broad View of Wuzhou Folklore*, Xining: Qinghai People's Publishers, 89.

Li, Banglin 李帮林 and Yang Zhuangwen 杨庄文 1996. "Fotang 'Mali' Jia Haoxiao" 佛堂"麻痢" 贾好笑. (Fotang's "Pockmarked Dysentery" Jia Haoxiao) *Yiwu Daily* May 17.

Li, Hua 李骅 1982. "Jinhua Daoqing Mantan" 金华道情漫谈 An informal discussion of Jinhua Daoqing *Yishu Guan* 艺术馆 *(Arts Bureau)*, 6.

Li, Taisong 李太松 and Yan Shishan 严世善 1992. "Dangdai Miaohui de Xin Tedian ji qi sikao" 当代庙会文化的新特点及其思考 (Some Thoughts on the New Characteristics of Contemporary Miaohui Culture). In Zhanxiang Gao 高占祥, ed. 1992. *Lun Miaohui Wenhua* 论庙会文化 (A Discussion of the Culture of Temple Fairs). Beijing: Xinhua Shudian.

Lin, Yongzhong 林用中 and Zhang Songshou 章松寿 1936. Lao Dongyue Miaohui Diaocha Baogao 老东岳庙会调查报告 (A Report on the Investigation of the Lao Dongyue Temple Fair). Hangzhou: Zhejiang Mass Education Experimental School.

Liu, Hui. 1999. Taishan Miaohui 泰山庙会 (Taishan Temple Fairs). Jinan: Shandong Jiaoyu Publishers.

Liu, Kexiang. n.d. "Jindai Nongcun Miaohui ji qi Gongneng yu Zuoyong" 近代农村庙会及其功能与作用 (Modern Rural Temple Fairs, Their Function and Utility). Conference paper, Wuhan, 8/2000.

Liu, Kezhong and Sun Yi. 1991. *Jiangnan Fengsu* 江南风俗 (Custom and Convention in the Jiangnan Region). Shanghai: Jiangsu Provincial Publishers.

Liu, Qiyin 刘其印 1997. "Long Chongbai de Huashi: Fanzhuang [township's] 2/2 Longpai Hui Lungang". 龙崇拜的活化石：范庄 2月2 龙牌会论纲 (The Living Fossil of Dragon Worship: the Longpai Festival of 2/2). *Minsu Yanjiu* 41 (1): 87–91.

Liu, Tieliang 刘铁梁 1996. "Cunluo jiti yishixing wenyi biaoyan huodong yu cunmin de shehui zuzhi guannian" 村落集体仪式性文艺表演活动与村民的社会组织观念

"Village Cultural Performance Activities of a Collective and Ceremonial Nature and the Concept of Rural Folk Social Organization." In Xicheng Liu ed., *Miaofeng Shan: Shiji zhi Jiao de Zhongguo Minsu Liubian* 妙峰山：世纪之交的中国民俗流变 (Miaofeng Shan: changes in Chinese Folklore at the turn of the century). Beijing: China Chengshi (Urban) Publishers.

Liu, Xicheng 刘锡诚 1996. "Looking Back on the Century: The Choices Faced by Chinese Folklore Studies on the Occasion of the 70th Anniversary of Gu Jiegang and Others Investigations of Miaofeng Shan." In Liu ed., *Miaofeng Shan: Shiji zhi Jiao de Zhongguo Minsu Liubian* 妙峰山：世纪之交的中国民俗流变 (Miaofeng Shan: changes in Chinese Folklore at the turn of the century). Beijing: China Chengshi (Urban) Publishers.

Liu, Xicheng 刘锡诚, ed. 1996. *Miaofeng Shan: Shiji zhi Jiao de Zhongguo Minsu Liubian* 妙峰山：世纪之交的中国民俗流变 (Miaofeng Shan: changes in Chinese Folklore at the turn of the century). Beijing: China Chengshi (Urban) Publishers.

Liu, Xun. n.d. "Visualizing Female Perfection: Daoist Painting of Our Lady, Court Patronage and Elite Female Piety in Late Qing (1862–1908)." Pre-publication draft of paper.

Lou, Zirong 楼子荣 ed. 1997. *Yiwu Shichang Shiwunian* 义乌市场十五年 "Fifteen years of the Yiwu Market" Yiwu: Bureau of Industry and Commerce.

Lü, Hongnian 吕洪年 n.d. 重视民俗调查的历史经验 (A Review of the Historical Experience of Folklore Investigations).

Lü, Ji Xiang 吕继祥 1994. "Taishan Miaohui Shulun" 泰山庙会述论 "A Discussion of the Taishan Miaohui" *Minsu Yanjiu* 29 (1): 55–62.

Lü, Wei 吕威 1996. "Minguo Shiqi de Miaofeng Shan Minsu Yanjiu: jinian Gu Jiegang deng ren de Miaofeng Shan Jinxiang diaocha 70 zhounian" 民国时期的妙峰山民俗研究：纪念顾颉刚等人的妙峰山进香调查70周年 (Folklore Study of Miaofeng Shan in the Repubican Period: In Celebration of the 70th Anniversary of the Investigation of the Miaofeng Shan Incense Presentation by Gu Jiegang and Others). In Xicheng Liu ed., *Miaofeng Shan: Shiji zhi Jiao de Zhongguo Minsu Liubian* 妙峰山：世纪之交的中国民俗流变 (Miaofeng Shan: changes in Chinese Folklore at the turn of the century). Beijing: China Chengshi (Urban) Publishers.

Lü, Weida 吕伟达 1994. "Fushan Taipingding Miaohui" 福山太平顶庙会 (The temple fair of Fushan Taiping peak). *Minsu Yanjiu* 29 (1): 82–84.

Lu, Xun. 1922. "She Xi" (The temple fair opera) in *Lu Xun Xiaoshuo Xuanji* (Selected Short stories of Lu Xun) *1995*. Beijing: Minzhu Publishers.

Luo, Mingcheng 罗明成 1996. "Miaofengshan Xianghui de Shisu Jiazhi" 妙峰山香会的世俗价值 (The Secular Value of the Miaofengshan Incense Societies). *Minsu Yanjiu* 38 (2): 52–55.

Luodian Township Government. n.d. Luodian People Welcome You 罗店人民欢迎你 (brochure published by Luodian government).

LXSZ (Lanxi Shizhi Lanxi City Annals Editorial Committee), ed. 1988. *Lanxi Shizhi* 兰溪市志 (Lanxi City Annals). Hangzhou: Zhejiang People's Publishers.

Ma, Caicai 马彩才 1997. "The rise of Ershisan Li 二十三里 commodities market." In ZWSZL, Zhejiang Wenshi Ziliao Weiyuanhui. Xiao Shangpin Da Shichang 小商品大市场：义乌中国小商品城创业者回忆. *Small Commodities, Big Market: Reminiscences of the Pioneers of Yiwu Small Commodities City Zhejiang Wenshi Ziliao* 60 Hangzhou: Zhejiang People's Publishers.

Ma, Gengcun 马庚存 1994. "Qingdao shiqude Miaohui yu Shanhui" 青岛市区的庙会与山会 (The Temple Fair and Mountain Fair of Qingdao Urban District). *Minsu Yanjiu* 29 (1): 77–81.

Ma, Lieshang 马烈商 1997. "Shizi lianhua yu Lianhua tou" 十字莲花与莲花头 (Ten character lotus flowers and lotus flower leader). In Xicheng Liu ed., *Miaofeng Shan: Shiji zhi Jiao de Zhongguo Minsu Liubian* 妙峰山：世纪之交的中国民俗流变 (Miaofeng Shan: changes in Chinese Folklore at the turn of the century). Beijing: China Chengshi (Urban) Publishers, 173.

Mao, Xufeng 毛旭峰 ed. 1996. Ke Ai de Yiwu 可爱的义乌 (Loveable Yiwu) Yiwu: Xinhua Publishers.

Mauss, Marcel. 1928. *The Gift.* New York: Norton Publishers.

Naquin, Susan. 1992. "The Peking Pilgrimage to Miao-feng Shan: Religious Organizations and Sacred Site." In Susan Naquin and Chun-fang Yu, eds. *Pilgrims and Sacred Sites in China.* Berkeley: University of California Press.

Naquin, Susan and Yu Chun-fang. 1992a. *Pilgrims and Sacred Sites in China.* Berkeley: University of California Press.

Naquin, Susan and Yu Chun-fang. 1992b. *Introduction to Pilgrims and Sacred Sites in China.* Berkeley: University of California Press.

New Market New Yiwu. 2004. DVD.

Nie, Fengjun 聂凤峻 and Liu Junjie 刘俊杰 1994 "Yin shi Lidao, Fahui Xiandai Miaohui de Jiji Zuoyong" 因势利导，发挥现代庙会的积极作用 (Guide Action According to Circumstances, Give Free Rein to the Positive Functions of Contemporary Miaohui). *Minsu Yanjiu* 29 (1): 44–47, 73.

Overmyer, Daniel L. 1972. "Folk-Buddhist Religion: Creation and Eschatology in Medieval China." *History of Religions* 12 (1): 42–70.

Overmyer, Daniel L. 2003. "Religion in China Today: Introduction." *China Quarterly* 174: 307–316.

Overmyer, Daniel L. 2009. *Local Religion in North China in the Twentiety Century: The Structure and Organization of Community Rituals and Beliefs.* Leiden: E.J. Brill.

Potter, Pitman B. 2003. "Belief in Control: Regulation of Religion in China." *China Quarterly* 174: 317–337.

Raben, Estelle M. 1992. "Peking Opera: the Persistence of Tradition in the People's Republic of China." *Journal of Popular Culture* 25 (4, Spring): 53–61.

Sai, Ren 塞人 1992. "The Function and Change of Miaohui Activity and Its Administration" (Shilun miaohui huodong de gongneng, bianhua ji guanli — 试论庙会活动的功能，变化及管理) in Zhanxiang Gao 高占祥, ed. *Lun Miaohui Wenhua* 论庙会文化 (A Discussion of the Culture of Temple Fairs). Beijing: Xinhua Shudian, 111.

Sangren, P. Steven. 1987. "Orthodoxy, Heterodoxy, and the Structure of Value in Chinese Rituals." *Modern China* 13 (1): 63–89.

Schneider, Laurence A. 1971. *Ku Chieh-kang and China's New History: Nationalism and the Quest for Alternative Traditions.* Berkeley: University of California Press.

Schoppa, R. Keith. 1982. *Chinese elites and Political Change: Zhejiang Province in the Early Twentieth Century.* Cambridge: Harvard University Press.

Scoggard, Ian. 1996. *The Indigenous Dynamic in Taiwan's Postwar Development: the religious and historical roots of entrepreneurship.* New York: M.E. Sharpe.

Scott, James. 1985. *Weapons of the Weak: everyday forms of peasant resistance.* New Haven: Yale University Press.

Scott, James. 1992. *Domination and the Arts of Resistance.* New Haven: Yale University Press.

Shen, Jing. 2003. "Role Types in the Paired Fish, a Chuanqi Play." *Asian Theater Journal* 20 (2, Autumn): 226–236.

Shen, Ruilan 沈瑞兰 1997 Tanhuang (Shoal Reeds) Taizi Ban 滩簧太子班. In Qihua Shu 舒启华, Zhu Peiyue 朱佩(王乐) and Shi Huaide 施怀德, eds., *A Broad View of Wuzhou Folklore*, Xining: Qinghai People's Publishers, 95.

Shi, Huaide 施怀德 1997. "Surviving Customs in the Worship of Huang Da Xian." In Qihua Shu 舒启华, Zhu Peiyue 朱佩(王乐) and Shi Huaide 施怀德, eds., *A Broad View of Wuzhou Folklore*, Xining: Qinghai People's Publishers, 126.

Shi Zhangyue 施章岳 1997a. Yiwu Daoqing 义乌道情. In Qihua Shu舒启华, Zhu Peiyue 朱佩(王乐) and Shi Huaide 施怀德, eds., *A Broad View of Wuzhou Folklore*, Xining: Qinghai People's Publishers, 102.

Shi, Zhangyue 施章岳 1997b. "Luo Gu Ban" 锣鼓班 Gong and Drum Troupes. In Qihua Shu 舒启华, Zhu Peiyue 朱佩(王乐) and Shi Huaide 施怀德, eds., *A Broad View of Wuzhou Folklore*, Xining: Qinghai People's Publishers, 78.

Shu, Qihua 舒启华, Zhu Peiyue 朱佩(王乐) and Shi Huaide 施怀德, eds. 1997. *Wuzhou Minsu Daguan 婺州民俗大观 (A Broad View of Wuzhou Folklore)*. Xining: Qinghai People's Publishers.

Skinner, G.W. 1964–5. "Marketing and Social Structure in Rural China." *Journal of Asian Studies* 24: 3 and 4.

Skinner, G.W. 1977. *The City in Late Imperial China*. Stanford: Stanford University Press.

Song, Bo 松波 1983a. Zhouchunju Wutai Chunqiu 周春聚舞台春秋 (The Spring and Autumn of Zhouchunju Opera Troupe), Part 1, *Yishuguan* 艺术馆 5: 83–93.

Song, Bo 松波 1983b. Part 2, *Yishuguan* 艺术馆 8: 55–68.

Song, Bo 松波 1983c. Part 3, *Yishuguan* 艺术馆 9: 59–78.

Song, Bo 松波 1984a. "Dongyang Sanhe Ban Wutai Chunqiu" 东阳三合班舞台春秋 (The Spring and Autumn of Dongyang's "Three Combined" Opera Troupes). *Yishuguan* 艺术馆 7 (Part 1): 72–79.

Song, Bo 松波 1984b. "Dongyang Sanhe Ban Wutai Chunqiu" 东阳三合班舞台春秋 (The Spring and Autumn of Dongyang's "Three Combined" Opera Troupes). *Yishuguan* 艺术馆 8 (Part 2): 78–103.

Song, Bo 松波 1984c. "Dongyang Sanhe Ban Wutai Chunqiu" 东阳三合班舞台春秋 (The Spring and Autumn of Dongyang's "Three Combined" Opera Troupes). *Yishuguan* 艺术馆 9 (Part 3): 65–74.

Sutton, Donald S. 1990. "Ritual Drama and Moral Order: Interpreting the Gods' Festival Troupes of Southern Taiwan." *Journal of Asian Studies* 49 (3): 535–554.

Tan, Dehui 潭德慧 1988. "Ye Tan Wuju zhi Ming Youlai" 也谈婺剧之名由来 (More on the Origin of the Name Wuju: a Discussion with Comrade Hong Bo). *Wuxing* 婺星 3: 59–60.

Teiser, Stephen F. 1995. "Popular Religion" *Journal of Asian Studies* 54 (2): 378–395.

Union Research Service. 1962. "On Commodity Exchange Fairs." 33 (22, December): 13.

Walker, Kathy Le Mons. 1999. *Chinese Modernity and the Peasant Path: Semi-colonialism in the Northern Yangzi Delta*. Stanford: Stanford University Press.

Wang, Hongxing 王洪星, ed. 1997. *Yongkang Lan Sheng* 永康揽胜 (Scenic Spots of Yongkang). Yongkang: People's Publishers.

Wang, Jiucheng 王九成, ed. 1998. *Dongyang Shi Wenhuazhi* 东阳市文化志 (Cultural Annals of Dongyang City) Dongyang: Ministry of Culture.

Wang, Yonghua 王庸华, ed. 1993. *Dongyang Shizhi* (东阳市志 Dongyang City Annals). Shanghai: Hanyu Dazidian Publishers.

Wang Zhaoxiang 王兆祥 and Liu Wenzhi. 刘文智. 1997. *Zhongguo Gudaide Miaohui*, 中国古代的庙会 (China's Ancient Temple Fairs) Commercial Press International: Beijing.

Wei, Xilong 韦锡龙 and Cai Gongxing 蔡拱星 n.d. "Cong Dongyang Daoqing Shuoqi: Tan Minzu Minjian Wenhua de Zhuancheng he Fazhan." 从"东阳道情"说起：谈民族民间文化的传承和发展 (Speaking of Dongyang Daoqing: a Discussion of the Transmission and Development of Ethnic Folk Culture).

Wu, Cheng-han. 1988. *The Temple Fairs of Late Imperial China*. Ph.D. Dissertation, Princeton University.

Wu, Gangji 吴刚戢 1993. *Kuo Cang Qing Yuan* 括苍情缘 (Gather the Old with Affection and Reason). Yongkang: People's Publishers.

Wu Zhongwen 吴钟文 1997. "The Ranking of Daoqing Yugu (drums)". In Qihua Shu 舒启华, Zhu Peiyue 朱佩(王乐) and Shi Huaide 施怀德, eds., *A Broad View of Wuzhou Folklore*, Xining: Qinghai People's Publishers.

Xie, Yuanli 谢元鲤 1996. "Jindai Tancheng Miao Hui" 近代郯城庙会 (The Temple Fair of Modern Tancheng). *Minsu Yanjiu* 38 (2): 30–39.

Xu, Hongtu 徐宏图 2005. "Zhejiang de Daojiao yu Xiju" 浙江的道教与戏剧 (Daoism and Drama in Zhejiang) 杭州师范学院学报 (社会科学版). *Hangzhou Normal Academy Social Science Journal* 6 (Nov.): 37–41.

XWXWHZ (Xiawang Xiang Cultural Annals Editorial Committee) 1987. Lanxi Shi Xiawang xiang Wenhua Zhi 兰溪市下王乡文化志 (Cultural Annals of Xiawang Township of Lanxi City). Lanxi: Xinxin printers.

Yan, Yunxiang 2003. *Private Life Under Socialism*. Stanford University Press.

Yang, C.K. 1967. *Religion in Chinese Society*. Berkeley: University of Californai Press.

Yang, Fenggang. 2006. "The Red, Black and Gray Markets of Religion in China." *Sociological Quarterly* 47: 93–122.

Yang, Yabin 杨雅彬 1992. "Duiyu Miaohui Wenhua de jidian xiangfa" 对於庙会文化研究的几点想法 "Several ideas concerning the study of miao hui culture." In Zhanxiang Gao 高占祥, ed. 1992. *Lun Miaohui Wenhua* 论庙会文化 (A Discussion of the Culture of Temple Fairs). Beijing: Xinhua Shudian.

Yang, Zhongxiang 杨中祥 2006. Zoujin Yiwu 走进义乌 (Step into Yiwu). *China Air Magazine* 6/06.

Yao, Ping 2011. "Cousin Marriage in Tang China (618–907)". *China Historical Review* 8 (1): 25–55.

YCZX (Qianxiang Merchant's Association) n.d. "Yaocai zhi Xiang" (药材之乡 The township of medicinal herbs) mimeo.

Ye, Zhilin, ed. 1997. *Xiao Shangpin, Da Shichang: Yiwu Zhongguo Xiao Shangpin Cheng Zhuangyezhe Huiyi* 小商品，大市场：义乌中国小商品城创业者回忆 (Reminiscences of the pioneers of the China Small Commodities City). *Zhejiang Sheng Wenshi Ziliao* 60. Hangzhou: Zhejiang People's Publishers.

Ying, Baorong 应宝容 and Hu Guojun 胡国钧1983. "A Record of Major Events in the Life of Fangyan's Hugong." 方岩胡公大事记. *Yishu Guan* 艺术馆 (Arts Bureau) 8: 85–86.

Ying, Jiadeng 应加登 1991. "Fangyan Miaohui" 方岩庙会 (Fangyan's Temple Fair) *Wu Xing* 婺星 (Jinhua Star) 77: 45–48.

Ying Jiadeng and Hu Guojun, eds. 1990. *Fangyan Minjian Gushi Zhuanshuo* (方岩民间故事传说 — Folk stories and myths of Fangyan). Yongkang: Zhejiang Wenyi Publishers.

Yiwu Commodity City Group DVD (2002).

YKXZ (Yongkang Historical Annals Editorial Committee) 1991 *Yongkang Xianzhi* (永康县志 Gazetteer of Yongkang county). Hangzhou: Zhejiang People's Publishers.

Yongkang City Government webpage: www.yk.gov.cn/ykgk/jjfz_01.htm.

YWFSZ (Yiwu County Cultural Center 义乌文化馆), ed. 1985 *Yiwu Xian Fengsu Jianzhi* 义乌县风俗简志 (The Habits and Customs of Yiwu County). Yiwu: People's Publishers.

Yiwu Chenlie guan (Exhibition Hall). 2006. Script from the Museum Exhibition. Guide to the Yiwu Museum.

YWXZ (Wu, Shichun 吴世春), ed. 1987. *Yiwu Xianzhi* 义乌县志 (Yiwu County Gazetteer). Hangzhou: Zhejiang People's Publishers.

Zhang, Bengao 张本高 2005. "Tan Qing Houyi Shuo Wuju" 深情厚意说婺剧 (Deeply Felt Kind Thoughts about Wuju). *Wuxing* 婺星 127: 34–38.

Zhang, Cuiling 张翠玲 1996. "Xihua Nuwacheng Miaohui Diaocha Baogao" 西华女娲城庙会调查报告 (Report on an Investigation of the Xihua Nuwa City Temple Fair, Part 1). *Minsu Yanjiu* 36 (2): 40–45.

Zhang, Hanzhen 张含贞 and Fu Jian 傅健 1998. "Youyoude Yugu weile Qing: Yiwu Jiang [yan jiang hang] Caifang zhi ershiwu" 悠悠的渔鼓未了情：义乌江[沿江行]采访之二十五 (The Leisurely Sound of the Yugu Drum: Walks on the Banks of the Yiwu River 25). Yiwu: *Yiwu Daily News* 义乌日报.

Zhang, Shi 张适 1996. "Yangzhou Guanyinshan Xianghui" 扬州观音山香会 (The Incense Fair of Yangzhou's Guanyin Mountain). *Minsu Yanjiu* 39 (3): 54–5.

Zhang, Shousong 章寿松 and Hong Bo 洪波 1985. *Wuju Jianshi* 婺剧简史 (Brief History of Wu Opera). Jinhua: People's Publishers.

Zhang, Zhulin 张竹林 1990. "A Brief Discussion of Jinhua Daoqing." 金华道情浅谈 In Jinhua Cultural and Historical Materials Committee, ed. 金华县文史资料 #3：181–185 (November). Jinhua: Xinhua printers.

Zhang, Zhulin 章竹林 1997. "Daoqing Artists Pay Respects to Their Master and Meet as a Profession." In Qihua Shu 舒启华, Zhu Peiyue 朱佩(王乐) and Shi Huaide 施怀德, eds., *A Broad View of Wuzhou Folklore*, Xining: Qinghai People's Publishers, 107.

Zhang, Zhulin 张竹林 2003. *Jinhua Quyi Zhi* (金华曲艺志—A record of the musical forms of Jinhua). Hong Kong: Tianma Books.

Zhao, Denggui 赵登贵 and Ma Lieshang 马烈商 1997 "Foxi (Xifang Yue)" 佛戏 (西方乐) In Qihua Shu 舒启华, Zhu Peiyue 朱佩(王乐) and Shi Huaide 施怀德, eds., *A Broad View of Wuzhou Folklore*, Xining: Qinghai People's Publishers, 174–5.

Zhao, Shiyu. 赵世瑜. n.d. "The Religious Activities, Leisure Life of Women and the Female Sub-culture since the Ming Qing Period." Unpublished paper.

Zhao, Shiyu 赵世瑜 1996. "Ming Qing Shiqi Jiangnan Miaohui yu Huabei Miaohui Jidian Bijiao" 明清时期江南庙会与华北庙会几点比较 (Several Points of Comparison between the Temple Fairs of South and North China during the Ming and Qing periods). In Liu Shicheng, ed. *Miaofengshan: Shiji zhi Jiao de Zhonngguo Minsu Liubian* (Miaofengshan: the Evolution of Chinese Folklore at the Turn of the Century). Beijing: China Urban Publishers.

Zhao, Shiyu 赵世瑜 2002. *Kuanghuan yu Richang — MingQing yilai de miaohui yu minjian wenhua* 狂欢与日常 — 明清以来的庙会与民间社会 Carnivals in Daily Life: Temple Fairs and Local Society since the Ming and Qing Dynasties. Beijing: Sanlian Shudian.

Zhejiang Folklore Society, ed. 1991. *Zhejiang Minsu* 浙江民俗. Shanghai: Shanghai Culture and Arts Publishers.

Zhejiang Ribao. "Fotang city." June 14, 2006: 14.

Zhejiang Wenshi Ziliao Weiyuanhui. 1997. *Xiao Shangpin Da Shichang: Yiwu Zhongguo Xiao Shangpin Cheng zhuangyezhe Huiyi* 小商品大市场：义乌中国小商

品城创业者回忆 (Small Commodities, Big Market: Reminiscences of the Pioneers of Yiwu Small Commodities City). Zhejiang Wenshi Ziliao #60 Hangzhou: Zhejiang People's Publishers.

Zhejiang Yiwu Museum: extract from 义乌日报 Yiwu Daily.

Zhong, Jingwen 种敬文. 1999. *Zhong Jingwen Wenji* 种敬文文集 (Collected Writings of Professor Zhong Jingwen). Hefei: Anhui Educational Publishers.

Zhou, Yaoming 周耀明, ed. 1987. *Dongyang Xian Gushi Juan* 东阳县故事卷 (A Collection of Stories from Dongyang County). Hangzhou: Zhejiang Province Office of Popular Literature.

Zhu, Haibin 朱海濱 2005. "Belief in Hu Ze in Modern Zhejiang" 近世浙江の湖則信仰 *Tōyō gakuhō* 東洋學報 86 (2): 67–96.

Zhu, Junzhi 朱君之 and Ye Tao 叶涛 1994. "Haiweiwang Dao Xiangumiao yu Xianguding Miaohui Kaocha Ji" 威海望岛仙姑庙与仙姑顶庙会考察记 (Haiwei Wang Island Xiangu Temple and the Xiangu Peak Temple Fair: Notes from an Investigation) *Minsu Yanjiu* 29 (1): 66–73.

Zhu, Wenqiang 朱文强 n.d. "Jian Guo Hou Huabei Nongcun Jishi de Fazhan Yanjiu." 建国后华北农村集市的发展研究 (A Study of the Development of Rural Markets in Post-1949 North China). Unpublished paper presented at the conference on Commercial Organization and Market Development, Wuhan, July 29, 2000.

Index

Academy of the Five Peaks 153–5
agricultural slack season 26, 75, 132, 139, 203
alcohol 85
allegory 95, 97, 211, 213
amateur troupes 130–31
anti-Japanese war 14, 27, 77, 105, 117, 140–41, 165
anti-religion campaigns 35–6, 45–6
armed rebellion 186
Assassin, The 22
autonomy 187

Bai Bu Jun (百步峻) 160
Bakhtin, Mikhail 2, 5, 94–7, 113
Bamian Shan 19
Banbi Street 13–14
begging 152
Beijing 13–14, 24–5, 166, 202
"big year pig" 81
Binwang 21st Century Trade Center 31
birthdays 5, 38, 43–4, 67, 78, 80, 88, 103, 132–4, 139, 165, 167, 171, 182, 195
Bixia Yuanjun 59–60
Black Dragon Temple 53
blind artistes 87, 102, 104–6, 108–110, 212
Boas, Franz 58, 61
Bol, Peter 35, 40, 193
Bolang Gu (拔浪鼓) drum rattle 26–8
Borrowed Umbrella (借伞记) 106, 219–20
Bourdieu, Pierre 1–2, 216
Bringing Together of the Pearl 222–3
Brook, Timothy 2, 6, 185, 187, 189, 214
"Buddha hands" 77
Buddhism 5, 34–8, 45–9, 53–5, 67–8, 82, 88, 102, 161–2, 165–9, 180, 185, 194–7, 203, 208;
  Three Buddhas and Five Marquises of Jinhua 36–8

Buddhist Warrior Attendants (金刚) 161
burning money 52
Buyun Ting (步云亭) 161

calligraphy 152
Cao, Songye 36, 38, 157, 196
capitalism 51–2, 65
cargo cult mentality 31
carnival spirit 97
Catholicism 34, 46
central provisioning center for merchants 33
Chan, Selina Ching 42–4
Chao, Emily 50
chaotic playing 118
Chau, Adam Yuet 2, 34, 46, 48–53, 135, 187–9
Chen, Chongren 29–30, 32, 103, 105, 126, 173, 177–8 (see below)
Chenghuang 45, 148
Chen Hou (陳侯) 38
Chen Kaige 22–3
Chen Liang 153
Chen, Ming 30
Chen Yisi 158–60
Chen, Yongyua 85–9
Chenlie guan 29–30, 32
Chiang Kaishak 165
China's Hollywood *see* Hengdian
Chinese folklore studies 54–62
Chongyang festival 155, 170–71
Christianity 6, 47, 49, 69
circumscribed toleration 6
civil war 14, 62, 80, 196
Cloud Yellow Mountain 195–6
Cloud Yellow Temple 196
coffee-house gossip 183–4

Index

Cohen, Alvin P. 1
combined troupes 119–21
commercial associations 13–14, 199
commercial/economic dimension of secular fairs 65–94
commercialization 183–4
commodity exchange fair 1, 3, 65–5, 138
commodity trade fair 3, 65, 113
communism 1, 3–4, 6, 34, 42, 45–8, 50, 65–6, 100, 106, 108, 113, 146, 165–6, 177, 185–6, 188, 192–3, 212–16
Communist Party 3, 66, 100, 107, 146, 166, 177, 186, 202, 214–5, 220
Competition for the Stage (斗台) 135–6
compliance 52
concept of Wuju 140–41
conceptual framework 1–6; fairs 3–6
Conference of National Medicinal Herb Markets 73
Confucianism 5, 35, 39, 45–9, 57, 78, 155, 168, 185–6, 196
conspicuous efficacy 159–60
consecrate the stage 134–5
constituent genres of Wuju 114–21; Gaoqiang (高腔) 114; Houyang Gaoqiang 114–15; Huixi (徽戏) 117–18; Kun Qiang (昆腔) 116–17; Luantan (乱弹) 118; Shidiao (时调) 119; Songyang Gaoqiang (松阳高腔) 115; Tanhuang (滩簧) 118–19; Xi An Gaoqiang (西安高腔) 115; Xiwu Gaoqiang (西吴高腔) 115
consumerism 3
continuity paradigm 50
contortionists 5, 69, 84–5, 94, 96–7, 211
Convent of the Seven Buddhas 196
Cooper, Eugene 9, 41, 67, 69
cooperativization 107
corruption 99, 181
counter-revolutionary mobilization 214
Cross the River for Murderous Revenge 225
cult center 160–71
Cultivating Li Mountain 223
Cultural Revolution 3, 27–8, 36, 42, 44, 65, 81–2, 100, 106, 108–110, 139–40, 147, 155, 165–7, 171–2, 176, 187, 192, 195, 197, 212; and Hugong 166–7
cymbal and drum troupe 130–31

Da Bei Si 156, 158, 161, 164–5, 180
da Bianqiu (打边球) 97
Da Tai (打台) 126
Da Yu Shan *see* Bamian Shan

Dagong Bao 21
Dai, Rucai 14, 78
Damo (天竺僧达摩) 194–5, 203
Dance of the Eight Immortals 41, 126–7, 131–2, 173
Dance the God of Wealth 129–30
Daoqing 25, 80, 87, 98, 101–10, 208, 212
Daoism 5, 34–5, 38–49, 53–5, 88, 128, 161, 185, 196, 213; Huang Daxian (黄大仙) 41–4
Dashi 34–5
Dashi Fo *see* Fu Dashi (傅大士)
Dean, Kenneth 2, 45–7, 49, 51–2, 188–9, 213–14, 216
decadence 181
deification of Hugong 158–60
deity niche 172–5, 183–4
deity of the eastern peak 192
delegitimization of Communist orthodoxy 216
descend the spirit servant 173
didactic content of repertoire 139–40
Die Luohan (叠罗汉) 178
different kind of movement 51, 214
Ding, Yibin 79, 115–16, 118, 121, 124, 131–2, 136–7, 139
Dingguang Fo (定光佛) 36–8
divination 187
divination poem 169
divination slip texts 152, 169
divine fate using bamboo slips 169
doctrinal purity 49
Dong Yue (东岳) 192
Dongyang county 19, 34, 36, 39, 65–7, 145, 156
Dongyang Shizhi 36, 39–40
Dongzhi 28
Doutai (斗台) 135–6, 212
dowry goods 4
drum-rattle Bolang Gu (拔浪鼓) 26–8
Du Baolin 98
Duara, Prasenjit 49–50
Duqing Si temple (渡磬寺) 194–7
Durkheim, Émile 47, 49

early years of PRC 145–7
Eastern Han dynasty (AD 58–75) 4
Eastern Jin 34, 41
Eberhard, Wolfram 59, 163, 175
economic background of Jinhua 15–17
economic reform 1, 4, 15, 19–20, 25, 43, 54, 65–6, 72, 77, 81, 86, 90, 151, 176, 198, 200, 204, 215

effervescence 4
egalitarianism 96
Eight Immortals 41, 103, 130–31, 173
18 Foxes 180–81, 213
elite vs. popular religion 45–6
embeddedness 48–9
Enjoy the Moonlight Garden 21
enlightenment 37, 49–50
"entertaining the deity" 5
entertainment 132
Erheban Ban (二合半班) 117, 119, 141
Ershisan Li village 28–9, 108
Evans-Pritchard, E. E. 2
"everyday" forms of resistance 52, 95, 211
exchange of incense and fire 38, 172, 175–6
exorcism 39–40, 48, 52
extravagance 56
eye openings 132, 138

facial make-up 97, 122–4
Falun gong 6
famine 3
Fan Zhongyan 156–8, 191
Fang La uprising 158–60
Fangyan 152–3, 160–71; Hugong temple at 160–71
Fangyan Huo (方岩货) 163
feathers 26–8, 32, 108
fee for service 39, 52
Fei Qiao (飞桥) 160–61
feudalism 3, 187
feverish gibberish 98
Fine Accommodation of the Beautiful Pool at Peach Bluff 155
fire leg huotui 26
First Harassing the Stage 126
Five Dynasties 197
"Five Great Folk Arts of Zhejiang Province" 98, 101
Five Marquises of Jinhua 36–8, 196, 212
Flath, James 96, 188–9
Float on the Clouds Pavilion 197
flower drum 110
Flower God Temple 78
Flying Bridge 160–61
folk custom 51
"Forbidden City" 25
foreign investment; Jinhua 18–19
foreign trade 73; Jinhua 17–18
Forster, Keith 15, 31
Fortune 500 18

Index 241

fortune telling 69, 75, 84, 187
Fotang town 194–209; about the town 198–200; Duqing Si (渡磬寺) Temple 194–7; historic preservation of the Old Town 202–3; market/temple fair of 203–8; origins 194–7; post-reform Fotang 200–202; Shuanglin Si (双林寺) Temple 194–7
"four allows" 29
Four Great Jin Gang 161
"four olds" 3, 108, 147, 203
"four withouts" 162
"four Zhejiangs" 12–13
freak shows 5, 70–71, 84, 91–2, 94, 96–7, 205, 211
free-market reform 3
Frontline 108
Fu Dashi (傅大士) 36–8, 196–7, 208, 210, 213
Fu, Jian 27, 106–9
"full sand, flaming mouth" 40
functional expansiveness 48, 189
Fuxi (傅禽) 34–8
Fuyun Ting (浮云亭) 197

Gamble, Sidney 59–60
gambling 75, 82–3, 91, 94, 109
Gang of Four 29, 100, 108, 147, 149
Gao, Youpeng 39, 45, 54–7, 59–62
Gaoqiang (高腔) 114
Gaozong 26
Gates 5–8 130
Gates, Hill 2, 52–3, 186, 214
Ge yao zhoukan (歌谣周刊) 58
Geng Lishan (耕历山) 223
Geng, Rong 60
geographical background of Jinhua 9–15
globalization 19
God of Wealth 129–30
golden age 149
Gong Li 23
Gongshang Ju (工商局) 66
Gongshang Suo (工商所) 29
Goossaert, Vincent 2, 44–7, 49–52, 95, 185–7
Great Emperor Uncle Hu 38, 155–60
Great Immortal Huang *see* Huang Daxian (黄大仙)
Great Leap Forward 3, 65, 166, 197, 208
Greet the Dragon Lantern procession 132
grotesque 2, 5, 94, 96–7, 113, 122, 205, 211
grotesquery 7, 50, 97, 211–12

Gu Jiegang 58–61
Guangzhou Street 21–2, 25
guardian of the dharma 80–81, 163
Guojiang Sha Xiang (过江杀相) 225
Guomindang 13, 165, 186; and Hugong 165

habitus 1, 6, 216
Han dynasty (206 BC–AD 220) 54
hang xiang 54
Hangzhou politics 13
He Ling (赫灵) 159–60
head tax 157–8
Heaven Street (天街) 162–3
Heaven's Gate 161
Heban (合班) 119–21
hengban 55
Hengdian 19–25
Hengdian Industrial Group 20–22, 24–5
Hengdian Jituan Bao 23–5
heterodoxy 45–6
Hezhu Ji (合珠记) 222–3
historic preservation of Fotang 202–3
history of fairs 3–6
history of Fotang town 198–200
Hit the Stage 126
Hong, Bo 14, 42, 113–24, 126–37, 139–41, 143–7, 149, 203–4, 223, 225
"Hong Kong Street" 23
Hong Wu 45
honghuo 4, 53, 126, 132, 134–5, 138, 204, 208, 214
houses of horror 5, 96–7, 205, 211
Houtang Nong village 171–2
Houyang Gaoqiang 114–15, 221–2
Hu Gong Associations (胡公会) 171–6
Hu, Guojun 152–9, 162–5, 167–83
Hu Hou (胡侯) 38, 155–60
Hu Ze (胡则) 155–60, 182, 193; Fang La uprising 158–60; official career during Song dynasty 156–8; the person 155–6
Huagu (花鼓) 110
Huaizhong Ge (怀忠阁) 190–91
Huang Daxian (黄大仙) 41–4, 213
huan xianghuo (换香火) 38, 172, 175–6
Huashen Miao (花神庙) 78
Hugong Associations 169, 171, 214
Hugong Dadi 5, 112, 150–84; coffee-house gossip 183–4; Fangyan 152–3; Hu Gong Associations (胡公会) 171–6; Hugong temple at Fangyan 160–71; Hugong temples and fairs past and present 182–3; Luohanban (罗汉班) martial arts troupes 176–8; ritual song and dance repertoire 178–82; saga of Hugong Dadi 155–60; Wufeng Shuyuan (五峰书院) 153–5; Yongkang 150–51
Hugong Hui (胡公会) 169, 171, 214
Hugong temple at Fangyan 160–71; and the Cultural Revolution 166–7; Heaven Street (天街) 162–3; Heaven's Gate 161; Hugong and the Guomindang 165; Palace of the Four Heaven Kings (天王殿) 161–2; and the People's Republic 165–6; rituals of worship 167–71; temple complex 163–5
huiguan (会馆) 13–14, 199
Huiguang Fo (慧光佛) 36–8
huimiao banxue (毁庙办学) 46
Huiqin Ji (悔亲记) 218
Huixi (徽戏) 117–18, 225
Huku 155, 170, 175, 183–4, 189–92, 214–5; "Lower" Huku (Huku Xia 胡库下) 184, 190–92, 215; "Upper" Huku (Huku Shang 胡库上) 184, 191–2, 215
Huku Shang (胡库上) 184, 191–2, 215
Huku temples 189–93, 214–15
Huku Xia (胡库下) 184, 190–92, 215
Huqi fair 1988 69–70
Huqi fair 1998 70–71
Huqi town 66–71; Huqi fair 1988 69–70; Huqi fair 1998 70–71 (Do we need to repeat these? Del.)

immortality 39, 41, 44, 55, 81–2, 140
Imperial Prince troupes 79, 130
indigenous religion 39; *see also* Daoism
indirection 52, 95, 97, 211, 213
industrial background of Jinhua 15–17
Industry and Trade Office 29, 66
innuendo 95, 97, 211, 213
institutional dichotomy 46–9
insurrection 186
intermarriage 86
International Trade City (Yiwu) 31–2
Islam 34

Japan 35, 62, 73, 80, 197
Japanese occupation 14, 142
ji cha (祭叉) 173
Ji Gong (济公) 162
Jia Weicheng (贾惟承) 26
Jia Youfu 99–101, 205, 211–12
Jianban (简板) 103–104

Index 243

Jiang Heyi (江和义) 115, 144–5
Jiang Qing 147
Jiang, Yinhuo 19, 41, 67, 69, 156–7, 175
Jiangshen Tong (降神僮) 173
Jiaxiang rou 26; see also Jinhua ham
Jidao Mountain (积道山) 37
Jin dynasty (AD 265–419) 54
Jinhua Daoqing (道情) 101–6
Jinhua Foshou (金华佛手) 77–8
Jinhua ham 12, 19, 25–6, 70, 200
Jinhua opera 113–49; amateur troupes 130–31; concept of Wuju 140–41; constituent genres 114–21; custom 133–6; facial make-up and its symbolism 122–4; minor leagues of 131; organization of troupes 121–2; present circumstances of Wuju 149; repertoire and didactic content 139–40; structure of performance 124–30; Taizi Ban (太子班) 131–2; venues and occasions 136–9; what happens where 132; Zhouchunju Ban 141–9
Jinhua opera custom 133–6; Doutai 135–6; Jitai (祭台) 134–5; professional association 133–4; Tang Minghuang (唐明皇) 133
Jinhua region 9–53; central provisioning center for fairs 33; economic/industrial background 15–17; foreign investment 18–19; foreign trade 17–18; Hengdian, China's Hollywood 19–25; physical/geographical background 9–15; religion 34–53; Yiwu 25–33
Jinhua Regional Opera Federation (金华地区戏曲联合会) 146
Jinhua Shizhi 14, 18, 34–6, 39–42, 65, 119, 122–3, 138–9, 145, 147
Jinshi degrees 56
Jitai (祭台) 134–5
Johnson, David 2–3
joint ventures 18

Kaifeng 23, 25, 156 – 7
Kang Youwei 46
kanxiang (看相) 69
Kaoshan Sumeng (靠山宿梦) 167–8
kinship 2
Korean War 106
Kun Qiang (昆腔) 116–17

Lady Meng Jiang 58
Lang, Graeme S. 42–4
Lanxi county 13–15, 41, 98

Lanxi Shizhi 39–40, 112, 119, 136
Laolang Guan (老郎馆) 133–4, 145
Lee, Junghwan 154
legitimacy 187
Lei, Guoqiang 134–5
letting off steam 186
Li, Banglin 100–101, 104
Li, Hua 109
Li, Taisan 1
Li Yu (李渔) 116
Lianhua Tou (莲花头) 179
liberation 14, 66, 78, 113, 116–17, 137, 148, 176–7
Lin, Yongzhong 61–2
Lion Pair 217
Little Shanghai 14, 199
Little Shepherd 144
Liu, Kezhong 138–9
Liu, Tieliang 57–60, 62, 181
Liu, Wenzhi 54–6, 62
local market town fairs 182–3
Longevity Mountain Hollow 153–4, 156
Longjing 115, 158–9, 190–91
lotus leader 179
"Lower" Huku 184, 190–92, 215
Lü Zuqian 153–5
Lü, Wei 57, 59–61
Lu, Xun 5
Luantan (乱弹) 118, 224–5
Luhua Xu (芦花絮) 223–4
Luo Binwang 31
Luodian fair 79–80
Luodian town 76–80; Luodian fair 79–80
Luogu Ban (锣鼓班) 130–31
Luohan grandchildren 110, 174
Luohan sun (罗汉孙) 110, 174
Luohanban (罗汉班) martial arts troupes 110, 173–8, 214

Ma Lieshang (马烈商) 105
Ma, Caicai 29, 179
machismo 177
macro-political dimension 185–93
Mafu Dian (马夫殿) 81–2
Mafu Niangniang (马夫娘娘) 81, 88–90, 94
Mahayana 196
making sense of the phenomena 210–216; economic dimension 211; political dimension 213–16; popular cultural dimension 211–12; popular religious dimension 212–13

Index

Mao Fumei 165
Mao, Xufeng 25–9, 31–2, 101–9, 132, 177–8, 189, 195–7, 203, 208
Mao Zedong 3, 15, 50, 108, 146–7, 166–7, 186–7, 193, 212, 214
market/temple fair of Fotang 203–8
Marquis Hu *see* Great Emperor Uncle Hu
Marvel comics 139
Marx, Karl 52
Mauss, Marcel 1–2, 4, 47, 210, 215
May 4 Enlightenment Movement 57–62; *see also* Chinese folklore studies
meaning of "Wuju" 145
medicinal herb markets 4, 69, 72, 79, 140, 207
Mei Lanfang 117, 146
metaphor 52, 95, 97, 211, 212
micro-political dimension 185–93
micro-politics of temple fairs 189–93
Mi Le An convent (弥勒庵) 195
Miaofengshan 58–62
Miaohui 167
millionaires 73
Ming dynasty 12–13, 21, 35, 40, 45, 55–7, 77, 79, 104, 114–18, 137, 153–5, 171, 185, 212
minjian xinyang (民间信仰) 51, 187
minimalist religion 48–9
minor leagues of Wuju 131
minority nationality status 85–8
Minsheng Wutai (民生舞台) 117, 136
minstrelsy 101
Minsu 60–62
MishaFang Yankou (弥沙放焰口) 40
mockery of the quotidian 96–7
modern Chinese religion 44–52
modernity 51
money 52–3
morning light opera 124
Mute Carries the Crazy One 116, 147–9, 181–2, 213

Nanxi 55, 114
Nao Toutai (闹头台) 126
Naquin, Susan 58, 60
nationalism 13, 59
negotiation paradigm 50–51
networking 4, 48
New Culture Movement 58
"new singing method" (新派唱法) 109
nexus of power 49, 189
Nine Gates 124–30, 137; Da Tai (打台) 126; Gates 5–8 130; Nao Toutai (闹头台) 126; San Tiao (三跳) 127–30; Ta Baxian (踏八仙) 126–7; Zhuangyuan pays respects (状元拜堂) 130
Northern dynasty 34, 54, 194
Northern Song Dynasty (AD 960–1126) 34, 150, 155–6, 158, 165–6, 177, 197

occasions for performance 136–9
occupational associations/guilds (同行工) 199
official symbolic system 97
one hundred step mountain 160
one-man band 5, 205, 207, 211
openness 29, 36
opera 5–6, 17, 25, 36, 41–4, 52–6, 67–8, 70, 76–81, 84–9, 94, 97–8, 101, 105–49, 167, 172–4, 187, 196, 199, 203–205, 211–12
operatic themes 140
Opium War, The 21–2
organization of troupes 121–2
origins of Fotang 194–7
orthodox religions 34–44; Buddhism 34–8; Daoism 38–44; vs. heterodox religions 45–6
Overmyer, Daniel L. 2, 47

Pacification Campaign East 222
Pair of Bloody Garments 225
Palace of the Four Heaven Kings (天王殿) 161–2
Palace of Qinshi Huang 23
Pannong, Liu 58
Paper Fan Mountain 37
paradigms of modern Chinese religion 44–52
paternalism 187
patron founder of operatic tradition 133
Pavilion of Cherishing Loyalty 190–91
Pear Garden 133
Pearl Pagoda 224–5
Peng Dehuai 166
pentatonic scales 101, 122
People's Republic of China 5, 36, 40, 46, 65, 87–8, 106–7, 110, 113–15, 126–7, 134, 141, 145–7, 165–6, 192, 203; early years 145–7; and Hugong 165–6; transition to PRC 145
"people's unofficial truth" 95, 211
performance at Fangyan Hugong Miaohui 167–71

performing sevens 40
perspectives for understanding religion 34–55
physical background of Jinhua 9–15
"Pile up" the Luohan 178
pilgrimage 43–4, 182, 189–93, 208
Pingfeng Ge (屏风阁) 164
Pingzheng Dong (平征东) 222
Plum in the Snow 147–9, 181–2
political dimension 185–93; Huku temple(s) 189–93; temple fairs and pilgrimage 189–93
popular belief 51, 187
popular cultural dimension 95–112; Huagu (花鼓) 110; Jinhua Daoqing (道情) 101–6; Taige (抬阁) 110–112; Xiaoluo Shu (小锣书) 98–101; Ye Yingmei (叶英美) 106–110
popular culture 6, 41, 51, 57, 113–49
popular religion 1–2, 5, 46–52, 55, 185–9, 194, 214–5
post-reform Fotang 200–202
Potter, Pitman B. 2, 187–8
PRC see People's Republic of China
"prefecture of 100 skills" 12; see also Jinhua region
present circumstances of Wuju 149
privilege 44, 46
procession 38, 53–4, 78, 110, 112, 132, 167, 172–6, 189, 213–18
professional association 133–4
prohibition 56–7, 108, 187, 214
promotion of tourism 6
propaganda 99, 108, 140–41
Protestantism 34, 46, 69
purgatory 40, 69
pusa 37, 44, 54, 67, 78–9, 82, 89, 121, 138, 165, 183, 196

Qian Hou (钱侯) 38
Qianxiang fair 74–6
Qianxiang town 71–6; Qianxiang fair 74–6
Qifo An (七佛庵) 196
Qingtong (情筒) 101, 103
Qing Ming on the River festival 23–4
Qing dynasty 12–13, 21, 35, 40, 45–6, 55–7, 66–7, 79, 81, 86, 98, 104–5, 117–18, 137, 140–41, 153, 185–6
Qinshi Huangdi 22
Qiujian Wenyun (求签问运) 169
Quan Shi Yi (全十义) 221–2

Quzhou 9, 12–15, 25, 37, 115, 117–20, 130, 143–8, 182, 198, 217
Quzhou Experimental Wujutuan (衢州试验婺剧团) 145–6

reciprocity 52, 54
reconnaissance 186
Red Guard 100, 166, 171–2
red sugar 26–8
Reed Catkin Padding 223–4
reform 28–9, 36
Regret the Marriage 218
relaxation of trade regulations 28–31
religion in Jinhua 34–55;
continuity paradigm 50; institutional/diffused dichotomy 46–9; money as symbol 52–3; orthodox religions 34–44; orthodox/heterodox religion and superstition 45–6; renewal paradigm 50; repression and resistance paradigm 51–2; secularization paradigm 49–50; sociothermic theory of sociality 53; something different 51; something new 50–51; syncretism vs. doctrinal purity 49; understanding modern Chinese religion 44
religious dimension 150–84
renewal paradigm 50
repertoire 139–40
repression 51–2, 185, 214
Republican period (AD 1911–1949) 21–15, 35, 39, 54, 57, 67, 98, 102, 105, 117–21, 136, 141, 171, 179, 198, 202–203
resacralization of commercial fairs 194–209
resistance paradigm 51–2, 185, 188–9
revolution 62
rhetorical subversion 51, 95
ritual bricolage 50
ritual song and dance repertoire 178–82; 18 Foxes 180–81; Sanshiliu Hang (三十六行) 178–9; Ten Character Lotus (十字莲花) 179–80; Ya Bei Feng (哑背疯) 181–2
rituals of worship 167–71

"sacrifice the stage" 134–5
sacrifice the trident, 173
sacrifices 53–4
safety valve 186
saga of Hugong Dadi 155–60; Hu Ze the person 155–6; Hu Ze's official career during the Song dynasty 156–8

Sai, Ren 40
San Tiao (三跳) 127–30; Tiao Caishen 跳财神 (Dance the God of Wealth) 129–30; Tiao Jia Guan 跳加官 (Dance Jiaguan) 128–9; Tiao Kuixing 跳魁星 (Dance Kuixing) 127–8
Sanhe Ban (三合班) 115, 117–19, 132, 141
Sanshi Chou (三世仇) 220
Sanshiliu Hang (三十六行) 178–9
Schneider, Laurence A. 46, 57–61
Schoppa, R. Keith 10, 12–14
Scott, James 1–2, 6, 95, 98, 216
Screen Pavilion 164
sectarianism 49
secular fairs 65–94; Huqi town 66–71; Luodian town 76–80; Qianxiang town 71–6; summary 94; Xiawang township 80–85; Zhudaishi town/village 85–94
secularization paradigm 49–50, 203
setting 7–62; Jinhua region 9–33; religion in Jinhua 34–53; temple fairs in Chinese history 54–62
Shanghai Buddhist Association 67
Shangwang 81
Shangyue Yuan (赏月园) 21
She (minority people) 86, 88–9
She ri (社日) 88
shen kan (神龛) 172–5, 183–4
Shen, Ruilan 118–19, 122
shending shui (身丁税) 157–8
Shexi (社戏) 88, 138
Shi, Huaide 42, 44, 130–32, 136
Shi Yi Ji *see* Quan Shi Yi (全十义)
Shi, Zhangyue 101
Shidiao (时调) 119
Shishan, Yan 1
Shixiang Ban (十响班) 130
shoals reed 118–19
Shuang Shizi (双狮子) 217
Shuang Xueyi (双血衣) 225
Shuangdao Ji (双刀记) 218–19
Shuanglin Si temple (双林寺) 5, 194–7
silk production 66
"Sing the News" 101–2
Siu, Helen 50
Si wu (四无) 162
"six medicinal herbs" 72
Skinner, G.W. 4
small commodities market (Yiwu) 25, 28, 31, 94
small cymbal narrative 87, 97–101, 109, 205, 208
socialism 15, 108

Sociology Magazine 60
sociothermic theory of sociality 53
something new 50–51
Song, Bo 114, 122, 124, 126–30, 133, 136, 139, 141–9, 181
Song dynasty (AD 960–1278) 12, 23, 25–6, 35, 37, 42, 55–6, 104, 114, 116, 154–9, 171, 194, 197; Hu Ze's official career during 156–8
Songs and Ballads 58
song and dance troupes 170, 174–5, 178–82, 191
Songyang Gaoqiang (松阳高腔) 115, 223
Southern dynasty 34, 54, 194
spontaneity 57, 66
Spring Wind 108
sprouts of capitalist restoration 3
stability 14, 54, 57
"standard" market 3–4, 211
Step on the Cloud pavilion 161
storytelling 87, 109
strands of total social phenomenon 63–209
structure of performance 124–30; *see also* Nine Gates
sub-insurrectional resistance 2, 52, 95, 185, 211, 213
subversion 52–3
sugar clique 26–8
"sugar for feathers trade" 27
Sui dynasty (AD 589–618) 54, 128
summary of secular fairs 94
Sun, Yi 138
superstition 3, 5, 34–6, 45–6, 50–51, 57, 78, 152, 165–6, 176, 187; anti-superstition campaigns 35–6
suppression 28–9, 65, 186–7
surveillance 3–4
symbolism of facial make-up 122–4
symbolism of money 52–3
syncretism vs. doctrinal purity 49, 186

Ta Baxian (踏八仙) 126–7
Taige (抬阁) 110–112, 196
Taiping rebellion 115
Taizi Ban (太子班) 79, 87, 130–32
Tale of the Pair of Knives 218–19
Tale of the Pearl *see* Bringing Together of the Pearl
Tan, Dehui 141
Tang Bin 56
Tang dynasty (AD 618–907) 2, 12, 31, 38, 54–6, 66, 84, 103, 116, 126, 128, 181, 197, 212

Tang Minghuang (唐明皇) 103, 128–9, 133–4
Tanhuang (滩簧) 118–19
Tao Yan Lize Jing She (桃岩丽泽精舍) 155
tea houses 87, 102–3, 105, 137, 183–4
temple complex at Fangyan 163–5
temple fairs in Chinese history 54–62; Chinese folklore studies 57–62
Temple of Great Mercy (大悲寺) 156, 158, 161, 164–5, 180
Temple of Lady Ma 81–2
temple-less temple fair 81, 213
temporary autonomous zones 2, 188, 213
Ten Character Lotus (十字莲花) 179–80, 213
Ten Times Righteous 221–2
Ten Tone troupe 130
Third Plenum of the Eleventh Central Committee 3, 29, 108
36 Professions 178–9, 213
Three Buddhas of Jinhua 34, 36–8, 196, 212–13
Three Dances 127–30; Tiao Caishen (跳财神) 129–30; Tiao Jia Guan (跳加官) 128–9; Tiao Kuixing 127–8
Three Kingdoms era 34
3 in 1 combined troupes 115, 117–19, 132, 141
Tian Men (天门) 161
Tian Wenqing 56
Tianliang Xi 天亮戏 124
Tiantai Guoqing Buddhist sect (天台国清) 165
Tiao Caishen (跳财神) 129–30
Tiao Jia Guan (跳加官) 128–9
Tiao Kuixing 127–8
Tieling Guan (铁灵关) 224
total social phenomena 5, 63–209; Fotang town 194–209; more popular culture 113–49; political dimension 184–93; popular cultural dimension 95–112; religious dimension 150–84; secular fairs 65–94
"town of 100 skills" 12, 66
"town of 1000 strengths" 202
transcendence 39, 55
transition to PRC 5, 145
Triple A Ball 131–2
Triple Revenge 220

2 1/2 in 1 combined troupes 117, 119, 141
Two Immortals Well 41–2

underground markets 28–9
underground performances 108
understanding modern Chinese religion 44–52; continuity paradigm 50; institutional/diffused dichotomy 46–9; orthodoxy/heterodoxy 45–6; renewal paradigm 50; repression/resistance paradigm 50–51; secularization paradigm 49–50; syncretism/doctrinal purity 49
"Upper" Huku (Huku Shang 胡库上) 184, 191–2, 215

vandalism 36, 44, 155, 166–7, 176
venues for performance 136–9
vigilance 56
Village of Culture 21

Wang Yangming 154–5
Wang, Jiucheng 114, 116–17, 124, 126–9, 133, 136, 138–9, 145, 149, 153–67, 174, 176–8, 181, 186, 191, 222–5
Wang, Zhaoxiang 54–6, 62
weapon of the weak 97–8, 211–12
Wei dynasty (AD 220–264) 54
Weituo (韦陀) 80–81, 163
Wenchang Dijun 14
Westlake Exposition 27
winter solstice 28
World Trade Organization 31
Wu, Gangji 155–9, 163, 165, 168, 171–6, 188–9, 196–7
Wufeng Shuyuan (五峰书院) 153–5
Wuju (婺剧) 113–49; see also Jinhua opera
Wuju Improvement Committee 134, 145–6
Wuju repertoire items 221–5; Geng Lishan (耕历山) 223; Guojiang Sha Xiang (过江杀相) 225; Hezhu Ji (合珠记) 222–3; Luhua Xu (芦花絮) 223–4; Pingzheng Dong (平征东) 222; Quan Shi Yi (全十义) 221–2; Shuang Xueyi (双血衣) 225; Tieling Guan (铁灵关) 224; Zhenzhu Ta (珍珠塔) 224–5

Xi An Gaoqiang (西安高腔) 115, 223–4
Xia dynasty 19

Xiaoluo Shu (小锣书) 97–101, 211–12
Xiawang township 80–85; Xiawang fair 82–5
Xie Jin 21–2
Xing Hou (刑侯) 38
Xiwu Gaoqiang (西吴高腔) 115
Xiwu village (西吴村) 78–9, 114–15
Xueli Mei (雪里梅) 147–9, 181–2

Ya Bei Feng (哑背疯) 147–9, 181–2
Yang, C.K. 4–5, 46–9, 96, 213
Yang, Fenggang 28, 32
Yang, Yabin 2
Yang, Zhuangwen 100–101
Yao, Ping 2
Ye Yingmei (叶英美) 106–110
Ying An troupes 169–72
Ying, Jiadeng 149, 156, 158–9, 162, 165, 181
yinong yigong (亦农亦工) 66
Yinsi 45–6
Yiwu 25–33; central provisioning center for merchants 33; drum rattle Bolang Gu (拨浪鼓) 26–8; International Trade City 31–2; relaxation of trade regulations 28–31; small commodities market 25
Yiwu Bao 26
Yiwu Daoqing repertoire 217–20; Borrowed Umbrella (借伞记) 219–20; Huiqin Ji (悔亲记) 218; Sanshi Chou (三世仇) 220; Shuang Shizi (双狮子) 217; Shuangdao Ji (双刀记) 218–19
Yiwu Folk Artists' Association 104, 106
Yiwu International Trade City 31–2
Yiwu Sugar and Paper Factory 27
Yiwu Xianzhi 36, 40
Yongkang 150–51
Yongkang Xianzhi 65, 149
Yongzheng period (AD 1723–1736) 37, 56–7
Yuan dynasty 12, 40, 55–6, 197
Yuanhu 72–3
Yueju 132, 141–3
Yugu (渔鼓) 87, 101–103, 106–107

Yunhuang shan (云黄山)
Yunhuang Si (云黄寺)

Zhang Bengao 140
Zhang Guolao 103
Zhang Jingsheng 58
Zhang Yimou 23
Zhang Zeduan 23
Zhang, Hanzhen 106–9
Zhang, Songshou 14, 61–2, 80, 113–24, 129–37, 139–40, 143–7, 149, 178–80, 203–4, 217–20, 223, 225
Zhang, Zhulin 98, 101, 103–110, 118
Zhao, Shiyu 2, 35, 45, 55–7, 62, 96–7, 137, 168, 186, 188, 213
Zhaoli Hou (招利侯) 38
Zhejiang Province Wuju Experimental Troupe 146
Zhejiang Ribao 201–2
Zheng De (Chan Buddhist master) 113, 160–62
Zhengyi Daoism 39–40
Zhenzhu Ji *see* Hezhu Ji (合珠记)
Zhenzhu Ta (珍珠塔) 224–5
Zhong Jingwen 60–62
Zhongshan University 60–61
Zhou Yuexian (周越仙) 141–9, 212; and early years of PRC 145–7; and her sisters 141–2; and Jiang Heyi 144–5; rewriting Ya Bei Feng and Xueli Mei 147–9
Zhouchunju Ban 141–9; rewriting Ya Bei Feng and Xueli Mei 147–9; transition to PRC 145; Yuexian and early years of PRC 145–7; Zhou Yuexian 142–4; Zhou Yuexian and her sisters 141–2; Zhou Yuexian and Jiang Heyi 144–5
Zhu Yuanzhang 45, 55, 185
Zhuangyuan pays respects (状元拜堂) 130
Zhudaishi town 85–94; Zhudaishi fair 90–94
zifa (自发) 66
zones of indifference 188
Zong Ze 25
Zuochang Ban (坐唱班) 79–80, 86–7, 118, 130–31
zuofang 27

A World of Online Content!

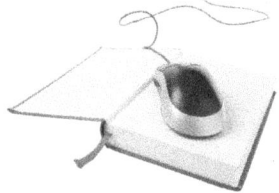

Did you know that Taylor & Francis has over 20,000 books available electronically?

What's more, they are all available for browsing and individual purchase on the Taylor & Francis eBookstore.

www.ebookstore.tandf.co.uk

eBooks for libraries

Free trials available

Choose from annual subscription or outright purchase and select from a range of bespoke subject packages, or tailor make your own.

www.ebooksubscriptions.com

For more information, email
online.sales@tandf.co.uk

Taylor & Francis Group